Palgrave Philosophy Today

Series Editor: **Vittorio Bufacchi**, University College Cork, Ireland

The *Palgrave Philosophy Today* series provides concise introductions to all the major areas of philosophy currently being taught in philosophy departments around the world. Each book gives a state-of-the-art informed assessment of a key area of philosophical study. In addition, each title in the series offers a distinct interpretation from an outstanding scholar who is closely involved with current work in the field. Books in the series provide students and teachers with not only a succinct introduction to the topic, with the essential information necessary to understand it and the literature being discussed, but also a demanding and engaging entry into the subject.

Titles include:

Helen Beebee
FREE WILL: An Introduction

Shaun Gallagher
PHENOMENOLOGY

Simon Kirchin
METAETHICS

Duncan Pritchard
KNOWLEDGE

Mathias Risse
GLOBAL POLITICAL PHILOSOPHY

Don Ross
PHILOSOPHY OF ECONOMICS

Joel Walmsley
MIND AND MACHINE

Forthcoming Titles:

James Robert Brown
PHILOSOPHY OF SCIENCE

Pascal Engel
PHILOSOPHY OF PSYCHOLOGY

Neil Manson
ENVIRONMENTAL PHILOSOPHY

Chad Meister
PHILOSOPHY OF RELIGION

Lilian O'Brien
PHILOSOPHY OF ACTION

Nancy Tuana
FEMINISM AND PHILOSOPHY

Palgrave Philosophy Today
Series Standing Order ISBN 978-0-230-00232-6 (hardcover)
Series Standing Order ISBN 978-0-230-00233-3 (paperback)
(*outside North America only*)

You can receive future titles in this series as they are published by placing a standing order. Please contact your bookseller or, in case of difficulty, write to us at the address below with your name and address, the title of the series and one of the ISBNs quoted above.

Customer Services Department, Macmillan Distribution Ltd, Houndmills, Basingstoke, Hampshire RG21 6XS, England

Also by Don Ross

METAPHOR, MEANING AND COGNITION

I NOUVI PERCORSI DELL'INTELLIGENZA ARTIFICIALE (New Frontiers in Artificial Intelligence)

WHAT PEOPLE WANT: The Concept of Utility from Bentham to Game Theory

DENNETT'S PHILOSOPHY: A COMPREHENSIVE ASSESSMENT (*editor with David Thompson and Andrew Brook*)

DANIEL DENNETT (*editor with Andrew Brook*)

DEVELOPMENT DILEMMAS: The Methods and Political Ethics of Growth Policy (*editor with Melvin Ayogu*)

ECONOMIC THEORY AND COGNITIVE SCIENCE, VOLUME ONE: Microexplanation

EVERY THING MUST GO: Metaphysics Naturalized (*with James Ladyman*)

DISTRIBUTED COGNITION AND THE WILL (*editor with David Spurrett, Harold Kincaid and G. Lynn Stephens*)

MIDBRAIN MUTINY: The Behavioral Economics and Neuroeconomics of Disordered Gambling (*with Carla Sharp, Rudolph E. Vuchinich and David Spurrett*)

THE OXFORD HANDBOOK OF PHILOSOPHY OF ECONOMICS (*editor with Harold Kincaid*)

WHAT IS ADDICTION? (*editor with Harold Kincaid, David Spurrett and Peter Collins*)

SCIENTIFIC METAPHYSICS (*editor with James Ladyman and Harold Kincaid*)

Philosophy of Economics

Don Ross

University of Cape Town, South Africa
Georgia State University, United States

First published 2014 by
PALGRAVE MACMILLAN

Palgrave Macmillan in the UK is an imprint of Macmillan Publishers Limited, registered in England, company number 785998, of Houndmills, Basingstoke, Hampshire RG21 6XS.

Palgrave Macmillan in the US is a division of St Martin's Press LLC, 175 Fifth Avenue, New York, NY 10010.

Palgrave Macmillan is the global academic imprint of the above companies and has companies and representatives throughout the world.

Palgrave® and Macmillan® are registered trademarks in the United States, the United Kingdom, Europe and other countries.

ISBN: 978–0–230–30296–9 hardback
ISBN: 978–0–230–30297–6 paperback

This book is printed on paper suitable for recycling and made from fully managed and sustained forest sources. Logging, pulping and manufacturing processes are expected to conform to the environmental regulations of the country of origin.

A catalogue record for this book is available from the British Library.

A catalog record for this book is available from the Library of Congress.

This book is dedicated to my wife, Dr Nelleke Bak. A happy life partnership produces a unique economic effect, pervasive endogeneity of utility. In other words: Nelleke's presence and support makes everything I like better than it would otherwise be.

Contents

List of Figures

Preface and Acknowledgments

This book is an opinionated tour through what I consider to be the most important issues in the philosophy of economics. It asks: What is economics fundamentally *about?* It appears to be about aspects of behavior and social organization. But then how and why does it differ from other sciences – in particular, psychology and sociology – that study these topics?

In calling the book 'opinionated' I refer to the fact that although I try to be fair and accurate in stating the views of others whom I criticize, I have not tried to represent or survey all or even most of the leading positions in the literature. This is therefore not an even-handed survey of 'the' philosophy of economics. It states *my* philosophy of economics.

Chapter 1 explains the distinctive philosophical ground on which I stand, and contrasts it with some alternative philosophical attitudes. So I will not outline or defend that in this preface. And throughout the book I make clear whenever I align myself with one side of a currently live controversy among economists.

However, a prospective reader looking quickly at the book to determine whether she is likely to find opinions sympathetic or contrary to her own might appreciate some simple slogan statements. My general philosophical stance is that of a naturalistic philosopher of science. It is the mission of scientific institutions to strive to provide a complete objective account of the universe at all scales of description. This ambition can never be realized, but that is only because scientists will never be able to make every possible observation or take every possible measurement – not because there is a rival path to knowledge, such as religion or intuitive insight, that performs better in some domains of inquiry. Economics is part of science, though economists, like most other scientists, often engage in activity other than seeking objective knowledge. In particular, they are often preoccupied with offering practical and policy advice that should be crucially based on such objective knowledge as they have obtained. As for grand economic doctrine, my views are in the tradition usually called 'mainstream'. That label mainly just conveys a set of negatives: I am not a Marxist, nor an Austrian, nor a critical realist. But I think that all of the leading mainstream economists, including Smith, Walras, Marshall, Keynes, Hayek, Frisch, Tinbergen, Schumpeter, Samuelson, Arrow, Schelling, Friedman, and Stiglitz, are 'leading' because they have contributed lasting and important insights, notwithstanding their sharp disagreements with one another on many questions.

This book is intended to be accessible to a senior student of philosophy or economics – or, for that matter, of psychology, or sociology, or any other social or behavioral science. What I mean by this is that it does not contain specialized mathematics, and when it addresses or uses technical concepts that are unique to a particular discipline these are introduced and explained in the text. (Sometimes this happens in footnotes, however, so a reader who encounters something she doesn't understand should check those.)

At the same time, the book defends an original and distinctive view of economics, and of a number of methodological controversies in economics, that I hope will interest professional scholars. They will know where they can speed-read while familiar concepts are being explained for the benefit of less expert readers, and they can judge for themselves where it is worth slowing down to digest and engage with a novel perspective.

Some student readers may want to read this book alongside a more conventionally constructed textbook on the philosophy of economics. The only truly up-to-date such book currently on the market is Julian Reiss's *Philosophy of Economics* (Routledge, 2013). I recommend it, though noting that there is much in it with which I disagree, and that I am less sympathetic than Reiss is to the style of philosophy called 'analytic'.

Other student readers may want a less philosophical and less dialectical non-technical survey of the contemporary state of economics. There is a splendid such source on the market, Diane Coyle's *The Soulful Science* (Princeton University Press, 2007). I urge everyone with any interest in economics to read Coyle. It is ideal preparation for this one.

Finally, some student readers may want to complement this book with a concise history of economic thought that narrates the story 'straight up' and is less preoccupied with critical questions of methodology. To these readers I recommend Roger Backhouse's *The Ordinary Business of Life* (Princeton University Press, 2002).

I am grateful to a number of people whose assistance was crucial to the production of this book. Vittorio Bufacchi commissioned it on behalf of the publisher, and was tolerant – indeed strongly supportive – when I requested indulgence to go beyond the original (generous) timeframe he set for the project, and when I asked if I could make it substantially longer than initially agreed. My regular collaborator and friend Glenn Harrison commented extensively on each chapter draft and suggested numerous improvements, refinements and corrections. I have learned more about economics over the years from Glenn than from any other single person. The book also profits from comments I gratefully received from Ken Binmore, Harold Kincaid and Andreas Papandreou. Carsten Hermann-Pilath read the manuscript after I sent it to him with little time remaining for further work on it (at least if I was not to abuse the patience of Vittorio intolerably), and reassured me with his response. Of course some errors will still have slid past all of these first-rate intellectual filters, and they are my fault.

The general philosophy of science that forms the backdrop to my view of the philosophy of economics was developed with another treasured collaborator, James Ladyman, mainly in our book *Every Thing Must Go* (Oxford University Press, 2007). I did not burden James, whose main interests are in physics and mathematics, with drafts of the present book. But his learning and wisdom nevertheless strongly inform it.

My deepest debt of all is to my wife, Nelleke Bak. Nelleke is a philosopher of education, and what she knows of economics is mainly based on putting up with impolite shop-talk when we dine with my colleagues. She was thus an excellent filter for testing my effort to write a book that could be followed by a – very studious and intellectually alert – non-economist. She read every sentence of the book and made many of them less mysterious. Along with that she checked the concordance of the references and prepared the whole package nicely for the publisher. All of this she did *for no pay*, thus refuting a generalization about people that is frequently attributed to economists.

Parts of Chapter 3 are drawn from my article 'Game theory' in *The Stanford Encyclopedia of Philosophy* (SEP), available at http://plato.stanford.edu/archives/win2012/entries/game-theory/. SEP holds exclusive electronic distribution rights to this material, not superseded by the copyright on the present book. I thank the SEP editors for permission to distribute this material in any electronic version of the book that Palgrave Macmillan might choose to issue.

An outline of many of the themes of this book is due to appear as a chapter in Byron Kaldis, Ed., *Mind and Society: Cognitive Science meets the Social Sciences,* to be published by Springer. A few passages from the chapter reappear in this book. Some themes are treated more extensively in the book, others in the chapter; in the latter cases, this is noted in the text.

Series Editor's Preface

It is not easy being a student of philosophy these days. All the different areas of philosophy are reaching ever-increasing levels of complexity and sophistication, a fact which is reflected in the specialized literature and readership each branch of philosophy enjoys. And yet, anyone who studies philosophy is expected to have a solid grasp of the most current issues being debated in most, if not all, other areas of philosophy. It is an understatement to say that students of philosophy today are faced with a Herculean task.

The books in this new book series by Palgrave Macmillan are meant to help all philosophers, established and aspiring, to understand, appreciate and engage with the intricacies which characterize all the many faces of philosophy. They are also ideal teaching tools as textbooks for more advanced students. These books may not be meant primarily for those who have yet to read their first book of philosophy, but all students with a basic knowledge of philosophy will benefit greatly from reading these exciting and original works, which will enable anyone to engage with all the defining issues in contemporary philosophy.

There are three main aspects that make the Palgrave Philosophy Today series distinctive and attractive. First, each book is relatively short. Second, the books are commissioned from some of the best-known, established and upcoming international scholars in each area of philosophy. Third, while the primary purpose is to offer an informed assessment of opinion on a key area of philosophical study, each title presents a distinct interpretation from someone who is closely involved with current work in the field.

This book on philosophy of economics, by one of the world's leading scholars in the discipline, is both authoritative and highly original. Unlike most other books in the philosophy of economics, which aim to bring clarity to the key concepts that pertain to economic thinking, Ross takes an innovative approach, grounding his analysis in naturalistic philosophy of science.

This is an ambitious book, written by a scholar equally dexterous in the abstract reasoning distinctive to philosophy and in the technicalities of economics, which puts forward a completely novel way of presenting the philosophy of economics. The targeted readership for this book is not just the philosopher with an interest in making sense of economic realities, but also the economist interested in understanding the nature and logic of their discipline. This book could change the way we think about economics, and philosophy's contribution toward this paradigmatic shift.

Economics has evolved into a highly technical discipline, and philosophers writing about economics have not always kept pace with these developments. This is arguably the first book by a philosopher that engages with all the technical tools that are the modern economist's bread-and-butter. Don Ross has written a book that is destined to become pivotal for all future discussions in philosophy of economics.

List of Acronyms

BES	behavioural economics in the scanner
BOLD	blood-oxygen-level dependence
CGE	computable general equilibrium
CPT	cumulative prospect theory
CRRA	constant relative risk aversion
DE	development economics
DMRS	diminishing marginal rates of substitution
DSCGE	dynamic, stochastic computable general equilibrium
EMH	efficient markets hypothesis
EP	economic psychologism
EUT	expected utility theory
fMRI	functional magnetic resonance imaging
GARP	generalized axiom of revealed preference
GE	general equilibrium
GT	game theory
IKE	imperfect knowledge economics
IO	industrial organization
LLR	larger, later reward
MI	methodological individualism
NE	Nash equilibrium
ORT	ordinal utility theory
PD	prisoner's dilemma
PE	partial equilibrium
QRE	quantal response equilibrium
RDEU	rank-dependent expected utility
REH	rational expectations hypothesis
RPT	revealed preference theory
SARP	strong axiom of revealed preference
SPE	sub-game perfect equilibrium
SSR	smaller, sooner reward

SV	subjective value
vNMuf	von Neumann–Morgenstern utility function
WARP	weak axiom of revealed preference

1

Philosophy of Economics as Philosophy of Science

This book is about the philosophy of economics. Many readers will therefore be surprised to find that, after the first chapter, it will not seem to explicitly discuss much philosophy, but will describe the structures of theories and models in economics and in two neighboring disciplines, psychology and sociology. The purpose of this opening chapter is to explain why in my view that is how the philosophy of any science, including therefore the philosophy of economics, should be done. The reader should be alerted to the fact that this view of mine rests on a conception of philosophy that most philosophers do not share.

During the second half of the twentieth century it was common to divide the domain of philosophy into two largely estranged branches, analytic and continental.[1] Analytic philosophers, according to their self-image, wrote and thought more like scientists, proceeding methodically from empirical observations, whereas continental philosophers trafficked in the humanistic arts of metaphor and speculative generalizations based on intellectual insights and perspectival framing. My own early training in philosophy of science was squarely within the analytic idiom, and that is the idiom in which I remain a native. I nevertheless open this book by explaining why it will not be an exercise in analytic philosophy, why, indeed, I think that analytic philosophy is a barren enterprise.

My saying this relies on taking the word 'analytic' literally, as referring to efforts to produce more logically transparent but semantically equivalent renderings of concepts, theories or propositions. 'Transparency' roughly denotes replacing complex ideas by explicit constructions out

---

[1] For the stylized account of this split, see the manifesto that launched it, Ayer (1936). For actual history see Friedman (2000).

of simpler ones, replacing relatively abstract concepts by constructions using relatively more concrete and experiential ones, and, perhaps most importantly, sketching relationships between technical semantic fields and the semantic fields people use for expressing their most general and intuitive understandings of what exists and what happens. Most analytic philosophers of science think that such replacement helps us to understand science and therefore, at second remove, to understand the world that scientists study.[2]

This introductory chapter begins by explaining why I do not believe that analytic philosophy of science can be useful in these ways. It then moves on to explain what kind of philosophy of science I think *is* useful when done well, by members of a community of scholars who know a good deal about the sciences on which they write. The philosophy in question involves showing how different scientific specializations – disciplines or sub-disciplines – jointly constrain and influence one another to contribute to a general scientific worldview. The deepest of all my personal intellectual commitments is that such a worldview is the best one for all people to adopt, for the sake both of believing generally true things rather than false things, and for the sake of generally promoting rather than impeding human flourishing.

Some people who share my commitment to the value, indeed the superiority, of a scientific worldview doubt that economics, at least as it has been practiced by most academic and professional economists, makes a sound contribution to such a worldview. I do not share this doubt. There are some opinions maintained by many or most economists – for example, the opinion that all important properties of human societies ultimately 'boil down to' properties of individual people – that I think need profound adjustment when accumulated economic knowledge is placed in the wider context of the sciences. One main theme of this book will be explaining why I am convinced of this. In general, however, this book defends what is generally regarded as 'mainstream' economics as a crucial and powerful contributor to the scientific worldview. Explaining the basis of that opinion is the other main theme of this book.

---

[2] Not all philosophy written in the broadly scientific idiom counts as analytic in this restricted usage. Indeed, none of the work of my favorite contemporary philosophers – including among others Daniel Dennett, Mark Wilson, Kim Sterelny, Philip Kitcher, Penelope Maddy, Jenann Ismael, Paul Humphreys, James Ladyman and Harold Kincaid – falls under the label.

Unfolding these two themes will largely involve describing economics, along with aspects of the nearby disciplines with which economics must most directly be reconciled. In the last part of this opening chapter I begin to do this while still standing on the general philosophical terrain discussed in the first two sections. Thereafter self-conscious philosophizing will be left behind, and we will immerse ourselves in the details of current social and behavioral science.

1.1 What is philosophy of science for?

At universities all over the world, there are professional philosophers. As in all parts of the academy, they specialize. One of the ways in which many do so is as philosophers 'of' other recognized activities, including other academic disciplines. Thus we have philosophers of religion, philosophers of art, philosophers of sport, philosophers of sex, and also philosophers of physics, philosophers of biology, philosophers of mathematics – and philosophers of economics. I take it there isn't much mystery, at least in general, about the difference between playing sports and philosophizing about them, or about the difference between having sex and philosophizing about that. It is much less obvious how to draw the line between physics and the philosophy of physics or between economics and the philosophy of economics.

One common view is that philosophers distinguish themselves as experts on *concepts*. Thus a philosopher of physics might be someone who studies the explicit and implicit principles of application that physicists have in mind when they use their special concepts such as momentum or spin. But this view raises serious problems – not least of which is that scientists tend to find it very annoying. Some concepts used in physics are unsettled because the relevant empirical facts the concepts are used to structure are themselves unsettled – for example, the concept of dark matter. There are other physical concepts, such as that of the collapse of the wave function, that are partly 'open' because physicists aren't yet sure whether, in the empirically superior physics of later generations, they will be thought to apply to anything. But the 'settling' of these unsettled concepts is a process that will emerge in and through the design and interpretation of actual physical theories and experiments, done by physicists. They will not be 'settled' by armchair reflection on the 'logic' of the concepts. To most physicists, philosophers who try to 'explicate' the structures of unsettled physical concepts are doing something both useless – because it makes no possible contribution to objective knowledge – and presumptuous, since the only truly relevant expertise for the issue is working understanding of the *uses* of the concepts in day-to-day scientific activity, and in this respect philosophers are bound to be less well informed than physicists.

In the face of these worries, some philosophers concede that it is not their job to help scientists achieve more clarity in the way *they* (scientists) use their special, technical concepts. However, these philosophers might then point out that scientists' special concepts are often interpreted as partial contributors to a wider project of addressing broader, more traditionally rooted concepts that the scientists do not 'own' for themselves – for example, in the case of physics, 'space' and 'time.' Then the job of the philosopher as an expert on concepts might be to study the relationships between non-technical uses of broad concepts and related technical notions. This at least has the advantage of assigning to the philosopher a *distinctive* role, since scientists are not rewarded for doing this sort of thing as part of their professional activity (though many scientists do engage in it as a sideline, in popular books and articles).

The problem here is that scientists do not, and should not, think of themselves as under any obligation to preserve or vindicate the traditional conceptual structures of everyday discourse. Physicists talk about particles. So do non-physicists – for example we read in the media about how particles of human fecal matter in the ocean are harming coral reefs. But the physicists' particles and the marine ecologist's particles have *no* 'conceptual logic' in common; indeed *all* they have in common is that their individual direct effects on photons are beneath the resolution capacity of human vision. Reflecting on this seems to be a potential contribution to objective knowledge in only one possible way, as an aspect of the cultural anthropology and linguistics of different communities of people who talk about particles. Why should that inquiry be handed over to philosophers rather than to anthropologists and linguists?

A possible answer to this question is that the philosopher, unlike the anthropologist, aims to make concepts and their uses more coherent and consistent – she does not merely set out to *describe* use, but also has a normative project in mind. In that case, however, we should again not understand ourselves to be referring to technical concepts. The scientist hopes that the course of empirical discovery and theoretical refinement will make her technical concepts more coherent and consistent. She should not want – and if she is like most scientists she *will* not want – to adjust her structures for thinking and writing in accordance with normative pressure from philosophers. Reflection on many historical cases shows her that this pressure tends always to be a force for conservatism. Science, by contrast, is institutionally structured so as to transform and revolutionize our collective understanding of reality. We could only have learned from scientists, not from philosophers, that gravity is a consequence of the shape of the universe, that in the human brain 'wanting' something and 'liking' it are processed by separate systems, or that living things are not distinguished by having been injected with 'vital essence.' *Individual* scientists are required to be conservative, aiming at only incremental adjustments to the work on which they build. But to expect that scientists as a community should be tethered to the conceptual space of traditional culture and everyday practice would be to cripple science and implicitly deny its deepest source of importance.

Might the job of the philosopher of science then be to try to continually update the relationships between the moving frontier of scientific discovery and the non-technical, everyday conceptual space in which people understand and reflect on their practical projects and social interactions? As I will explain shortly, I think there is an *element* of truth to this idea – but at least as great an element of falsehood. The problem is with the emphasis on 'concepts.' Many philosophers think that their discipline is the home of professional expertise on a general 'logic of concepts.' But I see no convincing evidence, from linguistics or psychology or anthropology or the history of philosophy itself that any such general logic reliably connects with the ways in which people 'in general' actually talk and think. Nor do I find it persuasive – I find it, instead, grandiose – to suppose that anyone should sensibly set out to identify a *general* set of norms by which people *should* talk and think if they want to be regarded as 'rational.'

I therefore think that most of the historical agenda of philosophy as an academic discipline involves unreasonable ambitions. These ambitions, summarized very broadly, are to find universal and general norms of thought for the human species. A few rather banal, entirely negative, such norms can plausibly be identified: don't change the reference classes of words in the middle of a chain of verbal reasoning; don't generalize from what you know to be an unrepresentative sample. But these rules of thumb can all be identified in the first few chapters of a standard critical reasoning textbook. They aren't derived from deeper truths of mathematics or formal logic. Beyond them there is nothing reliable – and our main evidence for this is precisely that every other candidate for a general norm ever proposed has at some time been usefully disregarded by some community of scientists. The explanation for *that* is that the actual world is vastly more complicated and strange than human imagination can grasp in advance, so to be open to understanding it as we go along interacting with it in the new ways allowed by advancing technology, we should keep our minds open and unencumbered by rules and constraints imposed in advance.

At this point the prospects look bleak for identifying anything both distinctive and well motivated for a philosopher, and thus by special application for a philosopher of economics, to do. There is no useful mission for the philosopher of economics to perform that an economist could not in principle perform at least as authoritatively. So what am I doing writing a book on philosophy of economics? What are you doing reading it? Of what possible value could it be? What is it even going to be *about*?

I think there is just one general answer to this question, an answer that James Ladyman and I defend at length in our 2007 book on scientific metaphysics. One of the things that many people value is a general picture of how the innumerable kinds of processes in the world, on all their endlessly variable scales of measurement, 'fit together' into a coherent whole. This is obviously a metaphor, since the world isn't a kind of puzzle or machine with literal pieces that might or might not assemble neatly. Perhaps we might literalize the metaphor by reference to constructed models; 'fitting together' could then simply mean that all of the equations in a model have at least one simultaneous solution. However, that is almost never a realistic option when what is at issue is cross-disciplinary coherence, because movement across disciplinary borders typically involves shifts of scale that defeat the construction of transdisciplinary models with analytic solutions. For this reason, cross-disciplinary modeling often involves computer simulations. Since virtual worlds resemble the actual world with respect to their resistance to purely logical representation, this risks leading our present problem back around in a circle to where we started. If the construction of the scientific worldview isn't constrained by a general logic of concepts, what value can the philosopher think she usefully adds?

Fortunately, we can avoid this circle by declining to *analyze* the idea of 'fitting together,' and exemplifying it instead.[3] Like many dead metaphors, the 'fitting together' one has relatively uncontroversial conditions of use that most people understand. Let us consider an example.

Suppose you are told (correctly) by zoologists that birds are directly descended from dinosaurs. You are also advised (truly) by paleontologists that all dinosaurs died within a short time of the collision of the earth with a large asteroid at the end of the Cretaceous period 65 million years ago. Accepting *and fully understanding* these two facts together shouldn't be possible for a critically thoughtful person without a bit of intellectual work. If literally all of the dinosaurs perished, then how could they have left descendants? Perhaps some dinosaurs had already evolved into birds before the asteroid struck, and so all the dinosaurs then living died, while some already-evolved birds survived. This isn't too bad an approximation to the facts, but it's lazy in its attentiveness to general principles of biology. It implies that natural boundaries between kinds of organisms, such as dinosaurs and birds, are sharper than they really are. The better account is that there were many species, which lasted on earth for hundreds of thousands of years, that were dinosaur-like and bird-like at the same time. Some of these creatures survived the asteroid collision. Furthermore, survival rates were biased in favor of animals that were relatively more like modern birds in their genetic constitution, and relatively less like prototypical dinosaurs. In consequence of the sudden transformation, caused by the asteroid, of the distribution of gene frequencies in the relevant pool, the features we associate with birds, but not dinosaurs, were rapidly amplified during the evolutionary period following the catastrophe, while features

---

[3] For several decades the text most often presented to freshman students as their first example of original classic philosophy has been Plato's *Euthyphro*. One main point of this Socratic dialogue is to deny that exemplification can ever yield knowledge in the absence of analysis. I agree with Wittgenstein (1953) that Plato is wrong about this; that is the deepest reason why the project of analytic philosophy is misguided.

we associate with dinosaurs but not birds became much less salient (though many are still 'latent' in the genes of birds).

Those philosophers who take pride in referring to themselves as 'analytic' might diagnose the above example as boiling down to semantics. A problem is raised when we implicitly define the set of dinosaurs as not including birds. If we drop this restriction, then the statement 'All dinosaurs disappeared at the end of the Cretaceous' becomes false – dinosaurs are still with us, are indeed among the forms of life most of us see every day. Now, there is nothing scientifically wrong with regarding birds as a sub-type of dinosaurs if we want to. We are also welcome to think of the classic dinosaurs as early birds if we prefer. The problem with these purely semantic 'solutions' to the original problem is that they ignore the scientific character of that problem. Targets of scientific explanation are gaps in empirical knowledge, not questions about how to most consistently yet concisely *talk*. If someone intends their puzzle about dinosaurs and birds as a *scientific* question, rather than as a linguistic question, then a satisfactory answer to it must provide contingent information about some processes, structures or other real patterns discovered through observation. In the example, the key to such information is about how environmental shocks can suddenly change gene frequencies in populations, and about how such changes can in turn lead to rapid morphological changes in populations of organisms.

Another feature of the example that is typical of *unification problems* – that is, questions about how different parts of knowledge 'fit together' – is that it involves thinking simultaneously about patterns on different scales. Many of the asteroid's most dramatic effects occurred within a short interval similar to those in which people make plans. In particular, within this brief interval, a huge number of previously healthy animals of breeding age perished. That this happened is a vital part of the explanation of the disappearance of relatively non-birdlike dinosaurs. But the aggregate event 'extinction of the dinosaurs' was *not* confined to that sort of scale. When we say the extinction was 'sudden,' we mean this by reference to timescales appropriate for evolutionary modeling, which is seldom sensitive to any interval smaller than a century, and more often insensitive to intervals smaller than a millennium. (The recent re-making of the global ecology by humans happened so suddenly that it is, for many species, a catastrophic event like an asteroid collision, and so similarly forces chroniclers of the history of life to consider shorter scales than usual.) To properly understand what happened to the dinosaurs *along with* the origin of birds, one must direct one's attention to *both* scales of modeling, on each of which events are sorted into classes using different principles of organization.

The example satisfies the desire for explanation by drawing on principles from (at least) two sciences, ecology and population genetics. As such, it involves partially *unifying* these sciences for application to a problem. The unification in this case is one that is applied so often that its principles have become commonplace. To borrow a very useful idea from the philosopher of science Philip Kitcher (1981, 1984, 1989, 1993), this particular combination of sciences, as applied to species extinctions, has solidified through repeated use into a standard *argument pattern* that scientists know how to use without any explicit methodological reflection. They need not struggle to simultaneously think like ecologists and like population geneticists, because for them this is a familiar skill like riding a bicycle, so there is no reason why they would outsource some of this labor to philosophers (or to anyone else).

However, as sciences advance they continuously raise prospects for *novel* unifications. Here in the early twenty-first century, for example, we are collectively in the process of learning the best principles for unifying psychology and neuroscience in the contexts of application to various recurrent kinds of questions about the patterns and causes of behavior. This process has followed a broad course that is familiar to historians of science. Some scientists are attracted to the simplest form of unification, *ontological reduction.* This program encourages them to treat psychological structures and processes as just equivalent to neurophysiological structures and processes, even before they're sure just *which* possible neurophysiological pattern is the implementation of a particular psychological pattern. Such reduction is consistent with either the possibility that psychological generalizations, once translated into neuroscientific terms, are usually substantially vindicated, or with the possibility that they more typically turn out to be mere crude limiting cases of much more exact neuroscientific generalizations. In the former case we would say that psychology was being *intertheoretically reduced* to neuroscience; in the latter case we would say that neuroscience is displacing or *eliminating* psychology. Many philosophers of science reserve the term 'unification' for cases of intertheoretic reduction. In our book, however, Ladyman and I use 'unification' to apply to any joint application of patterns from different disciplines; so on our usage elimination is a limiting case of unification.

Scientists often pursue these logically simplest forms of unification – that is, reduction or elimination – because they provide practical methodological principles. If, in the end, the reality of the relationship between psychology and neuroscience will be more complicated than either smooth reduction or elimination – for example, many generalizations from psychology will survive but most will need some adjustment in light of neuroscience, while some neuroscientific generalizations will also need revision in light of psychology – then one practical way to discover this complicated resolution is to converge on it from efforts by different groups of scientists to achieve each of the simpler forms of unification. That is, some scientists pursue reduction while others aim at elimination, and the eventual collective result is mutual disciplinary adaptation. This is the most typical pattern in the joint histories of disciplines that become increasingly unified as they are repeatedly deployed together in furnishing explanations.[4]

I now link this sociological observation about science to a second one. Most scientists seem to work most efficiently by *not* trying to each personally incorporate the sophistication of eventual collective adaptations. That is, scientists engaged in unifying dynamics typically do not embrace intertheoretic reductionism or eliminativism as mere methodological heuristics while saying that they expect reality to be more complex and messy. Instead, reductionists and eliminativists intellectually quarrel with one another, each camp defending its favored corner solution as the *truth* about reality. I think there are readily understandable, and indeed good, reasons for this. No one can know the details of the complex unification on which consensus will settle until we actually get there through continuous refinements of structural models in the face of recalcitrant data. Thus to defend any *specific* version of complex unification *ahead of* consensus requires one to speculatively construct models that run far ahead of current

---

[4] For a treasure trove of examples mainly drawn from relationships between theoretical mechanics and various applied sciences, see Mark Wilson's beautiful 2006 book *Wandering Significance*. My present account implies a negative view of the value of most contemporary philosophy. But if someone espouses the view that philosophy *cannot*, in principle, yield knowledge and illumination, they can be refuted by reference to Wilson's book (and, of course, to some other good ones; see note 2 above).

evidence. Well entrenched norms of scientific practice discourage this particular *kind* of speculation. This is not to say that scientific norms discourage speculation altogether. To defend reductionist or eliminativist interpretations of current data is also to speculate, and indeed to assert speculative hypotheses that the wise historian of science could assure one are likely too simple to be true. But that is precisely the point. To allow oneself to be guided by a relatively *simple* speculation leads to sensible allocation of one's time as between philosophizing and getting on with experimentation, observation, and technical model refinement. Speculating on more complex possibilities away from the corner solutions is more intellectually challenging, but an ultimately inefficient way to do science.

This process of scientific evolution, whereby groups of intellectual rivals each defend competing corner unifications that are too structurally simple to usually have much chance of being true, works because scientific labor is massively divided. Adjustment of simpler hypotheses generally complicates these hypotheses; and since all scientists ultimately live in the same world,[5] the rivals' positions will tend to gradually be pulled into consensus as they deepen. This is obscured by the fact that primary attention is always focused on whatever is still contested, so it is *not* necessarily to be expected that as unification progresses the rate or salience of disputations and polemics reduces. The quarrels do, however, tend to focus on matters of progressively finer detail. Since there is no ultimately finest scale of reality, these processes of convergence never terminate. Yet as they develop, ever more phenomena that were once wholly or partly mysterious and speculatively contested come to be substantively explained. Thus there is progressive accumulation of knowledge, including conceptual knowledge.

We have now said enough about the ecosystem of the sciences to be able to identify the niche in which philosophers can make useful

---

[5] Some philosophers, known as 'disunity theorists', deny this; see Dupré (1993) and Cartwright (1999). Detailed critical discussion of disunity theory would carry us too deep into meta-philosophical complexities for indulgence in the present book. The reader in search of more background to this issue, from the point of view developed here, can consult Ladyman and Ross (2007, chapters 1 and 5). Here, I will summarize my view of disunity theory briskly. I do not think there is any knock-down argument against it. I think, however, that it mis-describes the most common pattern of development across the sciences by under-emphasizing the fact that competing models become steadily more precise, and as they do so expose formerly hidden complementarities. Disunity theorists stay closely attentive to specific growing trees at the cost of missing emerging forests.

contributions to the accumulation of objective knowledge. The progress of science unifies initially isolated patches of explanatory modeling without most of this being localized in the writing of any *individual* scientist. Individual scientists each try to squeeze as much explanatory work from the argument patterns in which they are expert as they can, in partial competition and partial cooperation with other scientists trying to do the same. The institutional norms that regulate their work do not strongly reward them for trying to rise above the fray and explicitly consolidate the unifications on which consensus has been achieved. But if *no one* did that then the resulting state of affairs would be quite strange. We would have, at any given time, a scientific worldview (including, of course, many patches of ignorance, some large), but it would be mainly *tacit*. That is, it would be implicit in the many unifying argument patterns over which scientists had ceased to quarrel, but it wouldn't be explicitly recorded anywhere by anyone.

What about historians of science? Isn't this recording of consolidation *their* obvious job? Up to a point, it is indeed. Some historians of science focus on relations between sciences, and thereby contribute to explicit unification of the scientific worldview. But this role for historians is constrained by special normative limitations that govern their work. First, the values of their profession strongly discourage speculation about the future. But if part of our motivation for unification is that we *want to* have a general worldview – and why shouldn't we want that? – then it is important to allow a sense of projective *telos*,[6] even if that is something that historians regard as anathema.[7] Second, historians do not pronounce on consensus among scientists until its achievement is very clear. In consequence, their clearest unifying work tends to concern developments that are well back in the rearview mirror.

Insofar as a rigorous thinker about the relationships among sciences evades these constraints, the history of science tends to blur

---

[6] Interpreting history teleologically involves narrating it as if the actors living in it and producing it by their actions were adhering to a prior rational script with an identified end state. People who think that the world is governed by supernatural intelligence can take teleological history as literal truth. Atheists should not.

[7] They *should* so regard it, because *telos* is a deadly enemy of historical objectivity. However, it doesn't follow that everyone who thinks about science should do so under the professional historian's constraints.

imperceptibly into the philosophy of science. To put the matter the other way around, the philosopher of science as I am characterizing her role is a *speculative, forward-looking historian of science with a special focus on interdisciplinary unification.*

This conception of the philosopher of science is unabashedly normative, not descriptive of all or most philosophers as we actually find them. Many philosophers, and especially those who regard themselves as experts in the analysis of concepts, would deny that the characterization does or should apply to them. But in our book Ladyman and I give our reasons for thinking these philosophers are throwing to the wrong base. Our objection centres on our argument, supported by attention to the actual history of science and its relationship to philosophy, that scientists do not and should not *want* explicit conceptual analysis done for them. Such analysis, especially when it is guided by intuitions influenced by everyday linguistic usage and practical purposes, is always conservative. But the very point of science, according to the enlightenment ideology to which we are committed, is to discover new knowledge. Though most of what great past scientists, and authors of influential textbooks, thought they knew they really *did* know – pace Kuhn (1962), science *is* broadly cumulative across so-called revolutions – there is no room in science for taking the venerability of a hypothesis as additional evidence for it. The legitimate kind of conservatism in science is refusal to accept new theories without convincing evidence. But any other kind of conservatism, especially attachment to familiar concepts because they are familiar, is anti-scientific.

For this reason, the best scientists are ruthless pragmatists about concepts. The more central a concept is to a discipline – matter, in physics, or selection, in biology, or incentive, in economics – the more it will tend to be used in multifarious ways that tolerate inconsistencies across even subtle shifts of context. Scientists exploit the intellectual freedom gained through open possibilities for conceptual evolution allowed by logical diversity. Philosophers who see it as their role to police the conceptual landscapes of the sciences and 'clean them up' thus do a disservice to science, and should be resisted with the same attitude that I advocate against social conservatives who promote homogenous and frozen social roles based on sex or nationality (etc.). Philosophers of science as speculative, forward-looking historians of science should allow, indeed expect, that as science progresses the worldview that it causes to evolve will be ever more unlike the familiar ones of pre-Enlightenment thought.[8]

1.2   The metaphysical context of economics

A further difference between the historian and the philosopher of science has been passed over in the foregoing discussion. The philosopher has a special interest in the *generality* of the evolving scientific worldview. This is why philosophy of science, but not most history of science, is relevant to the themes that have traditionally been taken up in metaphysics; themes, that is, about the most universal patterns that limit every structural real pattern at every scale. Ladyman and I argue that a philosopher of science does scientific metaphysics whenever she focuses on interdisciplinary unifications that include aspects of fundamental physics among the inputs.

In this book I will not be engaged, except occasionally, in metaphysics of this kind. Specifically, I will not attempt to unify economics with parts of fundamental physics in any direct way. However, it is crucial to my thinking about economics that such metaphysics involving it is possible; it's why I think that economics is – or, at least, *often* is – about objective reality rather than merely practical and parochial human purposes.

Here, I will confine myself to describing the most general way in which the nature of the physical world establishes a domain for the economist to objectively describe. The most fundamental generalizations of physics can all be characterized as constraints on how *information* can be conserved and transferred. This does not mean that the world is 'made of' information, as some recently popular metaphysical slogans would have it; I consider it an unhelpful metaphor to speak of the physical world as 'made of' anything.[9] The

---

[8] For example, Ladyman and I argue that, in light of a consensus already achieved in quantum physics, our current worldview should not regard individual spatially concentrated objects as anything but useful hooks for keeping track of some local patterns that are practically important to people. In other words, such objects are not 'building blocks' of reality, as in most metaphysical models promoted by philosophers. See Ladyman and Ross (2007).

[9] The pre-Socratic philosophers launched a very long-lived project in speculating about the ultimate constituents of the physical world. Some thought it was ultimately composed of the classical

point, rather, is that no real patterns[10] can be influenced by patterns to which they are unconnected by an information-carrying channel that physics indicates to be possible and which physical instruments can in principle quantitatively measure. People and other animals are real patterns, which are identified as such by the fact that they are systematically sensitive to information carried in certain physical formats and systematically insensitive to information carried in certain other physical formats. In consequence of their selective informational sensitivities, and the constitution of their nervous and other biophysical structures, they transform the information to which they are sensitive in the production of behavior. This behavior itself transmits information, both to other information-sensitive systems and to their own nervous systems. Because people's behavior provides information to themselves, they can learn to adapt their information-processing to serve biologically inherited stability and comfort conditions – the basis for their *preferences* – and on the basis of this leverage they evolve new preferences which under some circumstances can displace their inherited ones.[11]

The objectivity of (some) economics, as with any other special science, rests on the fact that there are physical facts of the matter about what information can and cannot be computationally extracted, by any physically possible measurement process, from a given signaling event.

This is all very abstract, and for that reason may strike some readers as frustratingly evasive. My excuse for this is that in later chapters I will describe a number of explicit relationships between human neural information-processing architecture and patterns of economic response – patterns that economists call, in a special technical sense

---

elements, earth, air, fire and water. This way of thinking was taken over into the modern scientific age by traditions that sought the smallest indivisible particles, an endeavor that was initially encouraged by the discovery that atomic energy is expressed in quanta. Ladyman and Ross (2007), however, argue that contemporary physics rejects this entire image. To understand the idea that information is fundamental in the sense that atoms once were, would be self-evidently silly were the grip of the metaphor not so venerable and easily overlooked.

[10] This phrase was given a special meaning in a classic paper by Daniel Dennett (1991a). This special meaning refines rather than revises the natural meaning, i.e. that of a recurring structure of events and relationships that's objectively 'there in the data' instead of imposed upon it. Dennett's idea is further technically refined in Ladyman and Ross (2007), Chapter 4.

[11] For example, most people do not prefer to beget as many children as they possibly can. Many prefer to beget no offspring at all.

of their own, 'choices.' For now I am confining myself to abstraction in service of a single general point. This is that physics *constrains* behavior of organisms, including therefore their economic behavior, but it *determines* behavior only in case a grand eliminativist hypothesis is true. This grand eliminativist hypothesis would be that all of the real patterns of information transformation and transmission, including fed-back processing, can in principle be identified without loss at the scale of description in which fundamental physical generalizations are rendered. I characterize this as an *eliminativist* hypothesis because if it is true then all of the behavioral sciences are ultimately *redundant* in the scientific limit; only fundamental physics objectively describes reality and all other sciences are mere patchwork approximations used for practical purposes by beings who must act in ignorance of most physical facts and principles. According to grand eliminativism, only fundamental physics can aspire to identify objective states of affairs, while special sciences such as economics, psychology and biology are accounts of subjective – though generally intersubjectively monitored and compared – partial perspectives on reality.

No one can know that this grand eliminativist hypothesis is false. I suspect that many people who like to say that economics isn't a 'real' science have it implicitly in mind.[12] It has recently been vigorously defended by a leading philosopher of science, Alex Rosenberg (2011). Though I will not go into details here, I think that where Rosenberg's version of grand eliminativism precisely goes wrong is in his interpretation of the content of fundamental physics. More generally, I am ready to bet against grand eliminativism not on the basis of philosophical intuitions, or even philosophical arguments, but because science is currently trending in the opposite direction from it, and has been for some time. Contemporary sciences, including not only social and behavioral sciences but also such disciplines as chemistry and cell biology, increasingly identify objectively stable patterns that cannot be modeled using variables measurable at the scale of

---

[12] Others who say this clutch the opposite but even more hopelessly wrong end of the stick by supposing that human behavior transcends the limits of science because it is in principle unpredictable. Of course human behavior is complex and arguably will never be rendered completely open to perfectly reliable forecast. But this is true of the majority of interesting phenomena, most of which no one thereby supposes to lie outside the domain of science. Science is not foiled by nondeterministic patterns.

fundamental physical magnitudes and processes. The grand elimi-nativist must attribute this to our current ignorance. But this attri-bution stumbles over empirical explanations, in terms that refer only to causal processes independent of human interpretation, of *why* and *how* specific patterns stabilize and give rise to information on scales that fundamental physical models can't distinguish or that they cross-classify. (For some details of such explanations, see Batterman 2002; Ladyman and Ross 2007, chapters 3 and 4.)

1.3   Economics and its neighbors: psychology and sociology

It seems likely that economics has nothing to say about most of the universe. It applies only where some systems husband energy into limited stores that they then selectively spend in pursuit of outcomes that bring their current states or prospects into closer conformity with their preferences. By 'preferences' I do not restrict reference to rankings of alternatives that are or could be consciously compared. A female bird that moves into the nest of the local male with the most redolent plumage thereby expresses a preference for males with bright and sharply contrasted feather colors, even though we presume that she doesn't frame this preference for her own reflective attention. Economists model the behavior of non-human animals using the same techniques and conceptual resources they apply to people.[13] For example, Bshary and Noë (2003) model the interactions between reef-dwelling fish that eat parasites taken from the scales of other fish and their 'clients' who benefit from this by removal of their parasites. Members of client species that cannot travel significant distances between reefs, and thus have reduced choice of cleaner services compared with more pelagic species, are more likely to have their scales nipped by cleaners and are made to wait in longer queues when cleaners have backlogs. This is exactly what the theory of behavior in a competitive market with restricted supply predicts. In the model, fish on both sides of the market make choices in the standard economic understanding of this concept: That is, their

---

[13]   See, for example, the studies collected in Noë et al. (2001).

behavioral variation is sensitive to changes in incentives, specifically changes in relative opportunity costs.[14] But no one supposes that fish make these choices by conscious deliberation. Similarly, economists are not committed to the idea that most people make most of their economic choices consciously either.

If people don't make most economic choices consciously, this mustn't imply that the choices in question are made by internal agents whose motivations and deliberations are hidden from introspection. As long emphasized by the philosopher of mind Daniel Dennett,[15] one cannot make progress toward explaining an agent's purposeful, or as philosophers call it 'intentional,' behavior by hypothesizing another intentional agent inside her; for then we immediately confront the problem of explaining the basis of *that* internal agent's intentions and their relationship to actions. Both intentionality and consciousness, insofar as they are important to all or some behavior, must be accounted for as phenomena that emerge from processes that are not themselves intentional or conscious. As we will see in a later chapter, the interdisciplinary field of cognitive science has made a good deal of progress in furnishing such explanations. I will argue that although only a minority of economic choices are made consciously, all involve intentionality. Therefore, to understand how economics can be integrated into our general scientific worldview, we will need to give a plausible general account of its relationship with psychology.

As explained earlier, the useful role for the philosopher of science lies in exploring normative interconnections between disciplines – that is, not only how disciplines are historically related to one another, but how they might *best* be integrated given current empirical knowledge. As we will see throughout the book, the relationship between economics and psychology has been a major recurring issue in economists' understanding of the limits and structure of their enterprise for all of its modern history. The majority of commentators have, in somewhat

---

[14] Opportunity cost refers to the relative value of alternatives that an agent foregoes when she spends resources, including her time. In the example, pelagic fish, having more opportunities to get their scales cleaned, face lower opportunity cost in avoiding cleaners who nip their scales or make them wait in line. The cleaner fish thus give them discounts in the form of shorter queues and higher-quality service.

[15] See Dennett (1969) and numerous subsequent works that further develop this theme, especially Dennett (1991b).

different ways, worked to distance economics from psychology, while recognizing that such distancing cannot be a simple or transparent matter for a field that traffics in the modeling of choices.

Beginning in the 1980s, however, an increasingly influential minority of economists, known as *behavioral* economists, have argued on the basis of experimental evidence that economic choices just *are* psychological phenomena, and should be modeled and explained using the concepts and theoretical structures developed by psychologists. Still more recently, the debate between behavioral and more traditional economists has been infused with data and models coming from neuroscience, which has emerged since the 1990s as the dominant discipline in the wider enterprise of cognitive science. The interanimation of neuroscience and economics has become known as 'neuroeconomics,' which has been nurtured by a dedicated academic society[16] since 2004 and is currently the basis for the research mission of over a dozen well-funded laboratories worldwide.

Chapter 4 of this book will consist in a criticism of behavioral economics and of that part of neuroeconomics – which, as I will explain, is not the whole of neuroeconomics – that shares its assumptions. The criticism does not involve denying that economics and psychology are crucially related to one another, and need to borrow one another's insights if they are each to offer contributions to an internally consistent scientific picture of objective reality. However, I will argue that economic choices are not processes that are confined within the minds or brains of individual agents. Furthermore, many of the choices most important to economists are made not by individual people but by groups of them, often over timescales that are relatively extended by the standards of psychologists. A key storehouse of *elements* of the set of constraints on economic choices is the structure of relative event, object and action valuation in the brain, so economists certainly rely on scientific study of this neural structure. However, I argue that it is an open empirical question at the moment whether neural value computation is most fruitfully modeled using the approach characteristic of economics. And regardless of how this question is ultimately resolved, most behavioral economics as it is currently practiced would, I maintain, be more consistently conceptualized as a

---

[16] http://www.neuroeconomics.org/

proper part of psychology – specifically, as the psychology of individual valuation and motivation. Thus I reject the call that has been voiced by some behavioral economists for a revolution in the main methodology of economic modeling and data analysis.

If much economic choice occurs at the supra-individual scale, as I contend, this immediately raises another set of questions about inter-disciplinary unification. Traditionally, the science that has been most explicitly concerned with putatively irreducible social-scale dynamics of behavior is sociology.[17] In Chapter 5, I therefore turn to the normative relationship between economics and sociology. The conclusion for which I argue is that the traditional basis for dividing these disciplines has collapsed, and that the scientific enterprise would be well served by its institutional demise (i.e., by the fusion of economics and sociology departments and societies). Importantly, I do *not* claim that this fusion should involve a takeover of sociology by economic styles of modeling or by the conceptual framework with which economists are most comfortable. Sociologists, for good reasons, have increasingly been thinking and working more like economists over the past few decades; but, for equally sound reasons, economists have discovered that to do justice to the actual phenomena of choice under scarcity and uncertainty and the dynamics of markets, they need to accept the conceptual ontology that sociologists have long championed. To anticipate the conclusion in a bit more detail, I celebrate the fact that more and more sociologists endorse economists' reliance on formal modeling and hypothesis testing, while being equally enthusiastic about many economists' implicit (and occasionally explicit) abandonment of the dogma known as methodological individualism.

Recall the earlier point that behavioral and social sciences are constrained by physics through specification of the informational

---

[17] Other social sciences, particularly anthropology, are also mainly preoccupied with patterns at this scale. The boundary between sociology and anthropology is highly porous and indeterminate. For purely practical reasons, and with due apologies to anthropologists, in this book I will write as if sociology is the basic home of systematic social-scale modeling and explanation. I will be similarly brusque with respect to applied social sciences such as political studies and religious studies. Some practitioners of these disciplines rely on methodological strategies borrowed primarily from economics, and others hew more closely to the sociological approach as I will characterize it. In light of this, since my ultimate conclusion will be that the boundary between economics and sociology should be entirely erased, it is implicit that the philosophy of social science I defend would incorporate all of these disciplines on which I will not here focus explicit attention.

sensitivities and computational transformation capacities of the objects they study. From this perspective we can say a bit more about the relationship between familiar individualistic microeconomics and sociology. People are systematically sensitive to many informational formats only in structurally organized collectives of various kinds. Large markets register relative values – in the form of prices – that would be statistically undetectable in the absence of huge numbers of trades among millions of buyers and sellers. As Friedrich Hayek was the first to emphasize, such a market is, fundamentally, an information-processing machine that takes trades as its inputs and yields prices as its outputs. The frustrating elusiveness of successful quantitative prediction in macroeconomics stems in part from the fact that no model can capture the information-processing power of the actual market. This makes the point that a large market is an irreducibly collective phenomenon. To take another example, drawn from the historical domain of sociology, the behavior of almost all men working in urban corporate offices is now governed by a norm according to which winking at a female employee or colleague with whom they are not intimate would be normatively offensive and would put them at high risk of profound embarrassment.[18] No such norm prevailed sixty years ago. Yet how many men have ever *individually* cognitively processed the entrenchment of this specific norm at all? It is unlikely that many men, especially younger ones, consider winking at the office and then stop themselves as their brains simulate the probable consequences. Rather, it would never cross their minds to wink. There is an air of paradox around the idea that all members of a large population know something that only a small minority of them have ever thought about. The puzzle is dissolved by reflection on the myriad ways in which the contemporary social environment teems with information about expected relationships between professional life and sex, between men and women, between managers and their subordinates, between informal personal exchanges and those governed by HR codes, which collectively imply that a wink would typically be perceived as a violation. This fact is processed and established *as* a fact at the scale of society, not (in general) at the scale of individuals.

---

[18] This example is borrowed from the psychiatrist Gene Heyman (2009). I will revisit it later in service of the point to which Heyman applied it, which differs from the one made here.

No sociologist has doubted the existence of such irreducible social facts, but it has been part of the traditional philosophical rhetoric of economics to regard them as ultimately redundant, on grounds that they are parasitic without residue on facts about individuals' psychologies. I put the point in this hedged way, rather than saying outright that individualistic reductionism has been an assumption of economics, because most economists have never paid much attention to this putative constraint in their actual work. Before the 1930s it was common for economists to attribute this mis-match between rhetoric and practice to the fact that empirical psychology and neuroscience were young enterprises. Following the work of Jan Tinbergen and John Maynard Keynes, however, economics was institutionally partitioned into microeconomics, which retained the mission of discovering generalizations about individuals' responses to changes in incentives, and macroeconomics, which sought patterns in relationships between changes in summary statistics about whole economies, such as the supply of money, average prices, and proportions of people trying but failing to find buyers for their offers of labor services.[19] Once it became normal for economists to specialize as either microeconomists or macroeconomists, most found no occasions in which their philosophical opinions about the reducibility or irreducibility of social facts had any bearing on their professional activity. Sophisticated discussions about relationships between the behavioral and the social sciences at mid-twentieth century were largely confined to sociologists and philosophers of science.

This situation began to change in the 1970s, when some leading macroeconomic generalizations on which standard fiscal policy were based seemed to break down, and some economists attributed this to destabilization of the patterns in question by the effects of policies on microeconomic incentives. This made the question of the 'microfoundations' of macroeconomics into a practical research problem for the discipline as a whole. A profusion of schools of thought, with different associated policy biases, quickly developed. The overwhelming majority of economists, however, accepted a methodological rule of thumb to the effect that constraint relationships between microeconomics and macroeconomics are asymmetric in favor of microeconomics. That is, it was assumed that macroeconomic patterns that were inconsistent with

---

[19] This is what economists actually understand by the popular word 'unemployment'.

the incentives and learning capacities of large numbers of asset traders would break down, but no similar generalization held in the opposite direction.[20] This widespread view has been reinforced in popularity by the global financial and labor markets crisis that began in 2008. Most popular and academic commentators on this crisis take the view that supposedly autonomous and relatively stable macroeconomic relationships were subverted by correlated psychological dispositions in consumers, traders, lenders, regulators, and central bankers; but a general failure by all of these agents to appreciate this subversion before the fact led to decisions and policies that interacted to produce a general disaster.[21] This is sometimes taken to represent a vindication of Keynes's most general opinion,[22] yielding the ironic implication that the economist with the largest *causal* responsibility for the rise of autonomous macroeconomics was the very person who most clearly appreciated the impossibility of such autonomy and the inadequacy of policies based on it.

It is well beyond the scope or capacity of the philosophy of economics to try to justify, by itself, an opinion as to the most reliable basis for fashioning economic policy, either at the individual or the state level. What I will more modestly do in the closing chapter of the book is argue that the main debates on these issues have been distorted by undue emphasis on the integration of *psychology* with economics by comparison with attention to the unification of economics with *sociology*. A better balance in interdisciplinary integration, I argue, would suggest that the asymmetric constraint on macroeconomics by microeconomics is a mistake, and that there is at least as much influence in the opposite direction.

The financial crisis, I will conclude the book by suggesting, had both microeconomic and macroeconomic causes, which compounded one another. Partly for this reason, well trained economic journalists who are

---

[20] A limiting case of this logic, producing a kind of inversion of the principle, is the *rational expectations hypothesis*. According to this hypothesis large markets incorporate, at any given time, all available information about future relative asset values, and so correct microeconomic and macroeconomic models, being models of exactly the same phenomena at different scales, could not be in tension with one another in the first place. I will discuss this hypothesis in Chapter 5.

[21] Akerlof and Shiller (2009) is the most widely promoted of many such arguments.

[22] E.g., Skidelsky (2010).

required to pay attention to both sides of the great institutional divide in economics foresaw the coming trouble more clearly than many economists did. This offers a lesson for philosophers of economics. Had they directed their professional attention at what, according to me, *should be* their proper target, they might have been the counterparts within the academy to the writers and editors at *The Economist* and a few other newspapers who saw the causal nexus accurately. Philosophers of economics were instead mainly preoccupied with the concept of economic rationality, which the book argues is a deep distraction and red herring. It is important to add here that the fact that the best economic journalists sounded clear alarms did not avert the crisis, or even allow any institutional actor to mitigate it. I thus do not suggest that had philosophers of economics been concentrating their minds in the right place they could have saved the world. In the realm of human institutions, between understanding and efficacious actions fall many shadows. But I think that most philosophers will agree with my feeling that when we humans go over cliffs together, as we often do, it's best to know roughly how we did it this time.

2
Economics and Its Neighbors before 1980

2.1 The pedagogy of economics versus better philosophy of economics

The suite of modern human behavioral science disciplines – psychology, economics, linguistics, anthropology, sociology and political science – was born gradually between the scientific revolution and the end of the nineteenth century. A natural question for philosophers about this intellectual evolution hinges on realism versus social constructionism, to what extent does the division of labor it institutionalized reflect relatively deep and stable patterns in the structure of human society? To what extent is it a consequence of path-dependent accidents in the evolution of European and American universities? I will be arguing in the chapters ahead that there is no single overarching answer to this question. I will tell a mainly realist story about the difference between economics and psychology and a mainly constructionist story about the division between economics and sociology.

On the standard narrative of the history of economics, the first 'true' economist, the writer who gave expression to the most fundamental insight of the discipline, was Adam Smith (1723–1790). The breakthrough attributed to Smith – sometimes with nods at others who anticipated it less systematically, such as Mandeville (1723 and 1728 [1997]) – is that the selfish and uncoordinated pursuit of material gain by individuals, *if* it is regulated by legal protection of private property and allows returns on investments to accrue in the form of such property, tends to lead to convergent prices for goods and services that reflect the relative scarcities of the factors used to produce them. This in turn leads selfish agents to unintentionally promote the growth of social wealth by trying to increase the productive efficiency of the factors they themselves own. They do this by trying to produce more efficiently than their rivals, which in turn inspires them to innovate new products and production processes that increase the ratio of output value to input costs. This pressure also leads them to invest the main shares of their profits in such innovative efforts, rather than consuming them or giving them away to members of their personal support networks.

Though this idealized picture of competition must be qualified in numerous ways, to which we will return later, it indeed offers one of the most powerful and important insights in the social and intellectual history of the world. The growth of human wealth has mainly been driven by the spontaneous *and* institutionally organized sorting of human talents into complementary specializations.[1] A key point for future reference is that the subject matter of Smith's analysis is social structure and organization, not psychology. The analysis does incorporate an assumption about individual people's motivations, but the assumption in question is a banal one that had been patently obvious since the dawn of human self-reflection, namely, that people tend to do things that they expect will augment the stock of resources over which they have control. It has been a disputed question in economics as to whether economists need to assume anything less anodyne about psychology in order to frame their general theories. We will explore answers to this question both in this chapter and in later ones.

Economics students generally do not rigorously study the generalization of Smith's that they are told is fundamental unless they pursue the subject for a second or third year. Instead, they typically first focus on a single imaginary individual, originally Robinson Crusoe alone on his island prior to the arrival of his companion Friday,[2] trying to decide how to allocate his basic input resources of personal energy and time in such a way as to optimize his later flow of revenues in the forms of food, clothing and leisure. For example, provided there are enough fish that will take bait cast from shore, Crusoe might sensibly take time off from

---

[1] Specialization of labor is far older than capitalism. Haim Ofek (2001) marshalls evidence for the hypothesis that such specialization preceded and was a necessary condition for the evolution of large-brained modern humans. The first professionals, according to Ofek, were fire keepers.

[2] The most elegant specimen of this classic pedagogical approach to introductory economics is Robertson (1957), chapter 2.

harvesting coconuts to make a fishing rod; later he might have enough food supplies stored up in reserve to spend most of his time building a boat. The primary motivation for this pedagogy is that it emphasizes *opportunity cost* – the relative value foregone when someone chooses from a set of competing alternative uses for a resource, in this case labor time – as a core element of the subject matter of economics. This is in fact importantly connected with Smith's insight, since it refines his understanding of relative scarcity, and that idea is in turn important to understanding the efficiency effects of competition. However, few introductory textbooks make these connections explicit. The Robinson Crusoe opening to the study of economics thus *seems* to mainly signal that what economics is about is, in the first place, 'rational' individual decision-making. That message is amplified if, when Friday comes along and introduces the prospects for efficiency-promoting exchange of the fruits of specialized labor, this is presented as a *complication* to 'pure' economic analysis. By contrast, economics as framed by Smith only *begins* to apply when Friday appears.

Decades of teaching economics on a foundation of individual decision-making is reflected in many economists' working philosophy of their discipline. However, a main argument of the present book is that this individualistic philosophy is an ultimately confusing way to think about economics. It obscures the fact that what is truly central to economics are differences in information within markets, which in turn make it worthwhile for people to enter into relationships of mutual exchange (Hayek 1945; Martens 2004). People trade with one another because, most fundamentally, no one can know enough to be very good at fulfilling more than a small share of their own wants and needs. But Crusoe before Friday has no one with whom to trade.

Beginning with Crusoe not only obscures the status of markets as the basic subject matter of economics, but furthermore clouds the foundational distinction between economics and psychology. A reader might wonder whether this should matter to anyone but an academic worried about guild politics. Indeed there is no reason why we should resist the merger of disciplines in principle; and I will later argue in favor of a merger between economics and sociology. However, I will also argue that when economics is allowed to collapse into psychology we lose access to important real patterns in the world that economists have worked long and hard to bring to light.

In claiming that the fundamental ontology of economics is organized around markets rather than individuals, I am not stating a matter of fact; I am *proposing* a way of interpreting the activity and priorities of economists. That is what makes this book philosophy of science rather than history or sociology of science. As I insisted in Chapter 1, however, useful philosophy is not conducted independently of factual constraints. My proposal needs to be defended not from first principles about what economics 'should' be about, but as one normative lesson read from the actual history of the major ideas in economics – and the actual history of economies and economic policies. Philosophers are often and rightly criticized for analyzing concepts ahistorically. Other philosophers, notably Ian Hacking (1983) and Mark Wilson (2006), have emphasized the deep ways in which the theoretical structures of sciences, and subtleties in how scientists understand the concepts that feature in theories, are shaped by histories of practical application. Philosophy should be done not by analyzing concepts abstractly, but by *showing* concepts at work. Thus this chapter, and indeed this whole book, is structured out of philosophical reflections on some selected themes from the history of economic thought.

2.2   Marginalism

The view that economics begins with analysis of individual motivation and decision emerged over several decades from the triumph of so-called *marginalist* reasoning about economic value. Historians commonly honor the emergence of marginalism with the word 'revolution.' A complication of the story I will be telling is that I *reject* the principal philosophical spin that has been associated with the marginalist revolution while at the same time *accepting* the technical improvements that it brought to economic method. This distinguishes my approach from the majority of critics of the marginalist mainstream (e.g., Lawson 1997, Keen 2002), who attack marginalist analytical principles along with the standard philosophy of economics bequeathed from the marginalists. In my opinion these critics send babies down the drain with the bathwater.

The marginalist revolution is regarded as having been launched in the 1870s by three figures working independently, William Stanley Jevons (1835–1882), Leon Walras (1834–1910) and Carl Menger (1840–1921).

The marginalists are so named because their central insight was that transactions and investments occur against existing stocks of assets. The value of a new car to a person will differ, relative to the value of other things she could buy, depending on whether she begins with no car, with one car, with two cars, or with twenty cars. Thus if we compare a world in which most people have no car to a hypothetical world in which everyone has at least one car, leaving other wealth unchanged, then the relative value of cars in the second world will be lower than in the first. The proportion of investment allocated to the production of cars will correspondingly decline unless their price relative to other prices falls faster than relative demand.[3] Notice how all the comparisons in these relationships involve *relative changes*. The key insight of the marginalists is that everything the economist analyzes has this character. The marginalists recognized that evaluation of new potential assets against the stock of existing ones is just a special case of general opportunity cost analysis. This suggests that the core item in the toolbox that an economist carries from problem to problem should be practical knowledge of calculus. And that, in turn, is the basic reason why the teaching of economics begins with the lone Crusoe trying to decide whether he would be better off if he reallocated his time among the various ways in which he could harvest food and firewood. Although, as I contend, this gets the *philosophy* of economics off to a confusing start, it has the higher compensating value of immediately directing the student to what most economists spend most of their time doing: calculating optimum points in possible budget allocations.

The pre-marginalist economics of Smith and successive 'classical' economists such as David Ricardo (1772–1823) and Karl Marx (1818–1883), traced the values of complex goods back to fixed scarcities of the important factors that went into their specific production. Classical economists sought to understand economy-wide systems of prices in terms of the scarcity of those factors – principally land and labor – that entered into *all* production. The marginalists effectively eliminated this appeal to 'bedrock' factors for determining value. All

---

[3] In actual history, the relative (real) value of cars *has* steadily fallen, because average human wealth has risen much faster than the relative costs of the main inputs to car production. Steady improvements in car quality have disguised the price consequences of some, but certainly not most, of this relative value decline.

values, they maintained, derive from people's opinions about which possible changes in their consumption patterns they expect will make the most difference to their subjectively evaluated well-being. Such changes are conceptualized as increments or decrements in an abstract construct that economists refer to as *utility*. Subjective expected valuations, measured in terms of utility, are one element of the function that determines prices. They interact with the opportunity costs, also represented in terms of utility, of any contemplated or actual changes in the allocation of production factors.

Since utility as developed by the early marginalists and their successors refers to relationships between possible or actual rates of change, it is intrinsically abstract. To try to reduce it to a kind of substance involves changing its conceptual character. This point will be of profound importance throughout this book; the abstract character of utility crystallizes the separateness of economics, as a discipline, from psychology. Of course, from the perspective defended in Chapter 1 there is nothing *wrong* with allowing concepts to evolve, and they often retain their value for practical purposes in changing circumstances by adapting. In some instances, however, concepts are debased by change, especially if the change in question involves loss of precision. As we will see, different contemporary economists operate with different ideas of utility, which are implicated in deep disagreements about economic methods and research agendas.

The research program of marginalism consisted of representing (1) the demand side of any economic system as based on a set of *utility functions* that map consumption possibilities onto consumers' *preferences*, and (2) the supply side as based on *production functions* that map possible arrangements of factors onto outputs. What the economist then sought was a model consisting of simultaneous equations expressing consequences of shifts in demand or supply for the relative satisfaction of consumers' preferences and the relative profitability of producers. Solving such models involves deriving sets of prices and output levels at which consumers could not increase their utility by changing their consumption, and producers could not increase their profits by changing factor allocations. Such solutions represent *equilibria* in the system, toward which consumption patterns, production arrangements and prices should converge in the short-run. In the longer-run, changes in technology and population demographics cause equilibrium positions to move, which requires re-analyzing the system.

Before the coming of modern computing technology, models had to admit of analytic solutions that could be calculated on paper. Thus they necessarily involved, and were recognized to involve, considerable idealization. For example, the number of agents in the market, or the number of goods to be produced, or the relationships among inputs, or typically all of the above and more, would be drastically scaled down by comparison with a typical real market. Controversies over application of the method to real economic facts and processes typically hinged on alternative ways of aggregating ('adding up') utility functions on the demand side, and, on the supply side, alternative principles for distinguishing between short-run and long-run changes.

In their methodological remarks the early marginalists often refer to the role of differential calculus and linear systems of equations in driving the triumph of classical physics after Newton, and recommend their approach to economics as promising parallel breakthroughs. A number of critics of the marginalist inheritance, notably the historian of economics Philip Mirowski (1989), adopt a condescending attitude toward this 'physics envy.' Sometimes these critics go so far as to deny that this aspect of the marginalist revolution represented progress. Mirowski offends some scholars with irreverent rhetoric about canonical economists, but I personally find irreverence healthy. The main point Mirowski makes is worth briefly considering, both because it is centrally related to the main theme of this book and because there is a real philosophical argument behind Mirowski's punk attitude. The marginalists' admiration of classical physics, he maintains, led them to focus away from the actual economy and instead construct cartoon economies deliberately fashioned to resemble relatively simple mechanical systems such as boilers. Worse, he argues, the mechanics the marginalists borrowed was already obsolete in physics at the time of their borrowing. This criticism, updated by reference to more recent physics and the more complex mathematics used in contemporary economics, is often leveled against current, not merely nineteenth-century, economic modeling practices.[4]

---

[4] See, e.g., Ormerod (1994), which, despite its foolish title, is better informed and more balanced than most of the recent literature that attacks mainstream economics in general.

In my opinion Mirowski gives us illuminating critical history of economics, but greatly exaggerates the extent to which the early marginalists were guilty of an original sin that corrupts their discipline ever after. All scientific modeling involves idealization, and idealizations usually begin by pretending that a system to be understood resembles some other system that is already better understood. All scientists are both driven and limited by the technology available to them for building, testing and solving models of the real patterns they aim to study. We will see, later in this book how the development of fast, powerful, cheap data processors since the 1980s has enabled economists to study a range of phenomena that were formerly out of their reach. Economic theorists of the preceding decades are today often criticized as though they foolishly thought that these out-of-reach phenomena didn't matter. Such criticisms reflect badly on the critics. Most scientists do not bemoan their lack of knowledge of phenomena that they don't currently have the machinery to examine; they study what they can while waiting for the engineers to build better tools. In the case of economics, the engineers in question are mathematicians and (especially) statisticians. At the same time, we should acknowledge that analogies sometimes become dogmatic traps that impede progress. There is justice to Mirowski's substantive claim that there were important properties of the physics the early marginalists borrowed that they misunderstood or ignored. But this does not imply that we should regret their emphasis on calculus or on changes in relative valuations.

Discovering generalizations about ways in which relative, aggregate changes in market valuations are influenced by changes in institutions, technology and demographics, as channeled through incentives, is the basic business of economics. That, in a nutshell, is the philosophy of economics defended in this book.

2.3 Subjective value and decision theory

I have endorsed the mainstream view that it constituted progress in economics when privileged inputs to production (land and labor) were abandoned as anchors of value in favor of subjective utility. However, some non-essential marginalist assumptions about the nature of subjectivity turned out to be a Trojan horse, infusing a subtle pathogen into people's understanding of economic theory that has recently metastasized into a campaign for wholescale displacement of economics by psychology and neuroscience.

The marginalists, in shifting the conception of value from putatively objective determinants to subjective and varying preferences, thereby turned the focus of economists from institutional structures toward individual choice. When this was later combined with the science of probability, marginalist economics set off down the path that eventually made decision theory a part of the logical foundations of the discipline. In turn the most common view of decision theory, so long as it has existed, is that it is either part of psychology or intimately connected with it. The association of the foundations of economics with decision theory has also attracted philosophers, whose emphasis on normative rationality steers their inquiries into these waters. When philosophers encounter a discipline they can take to rest on foundations in individual decision theory they feel much at home, and some of these philosophers, notably the brilliant technical innovator Frank Ramsey (1903–1930) and later the logician Richard Jeffrey (1926–2002), have reflected this attitude back into the self-conception of economists.

That decision theory is important to economics is not open to doubt. For one thing, it shares some essential axioms with game theory, which, as we will see, in the next chapter, is the mathematical technology that has transformed microeconomics over the past few decades. However, the extreme view that decision theory is the very basis of economics has encouraged thinking that we might reconstruct by the following lazy syllogism: Economics is an application of decision theory; decision theory is a part of psychology; therefore economics is an application of psychology. In calling the syllogism 'lazy' I of course mean to signal that I'll reject it.

The science of decision falls into two broad branches, descriptive and normative. Descriptive decision theory attempts to mathematically model the processes by which actual people in fact weigh and choose between alternative options. The dominant historical figures in this field are Ward Edwards (1927–2005), Herbert Simon (1916–2001), Daniel Kahneman (1934–), Amos Tversky (1937–1996) and Paul Slovic (1938–). That this modeling is a proper province of psychology – or, in ways we will touch upon in some detail in Chapter 4, of neuroscience – is clear. Any effort to preserve relative autonomy of economics from psychology and neuroscience must block the reduction of economics to descriptive decision theory, while explaining how the two disciplines are related to one another.

Normative decision theory is the branch of decision theory that mainly preoccupies philosophers. It aims to identify principles for choosing and weighing practical alternatives that conform to ideals of logical consistency and statistical soundness. Philosophers' interest in normative decision theory derives from their dominant project of constructing the boundaries of rationality in general. For reasons sketched in Chapter 1, this is not a project I regard as well-founded or helpful. Why should we suppose that there is a single basket of cognitive strategies, superior to all others in all contexts, that could be discovered and set up as an ideal against which to measure all particular strategies that real agents might actually use? The belief in a single-peaked general rationality criterion is inherited from belief in the mind of God. That idea doesn't make sense and neither does its secular descendent. The philosopher's bad question 'What is a rational agent in general?' should not be mixed up with economists' many good questions about potential improvements in information-processing and utility-improving capacities in particular kinds of environments (especially particular kinds of markets).

In their involvement with normative decision theory, economists have mainly emphasized two aspects of all members of the family of rationality models: (1) consistency of preferences over outcomes; and (2) accurate projections of statistical frequencies and distributions in making inferences from samples. To the extent that an economic agent's choices reflect inconsistent valuations of consequences, or fail to respect the actual frequencies of contingencies in the environment, the agent will tend to lose resources if she is competing with other agents whose choices are more consistent or conform better to sound principles of statistical inference. This point is often expressed in ways that make it unnecessarily controversial. For example, it is sometimes said that normatively unsound agents will be driven to bankruptcy in markets, or to extinction in Darwinian fitness tournaments. These arguments imply that market competition and natural selection are optimizing filters for cognitive apparatus. However, this isn't true in general. One important reason it isn't true is that environments change, and in changing shift the pressures on different trade-offs that strategies embody as between accuracy, informational variety, processing speed, and forms of error tolerance. Real, relatively rational, agents must be *learning* systems, and there is no such thing as a learning program that is generically best in all types of environment.

Putting biological selection aside, where markets are concerned the motivation for emphasizing normative decision theory can be based on a more plausible general consideration. This is that *if* normative analysis can identify decision principles not currently present in some market, but which would earn higher long-run profit for their adopters if they were deployed, then we should expect an entrepreneur to sooner or later notice this and to search for a cost-effective way of implementing the principles in question. This search might of course fail, perhaps because of an insurmountable physical or institutional barrier. But prudent students of markets learn that the limitations of their imaginations are typically tighter than the limitations of entrepreneurial cunning. If the analyst can define a better mousetrap, and it isn't ruled out by physics, she should expect it to sooner or later appear on the market – and to influence the flow of investment into current mousetraps by its mere possibility.

This argument can be complemented by a philosophical one, which has been formulated with particular clarity by the late sociologist James Coleman (1990). Economics, along with sociology, is a study of *actions*. One difference between an action and a general change of state is that the former is directed toward a condition that is normatively advantageous for an agent, and is selected to occur for this reason. The possibility of identifying this kind of relationship presupposes some level of stability in the conditions of flourishing for the entity to which agency is ascribed. Agency also implies that the entity in question is an essential part of the causal sources of its actions, which in turn implies that information about what is better for the agent is in *some* manner encoded in its structure, and encoded in a way that systematically constrains its actions.[5]

---

[5] The philosopher of science Alex Rosenberg (2011) argues that no science of actions can succeed, because despite appearances there are no actions. All events are caused by preceding states, and these states cannot include favorable consequences that haven't happened yet. Thus, according to Rosenberg, the patterns studied by economists, sociologists and psychologists who appeal to such *intentional* states as aims and purposes are causally redundant. In the limit where science is complete, intentional patterns will be eliminated in favor of more exact and reliable generalizations from physics, biochemistry and neuroscience. I briefly indicated the general grounds on which I reject general eliminativism about high-scale patterns in Chapter 1. In Chapter 4, I will address more specific eliminativism about intentionality.

Clearly this does not imply that agent behavior must satisfy the demands of an ideal normative decision theory. Real agents must have finite computational resources and thus be limited in inferential power or access to information or both. But agency *does* imply some minimal thresholds of soundness in the functioning of the mechanisms that relate actions to probabilities of improved conditions (Dennett 1969). This in turn implies some minimal threshold of consistency in what an agent seeks. Economists and sociologists are therefore committed to investment in models of decision that honor at least these minimal norms. As we will see, later in this chapter, the axiomatic foundations of microeconomics are typically framed and motivated in exactly this way.

This recognition is the background for stating what I consider currently to be the most important question of debate in the philosophy of economics:

> Are the principles of normative decision theory, or at least those principles most relevant to identification of relative opportunity costs and opportunity values, more closely approximated by individual people making choices in relative isolation, or by groups of people making choices in particular kinds of institutional contexts?

The central conclusion of the book will be that our best evidence favors the second disjunct. Indeed, I will argue for the more specific claim that human choices are *only* likely to approximate the recommendations of normative decision theory when they are distributed across groups of people acting within institutional contexts that give them access to information about relative values of resources and where the information in question has been at least partly processed through markets.

It will take the rest of the book to pull together the argument for this conclusion. In the present chapter the objective is to continue showing that the bases of its key premises are well grounded it in the history of economic thought.

2.4 After the marginalist revolution: economists retreat from psychology

At the time the early marginalists wrote, atomism and reductionism were doctrines on the rise among philosophers of science. Atomism is the doctrine according to which complex structures and processes are aggregations of simple, basic ones, and (ontological) reductionism[6] is the view that we should seek to explain properties of complexes strictly by reference to properties of simples. These doctrines were opposed at the time by philosophers whose attitudes toward the primacy of empirical science were equivocal, such as followers of Hegel (1770–1830). They were hedged against in a more qualified way by John Stuart Mill (1806–1873) who thought that the biological and psychological domains might be governed by *sui generis* causal factors that don't operate in physics or chemistry. Finally, they were doubted for what I regard as the right reasons by the American pragmatist philosopher C.S. Peirce (1839–1914). But against these sites of resistance atomism and reductionism gained more converts than they lost through the last decades of the nineteenth century and at least the first five decades of the twentieth century.

An influential and representative figure in this intellectual tendency was Bertrand Russell (1872–1970); see especially Russell (1912) for the classic short encapsulation of the mainstream perspective.[7] Russell changed his mind on many points of detail over the course of his long career; but these shifts concerned which specific versions of atomism and reductionism best captured the epistemological and metaphysical implications of the physics, chemistry and biology that all underwent revolutions during his lifetime. The key principles of atomistic reductionism are that complex entities derive their systematic or causal[8] properties from those of simpler entities out of which they are composed; that the way to understand a complex phenomenon or process is therefore to analyze it into its constituent parts or processes; and that although no science other than fundamental physics carries its analyzes all the way down to the ground floor elements of reality, each science should find its foundations in characteristic regularities governing the interactions of the units that are treated as basic in its domain.

---

[6] Ontological reductionism must be distinguished from some other forms, especially reductionism about theories that aims to derive theories with relatively narrow scope of application from more basic theories with broader domains.

[7] For a philosophically shallower but more forthright and scientifically focused manifesto, see Oppenheim and Putnam (1958).

[8] Russell at one stage doubted that causation is a helpful idea in either physics or metaphysics. See Price (2007) and Ladyman and Ross (2007, Chapter 5) for discussions.

Like all dominant metaphysical paradigms, atomistic reductionism has had more influence and importance as a general structuring framework for thought than as a carefully articulated philosophical program. One feature that has helped it resonate is that it complements the dominant political and social ideology of the post-Enlightenment West, according to which the fundamental engines of social causation are the motivations of individual people, and social value is likewise derived additively from the valuations of individuals. Rhetoric that runs together metaphysical and ideological atomism is easy to find in the less rigorous writings of many economists, and has been much emphasized by radical critics of the discipline.

It presumptuously insults the philosophical seriousness, and the political morality, of philosophers such as Russell to depict metaphysical atomism as merely a projection of heroic individualism. But we must acknowledge the less paranoid point that modern economics was crafted within, and both reflects and refines, a broadly entertained Western philosophy that combines elements of social metaphysics and a conception of the locus of ultimate value. Coleman (1990, p. 300) characterizes this philosophy as follows:

> There is a broadly perpetrated fiction in modern society, which is compatible with the political philosophy of natural rights, with classical and neoclassical economic theory, and with many of the intellectual developments (and the social changes which generated them) that have occurred since the seventeenth century. This fiction is that society consists of a set of independent individuals, each of whom acts to achieve goals that are independently arrived at, and that the functioning of the social system consists of the combination of these actions of independent individuals.

Though this image is no longer dominant among philosophers or social scientists, and though more general atomism and reductionism have been under steady retreat in the physical sciences, Coleman's fiction remains the principal framing myth of Western political life. In the Victorian period of the early marginalist economists, it was arguably at its apogee, and was taken as seriously inside the academy as it was in corporate boardrooms and the offices of civic associations.[9]

---

[9] This myth should not be simplistically associated with the political right. Elster (1985) argues that it informs classical Marxist political theory as well. Marx's working class becomes mobilized for action

In sketching the philosophical assumptions that informed the early marginalists, I take Jevons (1871) as the representative figure, because he is most explicit about these assumptions and because he had the greatest influence on their expression in subsequent economic pedagogy. Jevons erects his program for marginal analysis on the platform of a theory of subjective preference, specifically on the claim that people are motivated to trade for new sources of reward because they experience diminishing marginal utility from consumption of any one source. For example, a person's second piece of pie at a sitting will be less rewarding than her first, and a third might be much less desirable to her. The same principle applies, Jevons claims, to sources of utility that don't involve physical satiation; consider listening to the same song over and over again, or repeatedly entertaining the same attractive fantasy without variation. Jevons took for granted that this feature of subjective preference is ultimately based on neurophysiology and that, therefore, economics would eventually find its detailed foundations in biological psychology. F.Y. Edgeworth (1845–1926; 1881) is another early marginalist who pronounced a view of economics as a place-holder for a future neuroscience of value that, he expected, awaited the invention of new technologies for observation and measurement of the active brain.

It turned out to take over a century for the machines Edgeworth predicted to become available. Economists did not, as it developed, spend the interregnum humbly keeping the oven pre-heated for the neuroscientists' eventual baking. Economists instead rebelled against the easy assumptions of reductionism and sometimes, in a more equivocal and sporadic way, against atomism also. By a series of incremental revisions of the standard theoretical foundations over a period of six decades, they developed a conception of economics as autonomous from psychology.

The story of this intellectual evolution is complicated, and its significance is disputed, along multiple dimensions, by historians and philosophers of economics. Giocoli (2003) describes it in detail but regards it as having led the discipline into a methodological cul-de-sac. Bruni and Sugden (2007) maintain a similar regretful view. Hausman (2011)

---

as class consciousness spreads among its individual members; and the communist state is supposed to be attractive mainly because, with their labor power no longer alienated, everyone's distinctive individuality will flower lavishly. Marx never suggests himself drawn to the 'merging into collective consciousness' of, e.g., Christian communalist ideals.

also adopts this attitude, but questions the extent to which the retreat from psychology went beyond rhetoric and was reflected in the actual practice of economists. On the other hand, Ross (2005, 2012b) and Binmore (2009) celebrate the disciplinary separation and interpret it as having been essential in the development of microeconomics as a progressive research program. A careful account that avoids taking sides is given by Mandler (1999).

Economists did not back away from reductionism or atomism because they became infused with philosophical convictions that opposed these doctrines. Such convictions were in fact held by the most important figure in the history of the retreat from psychology, Vilfredo Pareto (1848–1923). But had Pareto promoted his preferred way of modeling demand on the basis of philosophical considerations his influence would have been slight at best. Economists retreated from psychology for the kind of reason that usually drives scientific change: the scale of their standard modeling converged through its own dynamic upon the scale at which the data that most interest them are measured. This is the scale of markets.

Explaining this will require some work. It had *better* require some work, because if it didn't then we wouldn't be able to understand why few non-economists grasped the implications or significance of the retreat from psychology even after economists had carried it out. This in turn explains why so many people fail to recognize that revisionary behavioral economics and neuroeconomics, which will be the subject of Chapter 4, effectively turn the philosophical clock back to Jevons's day.

Jevons, in considering the psychology of the consumer, focuses the main part of his attention on the supposed direct observation, which he takes all of us to be able to confirm through introspection, that the change in satisfaction we derive from a good declines as we consume more of it. Why does this loom so large for him? The answer is surely not that such diminishing marginal satisfaction is the most vivid property of a typical person's experience from moment to moment. Folk psychology in English, which is replete with fine distinctions based on descriptive qualities of different feelings, doesn't even have an everyday word for it. The answer is that diminishing marginal satisfaction can explain why people move their consumption around, and do not devote all of it to whichever sources of their basic biological needs they can obtain with the least effort and cost. More specifically, Jevons's observation implies that investment by a person in being able to consume any specific stream of utility has decreasing returns, so that there must be a point at which she would derive greater marginal utility by re-allocating her personal capital – in the form of energy, time or money – to consumption of an alternative stream.

Let us imagine a consumer choosing between two 'pure' streams of consumption, for example a flow of cheese and a flow of chocolate. Decreasing marginal returns on both consumption streams ensures that there exists a point from which, with prices and the consumer's budget held fixed, a potential trade partner would have to offer her more chocolate than she gives up cheese *or* more cheese than she gives up chocolate in order to induce her to exchange. But to say that the consumer's budget is fixed (at least for these two goods) is to say that such trades are not available. Thus for any given budget allocation for chocolate and cheese for this consumer we can both identify the allocation that maximizes her utility from consumption, and identify hypothetical rearrangements of the allocation (beyond her budget) that would give her the same utility – as economists say, would leave her indifferent. The diagram still familiar from the first chapter of every economics textbook results as shown in Figure 2.1.

This way of presenting the basic elements of consumer theory makes visually salient the underlying mathematical structure: the function from the agent's expenditures to her utility is homogenous in the first degree, ensuring that changes in proportions of a budget allocated between chocolate and cheese move her along an indifference curve that is convex to the origin. This is turn guarantees existence of a unique maximizing allocation for each budget.

What is beautifully achieved by this pedagogy is the illustration of why economic theory should be developed as applied calculus. But, as always, there are trade-offs here. Utility maximization is introduced as a property of a lone agent abstracted from any market – prices are simply given, as implied by fixing the consumer's consumption constraints as a function of her budget. This makes it natural to follow Jevons and Edgeworth in identifying utility with a range of subjective psychological states of the agent. When the goods being consumed are chocolate and cheese, or scalp massages and orgasms, we might associate this range with changes in a one-dimensional construct of 'sensory pleasure.' If the goods are poetry and prose, the subjective value construct must

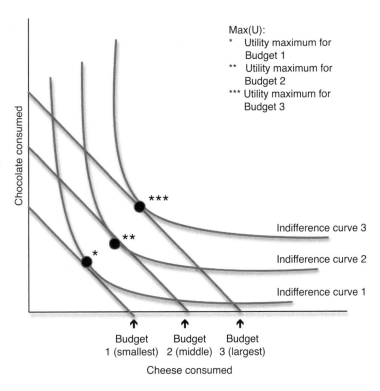

Figure 2.1 Indifference curves for two consumption goods

be something less familiar from folk psychology – say, 'feelings of sublimity.'[10] But in either case it seems immediate that the indifference curves are outputs of a function that takes psychological states as inputs.

The marginalists took the sources of value to be subjective. Indifference curves, it became canonical to say, represent an agent's *preferences*. But such preferences are not sufficient for the existence of a market. Suppose a second agent is considering investing in a chocolate factory, which would add to the total supply of chocolate. He may be able to profitably do so under one of two conditions. The more straightforward condition is one in which the consumer becomes wealthier,

---

[10] Recent neuroscience has empirically confirmed and modeled this distinction on the basis of distinct brain mechanisms that respond respectively to 'pleasure' and 'reward' (Berridge and Robinson 1998).

shifting her budget, say, from the middle straight line in Figure 1 to the northeast line. Then she consumes more of both chocolate and cheese and it might be possible for our investor, even if he cannot improve on the business models of already existing suppliers, to produce and sell the additionally demanded chocolate at a price that exceeds the costs of all the inputs to its production. The more interesting condition for present purposes is one in which the producer can *make* the consumer wealthier by producing chocolate more efficiently and so shifting the consumer's budget curves in the way shown in Figure 2.2.[11] By

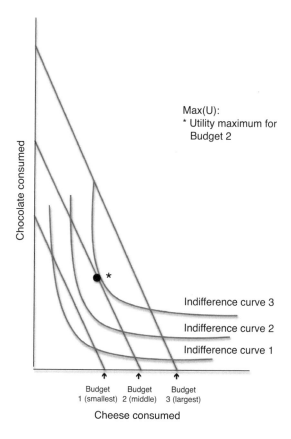

Figure 2.2   Demand responds to a supply shift

---

[11] This implies that the state of affairs before the investor opens the new chocolate factory is not a competitive market equilibrium; there must have been what the early marginalist literature called 'excess demand.'

assumption the consumer's monetary income remains the same, but she can now move to a higher indifference curve – gaining greater utility – by consuming more chocolate and less cheese.

In the context of this little market it is still as appropriate as before to regard the consumer's subjective valuations – her preferences – as the determinants of abstract valuation; she buys chocolate and cheese because they taste good to her and assuage her appetite. But what matters on the market are exchange values, measured in prices. In our example, the determinant of the shifted demand arises from the production side. If market relationships are the 'real' subject matter of economics, then we have evidently introduced some strain into the idea that economics reduces to psychology, at least in the context of the standard introductory pedagogy that is intended to lay bare the analytic operations involved in manipulating the theory.

I suggest that here, in a very early moment in the story, we come to the most delicate and portentous conceptual slippage point in the whole philosophy of economics. Indifference curves describe a systematic kind of relationship that exists between demand as expressed in actual exchanges on markets, and subjective valuations of consumers. Economics studies the properties of these objects under a diverse range of conditions and transformations. Folk ontology tends to be uncomfortable with treating constructs of this kind, which are devised by theorists to summarize *interfaces* between familiar domains of experience, *as objects*. In consequence, realist philosophers, given their usual self-assigned mission of squaring folk ontology with scientific practice (see Chapter 1), are typically inclined to try to analyze such objects 'out of' their literal ontologies. The philosophers do this by semantically reinterpreting interface objects as predicates of coupled systems – the coupled system being, in this case, a consumer and a market – and then granting full objective existence only to the independently observable, materially discrete, components of the system. This is the kind of Russellian analysis that supports a metaphysic of atomistic reductionism.

It is unusual for attention to be drawn to this analytical move that is made at the basic starting point of most philosophy of mainstream economics. This absence from gaze is explained by the fact that the assumption – that constructed interface objects are not *real* objects – remains merely implicit in every discussion of the ontology of economics that I am aware of. But the urge to analyze interface objects away is explicit and familiar from other domains on which philosophers have lavished attention. Consider the example of the *mind*. Many materialist philosophers have argued that if the mind exists, it must be identical with the brain. But this thesis wrestles with daunting challenges, the most important of which stem from the way in which minds are enmeshed in, and distinguished by reference to, external relationships. Brains are built by biochemical processes, whereas minds are jointly constructed by communities of observers and interpreters who stabilize the meanings of the elements of these constructions using public representational media (especially language) and shared semantic conventions. The stability of these elements is maintained in virtual social spaces that constrain and help to stabilize the responses of individuals' brains. Thus the currently most influential view of the ontology of mind among philosophers[12] is that minds are socially constructed and socially maintained *interfaces* between individual brains and domains of experience that people share. When we collectively ascribe a mind, with specific characteristics of personality, intelligence, opinions and sentimental affiliations, to (say) Barack Obama, what we're doing is describing observable and (relatively) distinctive patterns that his nervous system produces in response to events (including virtual events) characterized in terms that we others share with him to describe experience and behavior. The first explicit discoverer of this pattern was the philosopher Dan Dennett (1969). He has emphasized from the outset that when a person ascribes a mind to *herself*, as every normal post-infant person does, she constructs an interface object that bundles up relationships among her nervous system, her history of experiences and behavioral responses, and the expectations that she has observed in others and has learned through cultural training to co-describe with them.

Dennett has repeatedly been confronted by critics who insist that according to his view of minds they aren't truly *real* – they're just ways of *talking about* the good old visible, touchable, made-of-matter brain.

---

[12] A full list of citations here would be very long. I will cite only a few high-quality representative developments of the position: Dennett (1991b), McClamrock (1995), Clark (1997), Bogdan (2009, 2010), and Prinz (2012). Ross (2013b) argues that the virtual mind was a scientific discovery that should be credited to Dennett (1969).

This resistance to thinking of virtual reality as a kind of *reality* rather than a kind of *pretense* expresses the standard Western metaphysic, according to which the world as a whole is *composed of* entities that could 'in principle'[13] stand alone. These entities, that metaphysic pronounces, interact in various complicated ways that give rise to causal and other regularities. Science abstracts from the specific interactions and *represents* the regularities in statements, models, theories, equations etc. One of the tasks of the philosopher of science, on this conception, is reminding scientists and laypeople alike not to confuse representations with the underlying reality they represent. The philosopher stands guard against mistaking virtual reality for real reality.

I indicated in Chapter 1 why in my view this conception of the philosopher's mission is unhelpful to science, and indeed unhelpful to anything. But the better alternative is *not* to try to reify relationships of the kind described by interface constructions like minds and indifference curves as 'higher-level' things. It is rather to avoid in the first place cluttering science with questions about which kinds of things different groups of scientists study. This is easiest to do consistently if one follows Ladyman and Ross (2007) in dropping 'things' altogether from one's metaphysics, on grounds that science doesn't need self-subsistent distinct objects and there's no objective basis for metaphysics except scientific knowledge. But this discipline isn't easy to maintain, because we are all flesh-and-blood people who must constantly solve practical problems by manipulating our environment along the very limited dimensions that afford effective leverage for us. We do this by crudely partitioning the flux of reality into objects that we track from our shared practical and sensory perspective as humans. Analytic philosophy is the intellectual activity into which we naturally drift when we take this book-keeping system of pragmatic approximations too literally and elevate it into the basis for metaphysics. I stress 'naturally' here. Analytic philosophy isn't something people must work themselves into doing by adopting a strange attitude, as Wittgenstein (1953 and elsewhere) is sometimes read as claiming; analytic philosophy is something it takes effort *not* to do.

---

[13] This phrase usually expresses an intuition the writer expects the reader to share. Of course philosophers have devoted much effort to making the principle in question explicit; but there is no consensus among them on the preferred analysis.

The effort in question is easier in a domain like physics than in economics. It is true that we speak naturally of the Higgs boson as if it is a kind of thing. But it raises no practical challenge to anyone, except engineers working on the frontiers where quantum theory meets experimental manipulation of matter, to be reminded that the Higgs boson is really a statistical summary of generalizable relationships in the theory of matter, which is itself already a deep abstraction from the quantum fields described by more fundamental physical theory. The realm of high-energy physics is sufficiently bizarre from the perspective of folk ontology that many people who follow careful popular accounts can restrain their impulses to analyze it using the categories of folk metaphysics. The ontology of fundamental physics can be treated as effectively separated from the world of practical 'in-dwelling' (to paraphrase Heidegger).

By contrast, it seems that the very point of economics is to improve our individual and collective capacity to wisely allocate limited resources. Most of the discipline, if measured in person-hours of activity, is more a kind of engineering than a kind of theoretical science. Thus when we wonder how the elements of consumer theory relate to elements of human psychology, we are disinclined to give credence to the suggestion that economists might be exploring an esoteric domain of deep structures that have no straightforward description in the folk metaphysical category space. Indeed, if economics weren't *formalized* using mathematics – if it were informal, or formalized only by logic – this suggestion would be incredible. It would represent a kind of obscurantism, like astrology or numerology.

However, what economists in fact did, by increments over several decades following the marginalist revolution, was mathematicize their discipline, thus making a science out of it. Going down that road always involves departure from the folk ontology that mathematics doesn't respect. To the extent one hopes to understand the details of such work, and to integrate it into the general scientific worldview (i.e., weave it into a *scientific* metaphysic), one must resist the urge to deploy philosophical analysis. There is no good reason why the elements of economic theory should be expected to map directly onto kinds of objects and actions familiar to folk psychology.

The surest sign that late nineteenth and early twentieth century economists took their scientific mission seriously is that they stopped trying to understand indifference curves in terms of everyday concepts drawn from psychology, such as preferences. Instead, they gradually worked out how to understand indifference curves and related mathematical constructions on their own terms, and they were ultimately prepared to perform as much radical conceptual transformation on elements originally drawn from other domains – particularly from psychology – as the resulting scientific ambitions implied. In the end, the ideas of preference and choice, as adapted from folk psychology for use in economics, were made subordinate to models of market relationships that began with indifference curves. This made preference and choice, as economists model them, into technical tools that have interesting and complicated relationships with their ancestor notions but absolutely cannot be *identified* with them (Ross 2011). I here take direct issue with three of the leading philosophers of economics, who have little else in common with one another: Rosenberg (1992), Mäki (2009), and Hausman (2011). But in my view the intellectual evolution of economics away from folk ontology must be a central theme of any philosophy of economics that purports to do descriptive justice to the aims and practices of economists.

In saying that economists reconceived choice, preference and other psychological objects, our philosophical diagnosis has gotten well ahead of the details about economics related so far. But this anticipation is crucial to making sense of what the immediate successors to Jevons, Walras and Menger actually did. Specifically, they figured out over the course of several decades how to derive indifference curves from representations of preferences that are not based on and do not incorporate any information about the relative *intensities* of these preferences. All that is needed for construction of indifference curves is information about preference *orderings*. Thus, beyond the marginalist revolution some commentators on the history talk about an *ordinalist* revolution.[14]

What is important about this revolution for present purposes is the distance it put between economics and psychology, *both* practically and philosophically. According to Hume, the father of modern psychology,

---

[14] This piling up of 'revolutions' is standard usage from histories written in the twentieth century. Readers who came of intellectual age more recently might think that that century's intellectuals were morbidly preoccupied with violent, across-the-board change. Well they might have been, given the body count being piled up at the time by fomenters of non-metaphorical revolutions.

people distinguish their subjective preferences from the inside by experiencing and comparing their relative 'vividness.' Ordinalist economists proposed to altogether ignore this aspect of preferences – precisely their *essential* aspect according to Hume – and instead simply infer preference orderings from observed allocations of budgets in markets. An analytic philosopher might suggest that at that juncture the economists should have adopted a new label, because they were no longer referring to preferences at all. As usual with scientists, economists weren't constrained by such conservative semantic scruples.

Key steps along the road to the fully developed 'revealed' theory of preference now need to be described, so that we can understand how the divorce between economics and psychology really was based on technical analysis and *not* on philosophical ideology as far too many populist writers imagine. Of course this divorce had philosophical *consequences*, which are ultimately our subject of focus.

2.5   Ordinalism

In the previous section we encountered the basis for convex indifference curves as these were introduced by Edgeworth. We began to see how they might be applied to a tiny market that includes one consumer, some producers, and two goods. In our example we took the budget to be allocated to these two goods, which determines which of the consumer's indifference curves is tangent to her actual consumption of the goods, to be fixed. What fixes such budgets in the circumstances of a real consumer are her wealth, her income, and the relative values of the other commodities she would like to consume. The agent's choice behavior is taken as reflecting this complex and constantly evolving network of relative valuations. However, the task of measuring this network *directly* in terms of utility values would clearly be intractable for practical purposes. Even for theoretical objectives, since utility does not denote an independently measurable substance or quantity, but only a metric for recording trade-offs implied by a given consumer's choices, we cannot assign general utility values, at least as scalars, at the market level.[15]

---

[15] This correct insight, as we will see, got distorted during the 1930s into the overly strong claim that there can be no interpersonal comparison of utilities.

What we ideally need here is some one commodity for which our agent's demand on the margin incorporates both her expectations about total income, and all her pairwise indifference curves over the total set of commodities that she might consume. Available energy or time would be the most accurate such measurement instruments,[16] but are impractical because we can't decisively observe any living agent's stock of them. The need for economists to be able to at least approximately quantify relative demand schedules is shared by anyone who wants to trade on a market, which is to say, every post-infant person. Thus societies evolved money, which economists can use as their idealized 'numeraire' – that is, as a measuring rod for relative values that is influenced both by the distribution of utility functions and by market interactions.

Suppose we substitute money for one of the two commodities – say, chocolate – represented in Figure 2.1. This will give us a new set of indifference curves between cheese and money. Up to the limits of our idealization – that is, to the extent that all information about all of our agent's wants are expressible in money prices – and controlling for the agent's expectations about monetary inflation or deflation, these new indifference curves capture her demand for cheese for each possible income level she might have, the different income levels corresponding to different indifference curves.

As noted previously, the use of such indifference curves to model market demand incorporates no assumptions about relative magnitudes of individuals' utility. We assume only that agents have ordered preferences, and that they (and the economist) can in principle identify points of indifference. Equivalently, the early marginalists assume that we can compare *signs* of marginal utility, but presume no measurements of any quantitative sums or totals of these utilities.[17] Irving Fisher (1867–1947; 1892/1925) showed that relative price-levels at

---

[16] One of Mirowski's (1989) main theses is that a core commitment of neoclassicism is that the foundation of value is *literally* supposed to be energy, on an understanding of that idea that physics abandoned in the late nineteenth century. This is an interesting, and in my view plausible, interpretation of deep philosophical hunches that animated the early marginalists. But the usefulness of indifference curves as theoretical tools need not rise or fall with the cogency of this specific, doomed, unifying conjecture.

[17] Put technically: we assume only that measurement of relative utility is unique up to monotone transformation.

equilibria – points where agents could not improve their satisfaction by shifting their consumption – can be determined strictly by the gradients of indifference curves. Therefore, if we can derive families of indifference curves for all consumers and all consumption bundles, then we can do our economic analysis without having to know anything at all about the relative intensities of people's preferences – that is to say, about their degrees of Humean 'vividness.'

As long as our analysis is based on the primitive indifference judgment by an agent, we have not yet completely broken economics apart from psychology, though we have rendered most of the data that interested pre-behaviorist psychologists irrelevant to the economist. This slender connecting vine was further pruned by Pareto (1909/1971), who pointed out that indifference curves can be constructed on the basis of sequences of observed choices by agents. Suppose, controlling for price and budget changes, that our agent, given choices between different quantities of chocolate and cheese, always chooses 2 grams of chocolate over 4 grams of cheese, and always chooses 6 grams of cheese over 2 grams of chocolate, but chooses inconsistently – i.e., sometimes taking the cheese and sometimes the chocolate – when her alternatives are 2 grams of chocolate and 5 grams of cheese. The inconsistency can be taken to indicate observations in the neighborhood of indifference. To identify an entire indifference curve through this point we will have to do further work to determine how choice patterns are functionally related to increases and decreases of quantity ratios of chocolate and cheese – we should not simply assume that these functions are linear. But now suppose that the agent is embedded in a market where chocolate and cheese can be bought and sold using money, and where prices vary continuously with weight and there are no bulk discounts or transaction costs.[18] Regardless of any discontinuities in the agent's latent *psychological* preference structure over chocolate and cheese, it seems that in the marketplace she should operate a linear demand function anchored on the equivalence of 2 grams of chocolate and 5 grams of cheese.[19]

---

[18] Here is an example of the kinds of simplifying idealizations typical in economic models.

[19] Consumers in real markets don't behave this way with respect to goods like chocolate and cheese, because in general these goods can't be re-sold. But that is only to point out that something we knew to be a false idealization, the assumption of zero transaction costs, needs to be relaxed when the little model is applied.

Utility as a psychological construct has at this point *almost* dropped out of the picture. It is not quite gone altogether, though, because we might still wonder about how acutely the agent perceives differences in varying quantities of chocolate and cheese, *and* about the 'width' of her indifference zone. Is she no longer indifferent if a culinary alchemist turns 1/10th of a gram of chocolate (from her 2 optimal grams) into 1/10th of a gram (added to her 5 optimal grams) of cheese? Might she care in principle about such a change – yet can't detect it when faced with the actual choices that furnish the economist's evidence? In that case we would want to say that her indifference point is measurable only with some empirical margin of error. On the other hand, the assumption that indifference collapses to a true *point* seems motivated by nothing but formal convenience. Why not hypothesize instead that the agent doesn't care about the difference between 2 grams of chocolate and 2.1 grams of chocolate?

Wondering about these competing hypotheses seems to still leave us enmeshed in questions about the agent's psychology. As the philosopher Dan Hausman (2011) argues, it appears that we can't infer her preferences from her choices after all unless we know the extent to which she has accurate *beliefs* about the quantities of chocolate and cheese she encounters, and unless we can calibrate the *degrees* of accuracy in beliefs to which her preferences are sensitive. In fact, early marginalists were interested in the important work of the psychologist Gustav Fechner (1801–1887), who studied the relationships among scales of magnitude differences in quantities with which people physically interact, the accuracy of their judgments about such differences, and the effects of base points on these judgments. Contemporary economists who estimate utility functions based on experimental choice evidence wrestle with issues around systematically distinguishing perceptual error from indifference, and several have revisited the nineteenth-century psychology literature in search of models for refinement (Wilcox 2008; Andersen et al. 2010; Bardsley et al. 2010, Chapter 7).

A further barrier to the complete separation of economics from psychology in early ordinalist thought was the intended relevance of economics to the choice of policies that would promote human well-being. The economic analysis of comparative states of general flourishing – *welfare economics* – is clearly a continuation of Adam Smith's basic project, but is generally regarded as having begun in its modern form with the work of Arthur Pigou (1877–1959). Pigou's analysis treats every point to the northeast on an individual's indifference map[20] as an improvement in that agent's well-being. Social welfare improvement is then interpreted, following a suggestion due to Pareto, in terms of finding policies that pull some individuals in this direction on their indifference maps while moving no other individuals in the opposite direction on theirs. The basis of this might be thought obscure unless utility is associated in some sense or other with subjective psychological satisfaction. But what is this association?

The relationship between utility and subjective satisfaction was not imagined by any marginalists after Pareto to be one of *identity*. Rather, if utility and preference are inferred from choice, and we assume that individuals are the decisive experts on their own relative states of well-being, then we can interpret northeast movements on indifference maps as welfare improvements because individuals freely move their choices in that direction when their budgets expand. It may be objected that this reasoning is tautological. To this the economist can reply that she is not in the business of analyzing concepts of welfare or well-being; rather she is in the business of trying to identify, for replacement, policies that wastefully prevent people from shifting their consumption to higher indifference curves. Alternatively, one could object that an agent's own choice is not a reliable basis for policy preference, perhaps because of worries that in light of innumerable social constraints the ideal of 'freedom' being invoked is a shibboleth. But then one's objection is not to the economic analysis per se, but to identifying welfare improvements on the basis of normative individualism.

We will return to these issues in a less abstract and more contemporary setting in later chapters. For the moment the main point is historical. Early marginalists such as Pareto and Fisher weren't indulging in a *philosophical* campaign to make psychology something that economists could *ignore*. The evolution of economic concepts into technical notions that differed from their psychological ancestor concepts was driven by the value placed on general theory. By 'theory' here I refer

---

[20] This refers to an idealized abstraction, the 2-dimensional projection of the hyperplane on which all of an agent's indifference curves are represented. The core mathematics of economics for the past century has consisted of techniques for separating hyperplanes.

not to speculative empirical propositions but to mathematical structures. Once indifference curves are defined, then their mathematical properties, and properties of the formal operations that can be performed upon them, are open to formal investigation. Preferences were reconceptualized within this formal space not because economists imagined themselves to be discovering that psychologists – and everyday people – had been wrong about what preferences 'really are,' but simply because it turned out that the contribution of subjective valuation to the analysis of market demand doesn't require attention to most of the properties of psychological preferences; their mere ordering was sufficient.

The point of philosophical diagnosis that *is* relevant here is the following. Economists took their primary objects of study to be *markets*, not individual consumers or producers. This determined the relative strength of what we might call 'centres of conceptual gravity.' So the concept of preference was pulled away from its original psychological core toward a new core that emerged gradually into clarity as economists learned how to think more rigorously about markets. Later in this book I will tell a similar story about a concept that subsequently became more important to the relationship between economics and its neighboring disciplines, that of *choice*.

We can agree that economists are mainly interested in markets, rather than individual thoughts, perceptions, or decisions, without being led to the scorched-earth rhetoric[21] that has tempted some economists into declaring psychology *irrelevant* to economics. Markets, in a sense to be clarified later, are necessarily made by intentional agents. Intentionality is not merely psychological, but it crucially involves psychology. Furthermore, the early marginalists were right to think that psychophysics is relevant to modeling markets, though psychophysical modeling and economic modeling are different disciplines that draw on different resources and respect different constraints. The same should be said about economics and the richer domain of contemporary cognitive science, including neuroscience.

Before coming to that, however, there are further historical details at which we must glance. Though the ordinalists did not frame their program as a rejection of the relevance of psychology to economics,

---

[21] E.g., Gul and Pesendorfer (2008).

they *did* explicitly turn against the specific account of the relationship that had been promoted by Jevons. That is, they rejected what Mandler (1999) calls *psychological cardinalism.* We need to follow Mandler in adopting this anachronistic phrase because the name of the critical target the economists of the 1930s used, 'utilitarianism,' already involved misleading connotations then, and invites utter confusion in a reader removed from the intellectual context of that decade. The reader interested in untangling these complicated threads should consult Mandler (1999) and Ross (2005, Chapters 3 and 4). We may brusquely compress the details here as follows.

The methodological polemicists of the 1930s intended, in campaigning against utilitarianism, to reject three theses that later historians of thought have distinguished more clearly than they did. None of the three theses straightforwardly rise or fall together. The first thesis is psychological hedonism, the claim that people's choices are mainly motivated by the desires to obtain pleasing sensations and avoid painful ones. This empirically false thesis was an important issue in the early history of modern economics, and plays a newly interesting role in the development of neuroeconomics (so will be touched upon in Chapter 4); but it is unimportant in the present context. The second thesis is that the goal of economic policy should be the maximization of 'average' – or aggregate in some more precise sense – utility. The commentators of the 1930s tended to pummel what we now regard as straw man versions of this normative program;[22] in the present book we will restrict attention, in Chapter 5, to the more sophisticated contemporary debate. The third thesis is Mandler's psychological cardinalism.

Psychological cardinalism is the thesis that the basis on which the economist assumes the convexity of indifference curves and the downward slope of the compensated demand function is her belief that agents experience measurably different intensities of preference, for each specific source of utility, which decrease with marginal consumption. Pareto argued that this is false. Hicks and Allen (1934) formally verified Pareto's suggestion: indifference curves incorporate no presumption of cardinal comparability beyond primitive indifference judgments. Therefore their use does not imply commitment

---

[22] See, for a representative sample, Bergson (1938), Samuelson (1938), Hicks (1939a), Kaldor (1939) and Robbins (1938).

to underlying utility functions as these were understood by Jevons and Edgeworth. Thus, as Hicks and Allen made explicit, convexity of indifference curves does not require the psychological hypothesis of diminishing marginal utility. Convexity depends only on the logically weaker property of diminishing marginal rates of substitution (DMRS): the amount of commodity x an agent will exchange for a marginal increment of her stock of y declines with her stock of x. DMRS is at least in principle testable on the basis of behavioral observation, since it makes no direct reference to levels of inner satisfaction. It can also be supported by a logical rather than a psychological argument: violation of DMRS is consistent with the possibility that an agent could rationally decide to consume only one commodity. Economists have sometimes presented this possibility as a *reductio ad absurdum* on any hypothesis of DMRS violation. On that interpretation, the argument is straightforwardly invalid. But a more charitable interpretation of the argument is possible: economists are interested in markets, and a consumer for whom diminishing rates of marginal substitution doesn't hold lacks a motivation to trade. Thus the economist is interested only in that portion of consumption behavior consistent with convex indifference curves. This restriction is more plausible if the focus is on market demand rather than individual demand. There are surely some status-seeking consumers of vintage Jaguars who will buy more of them if their price rises; but aggregate demand for them will reliably fall.

This brings us to the milestone early achievement of the person whom I consider one of the ten most important economists of the twentieth century:[23] Paul Samuelson (1915–2009). Samuelson generalized Hicks and Allen's foundations of consumer theory, and in so doing completed the separation of economics from psychology along the lines envisaged by Pareto. The analytical framework for which he was chiefly responsible, known as *revealed preference theory*, is still taught – in more than one version, depending on the intended domain and scope of application[24] – to contemporary economics students.

---

[23] The nine others on my list are Hicks, Keynes, Friedrich von Hayek (1899–1992), Ragnar Frisch (1895–1973), Jan Tinbergen (1903–1994), Trygve Haavelmo (1911–1999), John von Neumann (1903–1957), Leonard (Jimmy) Savage (1917–1971) and Kenneth Arrow (1921–).

[24] Hands (2013) provides an astute survey of the versions of revealed preference theory, which is alert to the philosophical issues that are the focus of this book.

2.6 Revealed preference

The status of revealed preference theory (RPT) is intensely controversial among both historians and philosophers of economics. Some contemporary methodologists (Ross 2005, Gul and Pesendorfer 2008, Binmore 2009) regard it as still providing the core set of principles that demarcate economics from psychology, and the rhetoric of a number of widely used textbooks is consistent with this perspective. Other methodologists (e.g., Hausman 2011) present it as a fundamentally confused legacy of a dead version of psychological behaviorism, and argue that most economists fortunately never took it seriously in practice anyway. This attitude also finds expression in some newer textbooks (e.g., Frank 2009) by economists who think that students should learn the discipline on a foundation of descriptive decision theory that rests from the outset on rejection of revealed preference.

These widely divergent views of RPT among contemporary economists are *partly* expressions of substantial disagreements but also partly reflect that RPT has from its inception generated multiple versions and interpretations. When one scholar pronounces for RPT and another inveighs against it, one must often work quite hard to determine the extent to which they are talking about the same referent.

As we have seen, the ordinalist tradition steadily distanced the economist's technical understanding of preferences from the folk, and the psychologist's, conception of everyday subjective desires, yearnings and strivings. An obvious logical endpoint to this evolution was to break the association altogether by coining a new concept to denote *whatever* structural assumptions turned out to be necessary to link individual allocations of resources with estimations of aggregate demand. It is, after all, the latter that is directly relevant to analyzing both short-run market equilibria and longer-run market dynamics (i.e., movements from one equilibrium to another, or oscillations around ranges of equilibrium values).

Two developments in the wider context of economic thought, outside the main road of technical development from early marginalism to ordinalism, set the stage for Samuelson's effort to synthesize a unified set of formal foundations for the whole discipline, of which RPT was a basic element.

First, Lionel Robbins (1898–1984) married the evolving ordinalist break with psychology, following on Hicks's and Allen's technical work, to a so-called 'Austrian' tradition[25] that had always sought to explain market efficiency without reference to psychological models that its proponents regarded as unacceptably mechanical and deterministic. Robbins's 1932 book on the philosophy of economics, revised in 1935, was one of the two most influential works in the history of economic methodology.[26] Its persisting fame lies mainly in its proposed definition of the scope and subject matter of economics as 'the science which studies human behavior as a relationship between ends and scarce means which have alternative uses' (1935, p. 16). Many, perhaps most, economists still regard this as the most intuitively satisfying description of their discipline among those that can fit on a T-shirt.

Robbins's definition abstracts from foundations in individual decision-making in two senses: first, it directs attention to relationships between *behavior* and opportunity costs which might or might not be accurately represented by a decision-maker herself; and, second, it is carefully imprecise about the scale of analysis – individual or market – on which these relationships might be studied.

A second influence on the conception of economics that Samuelson synthesized stemmed from John Maynard Keynes's (1883–1946) analysis of the high involuntary unemployment – primarily of labor but also of other potentially productive assets – that characterized the great world depression of 1929–1939. Contrary to popular misconceptions, though Keynes indeed thought that folly and ignorance play important roles in the economic behavior of individuals, he did *not* attribute the depression, or fluctuations in economic performance generally, to the 'irrationality' of (many) individual people. Rather, he saw that any investor who could not afford to wait infinitely long to realize his or her returns would have to base his or her allocations on conjectures about future values of market-wide variables, particularly average rates of saving and investment. Such conjectures, in aggregation, determine the supply of credit, which in turn influences and interacts with exchange rates and interest rates to determine the employment of factors of

---

[25] The principal figures in the Austrian tradition are Menger (one of the trio of original marginalists), Ludwig von Mises (1881–1973), and Hayek (see note 22).

[26] The second is Friedman (1953).

production at a given point in time. No endogenously generated market pressure generally exists to stabilize these conjectures. Thus, Keynes argued, there is no unique equilibrium in the economy as a whole, and no standing expectation that the price of any given commodity, including labor, must fall until there is no unutilized supply of it. Contemporary behavioral economists sometimes read Keynes as among their progenitors because he attributed specific fluctuations in financial asset markets to 'animal spirits' (Akerlof and Shiller 2009). This has encouraged widespread mis-reading of Keynes's phrase as referring to contagious changes in emotional confidence. What Keynes in fact meant by it was merely the generic motivation of people to be economically active; it was *not* his view that individual psychological idiosyncrasies are a proper part of the economist's business. In any event, what Samuelson went on to draw into his synthesis were not the various opinions of Keynes per se, but the formalization by Hicks (1937) of one key strand in Keynes's work. This is the so-called IS/LM model, which defines a hypothesized equilibrium among the interest rate, the output of goods and services in the real (i.e., non-financial) economy, and the demand for and supply of money. This new *macroeconomics*[27] encouraged economists and policy-makers to conceptualize the economy as a complex machine that could be operated upon by manipulating system-level variables such as the interest rate or the level of public expenditure. In this environment, aggregate demand came to be widely regarded as a kind of system-level *force*. Samuelson followed Hicks's (1939b, p. 34) explicit agnosticism about whether aggregate demand is ultimately reducible to individual consumers' choices. After the work of Hicks and Samuelson, we accurately simulate the dominant economic image of demand by de-emphasizing its association with private, personal, heterogeneous schedules of primal – or even cognitively derived – *desire*.

In this setting, Samuelson aimed to build an empirically testable framework for modeling an economy as a deterministic *machine*. This required among many other features that demand has certain aggregate

---

[27] The distinction between microeconomics and macroeconomics was coined a few years before publication of Keynes's major work by Ragnar Frisch (Hoover 2012). But to most economists the original referent of the term 'macroeconomics' was to Keynesian analysis as formalized by Hicks and Samuelson.

characteristics – most importantly, that it be downward sloping. The origins of RPT lie in technical questions about the properties of individual demand functions that are consistent with aggregate demand as it featured in standard post-war macroeconomics and, later, in general equilibrium theory. In the context of the *philosophy* of economics it is important to emphasize that in Samuelson's opinion these questions are of little importance to applications of economics itself (Samuelson 1947, p. 117). We may interpret a later result due to Becker (1962) as supporting this hunch of Samuelson's. Becker showed that downward sloping demand for any good given constant real income depends on no claim about the individual rationality of any consumer; it depends only on the assumption that households with smaller budgets, and therefore smaller opportunity sets, consume less. The most extensive examination of the general issue has subsequently been provided in a 1994 book by Werner Hildenbrand. Hildenbrand demonstrates that there is no formal connection between the contribution to equilibrium stability of demand functions consistent at the aggregate scale with RPT, and individual utility maximization. (We will revisit Hildenbrand's important work in Chapter 5.)

I stress this historical point here because *most* of the philosophical literature on economics, and especially that part of the literature that aims to critically demarcate economics from other social sciences, focuses on the standard theory of the rational individual consumer. This is typically justified on grounds that economic analysis of markets depends on the assumption that aggregate demand is composed out of individual demand functions restricted by RPT. This is in turn identified as the modern (post-war) version of methodological individualism in economics; and that, finally, is often claimed to necessarily block any pretense by economists to adequately model social structures.[28] Let us thus note the deflationary tone with which Samuelson concludes his 1947 chapter on the theory of the individual consumer:

---

[28] A library's worth of examples could be cited here. A recent example is Fine and Milonakis (2009). They survey the frontier where economics meets sociology and critical social history, sneering all along the way at the crudity of economists' conceptions of society. Their contemptuous attitude is allegedly justified by repeated references to economists' 'methodological individualism.' This is never defined in the book, but is said to infect not only general equilibrium microeconomics, but game theory and its applications, imperfect information partial equilibrium analysis, and all formal adaptations of Keynesian ideas. The part of economics that, according to Fine and Milonakis, pumps the poison of methodological individualism through this entire well seems to be standard consumer theory.

Many writers have held the utility analysis to be an integral and important part of economic theory. Some have even sought to employ its applicability as a test criterion by which economics might be separated from the other social sciences. Nevertheless, I wonder how much economic theory would be changed if … [the conditions identified in the utility analysis] … were found to be empirically untrue. I suspect, very little. (Samuelson 1947, p. 117)

It should have puzzled philosophical and behavioralist critics more than it has that in Samuelson's synthesis of economics, the closest thing to a classic founding text in post-war mathematical economics, *there are no individual economic agents, rational or otherwise. Homo economicus,* the supposed star player of neoclassical economics who is routinely attacked by philosophers, psychologists and anti-establishment behavioralists, does not put in a single first-order appearance in the nearly 600 pages of *Foundations of Economic Analysis*; the one mention of him is an ironic reference to his role in the arguments of others.

A decade prior to writing the comment above, Samuelson (1938) had sought to eliminate the concepts of utility and preference from economics altogether, and thus to complete the philosophical project advanced by Edgeworth, Fisher, Pareto and Hicks. He showed that if an analyst knew a consumer's demand function for all possible budget constraints, where demand for each possible good is a continuous function of prices and possible incomes, then given three technical restrictions[29] *there is no additional content added by hypothesizing an underlying utility function* if the demand function satisfies what was later – but not in the 1938 paper – called the Weak Axiom of Revealed Preference (WARP). WARP may be intuitively glossed as follows. For any given set of prices, and for any two bundles of goods x, y: $x \neq y$ (which we may idealize as complete states of the world with respect to economic discrimination among such states), if the agent pays opportunity cost $c + y$ in exchange for x, then the agent will never pay opportunity cost $c + x$ in exchange for y.

There is good reason why Samuelson did not introduce the revealed preference terminology in the 1938 paper. At that point, as noted, he

---

[29] I do not give these here because the conditions Samuelson identified in his 1938 paper turned out not to be the most logically refined set. I will state that set with the mature formulation of RPT near the close of Section 2.6.

is aiming to *eliminate* reference to preference and utility. Before we go on to see why utility didn't disappear from economic theory then and there, we must pause for a bit of philosophy.

It is often pointed out that modeling economic agents on the basis of actually observed choices, instead of inferred mental states, echoes psychological behaviorism. And it is true that Samuelson's promotion of the idea that economic agency attribution should be based on observed choice coincided with the period in which behaviorism was most dominant in psychology. Furthermore, Samuelson was personally close to the philosopher W.V.O. Quine (1908–2000), who argued that *intentional* phenomena – states defined by reference to psychological attitudes to states of affairs such as believing in them or wanting them to come about – should not be mentioned in an objective account of the world because their identity conditions are context sensitive. Quine held that the determining condition for something to objectively exist as a kind of thing is for it to be an object of reference in the generalizations that science will confirm 'in the limit' (i.e., at the imaginary point in time when science is complete). Thus Quine was the first in a line of philosophers that includes Richard Rorty, Paul Churchland and Alex Rosenberg who deny the scientific value and the objective existence of such entities as preferences if these are understood as inner psychological states. Perhaps Samuelson discussed these ideas with Quine during the lunches together that they enjoyed;[30] and perhaps he was sympathetic to them.

For reasons to be discussed in Chapter 4, I think that a descriptively adequate scientific worldview must take account of intentional states, but should understand them as descriptions of coupled informational and behavioral patterns, not internal mental phenomena. (See also Ross 2005.) So I do favor a (broadly) behaviorist interpretation of preference. However, this view cannot be attributed to Samuelson on the basis of anything he wrote. Behaviorism as an *epistemological* principle depends on the idea that scientific generalizations should be based on actual observations, which are necessarily of finite sets of data. However, Samuelson's 1938 paper, and his initial formulations of RPT, rely essentially on the assumption of demand functions that are 'known' to apply over infinite sets of choices and prices. As Hands (2013) argues,

---

[30] Quine (1985) mentions these lunches in his memoirs. Unfortunately he doesn't say what he and Samuelson talked about during them.

this makes clear that Samuelson's analyses are not intended to provide economists with a new practical method for constructing models of agents, since no economist is ever blessed with an infinite set of choice data. Samuelson's 1938 paper was an exercise in formal definition: it was proof that purely formal microeconomic theory as conceived in the ordinalist tradition is not an application of psychological concepts. This suggests nothing one way or the other about the validity or empirical standing of those concepts in their own terms. Samuelson does not suppose that science consists in formal definitions; this is why he thinks, as indicated by his 1947 remarks quoted above, that the pure, formal, theory of the consumer is a kind of incidental commentary on economics rather than an 'important' *part* of economics.

It can be straightforwardly said why utility didn't vanish from the economist's lexicon after 1938. Samuelson thought he was preserving *part* of ordinalist theory in his 1938 analysis while throwing unnecessary 'utilitarian' baggage overboard. But it subsequently turned out that his larger, later project of synthesizing traditional marginalist (specifically, Marshallian) demand analysis with Hicksian macroeconomics incorporated the recovery of *all* of ordinalist theory. Utility theory, we might say, somewhat surprisingly turned out not to have any essential connection to utilitarian value theory.

The details are sketched briefly. A highly desirable property of the synthesis sought by Samuelson after the war is conformity to the so-called Slutsky equation for jointly representing substitution and income effects of price changes. Use of this equation implies that demand functions are restricted by the symmetry of the Slutsky matrix (that is, the full mXn matrix of substitution items in a demand schedule), which in turn helps establish uniqueness of equilibrium. Slutsky symmetry is *not* among the conditions used in Samuelson's 1938 elimination of utility.

Satisfaction of WARP deductively entails that the agent's choice of x over y is *consistent with* the hypothesis that she maximizes a utility function according to which $U(x) \geq U(y)$. In 1950 Hendrik Houthakker (1924–2008) extended WARP to apply not just to choices between pairs of bundles, but to choices over chains of bundles; the result is known as the Strong Axiom of Revealed Preference (SARP). This analysis implies Slutsky symmetry. But a much stronger relationship holds between ordinal utility theory (ORT) and WARP *with* Slutsky symmetry than between ORT and WARP *without* Slutsky symmetry: given Slutsky symmetry the former pair are *equivalent* – one applies exactly and only when the other does.

From this point in the technical development there is no reason to refrain from representing any equilibrium in an economic choice problem involving consumption as maximization of a utility function. Utility becomes simply the *name* of the abstract structure over certain choice sets that incorporates what we might call 'Samuelson consistency (1938)' *and* Slutsky symmetry. This synthesis is (modulo later improvements in elegance contributed by various authors) mature RPT. In mature RPT a 'utility function,' in general, simply refers to *any mapping from a sequence of choices onto the ordinal line.*

The mathematics of the ordinal utility function according to mature RPT can be stated transparently. Suppose that agent i prefers world-state A to world-state B and world-state B to world-state C. We map these onto a list of numbers, where the function maps the highest-ranked bundle onto the largest number in the list, the second-highest-ranked bundle onto the next-largest number in the list,[31] and so on, thus:

> World-state $A \to 3$
> World-state $B \to 2$
> World-state $C \to 1$

One may then *not* infer from the relationships among these numbers that i gets 3 times as much utility from World-state A as she gets from World-state C. We could represent exactly the same utility function by

> World-state $A \to 7,326$
> World-state $B \to 12.6$
> World-state $C \to -1,000,000$

This emphasizes that ordinal utility does not refer to a *quantity* of anything, such as relative levels of comfort that one might imagine measuring in a person's brain or biochemistry. In the next chapter we will encounter *cardinal* utility functions in which magnitudes of the utility indices *do* matter; but this will still not be because they are taken to represent real quantities.

---

[31] I will here represent the functions as deterministic. In empirical applications they should typically be stochastic. But that is unimportant for immediate purposes.

The ordinal mapping relation has two general sources of constraints. The economically motivated subset of the constraints derives from properties of the technical idea of a revealed preference. The remaining constraints derive from properties of the real numbers. First, following Rubinstein (2006), we can think of a preference relation (which is itself a function) as generalizing over an ordered set of answers to a series of evaluative questions about elements $x, y, \ldots, n$ of a set X, with one answer per question of the form 'x is preferred to y' ($x > y$), or 'y is preferred to x' ($y > x$), or 'x and y are interchangeable in preference ranking' (I). Two forms of generalization are equivalent. Rubinstein writes them as follows:

(1) Preferences on a set X are a function f that assigns to any pair (x, y) of distinct elements in X exactly one of $x > y$, $y > x$, or I, restricted by two properties: (i) *no order effect*: $f(x, y) = f(y, x)$; and (ii) *transitivity*: if $f(x, y) = x > y$ and $f(y, z) = y > z$ then $f(x, z) = x > z$ and if $f(x, y) = I$ and $f(y, z) = I$ then $f(x, z) = I$.

(2) A preference on a set X is a binary relation $\geq$ on X satisfying (i) *completeness*: for any $x, y \in X$, $x \geq y$ or $y \geq x$; and (ii) *transitivity*: for any $x, y, z \in X$ if $x \geq y$ and $y \geq z$ then $x \geq z$.

The completeness property implies that when we specify an agent by reference to her preferences over identified possible states of some world, we are claiming that there are no two distinguishable states in the identified set for which there is no fact of the matter as to whether the agent prefers one state over the other or is indifferent between them. If we are unsure about some such relation, then our specification of the agent will be said to be *incomplete* with respect to the states in question.

Now we can say that a utility function is a representation of a preference relation according to the following constraint: $U: X \to \Re$ represents $\geq$ if for all $x, y \in X$, $x \geq y$ if and only if $U(x) \geq U(y)$. That is, a utility function is simply a mapping of a preference function onto the real number line.

Philosophers will wonder about the principles for determining boundaries of these sets we are casually calling 'worlds.' In the classical post-Houthakker version of RPT, the set is all possible bundles of all possible consumable goods and services at all possible prices – that is to say, the set is infinite. So it seems reasonable to refer to it as 'the world.' But then, as Samuelson emphasized, the construction of RPT based on this set is a purely conceptual exercise that isn't of much practical significance. However, in a 1967 paper, Afriat, building on Samuelson (1948), showed that one can begin with a finite set of choice data – including, crucially, sequences of real empirical choices by agents at real prices under real budget constraints – and construct a utility function consistent with SARP. In the SARP context the objective was to prove existence of a unique utility *maximizing* function. Since Afriat's aim was an algorithm that would construct *some* ordinal utility function from choice data, the revealed preference relation was slightly relaxed, yielding the Generalized Axiom of Revealed Preference (GARP). GARP is essentially WARP plus independently imposed *monotonicity* and *convexity* of preferences. Monotonicity implies that for any element $x \in X, x + \varepsilon \succ x$ where ε is any further consumption increment. Convexity implies that we can represent consumption behavior by indifference curves as in Figure 2.1.

At this point we have a version of RPT we can actually use in economic modeling of empirical data. By a 'world' over which the revealed preference relation is defined for a modeling exercise, we now mean all and only the set of possible states we have chosen to attend to as motivated by some background knowledge, structural theory or pragmatic idealization.

The transitivity property implies that an agent's revealed preferences do not *cycle*: if she chooses bundle *A* over bundle *B* and bundle *B* over bundle *C* at some budget and for some set of prices, then she will not choose bundle *C* over bundle *A* at that same budget and prices. Philosophers (and some philosophically minded economists) have sometimes defended this as a 'rationality' criterion, on grounds that if it is not satisfied then an agent's choices are necessarily normatively inconsistent: we can't identify an ideal state of the world on which all her choices would, in the limit, converge. If satisfaction of classic RPT over the infinite consumption set is identified with rationality, then such transcendental consistency becomes something like the core of rationality. But this edifice of conceptual identifications is grandiose and bizarre. Rationality in general, as noted in Chapter 1, has historically been a place-holder for the set of ultimate norms of thought – a mystical idea. Classic RPT is a mathematical analysis of ordinal utility. Who would imagine that the latter might be the basis of the former?

But then, one might say that a general property of all mystical aspirations is that every proposal for their concrete realization is as arbitrary and deflationary as any other. The conclusion I draw from this is that we should not interest ourselves in mystical aspirations.

The identification of RPT satisfaction with rationality seems initially less mad in the context of what Hands (2013) calls 'empirical RPT,' i.e., RPT as a model of finite sets of real choices following Afriat. A substantial literature exists that aims to isolate consumption patterns that imply vulnerability to 'Dutch books' or 'money pumps.' An agent may fall victim to a Dutch book if her tolerance of risk could combine with restricted choice contexts in such a way that she would buy a series of lotteries that would be expected, given the laws of probability, to lead to her eventually having all her money extracted. The agent exploited by a money pump ends up similarly broke. Suppose that an agent chooses in accordance with the cyclical preferences $C \succ A \succ B \succ C$. Then another agent with acyclical preferences could offer him a sequence of trades in which he first surrenders his stock of C for some marginal gain in his stock of B, then surrenders his stock of B for some marginal gain in his stock of A, then finally surrenders his stock of A for some marginal gain in his stock of C. If for some real choice set the agent's utility function in fact conforms to the ordering $C \succ A \succ B$, and for some other real choice set his utility function corresponds to $A \succ B \succ C$, then there must exist a quantity of C he could be offered in the final trade such that the total value of his final endowment is smaller than that of the stock he started with. Thus by a series of such sequences the agent could be drained of all but an infinitesimal proportion of his initial asset stock. Preference structures that are open to Dutch books or money pumps thus have seemed to many to involve a restricted kind of logical pathology we might call *market irrationality*.

Market rationality and irrationality might be useful concepts for studying markets; we will investigate this question in later chapters. But we should resist temptations to identify market rationality with a norm of thought. One path to such identification involves substituting consumption bundles with epistemic states such as beliefs. Suppose an agent is choosing not between paying for one bundle or another of goods and services, but between 'paying' the effort to acquire one theory or another. Then the analogy of money pumping has her accumulating evidence while, in the end, having no coherent system of beliefs. Philosophers of science have made a minor industry out of this problem. (See Hájek 2008 for a high-level review.) But we can avoid inflating market rationality criteria into general normative rationality criteria simply by keeping in mind the differences between buying goods and services and 'buying' ideas. The road to bad philosophy is paved with simplistic conceptual identities.

Even as a norm *for markets*, market rationality has important limitations. If a person, over the whole course of her biography, is identified with a single economic agent then she will be found guilty of massive market irrationality; for example, in her youth she passed up good deals on dentures while buying undiscounted sports equipment, and in later life did the opposite. Again, this reminds us of the importance of not conflating RPT as a conceptual analysis of ordinal preference with RPT as a tool for modeling finite choice episodes. In the second context, the one that matters for actual economics, one is free to just be sensible. In modeling a younger person's choices over retirement fund investments one should identify her with her elderly self; in modeling her choices over jet skis one probably should not. Philosophers often criticize economists as if every practical application of RPT tests its value as a technical regimentation of concepts. This suggests that they confuse RPT as a *mathematical* theory with RPT as an *empirical* theory. (See Ross 2005, Chapter 4, for an extended development of this point.)

If pragmatism rules when empirically applying RPT, is this not tantamount to saying that RPT is nothing more than a modeling pretense? Answering 'yes' here is a move that has been popular among economists who have been impatient with complications from the philosophy of science and aim to wave them away. The classic source for justifying such impatience is the single most influential text in economic methodology, Milton Friedman's (1953) defense of the thesis that economic models should be evaluated on the basis of the success or failure of the predictions they generate, rather than on the basis of the accuracy or realism of the assumptions used to construct them.

It is common for books on the philosophy of economics to devote at least several pages to consideration of Friedman's argument. This is justified both by its abiding popularity among economists, and by the more specific point that it undergirds the famous and widespread suggestion that economists need not hypothesize that people are literally procedurally rational calculators of the maxima of utility functions, but merely that they tend to choose *as if* they were rational in this way. One of Friedman's vivid analogies is to leaves growing on a tree: they arrange themselves *as if* they deliberately acted so as to maximize their average daily exposure to sunlight. A gardener could successfully predict the relative leaf density on different parts of a tree by building a model that incorporated this evidently false 'assumption.' Friedman's idea is so widely touted and debated in economic methodology that it has a common label: as-if rationality. One could locate the debate over Friedman's philosophy, and the related but more specific debate over as-if rationality, by reference to almost any area of economics. I have chosen in this book to locate it here, with the discussion of RPT, for a reason.

All scientists who make use of models – which is to say, almost all scientists – build simulacra of the actual world that abstract from it by idealizing or even altogether ignoring some causally and structurally relevant aspects of the wider target reality. Such abstraction is a discipline-specific art that scientists learn during the apprenticeship phases of their careers. Great scientists are master judges in this art, who tend to be copied by scientists of merely average cognitive subtlety. For the special case of economics, the philosopher Uskali Mäki (1992 and elsewhere; see also Mäki 2009) has painstakingly produced a detailed critical typology of the styles of abstraction and idealization that form the templates economists inherit with their training and appreciate when they become journal referees and thesis supervisors. Mäki launched this project from the platform of reflection on Friedman's 1953 essay. A key insight about the essay that Mäki has emphasized is that philosophers tend to mis-read it by trying to shoehorn it into a more general, transdisciplinary philosophy of science known as 'instrumentalism.' According to this philosophy, scientists don't intend their theoretical ontologies to be understood as metaphysically objective descriptions of reality, but use them as mere tools for calculating predictions. According to some instrumentalists, for example, elements of physical theory that are too small to be directly observable, such as subatomic particles, need not be thought by physicists to exist independently of the theory that constructs them; they are built up as tools that allow physicists to predict events they *can* 'directly' observe.[32] Mäki has convincingly shown that

---

[32] An alert reader may wonder what interpretation of 'direct' observation would usefully characterize actual practice in physics. I think that philosophers who casually traffic in this idea demonstrate embarrassing naïveté about laboratory science.

Friedman was not an instrumentalist in this sense. Friedman took the ontology of economics to be simply the common sense world of traders, managers and market analysts, and then emphasized that economists try to generalize about this domain by abstracting away aspects of it that they, but not businesspeople, can afford to ignore. Friedman's is specifically a philosophy of economics, not an application of a more general philosophy of science.

I think that Mäki has got Friedman right. However, unlike Mäki, I do not agree with Friedman that economics is about phenomena that are properly distinguished on the basis of everyday, common sense observation. Economists have gradually unearthed a complex network of deep real patterns that common sense does not describe, even in simplified terms, though human behavior is implicitly sensitive to them. For example, few people think of themselves as having preferences over risk, let alone wonder to what extent these change when potential payoffs would take their wealth past certain thresholds (rank dependence). Even fewer imagine that they are averse to correlations of risk over time, or could even grasp what correlation aversion means without training in finance theory. Yet correctly identifying the distribution of risk preference functions in a population of interest is a crucial, and theoretically complex, aspect of modeling responses in that population to changes in prices and incentives.

Much human behavior in highly structured institutions of certain kinds, but especially in markets, conforms relatively closely to the restrictions of GARP. This is something that could only have been discovered by empirical study, and only after GARP had actually been formally constructed for testing. The structure of GARP is not at all obvious to everyday observation. Indeed, 'common sense' is skeptical of it. Anti-establishment behavioral economics, which we will review in Chapter 4, is persuasive and attractive to many non-economists, spurring brisk sales of rowdy popular books (e.g., Ariely 2008), because its framework conforms much more closely to folk conceptions of behavior. The reason for *that* is that most people's most intimate and reflective observations of human behavior (especially of their own behavior) are made in contexts *outside* the institutional constraints of markets; and in those domains behavior often does not correspond at all well to the patterns formalized by GARP. Behavioral economists usually run experiments that lift subjects out of market contexts they have learned, so violations of GARP are typically observed. Economists struggle to know how to frame responses to the resulting criticisms because most economists are products of a pedagogy that begins with the ultimate exile from a market context – Robinson Crusoe stranded alone on an island. Crusoe by hypothesis allocates his resources in accordance with GARP. But Crusoe is a fundamentally misleading fantasy person.

This point is not intended as a basis for defending as-if rationality. Economists should not try to duck the task of *specifically* explaining why GARP furnishes good descriptions of consumer behavior in some market conditions and bad descriptions in other market conditions. This requires some collaboration with psychologists. We should also like to know how the model gains traction as traditionally non-market contexts become more market-like; for this we must turn to ideas that have been developed, and to real patterns that have been discovered, by sociologists.

I have addressed these themes in the context of the discussion of RPT because, as nicely spotted by Hands (2013), commentators tend to be led astray here by failing to separate empirical RPT (applying GARP to finite real choice data) from mathematical RPT (applying SARP to hypothetical patterns over infinite choice sets). Human behavior, in or out of markets, should *not* be expected to conform to the latter. People do not have measurable preferences over infinite sets. A related, more prosaic but also more important, fact is that they don't have *stable* preferences over temporally extended or experientially highly disconnected sets of outcomes, as we would expect *if* we identified the abstract agents of mathematical RPT with flesh-and-blood people. Defenders of as-if rationality have rightly resisted that identification. That is a useful first move in defense of establishment economic theory, but by itself it is purely defensive and declines a task of explanation that economists must face. When economists neglect this job, they should not be surprised that psychologists and others come along to try to do it instead.

Until economists began turning their attention, in the late decades of the last century, to empirical facts about institutions, socialization and cognitive development, the underlying data generating processes that produce GARP-compliant choices remained inside a black box. All one could say is that in rule-governed markets *something or other* tends to integrate individual choices in temporally proximate choice sets. We can reasonably cite Samuelson's 1938 paper as a basis for denying a claim, made on purely conceptual grounds, that the something in question must be a private measurement of magnitudes of mental valuations, as Jevons had assumed. But this is a merely negative point confined to the plane of philosophy. As Samuelson said, it is not yet science. Some readers might nevertheless still feel the pull of the Jevonsian philosophical intuition. 'But what *else* could possibly be inside the black box?', such readers may be wondering. As indicated immediately above, this is a question that economists (and this book) need to answer, based on empirical evidence rather than a priori conceptual reasoning. A philosophical barrier we must try to set aside, which gives the question its rhetorical force as a seeming conversation-stopper, is the pre-scientific Western metaphysical impulse according to which causes must originate from 'inner' forces that push 'outward' to influence more complex systems built out of isolable parts. In Chapters 4 and 5, I will sketch an answer to the skeptical question based on a non-reductionist interpretation of various scientific experiments and observations.

But might there yet be a legitimate *semantic* complaint against the use of the phrase 'revealed preference'? Surely, it might be objected, it is natural to interpret this phrase as suggesting that a person (or, perhaps, other agent) makes some inner judgments about relative valuations which external observers can't directly access, but which are 'revealed' by observable choices. It is common for authors who join me in emphasizing that this is the wrong understanding of RPT (e.g., Binmore 2009) to concede that the language is pedagogically unfortunate. Ultimately, though, I will resist even this concession. As we will see in Chapter 4, something *is* revealed by the empirical identification of a utility function, namely, structural properties of some latent data-generating process. And I will furthermore present reasons for thinking that science – in this instance the science of developmental and social cognition – should lead us to recognize a concept of preference that *improves* on the folk idea of preference as an inner mental state. The scientific understanding of preference is an improvement because it allows us to dissolve what would otherwise be tensions in the pictures of the world presented by, respectively, our models of individual organisms and our models of social structures.

2.7 Economic theory, general equilibrium and welfare analysis

Because of philosophers' preoccupation with individual rational choice, a casual reader of the philosophy of economics literature might gather the impression that RPT was the central theoretical foundation stone of post-war economics. However, few economists award RPT that status. Mathematical RPT is merely the deep philosophical background to models of demand; and even empirical RPT is no more than a set of generic restrictions on such models. Furthermore, consumer theory characterizes only one strand of a theory of markets. As I have stressed repeatedly, markets are the basic subject matter of economics. Economists are centrally concerned with the *interaction* between demand and supply.

An aspect of economic theory that flowed from the early marginalists' work, especially Walras's, was recognition of the need to model *particular* systems of prices and opportunity costs – for example, a single industry with its producers, suppliers and customers – as derived from the network of such relations across the whole economy. Since every scarce consumption good is consumed at the expense of some other, and every factor allocated to one production process is withheld from a possible alternative, all costs and prices in an economy have implications for all others. Philosophy students who have read metaphysics will recognize this as the logic of holism; in economics it is referred to as the 'general equilibrium' (GE) perspective. This phrase reflects the idea that an economy's efficiency frontier, for a given set of natural and human resources, occurs when it reaches a point (if such a point can be uniquely defined) where no producers would improve their profits by reallocating some inputs, and no consumers would achieve higher marginal utility by reallocating their budgets. Since Walras, GE modeling has been the dominant framework within which economists have sought to mathematically refine Smith's insight that the 'invisible hand' of the market is an essential mechanism for growing a society's wealth.

Despite its origins in Walras, GE once stood loftily apart from most *applied* economics. The first great textbook of economics, which remained standard until the mid-twentieth century, was Alfred Marshall's *Principles of Economics* (1890). Marshall emphasized the impracticality of GE analysis as a basis for understanding the structures and problems of particular industries, and instead focused on what he called *partial equilibria* (PE). These are understood as conditions of temporary stability in a part of a system, which will tend to be maintained until governing variables at a wider scale of reality in which the part is embedded evolve new values. If the larger-scale variable evolution occurs much more slowly than variable change at the scale of the foregrounded partial system, then we can treat the former as a *long-run* process, and simply freeze it for purposes of modeling the latter. Mäki (1992), whose organization of the main styles of economic modeling was mentioned in Section 2.6, has identified PE analysis as a special kind of idealization, with distinctive properties for model testing. Following the philosopher Nancy Cartwright (1989), Mäki refers to it as *isolation*.

Isolation is exemplified by many possible illustrations; I choose one here by reference to an interesting and highly visible industry. Suppose that someone is wondering why passenger airlines throughout the world have, since the late 1990s, tended to consolidate and avoid head-to-head competition with one another in domestic markets, while competing strenuously over intercontinental routes. There are two key facts, exogenous to economic analysis, on which the explanation is based. First, the much higher rate of fuel consumed in take-off than in cruising makes it harder to make profits on, and thus reduces scope for competition in, services to and from smaller cities that don't produce passenger loads that fill large jets. Second, international regulations requiring passenger trips to originate on airlines owned by nationals of the country of departure strongly incentivize competition over access to airports that receive many visitors from abroad. Consider now the current global industrial structure, which features three full-service domestic carriers in the US, one major domestic carrier in most other countries, and three major international airline groupings competing to take people between continents. Should we regard this as a brief phase in a rapidly evolving market, or as a relatively persistent situation? 'Persistent' here doesn't mean changeless or eternal. For practical purposes, it means: probably sufficiently long-lasting to serve as a basis for decisions by airplane manufacturers over which mix of product development projects they should invest in, and by cities over which airports to support with new infrastructure. We may also want to pose specific questions about likely directions of change when, on different scenarios, it does come about. Should we or shouldn't we expect to eventually see the international airline groups reciprocally ceding monopoly positions on major intercontinental routes to one another, as they have been doing on domestic routes? Should we expect the alliance model to eventually draw in the independent challengers from the Middle East (Emirates, Turkish Airlines etc.) operating with a new business model, or should we expect their challenge to render the new equilibrium very short-lived?

The economist will typically address these questions, to begin with, by treating the regulatory environment as fixed, and by letting the price of fuel and the preferences of passengers vary independently of airline industry structure. If asked to defend these 'assumptions' she might do so by saying that fuel prices and passenger preferences are outside industry participants' influence. But this answer would be a bit misleading. The deeper point is that these variables move on time-scales that aren't tightly linked to airlines' strategic decisions.

Having thus selected relevant variables she will treat as *exogenous* *to* the isolated system, the economist then searches for an equilibrium that applies only to the airline industry by itself. Hence Mäki's choice of terminology: the exogenizing assumptions *isolate* the industry so it can be examined without regard to the entire political economy of the world. Of course, the assumptions are idealizations and they aren't true. The regulatory environment *will* change, in major ways, sooner or later, in response to airlines' strategies. Passenger preferences are *not* independent of industry structure: companies that pay to fly their employees around will gradually adapt their business practices to changes in the relative costs of travel on different kinds of routes. There is, indeed, no reason to believe that there is any *real* general equilibrium that renders the current values of the exogenous variables more stable than some other possible set of values they might have. But suppose it's just a general, contingent, non-mysterious fact that these variables treated as exogenous tend to change more slowly, or vary within smaller ranges, than some variables that are under the more direct management control of airlines. In that case it is worth investigating whether the airline industry is or isn't plausibly in a state of partial equilibrium that will keep its structure stable for as long as the variables treated as exogenous in the model haven't changed much. The economist's model isolates the airline industry in order to investigate that question.

Since Marshall's time, the line between GE and PE has simultaneously become sharper in *theoretical* economics and more indistinct in *applied* economics. This has generated considerable confusion, which often begins in semantics and ends in ideology, among external critics of economics. The deep source of the general muddle lies in the varying purposes to which economic theory and analysis are put. Some economic analysis, which we will call 'high theory,' is aimed at discovering general properties of markets in the abstract. This more closely resembles the conceptual analyzes of philosophers than it does empirical science. Then we have economic analysis that aims at comparing two or more possible states of affairs, typically distinguished in the first place by the application or non-application of some identified policy option, with respect to some *welfare* measure. Welfare is to be understood in terms of utility, but the welfare measures on which policy evaluation might turn are highly varied. Perhaps the policy-maker aims to improve *average* welfare (on one of several possible statistical understandings of 'average') in a whole country. Where this is the aim the policy-maker will tend to be drawn toward the holism associated with GE analysis. At the other extreme, the economist may only be concerned with discovering conditions under which a firm or industry improves its efficiency. This is the domain of old-fashioned PE analysis, though nowadays it will rely heavily on application of game theory (see Chapter 3), (Sutton 2001). In an intermediate instance, a policy analyst might want to know about effects on some disadvantaged minority, unconcerned with consequences for members of the better-off majority on grounds that their greater power will afford them with means for looking after themselves. Work of this sort typically shares core aspects of both GE and PE modeling.

Let us begin with high theory. Some economists think that the greatest achievement within the theoretical framework of GE is the 1954 proof by Arrow and Debreu that in every perfectly competitive market at least one equilibrium exists in which no agent can be made better off without another agent being made worse off. Intuitively, this condition, known as *Pareto efficiency*, is one sense in which we can say that an allocation of resources across an economy does not waste utility. If our focus is on Pareto efficiency, then we need not concern ourselves with controversies around how utility might be averaged or the gains and losses of different agents weighted; economics can be done without reference to psychology, institutions or political philosophy. The Arrow-Debreu result has often been touted as the formal culmination and vindication of an argument, often attributed to Adam Smith, in favor of policies that let the 'invisible hand of the market' operate without hindrance from government.

The connection between Smith's argument, which was about real policy choice in a real context, and high-theory GE is tenuous. We can agree that the Arrow-Debreu result represented vindication of a long-standing expectation among economists, clearly articulated by Walras, that if all agents are free to trade without extra-economic restrictions – institutional, political, financial or physical – then resources should be expected to move from inefficient to more efficient deployment until, in the absence of shocks, no further such movement is possible. However, there are a number of specific 'impediments' to perfect competition in real markets that must be assumed away to establish the Arrow-Debreu result. The most important of these are:

(1) *asymmetric information*: some agents know some facts relevant to supply and demand estimations while other agents don't yet know them;

(2) *non-decreasing returns*: there are some constant and increasing returns to scale available given some feasible innovations on the production side;

(3) *transaction costs*: implementing exchange typically involves physical and other costs (searching for exchange partners, traveling to meet them, taking time to bargain with them, paying contract lawyers, etc.);

(4) *market entry barriers*: most agents lack access to quantities of capital beyond certain thresholds, despite the fact that they could lower their investment risks if they could exceed the thresholds in question; and most people will pay premiums to trade with favored partners whom they know more about, and whom they trust, more than strangers;[33]

(5) *real monetary effects*: people and companies must deal with changes in relative monetary values that do not flow only from

---

[33] This incorporates the premium value associated with branded merchandise. In perfect competition there is no value in reputation or familiarity, and since all information is complete consumers do not pay for confidence in product quality or security of warranties.

changes in the relative supply and demand of currency and call deposits.

These features combine to produce *positive and negative externalities*: utility windfalls to some agents, and utility deficits to others, that are unrelated to these agents' responses to incentive shifts (i.e., their choices). Externalities are often regarded as morally problematic because they reward the unenterprising and punish innocent bystanders. But setting this concern aside for the moment, externalities are troubling to economic theory because they introduce noise into the relationship, which in perfect competition is seamless, between choice and outcomes.

Features (1)–(5) characterize all real economies, and are indeed the crucial variable conditions that differentiate economies from one another and frame the policy problems and alternatives facing their participants and regulators. It is empty rhetoric to say that some real *whole* market 'approximates' perfect competition, because 'approximate' here turns out to have no economic meaning. In a famous paper, Lipsey and Lancaster (1956) proved that a speculative corollary of the Arrow-Debreu result, to the effect that near-equilibrium allocations in perfectly competitive markets are more efficient than allocations farther from equilibrium, does *not* hold. One can sometimes usefully use perfectly competitive restrictions (not 'approximations' to such restrictions) to model narrowly isolated parts of the whole market, such as the raw sugar market, in which the effects of factors (1)–(5) are unusually small; but then one has obviously left the GE framework in favor of PE. Furthermore, there are relatively few real markets in this class; it consists only of markets for products in which production or extraction technology is mature, individual products are indistinguishable to consumers, demand is stable and capital costs are low. In general these are some global markets for raw materials (but many globally traded raw materials markets do *not* have these properties).

Despite all this, some economists regard the Arrow-Debreu result as the crown jewel of their disciplinary treasure chest. In expressing this attitude, an economist reveals aspects of her preferences concerning the relative importance of conceptual and empirical or policy engineering work. Arrow-Debreu as a contribution to conceptual clarification should delight any analytic philosopher. The proof, and the *specific* ways in which it is blocked by relaxation of its restrictions, may structure thought on what market mechanisms fundamentally *are*. In this light it is unsurprising that some leading philosophers of economics, notably Hausman (1992), have claimed to assess the science of economics while actually assessing high-theory GE. To a philosopher who thinks that sciences are 'founded on' their most rigorous conceptual definitions, it will seem as if high-theory GE must be the foundation of the discipline. Economists who value mathematics more than they value science – who certainly exist but who are a minority of the profession (Coyle 2007) – have encouraged such philosophers. As argued in Chapter 1, however, philosophy of economics that takes conceptual formalization as foundational reflects a mistaken underlying philosophy of science. Sciences are distinguished by experimental and mathematical (often statistical) traditions of practice, not by logical refinements of concepts.

What makes the philosophers' misunderstanding particularly beguiling in this instance is the *apparently* direct connection between the Arrow-Debreu result and the founding issues of modern economics. To fill in the context for thinking about high theory GE, and its contemporary relationship to PE, we will therefore step back not only to Adam Smith but, for a policy issue against which to ground all the abstractions, to the subject of practical controversy that most animated Smith – international trade.

Smith's second great book carried the abbreviated title *The Wealth of Nations* (1776/1986) because it was an argument against the common proposition that a country best maximizes 'its welfare' by regarding trade in the same way that a business does, treating exports like revenues from outputs and imports like costs of inputs. Then a country should try, to the extent that other countries will allow it, to minimize imports, through tariffs, quotas and other instruments while maximizing exports. This common proposition is known as *mercantilism*. I put quote marks around 'its welfare' in the sentence just above to signal that Smith's quarrel with the mercantilists turned partly on differing philosophical conceptions of what national welfare might reasonably mean. If one thinks of a country as a collective agency that makes itself best off by having substantial public deposits with which to quickly muster large armed forces for purposes of competition with other countries – and if, as in the eighteenth century, income and land taxes are difficult to collect without risking civil disorder – then the mercantilist position has some cogency. But Smith was an Enlightenment British (Scottish) empiricist, who conceived of national welfare as a function of the well-being of individual citizens. In that case, the argument for free trade as the best general or default policy is very strong. Citizens prosper by being able to afford more consumption rather than less. Their available consumption baskets are optimized if they can source tradable goods from wherever in the world they are most efficiently produced. On this individualist conception of welfare, imports rather than exports are the fundamental source of value; exports are the means to the end of earning foreign currency with which to pay for imports.

Any specific trade regime, whether mercantilist or free trading, will favor some industrial sectors and individuals more than others. Mercantilism benefits those who produce exportable goods at the expense of everyone else. Free trade disproportionately benefits those who are skilled at exploiting the country's least scarce factors of production, and can greatly disadvantage those who specialize in exploiting factors of production with which other countries are more liberally endowed. Thus *any* trade policy raises prima facie difficulties for a political morality that is broadly Kantian and associates the 'best' policy with minimization of the extent to which some citizens' interests are sacrificed as means for the realization of the ends of others.

Economists since Smith have had a response to this. Free trade as a general default policy grows wealth in a country to a greater extent – under some circumstances, to a dramatically greater extent – than mercantilism.[34] To the extent that a country or society as a whole has a

---

[34] This statement is disputed by many. The economic and political literature debating the empirical superiority of free trade is enormous, and at least a long chapter would be required to do it justice. Thus I will not attempt a balanced review here. There is a range of special circumstances in which specific interferences with free trade can be defended, but all of these are restricted to particular circumstances of time and place. Thus every mercantilist intervention needs to be periodically reviewed on the assumption that at some point it will become obsolete and counter-productive. But this is itself a problem, since when the time comes to repeal the intervention, the interests that benefit from it will spend resources defending it, and this will require others to spend resources trying to overcome the lobbying. This expenditure by both sides is what economists call a *deadweight loss* – a wasteful opportunity cost – to the society as a whole. It should be anticipated and set against whatever earlier benefits are derived from a limited-time and limited-scope mercantilist intervention. But this seldom happens in real political processes; and *that* is in turn an argument for maintaining the much simpler policy of generalized free trade. This states the considered opinion of a majority of economists, notwithstanding a substantial professionally legitimate literature of dissent (e.g., Rodrik 2007). For more extended non-technical defenses of generalized free trade, I recommend Irwin (1997) and Legrain (2002). The best current technical overview of international trade theory and relevant evidence is Feenstra (2003).

larger surplus of wealth, disproportionate 'winners' from the policy that fosters the surplus in question can transfer portions of their winnings to disproportionate 'losers.' This is the economic welfare criterion captured by the concept of Pareto efficiency. A state of affairs A is said to be Pareto superior to a state of affairs B if at least one individual is better off in A than that individual is in B and no one is worse off in A than they are in B. Then a policy P is *Pareto efficient* if its expected outcome O is such that there is no alternative feasible policy P' that produces an expected outcome O' that is Pareto superior to P. It is often pointed out that actually feasible Pareto efficient policies tend only to produce the underlying unambiguous welfare outcome if the necessary transfers are actually carried out (the *Scitovsky criterion* or alternatively the *Kaldor-Hicks criterion*); but then it is objected that in the real world they almost never are. This lavishly justified empirical point is grounds for mordancy about human selfishness, but it misses the point as an *objection* to the efficiency criterion itself. If a society has available to it a policy that would be Pareto efficient if it passes the Scitovsky criterion and the policy is not adopted, then the society in question is wasting utility. If one thinks in addition that, were that society to adopt the policy in question then it would not actually compensate the losers, one adds a second reason to be annoyed at that society. This all remains true even if all societies are (very) annoying. One has not thereby shown that the economist's analysis of efficiency is defective.

Much of the practical plausibility of this welfarist perspective as applied to international trade, and to other specific policy issues such as national publicly subsidized health insurance (countries should have it), national publicly subsidized universally accessible primary and secondary education (countries should have it), relatively simple tax codes (countries should have them), derive from the specificity itself, since this is crucial to actually estimating quantifiable effects. In these cases PE modeling will not suffice, because costs of a policy that improves outcomes in one policy sector might arise through secondary effects (distortions) occurring in any other sector. For example, addition of a new tariff might improve a country's terms of international trade, but exert a cost by diverting resources away from parts of the economy where capital is used more efficiently.

Since pioneering work by Taylor and Black (1974), this kind of analysis has involved application of *computable general equilibrium*

(CGE) modeling. CGE models build on the earlier development of whole-economy scale input-output models by the great mid-century economist Wassily Leontiff (1905–1999). To this framework they add empirically estimated elasticities of both consumption and production, which paramaterize the extent to which alternative goods and production technologies are treated by a given market as substitutes for one another. The extent of CGE work has grown apace with the development of computational technology, for it is this which allows economists to represent an entire economy in a model while relaxing some or all of the restrictions defining perfect competition. Such models cannot be solved by hand and were thus infeasible in earlier decades. Subsequent to the 1970s, economists have learned how to write dynamic CGE models, in which variables evolve through time, and to incorporate uncertain expectations. Such dynamic, stochastic computable general equilibrium (DSCGE) models have become the basic working technology of standard macroeconomics, though as we will see later this status is highly controversial. Clearly, DSCGE models preserve the impulse to Walrasian holism. However, they resemble PE models in having pragmatic foundations. All CGE models have more variables than equations, and thus may only be solved by fixing some variables. They therefore depend upon the pragmatic isolation decisions characteristic of PE modeling. Unless someone believes there is a standing, general hierarchy that structures variables governing whole economies into long, medium and short-run classes, the pragmatic foundations of CGE models in general, and of DSCGE models specifically, preclude the idea that any such model could ever be a complete description of an economy. This does *not* exclude them from being used to justify welfare assessments at particular times and places. To cite one of many possible examples from the international trade literature, Harrison et al. (2002) use a CGE model to identify plausible actual Scitovsky transfers to specific households that would be possible under various reform policies that would reduce or smooth excise taxes in Denmark.

Work of this kind is indeed in the Smithian tradition. But it has no meaningful relationship to any efforts, real or rhetorical, to use high GE theory to motivate a general welfarist argument for economic libertarianism or for a *laissez-faire* state that avoids interference with the consequences of voluntary market transactions.

Let us note first why this question even arises – it should not be considered obvious that it does, since economic libertarianism evidently prohibits forced compensation to satisfy the Scitovsky criterion. The answer is that the argument for free trade is based on a premise to the effect that growth of wealth depends crucially on efficient distribution of labor, which in turn depends on specialization. Specialization of labor was facilitated, both in Smith's time and to a much greater extent a few decades after him, by the organization of large enterprises. These required major concentrations and continuous reinvestments of financial and physical capital – hence the later term 'capitalism,' put into common coinage (though not invented) by Karl Marx. The separation of the functions of financing and producing that distinguished early capitalism from previous dominant forms of production is evidently an important kind of division of labor. Furthermore, Smith's argument against mercantilism, as we have seen, partly rests upon a decomposition of national well-being into the well-being of individuals. Economic libertarianism is most often promoted by its advocates as an extension of the principle that individuals are the best promoters of their own well-being, and so should be sovereign over such productive resources – including their own 'human capital' – that they come to control by means that don't involve theft from or coercion of others.

From the fact that capitalism fostered one efficiency-promoting kind of specialization of labor, it clearly does not follow that maximum welfare efficiency is achieved if the specialists in production financing are allowed to operate without restraints. The Lipsey-Lancaster result blocks any hope of being able to use the Arrow-Debreu result to supply the missing premises for such an argument. Non-confused libertarians depend on at least one of two further premises, which most of them accept jointly but which are logically independent of one another.

The first of these premises is *normative individualism*, the claim that what is most valuable to and about people are the self-conceptions that distinguish them, to themselves and in their social self-presentations, from other people. This is evidently not a factual premise, but an expression of a value judgment. Some empirical facts about human psychology and social structures are relevant to refining the understanding and scope of this sort of judgment. I will discuss some of these issues, in light of contemporary psychology and sociology, in Chapter 5. Smith shared the Enlightenment conviction that traditional European political and social organization based on hereditary hierarchies failed to place *enough* normative weight on the freedom of individuals to set their own objectives and guide their own life trajectories. To this extent, Smith was a normative individualist. But to categorize Smith as a libertarian, even in anticipation, requires highly selective reading of his corpus.

The conclusion of the main argument in *The Wealth of Nations* is that for purposes of growing a country's aggregate wealth, institutions that encourage individual agents to invest and exchange the commercial resources they control are generally preferable to institutions that grant partial monopolies to positionally privileged traders. This is not an argument for a de-institutionalized network of free moral atoms. Its implication, quite explicit in Smith, is that laws should foster certain institutions in preference to others. It thus entails the view, at least in any setting that has ever historically existed, that political and other authorities should do the fostering in question. Furthermore, as Smith explained with great subtlety of insight in his first major book, *The Theory of Moral Sentiments* (1759/1976), wealth is not the primary direct basis of utility[35] for most people. It is rather one important means to the more fundamental goods of social status and moral self-respect, where the latter in turn essentially involves a person's management of their human relationships. Therefore, there is important room in Smith's political philosophy for institutions that support these fundamental objectives directly, even if they limit the scope of market mechanisms. To cite obvious examples, Smith did not favor toleration of markets in slaves or poisoned wine, and his principles are compatible with banning markets in lethal weapons, injunctions to commit genocide, and various other products that generally cause more harm than good.[36] Smith is absolutely not an advocate of either the valorization of purely self-regarding preferences or a minimalist, laissez-faire state. Such advocacy is indeed not found in the writings of any of the classical or early neoclassical economists.

The second premise commonly invoked by contemporary economic libertarians is that efficiency requires private – ultimately

---

[35] In using this term, I characterize Smith's views using a later concept that was unavailable to him.
[36] This is the point of my insertion of the adjective 'commercial' in the first sentence of the present paragraph.

individual – control of productive resources because individuals are massively privileged in their *knowledge* of their own capabilities and levels of commitment to projects. This empirical claim about information was elaborated with great detail and ingenuity in the twentieth century by Hayek (1945 and elsewhere). Hayek's key insight is that the basic observation about asymmetric knowledge generalizes in such a way as to explain why markets can set relatively stable prices that at least approximately match the relative supply of goods and services to demand, whereas central planners cannot. Price setting through markets involves *distributed* processing of information about resource budgets, production functions and utility functions, whereas price setting by planners requires all this information to be aggregated and analyzed at one decision point. Evidence from multiple quarters, including twentieth-century experiments with non-market-based national economies (i.e., the Soviet Union and its imitators and client regimes), efforts to engineer artificial intelligence and other automated complex control systems, and recent discoveries about the organization of the human brain, has strongly confirmed Hayek's most general point. The most important social function performed by markets is *computation of information* about existing aggregate demand for goods and services, and about changes in opportunity costs of productive inputs that allow entrepreneurs to identify and assemble financing for viable innovations. As stressed with particular clarity and elegance by the great political economist and business theorist Joseph Schumpeter (1883–1950; see his 1942), the latter is an essential condition for sustained technological progress, and through that channel for growth of wealth.

Smith famously wrote that the coordination of supply and demand, and the consequent satisfaction of people's needs and wants that he equated with true national wealth, is 'guided as if by an invisible hand' (1776/1986), which he contrasts with explicit intentions by planners. Scholarly experts on Smith have studied the extent to which his invisible hand metaphor reflected anticipation of the much later Hayekian conception of the market as an aggregator of distributed information, or the Schumpeterian recognition of the market as a signaling instrument for innovators. Undoubtedly these ideas were glimpsed in less clearly articulated form by all or almost all modern economists. *Regardless* of what grounds it or of how its normative significance is exactly understood, the invisible hand encapsulates a question that must be of abiding interest to any student of markets: to what extent can markets be relied upon to produce optimally efficient distributions of consumption goods and productive resources automatically and without deliberate oversight and manipulation?

This is the context in which some economists view the Arrow-Debreu result as the culmination of the history of analysis in their discipline.[37] But, as I have said, this attitude treats economic *philosophy* as more important than economic *applications*. The key factor that limits the Arrow-Debreu result's practical value is that it relies on the restrictions of perfect competition. Had perfect competition turned out to be a limiting ideal, like the frictionless plane in classical mechanics, in which equilibrium results are approximated as the restricting variables get close to zero, the verdict would have been different. But the Lipsey-Lancaster proof demolishes this source of significance. We have no reason to think that even those few real markets that approximate perfect competition are more likely to contribute to a real general efficiency optimum than are markets for products with increasing returns to scale.

Another key limitation of the applicability of GE modeling in its high-theory (as opposed to computable, empirical) sense, and one that distinguishes it sharply from the basis of Smith's invisible hand, is that one of the key motivational mechanisms invoked in Smith's argument, the desire of producers to build profitable enterprises, is absent in the hypothetical perfectly competitive environment. In the imaginary conditions, producers can enter markets without facing capital constraints, and there are no variables for restricted control of scarce resources or patents on innovations. For Smith, emphasis on the profit motive is intended not as a contribution to psychology – the point that people are motivated by potential resource gains is hardly an insight – but as the basis for defending the legal enablement of institutions, such as limited-liability corporations, which channel that motive to build societal wealth. This issue cannot even be raised within the context of perfect competition. For these reasons, the Arrow-Debreu result has no applicability to the structures of real markets that interested Smith.

This point generalizes. In purely abstract GE models there is no role for any *institutions* – legal structures, firms, channels for advertising,

---

honest or biddable politicians or bureaucrats, labor unions, countries and customs barriers or even money – that are basic and recurrent restrictive factors and transmitters of influence in real markets. Arguably, institutions and the interacting expectations to which they give rise in both consumers and producers, rather than any imagined empirical analogues to formal equlibria in institutionless models, are the real stabilizers of prices and resource allocations.[38] To the extent that this is so, high-theory GE modeling abstracts away from an entire essential element of the class of phenomena that economists aim to understand.

It is ironic that, partly because of its name and partly because of its confused association with invisible hand arguments, perfect competition is often attacked by critics of laissez faire ideology as if it described the libertarian ideal. In fact, libertarians would not be very happy under a regime in which returns on investments were not protected by strong state institutions. We see followers of Ayn Rand periodically trying to create sheltered utopias beyond the reach of existing states, yet we never observe them moving to Somalia. The actual policy relevance, such as it is, of perfect competition analysis is mainly to advise a hypothetical or actual *central planner* about the optimal output target for a whole economy, in the short-run where technology is held fixed. This has sometimes been taken as setting an efficiency benchmark by which a planner might try to reduce waste within the limited time horizon of her control. During the heyday of central planning in both Soviet-style bureaucratic dictatorships and democracies, between 1945 and the late 1970s, such benchmark-identification was often set in imagined perfectly competitive environments. Nowadays any serious planner uses a CGE or specifically DSGE model for this purpose. In general, however, both perfect competition and general equilibrium acquire such practical value as they have because of the existence of governments as powerful economic agents; they do not characterize ideals that would reasonably be promoted by private corporations or entrepreneurs.

---

[38] As Colander (1996, pp. 60–61) points out, if one builds a CGE model that incorporates Keynesian monetary theory, which is a popular modeling approach among central banks, one faces the puzzle that *nothing* explains price stability; yet, in most times and places, prices are stable enough to allow for sensible investments in future money returns, and safeguarding such stability is the very core of a central bank's function.

We may thus summarize this section as follows. From the perspective of the philosopher of science, abstract GE models resemble RPT in being *conceptually* relevant to economists because they are used as reference points for restricting operational relationships among concepts. This has tended to cause philosophers of economics to overestimate their working importance in economics (though they have more excuse where high-theory GE is concerned, because economic theorists likewise tend to inflate its importance). The Arrow-Debreu result is best appreciated as technical conceptual achievement rather than as a contribution to practical policy economics. It is not best understood as a mathematical validation of Adam Smith's classic argument for anti-mercantilism and separation of the functions of capitalist and producer. That argument is essentially about social and legal organization of institutional structures.

It is fashionable in many quarters to make the point above and then to move swiftly to throwing rhetorical stones at 'Walrasians' or 'neoclassicists.' Such fashion is vulgar, and philosophers of economics should not join it. Separating Smith from Arrow-Debreu provides no grounds for disparaging the approach to economic analysis opened by the marginalists. The central tenet of the marginalist revolution, that economic analysis concerns marginal opportunity costs and benefits, is not open to serious question and is unlikely to be revised as the discipline goes forward. The technical tools of economics are always being extended and refined, but they are and will continue to be built on the solid base that the marginalists provided.

2.8 A note on macroeconomics

Every student of economics meets the subject as two separate inquiries, microeconomics and macroeconomics. The advanced student may later be taught that macroeconomics needs, or already has, 'microfoundations,' meaning that the generalizations and principles of macroeconomics can, or should be, constructed from some sort of aggregation of microeconomic models. Notwithstanding this – increasingly shaky – bridge between the two parts of economics, the division between them remains strongly entrenched in the institutions of the discipline. Microeconomists and macroeconomists largely occupy distinct mansions.

The familiarity of this disciplinary organization should not lead us to treat its basis as obvious or naturally given. Most sciences are not split, as economics is, into micro and macro wings with almost completely dissociated journals and theoretical frameworks. Is this division in economics mainly a historical accident, or does it reflect deep structural aspects of the economic domain? Though most economists prefer to remain uncommitted on such philosophical questions, this is one on which there have been substantial differences of opinion among them for decades.

Understanding the relationship between microeconomics and macroeconomics is particularly important to the main theme of this book, the place of economics in the wider scientific worldview. Someone might initially expect that microeconomics should be relatively more closely integrated with psychology than with sociology, and that the opposite should be true of macroeconomics. But this is *not* the picture I will eventually sketch in the final chapter of the book. Reversing the traditionally promoted relationship – but in agreement with the view of the inventor of the microeconomics/macroeconomics distinction, Ragnar Frisch (1895–1973) – I will argue that microeconomics has its foundations in macroeconomics. But psychology doesn't have sociological foundations (or vice versa). There is no master micro/macro distinction contributing to a generalized philosophy of the behavioral and social sciences.

The institutional divide between microeconomics and macroeconomics post-dates the Second World War. It stems from the great expansion of the role of the state in the management of whole economies during the 1940s, which attracted attention to the project of establishing scientific foundations for *national accounts*. These are efforts to model and estimate levels and changes in national output, assets, productivity, employment, outstanding credits and obligations, supply and circulation rate of money, rates of savings and investments, expectations about future prices, and other related variables, the range and sophistication of which grew as macroeconomics professionally matured. Major early figures in the enterprise of constructing and measuring national accounts included Jan Tinbergen (1903–1994), Trygve Haavelmo (1911–1999) and Wassily Leontief (1906–1999). As noted in the previous chapter, this strain of work was the precursor to CGE modeling.

Prior to the crisis of the Great Depression, the main agents whose actions were thought to be at least potentially guided by refinements in economic theory and measurement were corporations. Following

Marshall, most of the emphasis in applied economics was on partial equilibrium analysis of specific markets and industrial sectors. The economy as a whole was widely regarded as restricted by equilibrating forces of supply and demand that were independent of policy, with the main roles for governments being to maintain the material basis of wealth by keeping trade routes open, and defending price stability by ensuring that the supply of currency was regulated by the quantity of gold in the national treasury. This view was compatible with the existence of recurrent booms and slumps at the national and international scales, which were understood as limits in oscillation orbits around a dynamic but objectively real equilibrium anchor. During the early years of the world depression that began in late 1929, the standard opinion among economists was that, like previous slumps, this one would be corrected by automatic adjustments in corporate and consumer behavior. In particular, as industrial inventories wore down during the period of depressed output, labor would need to be engaged to replace it, which would in turn put resources in the hands of consumers who would resume buying – the expected pattern was familiar. Active government intervention was taken to be not only undesirable but in principle pointless, as equilibrium dynamics would naturally have their way.

Among leading economic analysts during the depression, Hayek prominently criticized *half* of this conventional opinion. Appreciating that prices are carriers of economic information, rather than merely nominal functions of supply and demand intersections that oscillate around equilibria, he argued that government action could fundamentally change the elements of national accounts. However, he believed that such action could only damage economic efficiency rather than improve it – essentially because he regarded markets as *accurate* transmitters of information that governments could not realistically attempt to centrally process. Thus, despite maintaining a non-standard philosophy of economics, Hayek shared the orthodox policy opinion of his time. (These views of Hayek's remain very popular, and strongly influential, among so-called conservatives[39] in the US Republican Party.)

---

[39] My use of 'so-called' reflects the fact that by comparison with opinions associated with conservatism in most of the world, American conservatism has evolved into an exotic and sui generis blend of hyper-individualism, rejection of business regulation, and moralistic authoritarianism about sexual behavior.

Famously, the most prominent economist who denied *both* aspects of the conventional view – who argued, that is, that governments both could and should intervene to change their nations' rates of output and employment for the better – was John Maynard Keynes. Keynes's learning and experience involved an unusual combination of canonical philosophy absorbed in the high British tradition, patronage of the arts, promotion of the extension of unconventional creative lifestyles beyond the aristocracy, and mastery of the then new art of professional investment asset management. As a sometime Treasury official and consultant, and Liberal Party insider, Keynes commanded the attention of senior policy-makers to an extent denied to purely academic economists. And as a former Cambridge don and member of the Bloomsbury Group of artists and thinkers, he also enjoyed an independence of intellectual status that reduced the pressure on him to remain within the ambit of conventional economic doctrine.

It is not possible within the scope of this book to characterize Keynes's views beyond broad generalizations. This is necessarily risky, because his opinions were unusually subtle and sensitive to changing influences. They were not derived from a distinctive philosophy of either psychology or social science; in my view his limited writings on these subjects reveal only casual and unsystematic attention. He did, however, have a deep and original grasp of the difference between, on the one hand, quantitatively forecastable risk and, on the other hand, uncertainty that is susceptible only to qualitative description.[40] For example, we can model and forecast, with decent accuracy, ranges within which major currencies will exchange over the course of the next year. Buying and selling currencies within this range involves quantifiable risk, which is reflected in the prices of currency options. On the other hand, we cannot know which of the current major financial institutions will still be in operation fifty years from now, though we can reasonably venture the qualitative expectation that some of them will suffer terminal disasters. Emphasis on this distinction led Keynes to

---

[40] This distinction is often attributed to a contemporary of Keynes's, the economist Frank Knight (1921), who articulated it in the context of investment decisions. Keynes arrived at the distinction independently and via a route less directly connected to economics, namely, philosophical reflection on the relationship between probability theory and inductive inference (Keynes 1921).

doubt that partial equilibrium reasoning scaled up reliably to applied general equilibrium on either the scale of time (from short-run to long-run) or of systemic scope (from individual industries to national economies).

Keynes's views are still the subject of heated polemics in popular economic policy debates, which leads to various currently advocated ideological tendencies being misattributed to him. Among these is the view that prices in large financial markets are mainly driven by irrational psychological fears and hopes and the view that economies are chaotic and entirely beyond the reach of equilibrium analysis. Keynes believed neither of these things. He thought that some investment decisions by a minority of purely speculative investors cannot be sensibly made on the basis of economic reasoning, that such investors *occasionally* cause serious harm to financial and political stability, and that their influence should therefore be regulated and contained; but he also believed that asset value is mainly driven by the underlying productive capacities of firms. He thought that large-scale economies generally oscillate within the orbits of equilibria, but held that such equilibria are not unique and that government and central bank policies can cause qualitatively predictable shifts among them. On neither of these matters did Keynes's opinions significantly differ from those of most current investors or applied economists.

Belief in multiple equilibria did, however, mark a major departure from the prevailing economic orthodoxy of Keynes's time. Equally revolutionary was his conviction that investors' attitudes to money exert causal influence on movements among these equilibria. These two unorthodox opinions were the basis of Keynes's policy advice, based on analysis in his epochal 1936 book, for politicians struggling to lift their nations' economies from the great depression. He argued that governments and central banks could and should act so as to steer economies away from equilibria that stabilize around low output, low employment, constrained credit availability and sluggish capital investment. They can do this, he maintained, by increasing the money supply during periods in which inventories of supply are high relative to demand, and constricting the money supply when the opposite relationship prevails. At the international scale, Keynes championed management of mutually destructive economic competition between nations – through competitive import tariffs and/or competitive currency devaluations – by global coordinating institutions.[41]

Contrary to widespread mythology, no major government in the 1930s seriously attempted to implement Keynes's policy therapy. The Roosevelt administration in the United States concentrated on regulating prices and output rather than the money supply directly, and in 1937 reverted to economic orthodoxy by trying to balance the national budget. In so doing it choked off a partial recovery to which its earlier expansionist policy had contributed. Meanwhile, in Germany, the Hitler regime did swell the money supply, but by massive investment in weapons which exaggerated an already negative balance of trade to the point where the country could ultimately secure vital imports only by setting out to conquer its neighbors.

Keynes was more immediately successful in persuading his fellow economists. During the ten years following the publication of Keynes's great book, Hicks and Samuelson built a loose but conceptually coherent theoretical structure in which the mechanisms and effects of Keynesian policies could be described in the familiar terms of optimization of neoclassical utility and production functions. Arguably, this reconciliation of theory with tools for policy application created the modern discipline as we have known it since, in which a global army of economic consultants models resource allocation using theoretical instruments refined by academic theorists. During their management of the giant war unleashed by Hitler, the governments of the US, the UK, Canada and Australia acquired a phalanx of technocrats to administer the newly orthodox fiscal and monetary machines, while monitoring their national accounts using the techniques invented by Tinbergen, Haavelmo, Leontief and followers. After the war such economic policy engines became essential components of the modern state. Understanding the normative logic of all this, after 1954, in terms of general equilibrium theory, reasonable people could believe that economists had collectively discovered the basis for reliable scientific engineering of perpetual growth in general wealth, under conditions of general relative stability of prices and employment.

---

[41] The World Bank, the International Monetary Fund and the World Trade Organization are institutions of this kind. Keynes was personally involved in the design and launch of the first two.

The reader of 2012 may be shaking her head ruefully at this. She has observed four years of dizzying instability in major global investment instruments, and she is anxiously warned on a continuous basis that structural dynamics seem to be relentlessly generating rising within-country inequalities that undermine consensus on principles of economic governance. In this atmosphere it has become common for people to regard the triumphant confidence of economists described in the previous paragraph as comical. Popular commentaries frequently give the impression that whereas we sadder but wiser twenty-first-century people appreciate the complexity of economic phenomena, our childish predecessors – including ourselves just a few years ago – allowed themselves to mistake simplistic cartoons for reality.

This attitude is subject to all the usual criticisms of arrogant ahistoricism. Keynesian monetary and institutional management appeared to work wonders in the rich Western democracies between the end of the Second World War and the mid-1970s. It is hardly surprising that finance ministers, central bankers and the applied economists who worked for them enjoyed growing confidence. Among economic theorists, however, there was general awareness that the deep context in which the new macroeconomics flourished harbored logical mysteries. As noted in the previous section, the mathematical consumer theory that was regarded as the conceptual core of microeconomics was recognized by Samuelson as having little empirical significance, notwithstanding that its proudest feature was its formal testability in principle. Macroeconomics and microeconomics evolved into barely related enterprises because in the world of practical application macroeconomics seemed to work brilliantly while microeconomics could be taken up as an intellectually exacting but irrelevant theoretical pastime. Those who worked most diligently at trying to assemble the pieces into a single view – most notably, Milton Friedman, Kenneth Arrow and Leonid Hurwicz, all economists who continue to be closely studied in 2012 – were naturally inclined to take the self-evident success of macroeconomics as their explanatory target and fixed point. They concentrated on rigor and incremental exploration because their mission did not seem practically urgent. (This is not at all equivalent to saying that, to devoted scholars, it didn't seem *important*.) Would any other attitude have then been reasonable?

We should not expect to have good philosophy of economics if we let ourselves spin dismissively simple narratives about the history of economics. The caricature of a monolithic 'neoclassical' orthodoxy into which we cram Adam Smith, Jevons, Walras, Pareto, Marshall, Samuelson and Friedman, and against which we contrast current, more enlightened conceptions, is a pernicious myth. The philosophy of economics sketched by Friedman (1953) should not be read, as it too often is, as a culmination of the thought of this invented ahistorical monolith. Friedman's philosophy is a sensitive reflection of the specific context of the mid-twentieth century state of the discipline. He assumed that economics was a highly successful science because it then certainly seemed to be one: growth was dramatically accelerating not only in the wealthy part of the world, but in Africa and Latin America. (Asia, wracked by political violence on a huge scale, was then the exception.) Better policy management seemed to be the explanation. But Friedman understood, like Samuelson, that this could not reasonably be attributed to the truth of the 'underlying' assumptions of microeconomic theory. It was well appreciated that the assumptions in question are not plausible descriptions of the plans or calculations of individual managers; and as descriptions of hypothetical consumers they played no obvious role in generating policy modeling except rationalizing downward-sloping demand curves. Thus Friedman took the leading problem of the philosophy of economics to be explaining how successful predictions could be generated by patently unrealistic assumptions.

This epistemological puzzle thrown up by the circumstances of the 1950s and 1960s – not a batty delusion to the effect that actual people are hyper-rational and purely self-regarding maximizers of their lifetime material wealth – is the accurate starting point for understanding the problems and debates of the contemporary philosophy of economics. Economics as Friedman – reasonably – saw it in 1953 was strikingly independent of all other disciplines, including its traditional neighbors. Its 'agents' didn't appear to be *simplified* or *distorted* models of empirical psychological phenomena; they didn't appear to be models of any such phenomena at all. Following a half century of steady separation from psychology, it was troublingly unclear that microeconomic theory was related to *any* normal human thought or motivation. Let it be stressed again, however, that the trouble was theoretical, not practical, as long as macroeconomists enjoyed smooth sailing. Furthermore, the formal completion of general equilibrium theory argued powerfully against efforts to walk back the technical dissociation from psychology, since the path of formal analysis launched by Pareto had culminated in logical triumph. The disappearance of models of individual human beings from economic theory was an abstract puzzle to be accounted for, not an obvious omission to be put right.

As we will discuss in the next two chapters, however, theory was moving vigorously in underground currents that would burst to the surface and transform economics again when, in the mid-1970s, the serene cruise of the Hicks-Samuelson synthesis encountered unexpected riptides of policy failure. Some readers might imagine that it should have been philosophers, worried about a policy science that had drifted free of conceptual or ontological relationships with any other disciplines, who might have preserved conceptual diversity for the harder times. No expectation could be farther from the truth; the philosophy of economics was almost completely moribund between Friedman's 1953 essay and a gradual re-emergence after economics encountered its practical crisis. The heroes of the next part of the story, those who produced the most vital conceptual innovations while economists were lulled into temporary complacency, were a mathematician and a statistician.

3 The Expansion of the Economic Toolbox

3.1 The information age

Standard histories of economics identify the 1970s as the decade of crisis for the distinctively Keynesian aspect of the Samuelsonian synthesis described in the previous chapter. This is often coupled with an emphasis on a shift in applied economics – that is to say, in policy analysis – from confidence in the economic management capacity of the state to a 'neoliberal' re-emphasis on the wealth-generating power of lightly regulated markets.

Academic writers often like to pour scorn on well-worn summaries like the one above, but I will not do that here. The standard gloss is broadly accurate. But it immediately raises questions for a philosopher of science. It would be important and disquieting, if, as is often suggested by critics, what happened in economics between the mid-seventies and the mid-eighties was recognition that the modeling approach of the discipline had been fundamentally wrong and needed to be rebuilt from new foundations. Contrary to widespread mythology associated with the work of the philosophical historian of science Thomas Kuhn (1922–1996), the structural cores of healthy sciences are *not* abandoned when major new discoveries or insights occur (Ladyman and Ross 2007, chapter 2). The philosophical extrapolation of classical physics to serve as the basis for a universal atomistic mechanism was shattered by the coming of relativistic and quantum physics, but the mathematical structures of fundamental physics were beautifully contextualized and explained, not overthrown. If, by contrast, it were decided that neoclassical economics was just a programmatic *mistake*, from which we must now recoil by going back to the drawing board in economics or turning it into psychology, this would have profound implications for the philosophy of social science.

A further complication is that the turn in economics is typically presented as originating in a policy problem. This must also cast doubt on the scientific credentials of the discipline. It would not be surprising to find that many economists, like other groups of people, have at various times changed their political views under a mix of influences. And it would be equally unsurprising if, in the economists' case, new insights from their own professional domain were among these influences. But if we could not account for the new insights themselves without invoking political preferences and motivations, we would be forced to concede substantial ground to enemies of economics who claim that it is merely ideology dressed up in mathematics.

This charge is frequently leveled from both conservative and progressive ideological standpoints. The unpopularity of economists across the ideological spectrum might be regarded as prima facie evidence for the relative political neutrality of mainstream economic theory. In Ross (2012a), I argue that this hunch stands up well under careful scrutiny, and that there is strong justification for viewing the guiding spirit of academic economics as anti-ideological. This is what we would expect to find to the extent that the institutional incentives of science have dominated the evolution of economic theory. In this book I will not repeat this mainly negative argument, which is based on detailed analysis of each of the ways in which economic theory has been or logically could be alleged to encode and entrench ideologically partisan assumptions. What I will instead provide here is the complementary positive argument: I will offer a philosophically critical narrative of the major changes in economics since (roughly) 1980 that emphasizes endogenous rather than exogenous influences.

This philosophical history will agree with some ideological accounts in depicting Hayek as the outstanding prescient thinker whose ideas, once they are distinguished from vulgar interpretations that Hayek encouraged by inveighing against the welfare state, continue to be fruitfully expanded upon. This is not because I think that most economists were persuaded to think and construct their models in new ways because they read Hayek. The point, rather, is that on the most important philosophical questions about economics as a discipline – namely, 'What is its distinctive subject matter?' and 'Why does it not reduce to the theory of rational decisions?' – Hayek has turned out to have been the first person to articulate the answers that look most plausible in light of developments since the 1980s.

Though he was explicitly not a conservative, Hayek was, famously, a leading libertarian[1] political philosopher – arguably history's most careful and important such philosopher.[2] I should therefore be clear that in celebrating Hayek's insights into the nature of the economic realm I do not imply endorsement of his libertarianism. I briefly explained in the previous chapter why economic theory cannot be taken to show that unregulated markets and minimal states tend naturally to generate efficient distributions of resources at the scale of whole societies. The most intellectually serious reason why some thoughtful people are libertarians is a function of a value judgment rather than scientific analysis: it has seemed to them that the freedom of the individual, notwithstanding the risks and perils that accompany it – indeed, partly *because* of those risks and perils – is the supreme source of value in human life. At the very end of this book I will indicate the specific context, partly based on scientific considerations, in which I join libertarians in celebrating individual freedom as *among* the basic, irreducible human goods. Where I cannot join libertarians is in thinking that this basic good, or any other basic good, generally *trumps* others. Political activity intended to implement the conviction that there is any one over-arching good for people in general amounts to *fanaticism*; and I am surer in my moral rejection of fanaticism than in my positive moral appreciation of liberty (or of anything else). This emotional distrust is complemented by my considered meta-philosophical opinion that rational argumentation cannot *in principle* establish a case for *any* context-free theory of the good.

In times and places where the value of markets is under-emphasized, or – a more widespread danger – profit-seeking is thoughtlessly

---

[1] Hayek struggled with ideological self-labeling. Living as he did in America after World War II, he did not want to call himself a liberal because the meaning of that word in US political culture has little relationship to its meaning anywhere else. He expressed discomfort with the libertarian label, but accepted it as the best of a non-ideal set of options. Late in his life he described himself as a Whig. Binmore (1994, 1998, 2005), whose anti-conservatism is much less ambiguous than Hayek's, also adopts this self-characterization.

[2] Hayek's best known and most popularly influential political book is *The Road to Serfdom* (1944). But the principal basis of his status as a serious political philosopher is the later *Constitution of Liberty* (1960). It is in a postscript to the latter that he explains why he should not be counted among conservatives.

regarded as immoral, it is useful to have articulate libertarians around to resist wealth-destroying populism. But I would not want to live in a state that based its constitution on libertarian principles. Often the lives and dignity of vulnerable people can be protected only by denying the putative 'rights' – and thus restricting the freedom – of some powerful individuals. Notwithstanding the frequent correlation of moral collectivism with economic ignorance, in real politics where debates rely on simplifications and slogans and do not resemble university seminars, we also need collectivists on hand to constrain exaggerated individualism.

I do not, then, think that Hayek was a great thinker because he was a great libertarian philosopher. His importance to the history and philosophy of economics lies in his having understood, with exceptional force and clarity, the respect in which the evolution of economic ideas through the whole neoclassical period was technically lopsided. From the work of the early marginalists through the post-war synthesis, it focused overwhelmingly on the identification of efficiency optima in static markets under varying specifications. This is why, as I said in the previous chapter, for decades one could have only semi-facetiously characterized economic theory as the science of separating hyperplanes. In the policy domain, it furnished an engineering manual for central planning. But a more complete and balanced economics, as understood by Smith and Marshall alike, is ultimately the scientific study of markets. Markets are special kinds of objects, worthy of attention by a whole scientific discipline, *partly* because of their special efficiency-related properties. But, as first emphasized by Hayek (1945 and elsewhere), the *other* fundamental property cluster that distinguishes markets is related to the remarkable ways in which they process *information*.

Various recurrent tensions in economic theory derive from a fundamental one between concepts of rationality and asymmetries of information. As discussed in the previous chapter, the core of economic rationality is consistency in choice; to the extent that a putative economic agent chooses inconsistently we cannot estimate a utility function for her – that is, cannot identify states in which she is better off or worse off according to her own evaluations. This undermines the extent to which the logic of agency applies to a person or other entity – e.g., an animal or structured group – at all. Consistency in choice in turn requires that an agent assemble, *in advance of choice*, relatively rich information about the implications of each of her options; a would-be agent that discovers most such implications only through trial and error will appear to choose randomly, unless the environment in which the agent acts is so simple in its (relevant) structure that its properties can be derived with minimal computational resources from the consequences of almost any arbitrarily selected behavioral probe. For this reason, theories of rationality that begin with consistency tend by their internal logic to 'grow' additional axioms and conditions that stipulate full sensitivity to available information. By 'sensitivity' I refer to both harvesting information through perception and inference, and using it accurately in generating decisions. This logic is the main force that has tended to pull economics toward dependence on psychology, since it is psychologists who are responsible for discovering and describing the general forms of human (and other animate) sensitivity to information. But then this rebounds against the *other* main element of the traditional rationality concept, conformity to sound principles of statistical inference, because psychologists find that the individual, de-institutionalized people that they take as their basic targets of study aren't very good at such inference.[3]

The core characteristic of the real markets that fascinated Adam Smith, and that constitute the basic objects of study for economics, is the specialization of the participants giving rise to the mutual profitability of exchange. Specialization partly involves differentiated access to material resources. An elderly rich person, for example, might have financial capital while a younger person has muscular force and stamina, incentivizing the former to purchase components that the latter assembles and operates. This aspect of specialization dominated the images of the exchange relation during the decades of development of modern industrial societies. But even Smith, at the dawn of the self-conscious study of markets, recognized that a more fundamental basis for specialization is cognitive and informational asymmetry. Professionals, including professional financiers, hold capital in the form of specialized *knowledge* that is complementary to different knowledge in the hands of others with whom they exchange services and form temporary or enduring partnerships. Smith emphasized that one crucial consideration to which every potential investor must attend is the *extent* of her

---

[3] We will review evidence for this conclusion in the next chapter.

market, which is in turn partly determined by the number of others who can benefit from the provision of services that she can provide for them, and in which they lack the expertise to provide for themselves.

Bertin Martens (2004) has nicely generalized *cognitive economics* in this Smithian vein. An effectively functioning market requires what Martens calls a *common knowledge interface*, that is, a domain of generally shared information. If there is no such interface, then potential traders cannot mutually recognize their opportunities for gainful exchange. But to the extent that an agent derives expected profit from information which she has and which her exchange partners lack, it is in her interest that the common knowledge interface does not become all-encompassing. Each agent thus tends to have incentives to make *limited* contributions to the common knowledge interface. For example, a tax lawyer who wants to optimize her income wants everyone who pays taxes to know that she could potentially save them more money than she will charge them for her services; but she does not want to explain the principles of tax law to them so thoroughly that they all acquire the capacity to be tax lawyers themselves. There will typically be some information that an agent cannot use as a basis for profitable exchange without adding it to the common knowledge interface whether she likes it or not. Economists refer to such additions as *positive spillovers*. To whatever extent agents happen to value their own welfare more than the welfare of others, information that spills over will tend to be under-provided by the market and may need to be discovered separately by each agent in the society. And then to the extent that they move along such isolated learning paths, adjusting as they go, agents will make choices that appear to reflect inconsistent preferences to better-informed observers.

This immediately implies that a person, over the whole course of her biography, cannot be identified with a single economic agent defined by reference to RPT. That is, when a person undergoes significant learning we should expect that her pattern of choices sampled from before and after the learning episode will often violate GARP. Some economic models avoid this problem by building in an assumption that all learning is deductive and respects the monotonicity restriction of classical logic, meaning that no new information ever overthrows old information. In that circumstance, learning causes agents to refine their preferences, reducing the thickness of indifference bands, but shouldn't reverse preferences. For example, I have always preferred acoustic jazz to electric jazz, but took some time to learn that what really matters is that the drums and bass be acoustic; an electric guitar is a better jazz instrument than an acoustic one. It is possible to justify the monotonicity assumption in certain problem settings. But most human learning is not deductive, and learning through induction (or what C.S. Peirce called *abduction*) often violates monotonicity. For example, the first Indian restaurant at which I ate, in the town where I went to university, was, unknown to me then, one of the best in the world; so sampling many more Indian restaurants since then has led me to revise my once unequivocal preference for Indian menus over all others. More generally, there is no reason to believe that the actual information in the world, as a complete science would characterize that world, is structured so as to be learnable by application of monotonic functions. The domain studied by fundamental physics is *known* not to be so structured.[4]

The fact that whole human biographies can't be successfully modeled as the careers of economic agents defined using RPT is an important application restriction for economic theory. As we will see in detail in Chapter 4, however, the implications of this restriction are often greatly exaggerated by critics of economics. Contrary to widespread claims, the applied economist is under no methodological or other obligation to treat each biological or psychological person as numerically identical to a single economic agent (Ross 2005).

The economics of information also raise deep complications for the applicability of equilibrium analysis, as Hayek was arguably the first to clearly appreciate. Perfectly competitive equilibrium is obviously incompatible with cognitive economics as characterized by Martens. If any agent can costlessly enter the market, this implies that no agent ever has anything to learn. And the need to make limited investments in a common knowledge interface cannot arise – spillovers, as transaction costs, are excluded by the definition of perfect competition. Of course, we already saw in Chapter 2, before introducing informational considerations, that perfect competition cannot characterize any (whole)

---

[4] This might be thought irrelevant on grounds that quantum physical effects don't 'percolate up' to the macro scale. This metaphysical intuition has no sound basis (Ladyman and Ross 2007). For evidence that the brain treats the world of the macro scale as having an underlying quantum statistical structure, see Pothos and Busemeyer (2013).

real market. The more practically significant limitation arises for the great workhorse of everyday applied economics, standard Marshallian equilibrium analysis. This relies on the restriction that the value of each output unit is entirely used to remunerate production factors proportionately to their marginal productivity. Put more technically, the standard neoclassical production function is homogenous in the first degree, allowing for the application of a mathematical principle, Euler's theorem, that is crucial to solving for equilibrium prices and quantities. But this restriction clearly doesn't apply to any production function that has knowledge as *either* an input or an output factor. Knowledge inputs typically deliver increasing returns to scale and knowledge outputs usually involve spillovers.

Hayek emphasized that market prices transmit information about supply and demand that is impossible for a central planner to accurately estimate. This information in turn enables agents to allocate capital where it will generate the highest returns, and enables all market participants to efficiently allocate their incomes between savings and consumption. Economists who build models in the general equilibrium framework have often disputed Hayek's informational argument against central planning, by arguing that production possibility frontiers can normally be analytically determined, and then the status quo distribution of inputs can be adjusted so as to move incrementally closer to this frontier by applications of lump-sum taxes and redistributions. But, as Hayek later argued, once knowledge is recognized as an input and an output of production, this response becomes implausible. And knowledge has a particularly important role to play where social wealth maximization is concerned: as the basis for technical innovation, it is arguably the principal factor that normally drives aggregate growth.

The crucial additions to the economist's tool-kit that have transformed the discipline since 1980, game theory, computational political economy, and econometric estimation of the utility and production functions of heterogeneous agents, which will be reviewed in this chapter, all rely on taking informational dynamics seriously. In Chapter 4, I will argue that it was recognition that information is a scarce economic resource that also explains the rise of behavioral economics as a methodological movement that, in its best known manifestations, aims to turn the clock back on the hard-won separation of economics from psychology that had been achieved by Pareto, Fisher, Hicks and

Samuelson. I will then explain how an insight known to Hayek, at least in general terms, provides the basis for answering the behavioral economists' radical methodological challenge. And finally in Chapter 5, we will see how full incorporation of informational asymmetries into economics dissolves the traditional basis for the distinction between economics and sociology.

3.2 The collapse of the Samuelsonian synthesis

In the first place, it was considerations about information and its use that generated the turmoil in macroeconomic theory that followed the collapse of the post-war policy consensus in the 1970s. These controversies continue to roil the field, with renewed force in the wake of the post-2008 global financial crisis. I will here summarize the older debates, saving reflections inspired by the very recent events for Chapter 5.

The Hicksian interpretation of Keynesian macroeconomics described in Chapter 2, supplemented by empirical analysis due to Phillips (1958), yielded a picture on which increases in the availability of credit in an economy lead to fuller employment of input resources, notably of labor. This is predicted to precipitate an increase in the rate of wage and price inflation, to which the monetary authority will respond by raising interest rates. In principle this should have a deflationary effect. But workers resist nominal pay cuts, and so do not consent to wage reductions even when prices are falling and the value of savings from income is increasing. The unemployment rate will thus rise back toward – and may indeed temporarily overshoot – its preferred level as workers are laid off and stock inventories accumulate. In this circumstance the monetary authority (typically the central reserve bank) can respond by lowering interest rates. Government can fine-tune this equilibrium maintained by the monetary authority through its fiscal behavior, expanding demand by building infrastructure when unemployment is rising and cutting its budget when unemployment is too low (when, as the popular phrase has it, the economy is 'overheating'). The point at which the actual trade-off should pivot was taken to be at the discretion of the monetary and fiscal authorities.

In the mid-1970s policy-makers in rich countries were confounded when growth fell, unemployment rose – and wage and price inflation also increased. Interest rates rose steadily higher, and yet inflation continued to surge. This situation, dubbed 'stagflation,' persisted for several years, eroding both the savings and the living standards of most households in rich countries and probably being the main factor that blocked the re-election of two American presidents, Gerald Ford and Jimmy Carter. The policy levers that had seemed to work just as Hicks and Samuelson predicted they would for three decades suddenly seemed to be disconnected from the gears of supply and demand. It was concluded that something had to be wrong with the standard model.

The debate triggered by this policy challenge has taken numerous twists and turns over the four decades since. The view taken by most commentators (leaving room for disputation about much else), beginning with Friedman (1968), was that the standard model had gone wrong because it failed to take into account that agents – specifically, in this instance, workers – would learn to anticipate the policies of the government and the monetary authority and would not wait for the inflation induced by monetary expansion before demanding wage increases. In other words, it was alleged that proponents of the standard model depended on the assumption that information about future prices that could be derived from observation of the policy regime was not used by some agents – who were thus, in this special sense discussed earlier, 'irrational.' Though it is a digression from the main point here, it is worth noting that the economists accused of this oversight, sometimes Keynes but more often Samuelson and his co-author Solow, were not in fact guilty of it.[5] I have tried but failed to find an instance of an important economist who clearly actually thought that monetary authorities could manipulate people like puppets. It is not unusual in the history of ideas for attacks on straw men to be subsequently celebrated as if they were victories over stubborn resistance.

---

[5] The issue hinged on whether the Phillips curve that represents the trade-off between inflation and unemployment is or is not stable at all levels of inflation. Friedman (1968) alleged that according to Samuelson and Solow (1960), it is. Thus, according to Friedman, Samuelson and Solow thought that the monetary and/or fiscal authorities could expand the money supply in a recession and improve the long-run rate of unemployment. Friedman argued that the only result in the long-run would be higher inflation. A reader who pays attention to the popular financial press will note that this argument is directly relevant to controversies that are raging as I write in 2013 over the US Federal Reserve's policy of quantitative easing. It is therefore important to point out that Samuelson and Solow say the opposite of what Friedman attributed to them; see Samuelson and Solow (1960), p. 193. But they also say, with much stronger justification than Friedman musters for his generalization about later inflation, that the long-run consequences are unpredictable.

Following Friedman's argument, the debate over the relationship between inflation and unemployment has been exceptionally convoluted, and its details must be passed over as properly belonging in a more directly historical and less philosophical book. The relevant point for present purposes is that it ultimately led macroeconomists into preoccupation with the *rational expectations hypothesis* (REH). This idea originated in a microeconomic context, with Muth (1961). Muth criticized a particular 'bounded rationality' model (see Chapter 4), in which farmers operate a heuristic to the effect that next year's prices will be predicted by last year's prices, on the grounds that the modeler should not reasonably suppose that farmers cannot understand the relatively uncomplicated and more accurate model based on supply and demand trend analysis. Over a decade later this critique was reiterated by Robert Lucas (1976) in application to macroeconomics. Lucas's normative version of the REH was that the policy authorities should not operate any policy that, to be successful, requires that the agents whose behavior is to be influenced by the policy, gather and use less information than the policy authorities themselves. This leads to the view that macroeconomic policy is essentially futile, as the anonymous traders on the market will bring about whatever good a policy-maker restricted by the REH might try to accomplish anyway, leaving *unintended* policy effects, which are more likely to be harmful than helpful, as the only possible ones. The reader will see that this conclusion was bound to appeal strongly to proponents of a minimally active or assertive state.

The view that if all information is symmetric among all market participants then macroeconomic policy is futile depends on a number of assumptions, including the assumption that there is a unique general equilibrium. If this assumption doesn't hold, then the policy-maker might see her useful role as being to *coordinate* the choices of agents who might otherwise struggle at cross purposes to select from among multiple equilibria. This consideration leads us into concepts drawn from game theory, the subject of the next section.

I will bring the discussion of the REH and of the efficacy of macroeconomic policy up to date in Chapter 5. The goal for the moment is the more limited one of indicating the pervasive importance of informational issues in main branches of economics from the 1970s onward. Closely related in its logic to Lucas's normative application of the REH to official policy is a descriptive generalization about strategic efficacy in asset markets known as the efficient markets hypothesis (EMH). This is the view that no agent without private information – of the kind that laws against insider trading are designed to prevent from influencing markets – can expect to out-perform the market itself in forecasting asset prices. The main basis for this hypothesis is that the current prices of all future options already incorporate all publicly available information; if they do not, then we must suppose there is an observable profit opportunity that no investor has noticed, but in an unrestricted market with many strongly motivated and well-capitalized participants this is implausible. Just as the REH implies that macroeconomic policy-makers cannot manipulate households or firms into producing the savings and consumption levels they want, so the EMH implies that investors cannot manipulate other investors into behaving so as to make them rich.

The 'efficiency' alluded to in the name of the EMH is twofold. First, as noted, it holds markets to process information about relative values more accurately than any individual participants, including, by direct implication, governments. This is Hayek's point as discussed earlier, with the qualification that Hayek did not assert that markets are perfect information processors; he claimed only that specific individuals or institutions are hopelessly clumsy processors of the information contained in prices. Second, if markets are the most efficient computers of values from prices, then this might be thought to be a reason for expecting them to be the most efficient mechanisms for allocating a society's scarce resources (i.e., capital).

Numerous empirical investigations of the EMH have yielded equivocal results. It provides the backdrop to a paradox, of the kind philosophers are particularly likely to appreciate, that highlights the distinctive nature of information as a source of value. Grossman and Stiglitz (1980) observed that if the EMH is true, and investors know that their market-derived model of asset prices cannot be improved upon, then they have no incentive to seek further information; but if no investors seek information then information must go missing from the market and the EMH must be false. I do not think that this paradox directly undermines the empirical plausibility of the EMH, because it incorporates an atomistic fallacy to the effect that if some information is not actively sought and processed by some specific people then it is not processed at all. Hayek would emphasize that if, for example, everyone who wants to buy a given kind of asset looks for the seller prepared to accept the lowest price, then the market as a whole will compute the 'true' aggregate value of that asset even if no individual tries or succeeds in directly determining that value for themselves. A central idea of the EMH is precisely that every individual's forecast of future prices can be wrong yet the market as a whole can be 'right'. But the Grossman-Stiglitz paradox usefully reminds us that the EMH must be formulated as a statistical hypothesis rather than a categorical proposition. If the EMH is to be rejected, it must be on the basis of empirical evidence about markets (and not evidence from 'behavioral finance' about how traders reason).

3.3 The call for microfoundations of macroeconomics

The uncertainties that roiled macroeconomics as a result of the stagflation phenomenon convinced the majority of economists that an adequate macroeconomic theory should be based on *microfoundations*. What this means is that the generalizations a macroeconomic model offers about relationships among aggregate economic indices (e.g., inflation, unemployment) should be explained on the basis of empirically verified incentives governing the choices of individual consumers and producers. Producers are of course to be identified with production functions and consumers with utility functions. No axiom requires that the latter be assumed to be purely self-interested. However, promoters of microfoundations generally suppose something related but weaker, namely that if the motivating interests of individual consumers and producers are identifiable at the micro scale, then macroeconomic effects of micro-scale choices should generally emerge as unintended consequences of choices based on these motivating interests. This is based on an empirical hypothesis about people, to the effect that they know that their own actions have only negligible impact on relationships at the macroeconomic scale, and that their preferences over these outcomes should therefore not motivate their actions. For example, I may prefer that the unemployment rate in my country be reduced. But this preference plays no role in my decision over whether to hire another technician for my laboratory. I do not thereby show that my preference about the unemployment rate is insincere, and that I am in that respect narrowly self-concerned and lacking in public spirit; I show only that I understand that my decision over hiring has an infinitesimally small effect on the state of the macroeconomy.

The above example shows how the disconnection between micro-economic preference structures and macroeconomic outcomes does not mainly derive from alleged narrow self-interest associated with the former. Let us now consider a more significant example of a macroeconomic outcome as an unintended consequence of preference structures at the microeconomic scale. Keynes famously argued that governments confronted with low-demand equilibria – that is, stubborn recessions that don't lift after producers clear debt overhangs and excess inventories – should attempt to move their economies to higher-demand equilibria through short-term borrowing from future receipts to inject more money into immediate circulation. Architects of such stimulus measures have generally believed that devoting $X to building infrastructure or hiring unemployed workers is more effective than reducing income taxes by $X, though both policies add the same quantum to the money supply. The explanation for this belief does not concern taxpayers' preferences over macroeconomic outcomes, which are generally assumed to align with the government's (i.e., that the stimulus work as quickly and effectively as possible to boost aggregate output). Rather, the explanation is that under recessionary conditions, when most taxpayers are battling with household debts, they tend to save tax rebates instead of spending them. The resulting under-performance of a stimulus based partly or wholly on tax cuts[6] is thus a consequence intended by no one, but is explained by reference to the incentives of the individual households considered separately.

The emphasis on macroeconomic outcomes as unintended consequences of micro-scale responses has always been a strong theme in economics – it is, after all, the essence of Adam Smith's invisible hand metaphor. But game theory, one of the two most important analytical technologies added to economists' tool-kit since the 1970s, has turned the metaphor into a surging research program. I will review game theory and its impact in Sections 3.5 and 3.6. First, however, more must

---

[6] President Obama's stimulus program of 2009 was criticized by many economists, notably including Nobel laureate Paul Krugman, for incorporating a significant temporary income tax reduction. The President's advisers were almost certainly aware of the basis of the criticism, but were forced into an inefficient mix of infrastructure investment and tax cutting by political pressures.

be said about the microfoundations principle at a more general and philosophical level.

In some instances economists' motivation for seeking microfoundations is purely technical, stemming from the view that formal theory in microeconomics is clearer and better developed than formal theory in macroeconomics, and that the former should therefore be brought to bear on the phenomena studied by the latter for the sake of precision (Ross and LaCasse 1995). General equilibrium theory,[7] by far the most important example of this kind of relationship, is built on microeconomic principles but is often taken as the standard framework within which to build macroeconomic models. In basic GE models, however, it is assumed that all agents make optimal use of all available information. In the context of an asset market with no transaction costs, idiosyncratic preferences of agents don't matter to their behavior, since every agent should first maximize her wealth, which she can then freely allocate to consumption, savings and investment as she sees fit. What maximizes wealth given uniqueness of general equilibrium is an objective fact, not a matter over which agents should differ. Thus all agents are identical so far as the modeler's purposes are concerned. Then the modeler can collapse the distinction between macroeconomics and microeconomics – so, automatically ensuring microfoundations in a purely technical sense – by analyzing the responses of an arbitrarily designated individual as the *representative agent*, and then modeling the market as a whole simply by aggregating the representative's responses across *n* such agents.

This approach has its uses whenever the economist is modeling a situation in which there is plausible reason to suppose that all agents really will all respond similarly, or reason to think that differences in agent responses will be random deviations from the representative agent's utility and production functions and will statistically cancel one another out as noise. This is one possible route to the EMH. Instead of supposing, as in the REH, that all agents are perfect computers of all information, one can suppose that many less-than-fully-rational market participants are 'noise traders,' random forces that supply volume to the market but contribute no information to it. But then it is necessary that the representative agent be assigned rational expectations.

---

[7] See Chapter 2.

There are a number of notable variants on representative agent models. Often the modeler will want to incorporate the fact that agents have finite lifespans, and that different information is available, or relevant, to different agents depending on when they live. Then one can follow an innovation originally due to Samuelson (1958) and build an *overlapping generations* model in which there is a succession of representative agents according to the following kind of structure. First, the timeline is divided into discrete periods. In the simplest variant of the structure this series is finite, so that there is a first period 1 and a final period k. In period 1 we find representative agent i_1. In period 2 i_1 is joined by i_2. Then in period 3 i_1 is dead, i_2 is in the prime of life and i_3 is born. This continues until period $k–1$ in which no one is born, and the world thus ends after period k (a general 'big T' as some economists like to call this terminus). There are then relatively simple mathematical devices by which a modeler could allow the timeline to have no beginning or end, and further variants of overlapping generations models in which no one ever dies so the population is effectively infinitely large or converges to an infinite continuum of traders.

A model with one representative agent and no generations, as applied to an empirical market, is obviously an extreme form of isolation, involving assumptions that are radically false characterizations of any markets populated by actual people. (They may be less radically false characterizations of markets populated by bacteria or insects or automated robot traders.) There can be no sound objection to an economist using such a model if she can muster a plausible argument for the claim that it isolates a phenomenon of interest to her without so badly distorting the representation of the phenomenon in question that it sacrifices all structural connection with external reality. Valid criticisms of uses of representative agents must strike at the plausibility of specific such arguments, and thus must be at least implicitly based on alternative models of the phenomena in question. For a review of more soundly grounded criticisms of leading traditions of representative agent model applications to the core problems of macroeconomics, the reader should consult Hartley (1997). But to object to representative agent modeling *in principle* is tantamount to objecting to isolation itself, and thereby to the whole enterprise of modeling. This is the kind of mindless naïve realism criticized in the work of the philosopher Uskali Mäki as discussed in the previous chapter.

The crucial point for the present discussion is that a model with a single representative agent abstracts away from all possible informational asymmetries, and in that respect may be regarded as an 'old-fashioned' kind of model. Once we consider overlapping generations models with more than one representative agent, we introduce informational variation. This point generalizes. An extremely common modeling strategy in economics is to have multiple *types* of agents, each of which is representative of a subset of the modeled population, all coexisting in one period. Typically these types differ from one another in the information they access or use. These differences may be explicit, or may be implicit in different comparative advantages the modeler assigns to them, or in transaction costs she imposes on them. For example, we might study preferences over public spending on education using a model that includes one representative rich household decision-maker with children, one representative poor household decision-maker with children, one representative rich household decision-maker without children, and one representative poor household decision-maker without children. If we had empirical evidence about different voting behavior among men and women, we might further divide each of the above representatives by sex and thus include eight of them in our model. (Of course, as we do this we make the model increasingly data-hungry when we want to use it to estimate real empirical values.) The differences among the types will be built into the construction of divergent utility or production functions that identify them. As we move further in this way from the radical isolation of the model with just one representative agent, we gradually open up our methodological framework and consider the whole domain of economic modeling. Since the various types of representative agents are not models of any actual individuals, we do not shift toward psychology. We do, however, converge with an approach that Max Weber (1864–1920) made popular in sociology, the methodology of 'ideal types.'

We will return to consider developments in this direction in Chapter 5. For the moment we restrict attention to a negative point: if a macroeconomist claims to have built her model on microfoundations by using one representative agent, she clearly cannot motivate this on the basis of a philosophical claim that she is thereby isolating causal relationships at the level of 'real' mechanisms. Every macroeconomy involves wide heterogeneity of agent types with respect to both utility and production functions. Again, if the motivation for ignoring this is simply a concern with precision and analytical transparency, then the philosophically appropriate critical attitude is the Mäkian one: does the specific isolation somehow improve our understanding of an aspect of the actual world or not? What is required for reliably addressing such questions is not conceptual subtlety of the philosopher's kind, but experience with microeconomic modeling.

Not infrequently, however, philosophically naïve economists *do* justify specifying a model's microfoundations on the basis of adherence to mechanistic realism. This implies an explicit or implicit commitment to metaphysical atomism about social and economic phenomena, and the philosopher can be on legitimate critical ground if she rehearses the problems with that commitment. Even in such cases, however, the critic should ask herself whether she can construct a more defensible alternative motivation for the economist's practice. What might appear at first glance to be an underlying metaphysical dogma might turn out to simply be casual, and epistemologically gratuitous, methodological boilerplate rhetoric. Any philosopher accusing a scientist of confusion always holds an extremely demanding burden of argument, to which she should expect the criticized scientist to hold her responsible.

3.4 Methodological individualism

As noted previously, economists have generally been coy about promoting methodological preferences on overtly metaphysical grounds. At the same time, there can be no serious doubt that many economists have been motivated by what can only be characterized as *metaphysical revulsion* against hypothesizing causal relationships that operate at the macro scale. Such hypothetical causation is not infrequently labeled as 'spooky,' clearly signaling atomistic metaphysical intuitions.[8] As applied to the social sciences, such atomism is expressed as the doctrine of methodological individualism (MI). In its strongest version, this is the claim that all macro-scale causal generalizations

---

[8] As discussed in Chapter 1, such intuitions have often been promoted by philosophers.

should be explained as arising out of (possibly highly complex) structural and causal relationships manifest in relationships among individual people. In the philosophy of social science literature, no single topic has received more attention than MI. The present book can be read as, in part, yet another intervention in this long debate. However, as explained in Chapter 1, my approach is not to review and analyze the dozens (or thousands!) of purely philosophical analyzes of general arguments for and against MI. The approach is instead to inductively arrive at a position on MI directly from reflection on economic modeling itself. This exercise will not be (provisionally) resolved until the conclusion of the book. For the moment I will sketch, at a very broad level, the main alternative positions that have been defended, and relate them to prevailing research traditions in economics, along with sociology. The best historical review is given by Udehn (2001), and the general philosophical overview I endorse, though not in every detail of application, is that of Kincaid (1997). The preliminary objective here is to show how the *contemporary* debate among working social scientists has come to be centered around the recent emphasis on information processing and information asymmetries.

To begin with, an economist who thinks that choices must find their 'concrete'[9] manifestation in deliberate conscious thought processes will tend to favor MI, at least to the extent that she regards these processes as *private*. One might think that the same must apply to more recently popular opinions that economic choices must be 'grounded' in neural processing in brains. As we will see in Chapter 4, however, intellectual options here are more subtle than one might at first suppose. The view that economic choices can always in principle be identified with discrete psychological episodes in the biographies of specific people (or other animals) is known as *economic psychologism* (EP). It is the subject of Chapter 4. One strand of it we will need to consider, up to a

---

[9] As someone who writes both on the metaphysics of science and on the economics of road surfacing, I find this ubiquitous metaphor personally amusing. It harkens back to the metaphysics of Descartes and his followers, who thought that physics was ultimately the science of hard little things banging into each other, and that all causation has to be channeled through such 'microbangings.' The metaphor did not have to wait for twentieth-century physics to become obsolete; it should have died with Newton. But both everyday people and philosophers still find it beguiling. See Ladyman and Ross (2007), Chapter 1.

point, in that chapter is the relationship between EP and the doctrine of *economic egoism*, the view that all economic choice is necessarily about maximizing the chooser's narrowly individual well-being. Though, as we saw in Chapter 2, economic analysis does indeed involve maximizing various kinds of functions, especially utility functions, it was recognized as far back as Sidgwick (1885) that egoism is logically completely distinct from the motivation, based in the mathematics of marginal estimation using calculus, for modeling economic agents as optimizers. The overwhelming majority of economists who have reflected systematically on methodology or philosophy have recognized that egoism is a gratuitous and self-defeating thesis to try to staple onto economic theory. Even thoughtful libertarians should avoid it if they wish to keep self-inflicted bullets out of their own feet.

It is very common to be told that the main difference between economics and sociology is that economists accept MI whereas sociologists don't. I will discuss the three-cornered relationship between MI, economics and sociology in detail in Chapter 5. For now it suffices to say that MI has historically been most interestingly and usefully discussed as a methodological controversy *within* sociology, while most arguments over MI *between* economists and sociologists have been parochial and philosophically crude. A good deal of distracting and unedifying rhetoric in economics might have been avoided over the years if more economists were familiar with the sociological literature on MI. Ironically, substantive methodological restrictions of the sort worthy of being taken seriously *and* deserving of the label 'individualism' have played a *smaller* role in economics than they have in sociology of the style descended from one of the discipline's three great founders, Max Weber. Among the other two members of this triad, Emile Durkheim (1858–1917) promoted a version of clear anti-individualism similar to what I will defend in Chapter 5. It finds echoes in the views of some important macroeconomists mentioned in Chapter 2, Ragnar Frisch and Werner Hildenbrand. Finally, Karl Marx's view of MI was sufficiently subtle – and perhaps inconsistent – that sociologists have been able to quarrel productively over whether he is better described as a methodological individualist or a methodological collectivist (Elster 1985; Udehn 2001, pp. 310–316).

Within economics the clutter of views on MI is equally complicated. Lionel Robbins, the leading weaver of Austrian threads into the post-war mainstream consensus, endorsed MI on the basis of EP (see Ross 2005, pp. 87–100). Hayek is often regarded as the individualist's individualist; yet, as Udehn (2001, pp. 120–121) and many other careful students of Hayek have made clear, his distinctive and most influential methodological theses developed after 1960 involve *denying* MI in favor of a view similar to those of Frisch and Hildenbrand.

Discussing this set of problems by lining influential thinkers up into teams is common practice in philosophy and intellectual history, but it is likely to generate complication without progress unless it is strongly anchored to more specific and directly empirical questions that feed into more general working research programs. I will thus now drop the name-dropping until coming back to it in Chapter 5 after more critical history of science has been sketched. But invocation of just one more famous thinker here will frame the next stage in the review. The greatest currently living economist, Kenneth Arrow, said late in his (continuing) career, that "the current formulation of methodological individualism is game theory" (Arrow 1994, p. 4). Some economists who would agree with this remark would do so – based on other things they believe – as a way of endorsing the near takeover of microeconomics by game theory since (roughly) 1980. The basis of this is that game theory, on one view, seems to be the true and ultimate implementation of economics as the study of the unintended consequences of individually considered choices – the study, that is, of invisible hands, both benign (as in Smith's metaphor) and malignant (as in much of the so-called *public choice* literature that applies game theory to political dynamics and outcomes; see Mueller 1996). Yet this is roughly the opposite interpretation to what Arrow intends, for his main conclusion is that game theory needs a *non*-individualistic interpretation if it is to perform the role in economic generalization for which its users have hoped.

We cannot possibly understand microeconomics since 1980 without considering game theory. The philosophical interpretation of it that I will sketch supports the interpretation that Arrow argues we need. I think this interpretation is also consistent with Hayek's philosophy of economics, because it sees game theory as a formalism for representing information asymmetries at multiple scales of agent aggregation, rather than as an extension of the theory of individual choice. I turn to that now.

3.5 Game theory

The mathematical theory of games was invented by John von Neumann and Oskar Morgenstern in 1944, and the most important elaborations on its foundations were made by John Nash (1928–) in the 1950s and by John Harsanyi (1920–2000) and Reinhard Selten (1930–) in the 1970s and 1980s. Following the mighty achievement of Leonard "Jimmie" Savage's (1917–1971) *Foundations of Statistics* (1954), game theory (GT) came to be regarded as an important extension of the formal and statistical theory of decision and choice, and for this reason has been explored in a variety of disciplinary literatures besides that of economics. GT was introduced slowly into economics via applications in specific areas, most importantly, for reasons to be explained shortly, the economics of market structures (industrial organization economics, usually referred to as 'IO'). Rapidly through the 1980s, however, it became the dominant mathematical technology for the construction of models across all of microeconomics outside GE modeling contexts. Recently, it has begun to be applied in macroeconomics, in models that represent policies as devices for coordinating the expectations of large sets of agents in markets with multiple equilibria.

There is not space in this book for a summary introduction to GT. A reader who is new to it can consult textbooks at various levels of assumed mathematical background. Dixit, Skeath and Reiley (2009) presume no such background at all. Though this feature makes it a useful entry point for many students, it obscures the fact that GT is a body of mathematics with economic applications, not an economic theory in itself. For a more philosophically sophisticated introduction, which presumes only minimal mathematical knowledge, the reader should turn to Binmore (2007). The definitive text for the mathematically prepared student remains Fudenberg and Tirole (1991).

As noted in Chapter 1, philosophers have historically been heavily invested in general theories of rationality, and GT has raised some new issues in that regard. In particular, a huge literature has arisen around the implications of one unusual game, the Prisoner's Dilemma (PD),[10]

---

[10] See Poundstone (1992) for a non-technical introduction.

for the relationship between rational individual and collective pursuit of well-being. Expanding from focus on the PD to a wider class of games that involve tension between individual and joint optimization, philosophers have extensively discussed mechanisms and methods of psychological self-manipulation by which people or other agents can aim to pre-commit to act against their individual self-interest, so as to induce others to reciprocate to achieve joint outcomes that are mutually beneficial.[11] Whereas philosophers have tended to be preoccupied with the implications of counter-selfish commitment for the relationship between rationality and morality, economists have studied the problem in the context of the more general logic of *coordination*, which is central to the efficiency of market exchange and investment.[12] I will discuss coordination within this frame later in the present chapter, and then more extensively in Chapter 5. Philosophers have also extensively reflected on the general logic of coordination, in a literature that begins with Lewis (1969), and extends through Bicchieri (1993), Skyrms (1996, 2004, 2010), and Weirich (1998) among other treatments. Once again, the main underlying topic of interest among these philosophers is the general concept of rationality. Some readers will expect that a book such as the present one on the philosophy of economics should engage closely with this thread of debate, particularly as it has drawn in some economists (e.g., Kreps 1990a, 1990b). Were I writing a book on the philosophy of GT, I would indeed need to review the literature just cited. But, as previously advertised, the focus here is on a philosophy of economics conceived as the study of markets. This study must be alert to the science – and philosophy – of rational decision, so from time to time themes from the philosophers who have written about that will need to be noted. But these themes are deep background rather than focal matter here.

Savage (1954) laid the groundwork for *both* the philosophers' project of developing the formal foundations of normative individual decision theory *and* the economists' project of developing the statistical theory

---

[11] This literature is very large. Gauthier (1986) and McClennen (1990) are early fountainheads. A representative sample of problems and perspectives from this first generation of literature is Danielson (1998). The general view of it that I endorse is presented and defended in Binmore (1994, 1998, 2005). Gauthier, McClennen and many others fall into what Binmore (2009, pp. 19–22) calls the 'causal utility fallacy.' I will say more about this in Chapters 4 and 5.

[12] For the most elegant and general economist's account, see Cooper (1999).

of incentivized choice in varying market structures. The philosophers' project frequently subjects Savage's foundations to critical pressure, whereas the economists' project as I am interpreting it takes Savage at face value.[13] By this I do not mean that economists must be dogmatic disciples of some or other 'Savage philosophy.' I mean rather that economists bypass consideration of the extent to which Savage furnishes the basis for an 'ultimate' theory of practical (or yet more general) rationality. (Following Binmore 2009, I would say that he *obviously* does not try to furnish such a foundation, as his theory doesn't apply to problems for which risks cannot be quantitatively estimated. Furthermore, it leaves a clear problem for investigation, which continues to be pursued by economists today: How do techniques for measuring subjective beliefs about probabilities interact with techniques for estimating utility functions?) Rather, I mean that if someone wants to know what economists mean by utility maximization under uncertainty they should be referred to Savage. Binmore (2009) is the authoritative summary set in the contemporary problem space and idiom.

I noted above that GT is often regarded as the extension of normative decision theory into strategic contexts.[14] This is potentially misleading, however, both historically and mathematically. Savage's theory followed and built upon, rather than preceded, the mathematics of *expected utility* developed by von Neumann and Morgenstern (1944) as part of their invention of GT. It is thus most accurate to think of decision theory and GT as sharing a common definition of utility, which enriches the foundations provided by Samuelson and Houthakker, rather than to conceive of GT as a technical outgrowth of decision theory. Decision theory tells us how an agent should make choices in a way that is mathematically consistent under circumstances where all relevant event probabilities can be quantitatively estimated. GT must be incorporated into applications of this theory in which event probabilities depend partly on agents' subjective models of the motivations and beliefs of other agents. But GT also furnishes the mathematics for *descriptive* theory used to

---

[13] This would of course not extend to ignoring errors in Savage's mathematics, in the highly unlikely event that such errors are lurking to be discovered.

[14] By a strategic context we might informally mean a context in which what counts as one agent's best action (for her) depends on expectations about what one or more other agents will do, and what counts as their best actions (for them) similarly depends on expectations about her and about one another.

model the ways in which information asymmetries shape the relative efficiency and stability of different arrangements of institutions. And every real market, none of which are perfectly competitive, is based partly on institutionalized constraints.

The work of von Neumann and Morgenstern that introduced GT concentrated on two quite different applied problems, neither of which was drawn from the mainstream agenda of economists. The first of these was the identification of winning strategies in what are conventionally regarded as games, such as chess and poker. Two necessary conditions for the intellectual and emotional entertainment that people derive from such games are that they are purely competitive – one player improves her chances of winning precisely to the extent that she raises the other player's chances of losing – and that their rules are precisely specified in advance and are clear to both players. The second applied problem to which von Neumann and Morgenstern addressed themselves was that of identifying what plans it is possible for agents to agree to jointly implement once they have determined the scope of convergence and divergence in their preferences. Von Neumann and Morgenstern addressed the first problem by building a theory of *zero-sum games*, in which each player figures out how to minimize her possible losses on the assumption that the other player will do whatever would maximize those losses. They addressed the second problem by building a theory of *cooperative* games in which players exchange promises once they figure out what it is individually rational for them to aim to do together. (The assumption that such promises are effectively binding sidesteps the problem of commitment that, as noted above, has been of so much interest to philosophers.)

Zero-sum and cooperative games are fundamentally unlike the logical spaces in which businesspeople or political actors encounter their crucial problems. Let us consider a simple example. Suppose you are the manager of a new and growing business in an industry dominated by a larger, entrenched incumbent. Your own private data might tell you that at the rate you're converting customers, and improving your margins due to increasing economies of scale, you will begin making a significant dent on your large rival's attractiveness to investors within three years. Your rival, by reasonable hypothesis, doesn't know the results of your analysis. That informational asymmetry might be crucial for you if the three-year window in which your competitor has advantageous access to capital, a deeper network of relationships in the supply chain, and capacity to lobby for self-serving regulations or tariffs would allow them to sustain some temporarily reduced profits in order to drive you out of business before you can become a threat. Once you recognize this, you should appreciate the information asymmetry as a valuable asset that you need to protect. Some expansion strategies that might otherwise be optimal for you might also have the effect of *signaling* to the incumbent that you intend ultimately to challenge for industry leadership. (That is, you might do something that wouldn't make practical sense unless you had an ambitious eye on the main contestable market.) It might under these circumstances be better for you to confine yourself, while you remain vulnerable, to investments that signal an interest only in niche markets with high margins but lower potential for volume expansion. This kind of preemptive defensive positioning is sufficiently common that it has a name among business strategists, who refer to it as the puppy dog ploy.

This example is intended to illustrate a general point. Business managers seldom engage in zero-sum games. Indeed, such games are generally rare outside of contexts designed for entertainment. (Even wars are not zero-sum games except in unusual cases where the two sides are aiming exclusively at one another's total annihilation.) Nor are businesses involved in cooperative games with one another, because they generally lack any way of pre-committing to keep promises to one another if they arrive at a set of circumstances in which one or the other could increase profits or share values by breaking such promises. In the example above, the manager of the entrant firm would be foolish to adopt the strategy of opening her books to the incumbent, accompanied by a promise to forever avoid expansion into the main large-volume market segment. This promise would amount to what game theorists call cheap talk, which the incumbent should not allow to influence her behavior. The incumbent should know that if an opportunity for market-wide expansion arose after the entrant had consolidated capital access and supply chain relationships through operation in the niche markets, the entrant's obligations to her shareholders would require that she break her promise. Ghemawat (1998) suggests that something like this happened in the American steel industry in the 1970s and 1980s. The industry was dominated by a massive incumbent, US Steel. A nimble entrant, Nucor, began producing thin-slab steel using a new technology in so-called mini-mills. At first this process could not produce output of sufficient surface regularity for the large automobile chassis or household appliance industries. US Steel seems to have decided not to try to contain Nucor's growth by engaging in aggressive price competition in the niche markets Nucor initially served, on grounds that Nucor did not constitute a threat to US Steel's core business. Later, as a result of changes in the structure of domestic demand for steel and further technological refinements, Nucor usurped US Steel's position and pushed it to the margins of the industry. (US Steel saved itself from extinction by morphing into an energy company.)

The importance of information asymmetries in real markets can hardly be exaggerated. As noted in Chapter 2, almost no real markets resemble perfectly competitive ones. On the production side, most industries are dominated by small numbers of firms with much greater access to capital and much more influence over suppliers than a new entrant can initially match. In addition, entrenched firms have reputations for quality and reliability with customers that prevent the latter from switching their purchasing simply on the basis of lower price. (Note that such reputation is another example of an asset based on asymmetric information.) This is why the first branch of economics that game theory came to dominate was industrial organization (IO) theory, which analyzes and identifies equilibria in the structures of specific, typically oligopolistic, industries isolated for modeling purposes from wider contexts. GT thus entered economics through a distinctly Marshallian, rather than Walrasian, intellectual pathway (Sutton 2000). The best way for a non-economist reader to gain a feel for the way economists think about GT, even if they are not IO specialists, is by reading a contemporary IO textbook such as Shy (1995), and then moving on to a more advanced set of applications such as those presented by Sutton (1991, 2001). Philosophers are generally more likely to have first thought about GT in economics through high theory treatments such as that of Kreps (1990b), and this, I speculate, has contributed to philosophers' tendency to confuse economists' projects with theirs.

Economic theory as synthesized after World War II by Samuelson and others was of little practical relevance to business managers because it had no means of formally modeling situations in which prices were not determined by the interrelationship of marginal costs and demand; value deriving from private information was not represented in models.

It was partly for this reason that the primary consumers of economists' practical advice from the 1940s through the 1970s were governments, who were interested in the effects of policy choices on the overall efficiency and output mix of whole national economies. As we saw in Chapter 2, this use of economic theory by central planners in turn reinforced the centrality of perfect competition analysis and general equilibrium modeling in economic theory. GT as introduced by von Neumann and Morgenstern in 1944 offered no immediate prospect for changing this situation, since its models also incorporated common and symmetric information about the rules and conditions under which games were played. Political scientists showed more widespread interest in early GT than economists, because some political situations are usefully modeled as circumstances in which agents with common information, whose promises to one another can be enforced by constitutions or by the political costs of promise-breaking, have reason to identify prospective coalitions and the terms of exchange under which coalitions can be assembled.

I will now move ahead from von Neumann and Morgenstern to discuss the dramatic impact of GT on economists' conception of economic equilibrium. Following Sutton (2000) my basic contention here is that it has served as a counterweight to the rhetorical and institutional dominance of GE theory.[15] The Marshallian tradition would have held its own anyway in applied economics because of its vital use in economic consulting. But the fact that the most logically general equilibrium concept in all of economics – Nash equilibrium – emerged from the mathematics of GT, prevented GE from monopolizing the theoretical highlands of the discipline. After discussing Nash equilibrium and its associated solution concepts, I will then return in the following section to von Neumann and Morgenstern. Along with GT itself they introduced a second innovation, the reconciliation of utility as revealed preference with quantitative estimation of empirical

---

[15] This remark applies to the realm of theoretical economics. Many exercises in applied economics combine the mathematics of GT and GE to good effect. A sub-field that is particularly rife with examples of this is international trade modeling. Here economists confront complex modeling issues around the relationships between strategic dynamics *within* countries and strategic dynamics *between* countries, with no general principle that identifies one set of dynamics as short-run or long-run relative to the other. Pragmatic modelers commonly achieve needed simplification here by locking one level or the other into general equilibrium while applying GT to the other level. Full understanding then requires consideration of families of models, in some of which each level's dynamics are considered.

magnitudes, which has been equally important to the development of economics over the past three decades.

3.6 Solving games

The form of GT that since the 1980s has become the primary mathematical technology of microeconomics is called *non-cooperative* GT. This expresses the idea that an agent will not keep a promise, or follow through on a threat, if she gains higher utility by breaking her promise or letting someone who has ignored her threat go unpunished. It is important to be clear about what this restriction does *not* say. It does not imply that no agent will ever make or keep a promise, or make or follow through on a threat. If agents expect to strategically interact with one another in the future, they will often maximize their utility by establishing reputations with one another as promise-keepers and threat-enforcers. We can allow that an agent might suffer damage to her self-reputation if she uttered the words "I promise" and then failed to follow through, and that anticipation of this cost would incentivize her to keep the promise at the cost of a material loss. This would still be consistent with application of non-cooperative GT as long as the disutility of the agent's feeling of shame were incorporated into the utility function the analyst modeled her as maximizing. For a similar reason, the idea that agents play games 'non-cooperatively' should not be treated as synonymous with the idea that they behave selfishly or asocially. As discussed in Chapter 2, their utility functions must be understood as incorporating *all* of their preferences, including their preferences over the maintenance of solidarity, friendship and stability of social norms. Of course, people vary considerably in the extent to which their behavior reveals concern for these commonly moralized goods. Some people attach little weight to them under any circumstances. Most people attach varying weights to them in different contexts. In markets where people exchange money for goods and services with anonymous others, or with known people not linked to them by other ties, moral concerns extending beyond what is required by law are often set aside, and this should generally be welcome to participants who rely on the market to signal accurate information about relative values through prices.

We can back into the topic of *solutions* to non-cooperative games by considering what it is about the equilibria of imaginary perfectly competitive markets that give these equilibria their stability properties. In such models, the hypothetical agents need not speculate about what others will do with their resources because everyone knows all prices, and everyone has equal access to as much capital as they can invest without loss. Thus all production niches will be occupied but never over-crowded, each producer will produce the quantity that maximizes her balance of revenues over costs, and everything produced will be sold at prices that allow all consumers to maximize their utility given their budgets. What makes this state an equilibrium – that is, a solution to the equations that define the model – is that no producer could change her quantity, and no consumer could change the allocation of her budget, without making themselves worse off, *given what all the others are deterministically guaranteed to do.* Non-cooperative GT can then be understood as the body of mathematics that allows one to find equilibria of this kind in more realistic conditions where people or other agents – e.g., firms – do *not* necessarily know all about everyone else's preferences, where the number of agents is small enough that differences in preferences do not all cancel out statistically, and where restricted access to capital, varying from agent to agent, means that agents are not perfectly insured against risk.

Following convention, any situation in which at least one agent can only act to maximize her utility through anticipating, either consciously or just implicitly in her behavior, the responses to her actions by one or more other agents is referred to as a *game*. Agents involved in games are referred to as *players*. We assume that players can (i) assess outcomes; (ii) calculate paths to outcomes; and (iii) identify actions that yield their most-preferred outcomes, given the actions of the other players. These assessments, calculations and identifications might in some cases be explicitly computed by the players in question. In other cases, the assessments etc. might simply be embodied in behavioral dispositions built by natural, cultural or economic selection. In particular, in calling an action 'chosen' we do not necessarily imply deliberation, conscious or otherwise. We mean merely that the action was taken when an alternative action was available, in some sense of 'available' normally established by the context of the particular analysis. I will say much more about this point, which is fundamental to an adequate philosophy of economics, in Chapter 4.

Each player in a game is modeled as facing a choice among two or more possible *strategies*. A strategy is a predetermined 'program of play' that tells her what actions to take in response to *every possible strategy other players might use*. A GT analysis does not directly model choices over outcomes; it models choices over strategies.

A crucial aspect of the specification of a game involves the information that players have about other players' strategies when they choose theirs. The simplest games from the perspective of logical structure are those in which agents have *perfect information*, meaning that at every point where each agent's strategy tells her to take an action, she knows everything that has happened in the game up to that point. A board game of sequential moves in which both players watch all the action (and know the rules in common), such as chess, is an instance of such a game. By contrast, a football coach developing strategies for the upcoming match is involved in a game of *imperfect information* with the rival coach, since the choices of each will be revealed to the other only after it is too late for properly prepared revision.

What makes games of perfect information the logically simplest sorts of games is that if such games terminate after a fixed number of actions then the analyst can use a straightforward procedure for predicting outcomes. We model a player in such a game as choosing her strategy by considering each series of responses and counter-responses that will result from each initial action open to her. She then asks herself which of the available final outcomes brings her the highest utility, and chooses the action that starts the chain leading to this outcome. This process is called *backward induction* (because the reasoning works backwards from eventual outcomes to present decision problems).

Finite games of perfect information can be represented as directed graphs with additional structure, known as *game trees*. That is, a game tree is a set of connected nodes in which the overall graph has a direction because the connections are uniformly asymmetric. We can draw trees from the top of the page to the bottom, or from left to right. In the first case, nodes at the top of the page are interpreted as coming earlier in the sequence of actions. In the case of a tree drawn from left to right, leftward nodes are prior in the sequence to rightward ones. An unlabeled top-down tree has a structure of the following sort shown in Figure 3.1.

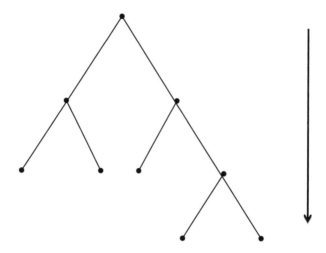

Figure 3.1 A directed graph

The point of representing games using trees can best be grasped by visualizing the use of them in supporting backward-induction reasoning. Imagine the player (or analyst) beginning at the end of the tree, where outcomes are displayed, and then working backwards from these, looking for sets of strategies that describe paths leading to them. Since a player's ordinal utility function indicates which outcomes she prefers to which, by this method we can work out which paths she will prefer. Of course, not all paths will be possible because the other player has a role in selecting paths too, and won't take actions that lead to less preferred outcomes for him.

A directed-graph representation is said to show the *extensive form* of a game. The alternative *strategic* or *normal* form represents a game as a matrix. The simplest such game is a 2-player matrix in which all of the elements of one player's strategy set are the rows and all elements of the other player's strategy set are the columns. Extensive and strategic forms are not merely alternative displays of the same mathematical object, because extensive-form games include specification of players' information about the game structure that strategic-form games do not. In general, a strategic-form game could represent any one of several extensive-form games, so a strategic-form game is best thought of as being a *set* of extensive-form games.

We best illustrate this distinction, which is of fundamental importance to applications of GT in economics, by reference to the most famous of all games, the Prisoner's Dilemma (PD). Most readers of this book have likely encountered the standard example from which it takes its name. We imagine that the police have arrested two people whom they know have committed an armed robbery together. Unfortunately, they lack enough admissible evidence to get a jury to convict. They do, however, have enough evidence to send each prisoner away for two years for theft of the getaway car. The prosecutor makes the following offer to each prisoner: If you will confess to the robbery, implicating your partner, and she does not also confess, then you'll go free and she'll get 10 years. If you both confess, you'll each get 5 years. If neither of you confess, then you'll each get 2 years for the auto theft.

The ordinal utility functions of the two players i, j over the four possible outcomes are symmetrical reverse images:

Player i:

i goes free, j gets 10 years → 4 (highest payoff for i)
i gets 2 years, j gets 2 years → 3
i gets 5 years, j gets 5 years → 2
i gets 10 years, j goes free → 1 (lowest payoff for i)

The rankings indexed to the utility functions are referred to in the GT context as *payoffs*.

The strategic form of the PD is then shown in Figure 3.2.

Each player receives a higher-ranked payoff from confessing regardless of the strategy choice of the other. Thus for each player confessing is said to be a *strictly dominant* strategy. If we think it is a plausible principle that an agent who understands the situation would not choose a strictly dominated strategy, then we would regard (Confess, Confess) as a *solution* to the game.

In popular discussions of the story that illustrates the PD, it is frequently said that the prosecutor should lock the prisoners into separate rooms so that they can't communicate with one another. The reasoning behind this suggestion is that if the prisoners could communicate, they would share their mutual understanding that the Pareto efficient outcome is brought about by (Hold out, Hold out), so they should exchange promises to play their dominated strategies. But this

Player II

		Confess	Hold out
	Confess	2,2	4,1
Player I			
	Hold out	1,4	3,3

Figure 3.2 Strategic-form PD

violates the assumption of non-cooperative GT that binding promises are cheap talk, unless the players' utility functions assign low ranking to outcomes classified by them as breaches of promises. Either of the two possible members of the set of extensive forms of the game with perfect information make this clear. Suppose that the prosecutor asks Player I to declare her choice first. Then we have the extensive-form game shown as Figure 3.3.

Some standard terminology will aid the discussion of this game. A *node* is a point at which a player has a choice of a primitive element of a strategy, known as an *action*. Roman numerals beside each node indicate the player to whom the action in question 'belongs.' Arabic numerals simply name the nodes for subsequent textual reference. Node 1, the *initial node*, is the point at which the first action in the game occurs. Nodes 4–7 are *terminal nodes*, nodes that, if reached, end the game. Each terminal node corresponds to an *outcome*. A *subgame* is any set of nodes and branches descending uniquely from one node; thus the game has three subgames, beginning at nodes 1, 2 and 3 respectively. A *payoff* gives a player's ordinal utility ranking to an outcome. Thus an outcome is an assignment of a set of payoffs, one to each player in the game. A *strategy* is a program instructing a player which action to take at every node in the tree where she has an action.

The conventional solution procedure for an extensive-form game with perfect information is *backward induction*, also known as *Zermelo's algorithm*. Consider the subgame that arises last in the sequence of play, that descending from node 3. Here Player II faces a choice between a payoff of 4 and a payoff of 3. She maximizes her utility by playing C. We may therefore replace the entire subgame with an assignment of the outcome (0,4) directly to node 3, since this is

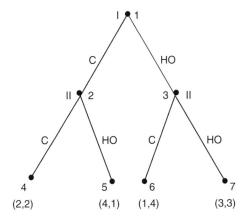

Figure 3.3   Extensive-form PD

the outcome that will be realized if the game reaches that node. Now consider the subgame descending from node 2. Here, II faces a choice between a payoff of 2 and a payoff of 1. She maximizes her utility by playing C. We may therefore assign the outcome (2,2) directly back to node 2. Now we move to the subgame descending from node 1. (This subgame is identical to the whole game; all games are subgames of themselves.) Player I now faces a choice between outcomes (2,2) and (1,4). He maximizes his utility by playing C, yielding the same outcome, (2,2), and the same solution, (C,C) as in the strategic-form representation. What this represents intuitively is that Player I sees that if he plays HO at node 1, as per his cheap talk promise to Player II, then Player II will maximize her utility by breaking her promise and playing C. This leaves Player I with his least-preferred outcome payoff, which he avoids only by playing C. Keeping his promise would be inconsistent with maximizing his utility.

Only finite extensive-form games of perfect information can be solved using Zermelo's algorithm. But games of imperfect information can also be represented in extensive form. We do this by generalizing the idea of a node, which should be understood as an *information set* with only one member. Consider the directed graph in Figure 3.4.

The oval drawn around nodes 2a and 2b indicates that they lie within a common information set. This means that when Player II makes her choices at these nodes, she does not know what Player I has chosen at

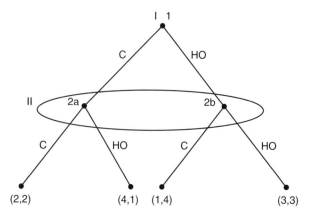

Figure 3.4   A non-singleton information set

node 1, and thus does not know whether she is at 2a or 2b. Her strategy must therefore direct her to take the same action at node 2b as at node 2a. The strategic form corresponding to this game is thus the matrix of Figure 3.1. By contrast, in the game of perfect information shown in Figure 3.2, because Player II knows what Player I chooses at node 1, when she chooses she can distinguish between four different strategies for herself, and the strategic form of the game is given by the matrix shown in Figure 3.5.

Changing the informational structure of the PD makes no difference to its intuitive solution, which always corresponds to the outcome (2,2). As we will illustrate shortly, this is not true of games in general. Indeed, for purposes of the main themes of this book, that is among the most important points about games to understand. But before we turn to that, we will use the example of the PD to discuss the critical history of the concept of a game's solution.

Mutual confession is said to be the 'solution' to the PD because the strategy pair that produces it represents each player's best response to any strategy chosen by the other player. This fact – that confessing is strictly dominant for each player considered *individually* – can obscure the property of the solution that leads it to be regarded as an *equilibrium*, which is a state of the *system* of players rather than of either player considered in isolation. Consider the extensive-form game shown as Figure 3.6.

		Player II		
		Confess, Confess	Confess, Hold out	Hold out, Confess	Hold out, Hold out
Player I	Confess	2, 2	2, 2	4, 1	4, 1
	Hold out	1, 4	3, 3	1, 4	3, 3

Figure 3.5   Strategic form equivalent to Figure 3.2

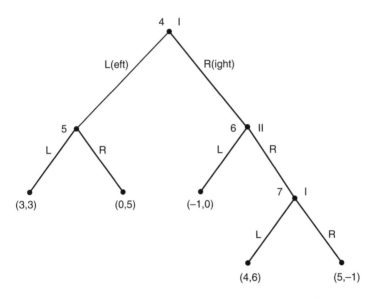

Figure 3.6   An extensive-form game with Pareto-superior non-solution

If one applies Zermelo's algorithm to this game, the unique solution is (LR,RL), yielding the outcome (0,5). (If the reader is confused here, the key to enlightenment is remembering that a strategy tells a player what to do at every node assigned to her, not merely at every node along a possible path of play.) But one can see that there is an alternative outcome, (4,6), obtained by either of two strategy combinations (RL, LR) or (RL, RR), which is Pareto superior to the solution because both players are better off. In the extensive form it makes intuitive sense that the Pareto superior state can't be reached. Player II would have to choose R at node 6 in order that Player I could then choose L at node 7.

But this would require Player I to fail to maximize her utility function. Thus, just as in the PD, Player II cannot believe a promise by Player I to play L at node 7, so Player II can only avoid getting his worst possible payoff, −1, by playing L at node 6; and this makes the outcome (4,6) unreachable.

But now consider the strategic form of this same game shown in Figure 3.7.

We can reason our way to the solution using the matrix as follows. When Player I plays LL, Player II maximizes his utility function by playing either RL or RR. (He is thus indifferent between these strategies.) When Player I plays LR, the same holds. When Player I plays RL, Player II maximizes by playing LR or RR, yielding the socially efficient outcome. When Player I plays RR, Player II maximizes by playing LL or RL. Now, when Player II plays LL, Player I maximizes her utility function by playing LL or LR. (She is indifferent between these strategies.) When Player II plays LR, Player I maximizes by playing RR. When Player II plays RL, Player I maximizes by playing LL or LR. When Player II plays RR, Player I maximizes by playing RR. When we put all of this together, we find only two strategies that are best replies *at the same time*: (LL, RL) and (LR, RL), both yielding the outcome (0,5). One of these solutions corresponds to the unique solution of the game in Figure 3.6, and the other is an alternative solution with the same outcome.

We can intuitively grasp the solution to the strategic-form game by thinking now not about one player at a time, but about the two together. Imagine that they were collectively playing one of the strategy pairs that yielded the socially efficient outcome, either (RL, LR) or (RL, RR). In neither case is Player I maximizing her utility function; to do so she must switch to playing RR.

		Player II			
		LL	LR	RL	RR
Player I	LL	3, 3	3, 3	0, 5	0, 5
	LR	3, 3	3, 3	0, 5	0, 5
	RL	−1, 0	4, 6	−1, 0	4, 6
	RR	−1, 0	5, −1	−1, 0	5, −1

Figure 3.7   Strategic form of Figure 3.6

Recall now what is 'equilibrated' about competitive equilibrium, whether Walrasian or Marshallian: no producer improves profits by changing production quantity, and no consumer improves her utility by reallocating her consumption budget. We should see that this is the same equilibrium idea as can be applied to the solutions of the game in Figure 3.7: neither player can improve their outcome by switching to an alternative strategy. It is because that does *not* apply to the strategy pairs that produce the socially efficient outcome that we might say that those strategy pairs are *not* an equilibrium.

Recognizing that the economic concept of equilibrium applies to games was the Nobel Prize winning achievement of the mathematician John Nash. In two seminal articles written in the early 1950s, Nash (1950a, 1951) proved that *if* players are not required to play one of their possible strategies with certainty – that is, if they are allowed to play strategies with definite probabilities summing to 1, and then randomize among some or all of their strategies according to the probabilities in question (see Section 3.7 below) – then every non-cooperative game has an economic equilibrium. Indeed, it is in the context of a non-cooperative game that the idea of economic equilibrium truly *generalizes*. Let us henceforth define economic equilibrium as *Nash equilibrium* (NE). This applies (or fails to apply, as the case may be) to whole *sets* of strategies, one for each player in a game. A set of strategies is an NE just in case no player could improve her payoff, given the strategies of all other players in the game, by changing her own strategy. Then we can define a variety of special cases that are sufficient but not necessary for NE. All players having strictly dominant strategies is one such special case. It applies to the PD, and also to a perfectly competitive market, where the set of general equilibrium prices is the set of dominant strategies. The point also applies to partial equilibria in models of industries *if* the equilibria are unique and no player is large enough to have unilateral influence over market prices. (In oligopolistic markets the second condition is usually violated.) In the case of zero-sum games as analyzed by von Neumann and Morgenstern, a combination of security strategies in which each player minimizes the maximum damage the other can inflict on her, is yet another special case. In extensive-form games of perfect information such as Figures 3.3 and 3.6, applying Zermelo's algorithm gives us the special case of NE known as *sub-game perfect equilibrium* (SPE). A SPE is an NE of every sub-game of the game, including, by implication, the whole game.

The suggestion that NE is a unifying concept for economics is philosophically controversial. Many games – for example, the game of Figure 3.7 – do not have unique NE, as the PD does. In such instances analysis of NE alone would not allow us to forecast a unique economic state even if we were very confident that our model correctly captured all of the empirically relevant aspects of the situation. But could we even reliably predict in such circumstances that the situation, modeled as a game, would converge to *one* of its NE? No player has a reason to play one of her NE strategies unless she has reason to predict that all other players will play the strategies assigned to them on the same NE. But does this not imply that players must achieve prior agreement on which NE they will all play? Players will often disagree about this, because typically different NE of one and the same game make varying players worse off and better off. Must we analyze such situations by constructing a meta-game in which players non-cooperatively bargain over which NE to operate in the base game? If so, such *meta-games* must not violate the rules of non-cooperative GT by letting players make binding promises about play in the base game.

We need to distinguish here between philosophical questions about NE as solutions that are internal to the foundations of game theory, and broader questions about equilibrium modeling as an approach to economics, or indeed to sciences of interacting systems in general. I will deal with questions of the former kind here, reserving questions of the latter kind for discussion in Chapter 5.

Many philosophers, and some economists, have taken the view that many or most cases of multiple NE should be dealt with by applying stronger principles of normative rationality, so as to select subsets – ideally singleton subsets – of the multiple NE. Consider the strategic-form game below, taken from Kreps (1990b, p. 403) (Figure 3.8).

This so-called Hi-Lo game has two NE: (s1, t1) and (s2, t2). If NE is our only solution concept, then we are forced to say that either of these outcomes is equally persuasive as a solution. However, if game theory is regarded as a normative theory of strategic reasoning, this seems to be leaving something out: surely rational players with perfect information should converge on (s1, t1)? Note that this is *not* like the situation in the PD, where the socially superior situation is unachievable because it is not an NE. In Hi-Lo nothing should, it seems, prevent the players from converging on the situation in which both are better off. Yet NE analysis alone doesn't get them there. (The reader should aim to remember the Hi-Lo game, which will be discussed further in Chapter 5.

Consider another example from Kreps (1990b, p. 397) shown in Figure 3.9.

Here, (s3, t3) and (s4, t3) are both NE. No strategy strictly dominates another. However, s3 *weakly* dominates s4, since I does *at least as well* using s3 as s4 for any reply by Player II, and on one reply by II (t3), Player I does better. So should the analyst not delete the weakly dominated row s4? When she does so, the NE s3-t3 is selected as the unique solution. However, as Kreps goes on to show using this example, the idea that weakly dominated strategies should be deleted just like strict ones has odd consequences. Suppose we change the payoffs of the game as follows, shown in Figure 3.10.

Now, s4* is still weakly dominated as before; but of the two NE, (s4*, t3*) is the most attractive for both players; so why should the analyst eliminate its possibility? (Note that this game, again, does *not* replicate the logic of the PD. There, it makes sense to eliminate the socially efficient outcome because both players have incentives to unilaterally deviate from it, so it is not an NE. This is not true of (s4*, t3*).) The argument *for* eliminating the weakly dominated strategy is that Player I may be nervous, fearing that Player II is not completely sure to do 'the rational thing' (or that Player II fears that Player I isn't fully reliably rational, or that Player II fears that Player I fears that Player II isn't fully reliably rational, and so on ad infinitum) and so might play t4* with some

		Player II	
		t1	t2
Player I	s1	10, 10	0, 0
	s2	0, 0	1, 1

Figure 3.8 Hi-Lo game

		Player II	
		t3	t4
Player I	s3	10, 10	5, 2
	s4	10, 1	2, 0

Figure 3.9 Weak domination

		Player II	
		t3*	t4*
Player I	s3*	10, 0	5, 2
	s4*	10, 11	2, 0

Figure 3.10 Weak dominance and efficiency conflict

positive probability. Eliminating row s4* insures Player I against her worst outcome, (s4*, t4*). Of course, she pays a cost for this insurance, reducing her expected payoff from 10 to 5. On the other hand, we might imagine that the players could communicate before playing the game and agree to play *correlated strategies* so as to *coordinate* on (s4*, t3*), thereby removing some, most or all of the uncertainty that encourages elimination of the weakly dominated row s4*, and eliminating (s3*, t3*) as a viable NE instead. (This agreement does not violate the rules of non-cooperative GT because neither player makes a promise they might regret keeping.) Correlated equilibrium is likewise the 'intuitive' solution to the Hi-Lo game; but, as noted, it goes beyond NE.

Any proposed principle for solving games that may have the effect of eliminating one or more NE from consideration is referred to as a *refinement* of NE. In the game of Figure 3.10, elimination of weakly dominated strategies is one possible refinement, since it refines away one NE, and correlation is another, since it refines away the other NE instead. So which refinement is more appropriate as a solution concept? Philosophers and economists who think of GT as part of the normative theory of rationality have generated a substantial literature in which the merits and drawbacks of a large number of refinements are debated. In principle, there seems to be no limit on the number of refinements that could be considered, since there may also be no limits on the set of philosophical intuitions about what principles a rational agent might or might not see fit to follow or to fear or hope that other players are following.

An interesting sociological fact about recent intellectual history is that once economists realized that the pursuit of refinements based on intuitions about the concept of rationality was irresolvably philosophical in character, rather than empirical or mathematical, they abandoned the project; the 'refinement program', as they called it, has not been seen in the economics journals since the 1990s. Following the naturalistic restrictions on philosophy that I defended in Chapter 1, it follows that philosophers should also drop this project, because it is based on conceptual intuitions rather than objective considerations. The majority of philosophers will disagree with me about this. What is wrong, they will ask, with the project of investigating the general characteristics of rationality? But this objection presupposes that careful sense can be made of the claim that any analysis of rationality in general could be produced that would be deemed normatively satisfactory across all contexts (or, at least, all contexts that are possible according to physics). Of course I cannot show that this is impossible, because I cannot consider every physically possible context. But the fact that we can throw around phrases like 'rationality in general' (or 'principles God would think it best to always use') provides no evidence that the ambition to produce an analytical theory of it makes sense. Philosophers should be challenged to provide other grounds for considering the ambition reasonable.[16]

Crucially, however, not all possible refinements to NE are based on opinions about the meaning of rationality. SPE, notably, is based instead on applying the basic principle of NE, absence of any preferred strategy for any player, to the richer structure of a finite perfect-information game with no non-singleton information sets. And in Chapter 5 we will encounter a way of recovering the intuitive solution to Hi-Lo games that does not depend on any conceptual commitments concerning rationality. Note, we need that for Hi-Lo because our dissatisfaction with (s2, t2) in Figure 3.8 is based on more than normative considerations. We would *predict* that *actual* (as opposed to just 'perfectly rational') people would converge on (s1, t1); and experiments show that they indeed do (Bacharach 2006, pp. 42–43).

Another philosophical problem internal to the foundations of GT, and which will later prove to have some relevance to our reflections on the philosophical character of treating economic equilibria as solutions, is raised by the so-called 'paradox of backward induction.' I borrow an elegant illustration from Bicchieri (1993). Consider the game shown in Figure 3.11.

---

[16] Some philosophers do seek answers to this kind of general skepticism about non-naturalistic analysis. See for example Cappelen (2012). I am entirely unpersuaded; but explaining why would carry us into details far from economics.

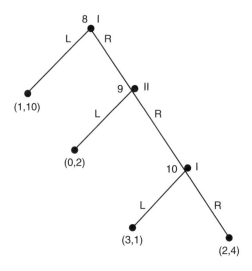

Figure 3.11 A virtual game

Zermelo's algorithm finds the NE outcome here at the single leftmost node descending from node 8. At node 10, Player I would play L for a payoff of 3, giving Player II a payoff of 1. Player II can do better than this by playing L at node 9, giving Player I a payoff of 0. Player I can do better than this by playing L at node 8, in which case the game terminates without Player II getting to move. This is a nice illustration of the way in which we can use equilibrium analysis to explain why we might observe a specific *failure* of action. But if we think about GT analysis as being a model of normatively restricted psychological reasoning, the game also illustrates logic that disturbs philosophers. (In addition to Bicchieri 1993, see Binmore 1987 and Pettit and Sugden 1989.)

Player I plays L at node 8 because she knows that Player II maximizes his utility function at node 9 by playing L, because Player II knows that Player I maximizes her utility at node 10 by playing L. But now we have the following apparent paradox: Player I must suppose that Player II, at node 9, would predict Player I's utility-maximizing play at node 10 despite having arrived at a node – 9 – that could only be reached if Player I were not playing so as to maximize her utility. If Player I is not maximizing her utility function then Player II is not justified in predicting that Player I will not play R at node 10, in which case it is not clear that Player II shouldn't play R at node 9; and if Player II plays R at node 9, then Player I is guaranteed of a better payoff than she gets if she plays L at node 8. Both players, we assume, use backward induction (Zermelo's algorithm) to solve the game; this requires that Player I knows that Player II knows that Player I behaves in conformity to GARP; but Player II can solve the game only by using a backward induction argument that takes as a premise the inconsistency of Player I.

A standard way around this paradox in the literature is to invoke the so-called 'trembling hand' due to Selten (1975). The idea here is that a decision and its consequent act may 'come apart' with some nonzero probability. That is, a player might intend to take an action but then slip up in the execution and send the game down some other path instead. If there is even a remote possibility that a player may make a mistake – that her 'hand may tremble' – then no contradiction is introduced by a player's finding equilibrium using a backward induction argument that requires the hypothetical assumption that another player has taken a path that a player choosing in accordance with GARP would not choose. In our example, Player II could reason about what to do at node 9 conditional on the assumption that Player I chose L at node 8 but then fumbled the execution of her plan.

As Gintis (2009) points out, a player also has reason to consider out-of-equilibrium possibilities if she attaches some doubt to her conjecture about his utility function. As Gintis also stresses, this issue with solving extensive-form games for SPE by Zermelo's algorithm generalizes: a player has no reason to play even a *Nash* equilibrium strategy unless she expects other players to also play Nash equilibrium strategies, and is confident in her conjectures about their utility functions.

When we use GT to model behavior of actual agents, including people, we must take account of a fact that has been repeatedly emphasized by Ken Binmore, namely, that people must *learn* the equilibrium strategies of games they play. Research shows that even a game as simple as the PD requires learning by people (Ledyard 1995; Sally 1995; Camerer 2003, p. 265). People encounter few one-shot PDs in everyday life, but they encounter many *repeated* PDs with non-strangers. As a result, when set into what is intended to be a (typically anonymous) one-shot PD in the experimental laboratory, people tend to initially play as if the game were a single round of a repeated PD. The repeated PD has many NE that involve holding out rather than confessing. Thus experimental subjects tend to play at first as if keeping promises to coordinate in these circumstances, but learn after some number of rounds to renege on such implicit promises (that is, in the standard parlance, to 'defect'). The experimenter cannot infer that she has successfully induced a one-shot PD with her experimental setup until she sees this behavior stabilize, indicating that learning has resolved.

If players of games realize that other players may need to learn game structures and equilibria from experience, this gives them reason to take account of what happens off the equilibrium paths of extensive-form games. Of course, if a player fears that other players have not learned equilibrium, this may remove her incentive to play an equilibrium strategy herself. This raises a set of deep problems about social learning (Fudenberg and Levine 1998). How do ignorant players learn to play equilibria if sophisticated players don't show them, because the sophisticated are not incentivized to play equilibrium strategies until the ignorant have learned? The crucial answer, invoking one of the main themes of this book to be discussed in much more detail in Chapters 4 and 5, is that, in the case of applications of GT to interactions among people, novice market participants are *socialized* by growing up in networks of *institutions*, including *cultural norms*. Most complex games that young people play are joined in progress, already institutionalized by generations who were socialized before them – learning of game structures and equilibria is mainly social rather than individual (Ross 2008a). Novices must then only copy those whose play appears to be expected and understood by others. Institutions and norms are rich with reminders, including homilies and easily remembered rules of thumb, to help people remember what they are doing (Clark 1997). Of course, young people famously make mistakes while learning, and take their lumps for it.

When observed behavior does *not* stabilize around equilibria in a game, and there is no evidence that learning is still in process, the analyst should infer that she has incorrectly modeled the situation she is studying. Chances are that she has either mis-specified players' utility functions, the strategies available to the players, or the information that is available to them. Given the complexity of many of the situations that social scientists study, we should not be surprised that mis-specification of models happens frequently. Applied game theorists must do lots of learning, just like their subjects.

Thus the paradox of backward induction is only apparent. Unless players have experienced play at equilibrium with one another in the past, we should predict that they will behave in a way that is consistent with attaching some positive probability to the conjecture that understanding of game structures among some players is imperfect. Apparently trembling hands may reflect either error or uncertainty, or a mix of them. Learning of equilibria may take various forms for different agents and for games of differing levels of complexity and risk. Incorporating it into game-theoretic models of interactions thus introduces an extensive new set of technicalities. There is an unfortunate tendency in some philosophical literature to then reason as if these technical complexities pose an insuperable barrier to using GT as a modeling technology. In one way, highly parochial to their own interests, the philosophers are right about this, for a reason I have indicated: GT does not furnish the basis for a compact, high-level theory of general strategic rationality. This doesn't reflect a limitation in GT as a body of mathematics. Rather, it reflects the residual theological ambitions of the disappointed philosophers. There is no reason to expect an overarching, normatively derived philosophical account of rationality to match any empirical phenomena.

In the meantime, economists who apply GT are not left at a loss. In a pair of important papers in the mid-to-late 1990s, McKelvey and Palfrey (1995, 1998) developed the solution concept of *quantal response equilibrium* (QRE). QRE is not a refinement of NE, in the sense of being a philosophically motivated effort to strengthen NE by reference to normative standards of rationality. It is, rather, a practical device for calculating the equilibrium properties of choices made by agents whose conjectures about possible errors in the choices of other players are uncertain. QRE is thus standard equipment in the toolkit of experimental economists who seek to estimate the distribution of utility functions in populations of real people placed in situations modeled as games. We should note, anticipating a point to be discussed more fully later in this chapter, that QRE would not have been practically serviceable in this way before the development of modern statistics packages such as STATA™ allowed computation of QRE given adequately powerful observation records from interestingly complex games involving substantial numbers of players. QRE is still chronically under-utilized by behavioral economists, and is almost never used by psychologists, in analyzing laboratory data. In consequence, many of these studies make apparently dramatic rhetorical points by 'discovering' that real people often fail to converge on NE in experimental games. But NE, although it is a minimalist solution concept in one sense because it abstracts away from much informational structure, is simultaneously a demanding expectation if imposed categorically (that is, if players are expected to play as if they are all certain that all others are playing NE strategies). Predicting play consistent with QRE is perfectly consistent with – indeed is motivated by – the view that NE captures the core general concept of an economic equilibrium. The key point is that if we want to use this concept to build a measurement apparatus for use in empirical science, we need to re-frame the concept in *statistical* rather than *logical* terms. (Philosophers, with the mighty exception of C.S. Peirce, have historically been very uncomfortable with this sort of move, which is one of the most serious barriers to more mutually sympathetic and productive relationships between philosophers and scientists. See Ladyman and Ross 2013.)

The crucial background to QRE had been developed as game theorists increasingly came to understand their project as, in part, an investigation into the relationship between changes in *information* available to agents and *frequencies* with which different mixes of economic strategies are observed in populations – most centrally, populations interacting in markets. Understanding this requires us now to return, as promised at the end of Section 3.5, to von Neumann and Morgenstern's original introduction of GT in 1944.

3.7 Expected utility and risk preferences

We have so far discussed the development of one key innovation of von Neumann and Morgenstern, the introduction of models of economic interaction in which agents have different utility functions from one another. Now we turn to their other most important novelty, their method for incorporating risk into the modeling framework of RPT. This required the introduction of cardinal structure – that is, relative numerical magnitudes – into the hitherto strictly ordinalist framework of RPT. Risk, unlike preference ranking, is a scalar quantity and larger risks that are recognized as such by agents have systematically stronger incentivizing effects on their behavior than what they perceive as smaller risks. But as extensively discussed in Chapter 2, after the maturation of the ordinalist understanding of utility, economists no longer followed Bentham or Jevons in regarding utility as measuring levels of psychological satisfaction; a utility function is merely a formal description of a set of choices satisfying certain mathematical restrictions (WARP or GARP or SARP). Therefore, the cardinal structure needed for GT modeling cannot be based on hypothetical differences in agents' subjective attitudes; it must be derived from observable properties of choices. That an agent is observed to choose a bundle X instead of a bundle Y cannot in principle reveal this. Von Neumann and Morgenstern showed how cardinalized preference structure is revealed if we can observe agents responses to quantifiable shifts in the riskiness of their choices.

Von Neumann – Morgenstern cardinalization is important to the argument of this book for two reasons. First, it is a core part of the technical background to the contemporary microeconomics of information. This turns Hayek's great insight about markets (including small markets involving only a few participants, as an experimenter might set up in a lab) into a practical modeling technology using GT. This synthesis is expressed in the measurement tool of QRE analysis as introduced at the end of the previous section. Second, in Chapter 2 we identified ordinalism as the key development in the separation of economics from psychology. Thus it behooves us to understand how any modification of ordinalism might bear on temptations to go back on this separation and embrace EP.[17] As we will see in Chapter 4, such temptations have captured many current researchers who conduct game-theoretic experiments with human subjects; but as we will also see, this is by no means naturally implied by the technical details.

We first need to understand why von Neumann and Morgenstern needed to bring risk analysis into the technical ambit of utility theory. After all, statisticians had been mathematically modeling risk for three centuries; some economists – notably Keynes – had been interested in probability; and every economist had always been aware of the importance of risk in investment decisions. The problem was that risk had

---

[17] In case the reader has forgotten, this stands for 'economic psychologism', the idea that utility is to be interpreted as a real psychological quantity.

been considered to be entirely independent of preference, and modern utility functions, as we have seen, were simply preference orderings with restrictions.

Let us set up a toy problem with which to work. Suppose that a person i wishes to cross a river that is spanned by three bridges. (Assume that swimming, wading or boating across are impossible.) The first bridge is known to be safe and free of obstacles; if i tries to cross there he will succeed. The second bridge lies beneath a cliff from which large rocks sometimes fall. The third is inhabited by deadly cobras. Now suppose i rank orders the three bridges with respect to their preferability as crossing-points. His task here is straightforward. The first bridge is obviously best, since it is safest. To order the other two bridges, i requires information about their relative levels of danger. If he can study the frequency of rock-falls and the movements of the cobras for a while, he might be able to calculate that the probability of being crushed by a rock at the second bridge is 10 percent and of being struck by a cobra at the third bridge is 20 percent. We say that his reasoning here is strictly *parametric* because neither the rocks nor the cobras are trying to influence his actions, by, for example, concealing their typical patterns of behavior because they know he is studying them. Although the different risks associated with the three bridges may influence – indeed determine – i's preference ordering of them (for example, yielding safe bridge > rocky bridge > cobra bridge), there is so far no more reason to incorporate these risks into the utility function than there is reason to incorporate representations of the different flavors of foods into utility functions that summarize ordinal preference relationships among them.

The most fundamental distinction that GT allows us to introduce into economics is between parametric choice over states of the world that do not respond to incentives and *non-parametric* choice over aspects of the world controlled by other choosers, who thus have incentive to try to anticipate and modify the choices in question. If we now complicate the bridge-choosing situation by introducing a non-parametric element, we move into the domain of GT. Suppose that i is a fugitive of some sort, and waiting on the other side of the river with a gun is his pursuer j. She will catch and shoot i, let us suppose, only if she waits at the bridge i tries to cross; otherwise, i will escape. As i reasons through his choice of bridge, it occurs to him that j is over there trying to anticipate his reasoning. It may seem to him that, surely, choosing the safe bridge straight away would be a mistake, since that is just where j will expect him, in which case his chances of death rise to certainty. So perhaps i should risk the rocks, since these odds are much better. But if i can reach this conclusion then j, who has all the information that i does, can anticipate that i will reach it, and will be waiting for him if he evades the rocks. So perhaps i must take his chances with the cobras; that is what j must least expect. But, then, no ... if j expects that i will expect that j will least expect this, then j will most expect it. This dilemma, i realizes, is general: he must do what his pursuer least expects; but whatever he most expects her to least expect is automatically what she will most expect. The fugitive appears to be trapped in indecision. All that might console him a bit is that, on the other side of the river, his pursuer is stuck in the same quandary, unable to decide which bridge to wait at because as soon as she imagines committing to one, she will notice that if she can find a best reason to pick a bridge, i can anticipate that same reason and then avoid her.

Pre-GT economists had not encountered this kind of problem because in markets as modeled in Walrasian or Marshallian competitive equilibria optimal budget allocations and production decisions are determined for all agents by exogenous preferences and budgets. Though all agents' utility-maximizing choices are conditional on the utility-maximizing choices of all others, all relevant computation is effectively done 'by the market' and revealed in prices. All agents predict the behavior of all others with certainty and all choice is parametric. It is still appropriate to call the agents' consumption and production behavior 'choices' because they are responses to incentives; but there is little temptation to think that latent choice *processes*, psychological or otherwise, should play any role in guiding analyzes.

Explanations of the intuitions behind GT analyzes, by contrast, tend to traffic heavily in sequences of reasoning. It is natural to think of these sequences as isomorphic to arguments that agents rehearse for themselves, just as in the standard pedagogy I employed above – and thus to regard them as real processes that occur "in" agents' minds. (The quote marks are intended to encourage the reader to pause for a philosophical moment. Is there any non-metaphorical content to the idea that processes are "in" people's minds? Are we trying to refer to hypothesized events in their brains? These issues will be taken up in Chapter 4.) Of course, people sometimes do consciously work through the probable consequences, both parametric and non-parametric, of options between which they are deciding. However, I will later be arguing for treating this kind of process as a special – and comparatively infrequent – kind of choice rather than as the model for choice in general.

Let us return to the fugitive and his pursuer. The fugitive i can escape only if his pursuer j cannot reliably predict which bridge he'll use. Symmetry of information on the part of the two agents – which we are simply assuming here – ensures that i can surprise j only if it is possible for i to surprise *himself*. This formulation might be regarded as a kind of verbal joke. In fact, I think it is often psychologically accurate. However, let us save our visitation of psychological themes for Chapter 4 and in the meantime speak more neutrally. The fugitive needs to partially de-couple the identification of his optimal *outcome* from the identification of his optimal *course of action* or *strategy*. Such partial de-coupling makes no sense in pre-GT economics; but it is the essence of any application of GT. I refer to 'partial' de-coupling because the valuation of outcomes must obviously be a crucial input to the choice of strategy. In pre-GT economics utility simply defines relationships among preferences over outcomes. In economics using GT, utility is still defined over outcomes, but choice is over strategies.

The games we encountered in Section 3.6 all involved players choosing from among *pure strategies*, in which each seeks a single optimal course of action at each node that constitutes a best reply to the actions of others. Often, however, a player's utility is optimized through use of a *mixed* strategy, in which she flips a weighted coin among several possible actions. (We will see later that there is an alternative interpretation of mixing, not involving randomization at a particular information set; but we will start here from the coin-flipping interpretation and then build on it later.) Mixing is called for whenever no pure strategy maximizes the player's utility against all opponent strategies. The river-crossing game exemplifies this.

Suppose that we ignore the rocks and cobras for a moment, and imagine that the bridges are equally safe. Suppose also that the fugitive has no special knowledge about his pursuer that might lead him to venture a special conjectured probability distribution over her available strategies given idiosyncratic preferences. In this case, i's best course is to roll a three-sided die, in which each side represents a different bridge (or, more conventionally, a six-sided die in which each bridge is represented by two sides). He must then pre-commit himself to using whichever bridge is selected by this *randomizing device*. This is what we meant above by 'surprising himself': i chooses to do whatever his die dictates before he rolls it. Since we are presuming j's epistemic situation to be symmetrical to i's, we may suppose that j rolls a three-sided die of her own. i now has a 2/3 probability of escaping and j has a 1/3 probability of catching him. Neither agent can improve their chances given the other's randomizing mix, so the two randomizing strategies are an NE. Note that if *one* player is randomizing then the other does equally well on *any* mix of probabilities over bridges, so there are infinitely many combinations of best replies. However, each player should worry that anything other than a random strategy might be coordinated with some factor the other player can detect and exploit. Since any non-random strategy is exploitable by another non-random strategy, in a zero-sum game such as our example, only the vector of randomized strategies is an NE.

Now let us re-introduce the parametric risk factors, that is, the falling rocks at bridge #2 and the cobras at bridge #3. Again, suppose that the fugitive is sure to get safely across bridge #1, has a 90 precent chance of crossing bridge #2, and an 80 percent chance of crossing bridge #3. We will now make some assumptions about the two players' utility functions over the possible outcomes of the game. Suppose that i cares only about living or dying (preferring life to death) while j simply wishes to be able to report that i is dead, preferring this to having to report that he got away. (In other words, neither player cares about how i dies, if he dies.) In this case, i simply takes his original randomizing formula and weights it according to the different levels of parametric danger at the three bridges. Each bridge should be thought of as a *lottery* over i's possible outcomes, in which each lottery has a different *expected payoff* in terms of the items in his utility function.

In the first example of an application of reasoning about expected payoffs, we will assume that the agents are risk-neutral, that is, that they are indifferent between a sure thing and an outcome in which the risk of non-payment exactly cancels out the extra marginal value of the prize, and also derive no utility from the thrill of gambling.

Consider matters from j's point of view. She maximizes the probability that i dies if she can find and choose a mix of probabilities over the three bridges that makes i indifferent among his pure strategies. (Were j to choose a mix that made one bridge a better option for i than the other two, this would clearly amount to allowing him an improved chance of living.) The bridge with rocks is 1.1 times more dangerous for i than the safe bridge. Therefore, on the assumption that all he cares about is living versus dying, he is indifferent between the rocky bridge and the safe bridge when j is 1.1 times more likely to be waiting at the safe bridge than the rocky bridge. The cobra bridge is 1.2 times more dangerous for i than the safe bridge. Therefore, he is indifferent between these two bridges when j's probability of waiting at the safe bridge is 1.2 times higher than the probability that she is at the cobra bridge. Suppose we use s1, s2 and s3 to represent i's parametric survival rates at each bridge. Then j minimizes i's net survival rate across any pair of bridges by adjusting the probabilities p1 and p2 that she will wait at them so that

$$s1\,(1 - p1) = s2\,(1 - p2)$$

Since p1 + p2 = 1, we can rewrite this as

$$s1 \times p2 = s2 \times p1$$

so

$$p1/s1 = p2/s2.$$

Thus j maximizes her expected payoff by solving the following simultaneous equations:

$$1\,(1 - p1) = 0.9\,(1 - p2)$$
$$= 0.9\,(1 - p2)$$
$$p1 + p2 + p3 = 1$$

Then

$$p1 = 49/121$$
$$p2 = 41/121$$
$$p3 = 31/121$$

Now let f1, f2, f3 represent the probabilities with which i chooses each respective bridge. Then i maximizes his expected payoff by solving

$$s1 \times f1 = s2 \times f2$$
$$= s3 \times f3$$

so

$$1 \times f1 = 0.9 \times f2$$
$$= 0.8 \times f3$$

simultaneously with

$$f1 + f2 + f3 = 1.$$

Then

$$f1 = 36/121$$
$$f2 = 40/121$$
$$f3 = 45/121$$

These two sets of probabilities (p1-p3 and f1-f3) tell each player how to weight his or her die before throwing it. Note the – perhaps surprising – result that i uses riskier bridges with *higher* probability. This is the only way of making j indifferent over which bridge she stakes out, which in turn is what maximizes i's probability of survival.

Following von Neumann and Morgenstern's original 1944 presentation, the solution procedure for this game relied on the fact that the players' utility functions are such as to make it *zero-sum*, or *strictly competitive*. That is, every gain in expected utility by one player represents a precisely symmetrical loss by the other. However, as explored in subsequent developments of non-cooperative GT after von Neumann and Morgenstern, this condition is a special case, not the general one. Suppose then that the utility functions are related to one another in a more complicated way. Imagine that j prefers an outcome in which she shoots i and so claims credit for his apprehension to one in which i dies of rockfall or snakebite; and j prefers this second outcome to i's escape. Suppose that i prefers a quick death by gunshot to the pain of being crushed or the terror of an encounter with a cobra. Most of all, of course, he prefers to escape. At this point the need for cardinalized utility measures confronts us. We cannot solve this game, as before, simply on the basis of knowing the players' ordinal utility functions, since the *intensities* of their respective preferences are relevant to their choices of strategies. But this looks at first glance like a philosophical crisis point for RPT, since the whole point of RPT was to generalize ordinalism and dissociate the idea of preference from psychological constructs such as intensity.

Von Neumann and Morgenstern's solution to this problem rested on using our independent access to relative quantitative risks of options to infer quantitative structure in utility functions from choices. Suppose we know that the ordinal utility function of the fugitive is compatible with the following numerical example:

> Escape → 4 (highest utility)
> Death by shooting → 3
> Death by rockfall → 2
> Death by snakebite → 1 (lowest utility)

One might think it a plausible conjecture that i's preference for escape over any form of death would be stronger than his preference for being shot over being bitten by a snake. But what might that conjecture actually mean? Hume (or, following him, Bentham and Jevons) would have understood it in terms of relative 'vividness' of internal perceptions. But unless we are convinced that we should completely abandon the program of Pareto and his successors and fold economics back into psychology – that is, return to EP – we must avoid any interpretation of that kind. Can we find some interpretation of relative preference strength in terms of choice behavior? Von Neumann and Morgenstern reasoned that in a situation such as the scenario of our example, a fugitive with the preference structure just conjectured should be willing to run greater risks to increase the relative probability of escape over shooting than he is to increase the relative probability of shooting over snakebite. His cardinal preference structure, that is, can be revealed by choices he makes over *lotteries*.

Suppose we asked the fugitive to pick, from the available set of outcomes, a best one and a worst one. 'Best' and 'worst' are defined in terms of expected payoffs as illustrated in the zero-sum game example above: an agent maximizes his expected payoff if, when choosing among lotteries that contain only two possible prizes, he always chooses so as to maximize the probability of the best outcome – call this **W** (for 'win') – and to minimize the probability of the worst outcome – call this **L** (for 'lose'). Now imagine expanding the set of possible prizes so that it includes prizes that the agent values as intermediate between **W** and **L**. We find, for a set of outcomes containing such prizes, a lottery over them such that our agent is indifferent between that lottery and a lottery including only **W** and **L**. In our example, this is a lottery that includes being shot and being crushed by rocks. Call this lottery **T**. We define a utility function $q = u(\mathbf{T})$ from outcomes to the real (as opposed to ordinal) number line such that if q is the expected prize in **T**, the agent is indifferent between winning **T** and winning a lottery **T*** in which **W** occurs with probability $u(\mathbf{T})$ and **L** occurs with probability $1 - u(\mathbf{T})$. Assuming that the agent does not gain utility from considering more complex lotteries rather than simple ones,[18] the set of mappings of outcomes in **T** to $u(\mathbf{T*})$ gives a von Neumann – Morgenstern utility function (vNMuf) with cardinal structure over all outcomes in **T**.

Intuitively, in this hypothetical procedure we've given our agent choices over lotteries, instead of directly over resolved outcomes, and observed how much extra risk of death he's willing to run to change the odds of getting one form of death relative to another form of death. Note that this cardinalizes the agent's preference structure only relative to agent-specific reference points **W** and **L**; the procedure reveals nothing about comparative extra-ordinal preferences *between* agents, which helps to make clear that we are not introducing a potentially objective psychological element. Furthermore, two agents in one game, or one agent under different choice circumstances, might display different attitudes to risk. Perhaps in the river-crossing game the pursuer, whose life is not at stake, will enjoy gambling with her glory while the fugitive is cautious. In general, a *risk-averse* agent prefers a guaranteed prize to its equivalent expected value in a lottery over that prize and less-preferred alternative. A *risk-loving* agent has the reverse preference structure. A *risk-neutral* agent is indifferent between these options.

In analyzing the river-crossing game, we don't have to be able to compare i's cardinal utilities with j's. Both agents can find their NE strategies if they can estimate the probabilities each will assign to the actions of the other. This means that each must know both vNMufs; but neither need try to comparatively value the outcomes of the strategies over which they're choosing.

---

[18] As an analogy for what we are excluding, think of someone who prefers harder crossword puzzles to easier ones.

Suppose we assume the restriction, which we will later relax, that an agent's aversion to risk is constant and relative to her wealth. Then we can represent it by the workhorse of the experimental literature, the constant relative risk aversion (CRRA) utility function:

$$u(x) = \frac{x^{1-r}}{1-r} \tag{1}$$

Then when $r < 0$ the agent is risk loving and the utility function is concave; where $r = 0$ the agent is risk-neutral; and where $r > 0$ the agent is risk-averse and the utility function is convex.

Imagine that we presented an agent with the following series of lottery choices shown in Figure 3.12.

Note that each lottery in the A series is 'safe,' in the sense of offering a larger minimum prize, by comparison with its counterpart in the B series. But in choices 1–4 the expected monetary value (EV) of the A choice is higher than the EV of the corresponding B choice, with the margin of EV(A) over EV(B) declining as we move down the choices. The difference EV(A) – EV(B) is shown in the rightmost column. From choice 5 onward EV(B) > EV(A), with the margin in favor of EV(B) increasing. Thus a risk-neutral agent will choose the A lottery in choices 1–4 and the B lottery in choices 5–9.

We can estimate the curvature of an agent's utility function given the choices above, provided they are made independently (or we know the function by which the agent integrates them).[19] First, we estimate the range of values of r in equation (1) that would predict indifference on each choice pair. For example, for choice 4,

$$EU(A) = (0.4)\left[\frac{\$250^{1-r}}{1-r}\right] + (0.6)\left[\frac{\$150^{1-r}}{1-r}\right] \tag{2}$$

---

[19] Since an experimenter typically does *not* know this function, it is wise not to present experimental subjects with entire tables of choices at once, which may make them more likely to frame their task as a single portfolio choice instead of 9 independent pairwise choices. Nor should one simply move up or down the ladder in offering the choices. But even this advice must be understood with due modesty. The experimenter should remember that her subjects might do anything she doesn't adequately incentivize them not to do – subjects are free systems, not elements in stipulated models. In particular, we cannot force subjects to treat their choices as independent; we can merely avoid accidentally encouraging them not to.

Choice	Lottery A	Lottery B	EV(A) – EV(B)
1	$250 X 10%	$400 X 10%	$84
	$150 X 90%	$40 X 90%	
2	$250 X 20%	$400 X 20%	$58
	$150 X 80%	$40 X 80%	
3	$250 X 30%	$400 X 30%	$32
	$150 X 70%	$40 X 70%	
4	$250 X 40%	$400 X 40%	$6
	$150 X 60%	$40 X 60%	
5	$250 X 50%	$400 X 50%	–$20
	$150 X 50%	$40 X 50%	
6	$250 X 60%	$400 X 60%	–$46
	$150 X 40%	$40 X 40%	
7	$250 X 70%	$400 X 70%	–$72
	$150 X 30%	$40 X 30%	
8	$250 X 80%	$400 X 80%	–$98
	$150 X 20%	$40 X 20%	
9	$250 X 90%	$400 X 90%	–$124
	$150 X 10%	$40 X 10%	

Figure 3.12   A list of lottery choices

$$EU(B) = (0.4)\left[\frac{\$400^{1-r}}{1-r}\right] + (0.6)\left[\frac{\$40^{1-r}}{1-r}\right] \tag{3}$$

yielding $-0.07 < r < 0.24$ as the estimated range consistent with the hypothesis of risk neutrality (since this is the range that includes $r = 0$). Estimating r values for the number of choices drawn from the A series consistent with the CRRA utility function yields the table shown in Figure 3.13.

Note that we can use this method not only to estimate an individual agent's utility function. As will be important to issues to be discussed in Chapter 4, we can use maximum likelihood estimation procedures to associate ranges of r values with models of populations, using pooled choice data. That is, we treat choices, rather than sets of choices by specified individuals, as the data against which models are estimated. Nor need we be committed to the simple CRRA function used in the example. We might instead, for instance, assume *rank-dependent expected utility* (Quiggin 1982, 1993), in which we transform the cumulative probability distribution function so as to allow for

Number of A choices	0–1	2	3	4	5	6	7	8	9
Range of relative risk aversion given CRRA	r < –0.87	–0.87 < r < –0.43	–0.43 < r < –0.07	–0.07 < r < 0.24	0.24 < r < 0.54	0.54 < r < 0.87	0.87 < r < 1.25	1.25 < r < 1.79	1.79 < r

Figure 3.13   Ranges of estimated risk aversion for choice set 3.12

overweighting of extreme outcomes conditional on the inverse of their probabilities. Finally, we need not impose the assumption that all agents contributing to a data set choose in accordance with the same form of utility function. We can use a *mixture model* to estimate the distribution of utility functions in a model of the population that has maximum likelihood given the data (Andersen et al. 2008). Thus we can allow for heterogeneity of utility functions in the population without having to drill all the way down to estimating an idiosyncratic utility function for each agent. When we apply mixture models to pooled choice data, we use demographic identifying variables to allow our statistical inference packages to test the extent to which particular utility functions are associated with recurring clusters of these variables. A utility function included in the mixture might be supported because some individual people always or almost always choose in accordance with it; or it might be supported because all or almost all individuals choose in accordance with it under some conditions. Thus the traditional a priori assumption that a person is a utility function for economic modeling purposes need not be maintained.

3.8   Equilibria and subjective probability

All reasoning in Section 3.7 presupposed that agents' beliefs about probabilities in lotteries match objective probabilities. In lottery choice experiments subjects are typically told these probabilities in hopes of making such matching as likely as possible.[20] But in real interactive

---

[20] The point in the previous footnote about free subjects is reiterated. A careful experimenter supplements hope with an empirical check. If hope turns out to not be quite realized, the default assumption should be replaced by what is empirically revealed. Risk aversion, for example, can interfere with a

choice situations – in real markets, for example – agents must often rely on their subjective estimations or perceptions of probabilities. Savage (1954) showed how to incorporate this into normative decision theory,[21] and Harsanyi (1967) showed how to incorporate Savage's theory into GT. We need to explain Harsanyi's idea because we will want to use it to finally close the main theme of the chapter and show how GT allowed economists to make methodological flesh out of Hayek's skeletal insight about information.

As we observed in the discussion in Section 3.6 of the need for people to learn equilibria, of trembling hands, and of QRE, when we model the strategic interactions of people we must allow for the fact that players are typically uncertain about their models of one another. This uncertainty is reflected in their choices of strategies. Furthermore, some actions might be taken specifically for the sake of facilitating learning about the accuracy of a player's conjectures about other players. Developing the foundations of these aspects of GT earned Harsanyi his Nobel prize.

Consider the three-player imperfect-information game of Figure 3.14. This is known as 'Selten's horse' for its inventor, Nobel laureate Reinhard Selten, and because of the shape of its tree (taken from Kreps 1990b, p. 426).

This game has four NE: (L, l_2, l_3), (L, r_2, l_3), (R, r_2, l_3) and (R, r_2, r_3) . Consider the fourth NE. It arises because when Player I plays R and Player II plays r_2, Player III's entire information set is off the path of play, and it doesn't matter to the outcome what Player III does. But Player I would not play R if Player III could tell the difference between being at node 3 and being at node 4. The structure of the game incentivizes efforts by Player I to supply Player III with information that would open up her closed information set. Player III should believe this information because the structure of the game shows that Player I has incentive to communicate it truthfully. The game's solution would then be its SPE: (L, r_2, l_3).

---

subject's incentives to accurately reveal her subjective probability assignments. Harrison et al. (2012) consequently present an experimental task for incentive compatible revelation of beliefs about probabilities that they urge should be run alongside lottery choice experiments to produce a control variable for joint estimation.

[21] This is not equivalent to showing how to incorporate subjective probability into *economics*. That project continues.

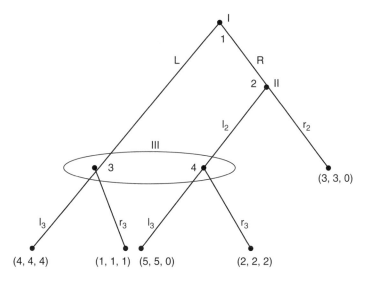

Figure 3.14 Selten's Horse

Theorists who think of GT as part of a normative theory of general rationality, for example most philosophers, and refinement program enthusiasts among economists, have pursued a strategy that would identify this solution on general principles. Notice what Player III in Selten's Horse might ask himself as he selects his strategy: "Given that I get a move, was my action node reached from node 1 or from node 2?" What, in other words, are the *conditional probabilities* that III is at node 3 or 4 given that he has a move? Now, if conditional probabilities are what III wonders about, then what Players I and II might make conjectures about when they select *their* strategies are III's *beliefs* about these conditional probabilities. In that case, I must conjecture about II's beliefs about III's beliefs, and III's beliefs about II's beliefs and so on. The relevant beliefs here are not merely strategic, as before, since they are not just about what players will *do* given a set of payoffs and game structures, but about what understanding of conditional probability they should expect other players to operate with.

What beliefs about conditional probability is it reasonable for players to expect from each other? If we follow Savage (1954) we would suggest as a normative principle that they should reason and expect others to reason in accordance with *Bayes's rule*. This tells them how to compute the probability of an event F given information E (written 'pr(F/E)'):

$$pr(F/E) = [pr(E/F) \times pr(F)] / pr(E)$$

If we assume that players do not hold beliefs inconsistent with this equality, then we may define a *sequential equilibrium*. An SE has two parts: (1) a strategy profile § for each player, as before, and (2) a *system of beliefs* μ for each player. μ assigns to each information set h a probability distribution over the nodes in h, with the interpretation that these are the beliefs of player $i(h)$ about where in his information set he is, given that information set h has been reached. Then a sequential equilibrium is a profile of strategies § and a system of beliefs μ consistent with Bayes's rule such that starting from every information set h in the tree player $i(h)$ plays optimally from then on, given that what he believes to have transpired previously is given by μ(h) and what will transpire at subsequent moves is given by §.

Let us apply this solution concept to Selten's Horse. Consider again the NE (R, r_2, r_3). Suppose that Player III assigns pr(1) to her belief that if she gets a move she is at node 3. Then Player I, given a consistent μ(I), must believe that Player III will play l_3, in which case her only SE strategy is L. So although (R, r_2, l_3) is an NE, it is not a SE.

The use of the consistency requirement in this example is somewhat trivial, so consider now a second case (also taken from Kreps 1990b, p. 429) shown in Figure 3.15.

Suppose that Player I plays L, Player II plays l_2 and Player III plays l_3. Suppose also that μ(II) assigns pr(.3) to node 6. In that case, l_2 is not a SE strategy for Player II, since l_2 returns an expected payoff of .3(4) + .7(2) = 2.6, while r_2 brings an expected payoff of 3.1. Notice that if we fiddle the strategy profile for Player III while leaving everything else fixed, l_2 could *become* an SE strategy for Player II. If §(III) yielded a play of l_3 with pr(.5) and r_3 with pr(.5), then if Player II plays r_2 his expected payoff would now be 2.2, so Ll$_2$l$_3$ would be an SE. Now imagine setting μ(III) back as it was, but change μ(II) so that Player II thinks the conditional probability of being at node 6 is greater than .5; in that case, l_2 is again not an SE strategy.[22]

---

[22] Bayes's rule cannot be applied to events with probability 0. Therefore its application to GT requires that players assign non-zero probabilities to all actions available in extensive form. This requirement is captured by supposing that all strategy profiles be *strictly mixed*, that is, that every action at every information set be taken with positive probability. This is just equivalent to supposing that all hands sometimes tremble. An SE is said to be *trembling-hand perfect* if all strategies played at equilibrium are best replies to strategies that are strictly mixed.

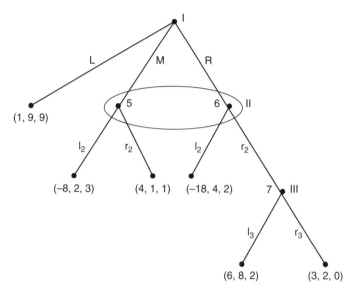

Figure 3.15 A game of conjectures

The concept of an NE that is an equilibrium in both actions and beliefs is the basis for formalizing the kind of cognitive economics discussed in Section 3.1. It should again be reiterated that an experimenter or forecaster of the behavior of actual people or firms should not predict that that they will play in strict conformity with equilibria in beliefs. She should instead predict that there will be a relationship between their play and the probabilities and expected costs of departures from such equilibria. That is, she should estimate the QRE that make the observed actions maximally likely. This investigative strategy is compatible with the expectation that multiple kinds of informational channels link different agents with the incentive structures in their environments. Some agents may actually compute equilibria, with more or less error. Others may settle within error ranges that stochastically drift around equilibrium values through more or less myopic conditioned learning. Still others may select response patterns by copying the behavior of other agents, or by following rules of thumb that are embedded in cultural and institutional structures and represent historical collective learning. Estimating QRE in a game is consistent with the standing hypothesis that a mix of these kinds of informational dynamics is operating in a population involved in a game or network of games.

An economist working with empirical data in this way should not be interpreted as 'testing the hypothesis' that the agents under observation are 'rational.' Rather, she conjectures that they are agents, that is, that there is a systematic relationship between changes in statistical patterns in their behavior and some risk-weighted cardinal rankings of possible goal-states. If the agents are people or institutionally structured groups of people that monitor one another and are incentivized to attempt to act collectively, these conjectures will often be regarded as reasonable, or even as pragmatically beyond question, even if always defeasible given the non-zero possibility of bizarre unknown circumstances of the kind philosophers, but not economists, sometimes consider (e.g., the apparent people are pre-programmed unintelligent mechanical simulacra that would be revealed as such if only the environment incentivized responses not written into their programs[23]).

The economist might assume that all of the agents respond to incentive changes in accordance with Savage expected-utility theory, particularly if the agents are firms that have learned response contingencies under normatively demanding conditions of market competition with many players. If her subjects are individual people, and especially if they are in a non-standard environment relative to their cultural and institutional experience, she would more wisely estimate a mixture model that allows that a range of different utility structures govern different subsets of the choice data. Reflecting the most important deep intellectual innovation in late twentieth-century economics, she should model the subjects' interactions in recognition of the fact that if some of the agents have strategically relevant information that other agents lack, then some of their actions are likely to be taken for the sake of signaling this private information to others, or extracting the private information of others, or blocking others' efforts to extract private information from them. To the details of such signaling, bluffing, screening and jamming we now turn.

---

[23] Economists working on very general theoretical questions sometimes reason just like philosophers in this respect. See Binmore (1987).

3.9 Institutions and information asymmetry

In the foregoing discussion, I have implicitly presented GT as important to economics *because* it is the body of mathematics that allows us to model responses to incentives among groups of economically interacting agents – that is, markets – in which no agent is representative of all others. I am *not* saying that this is the only kind of circumstance GT is useful for modeling; for the most important specific qualification see Section 3.10 below. However, it is why GT has transformed economics.

Over this and the next two sections I will set the discussion of the importance of GT in a wider intellectual context. Both professional and popular commentators on the history of economics often distinguish between *neoclassical* and *heterodox* economics. Unfortunately the principles on which this distinction is based vary from author to author. We can cut through the confusion by being very stringently restrictive on what we mean by neoclassicism. Such stringency has the rhetorical effect of turning almost all contemporary working economists into heterodox economists. That has the flavor of a joke, but (as one should never do with a joke) I'll explain it. The sound-bite explanation is that, as discussed early in this chapter, the establishment consensus against which the heterodoxy formerly defined itself evaporated almost forty years ago, but labeling conventions haven't caught up.

(Some critics of mainstream economics who call themselves heterodox mainly mean that they don't like the requirement that serious economics be done using mathematics. For example, Lawson (2009) is explicit about this. Though Lawson denies the charge, I think that such people effectively exile themselves from science. Ladyman and Ross (2007) give a philosophical account of why natural language is ill-suited to framing the objective accounts of reality that science pursues, and why, ultimately, the most powerful generalizations in all sciences consist of sets of equations that do not admit of literally non-mathematical paraphrase. As for metaphorical paraphrases, these are useful in early stages of pedagogy but have the unfortunate property of encouraging conservatism, because they tend to make the consequences of scientific investigation seem less strange to everyday experience and intuitions than they generally are. Ladyman and Ross refer to such metaphorical balm as 'domestication' of science. As promoters of enlightenment values, we prefer to emphasize wild science. It follows from this philosophy of science that people who promote the 'liberation' of economics from mathematics are actually urging the abandonment of scientific ambitions in economics.)

I will reserve the label 'neoclassical' for economic models that assign no role to *institutional* factors. Consider, for example, the hypothetical perfectly competitive market at general equilibrium. In this imaginary but precisely defined environment, every participant determines their own optimal consumption and production schedules independently of all others. There is no need for conventions or coordination because the equilibrium is unique. All agents know everything about the market that all other agents know, so there are no relevant informational dynamics. Crucially, there is no role for exogenous *rules* because no agent has any incentive to do anything other than consume what they most prefer and produce what their factor endowments and comparative advantage make most efficient for them to concentrate their energy upon. (The irrelevance of rules to perfect competition is the main reason why, even though analysis of perfectly competitive markets is practically valuable only to central planners, libertarians like to fantasize about worlds in which perfectly competitive markets could be real.)

This world without institutions is precisely the world in which economics is done without GT. The many important economists who emphasized the importance of institutional factors before GT was invented[24] were thus in the uncomfortable position of being empirically correct but methodologically bereft. This set of people is effectively coextensive (anti-mathematical luddites aside) with the pursuers of the various incomplete styles of economics labeled as heterodoxy before the 1980s. The maturation of GT relieved this unhappy condition. This is why, with almost all microeconomists now using GT as their basic tool, we arrive at the odd conclusion that the majority of economists are heterodox. If people actually used the phrase 'institutional economics' to mean roughly all of contemporary microeconomics then the phrase would disappear from use due to lack of a contrast class. What has happened instead, semantically, is that the meaning of the label has migrated to denote economists who use GT to study the economic

---

[24] There are many good accounts of the history of thinking about institutions in pre-GT economics. The reader with only a casual level of interest can consult Backhouse (2002, Chapters 8–9). A more detailed but still short account is Mercuro and Medema (2006, Chapters 1–4).

development of nations and other political communities (e.g., North 1990, 2005; Ostrom 1990; Bates 2001; Greif 2006; Banerjee and Duflo 2011; for books on related methodology see Bates et al. 1998; Wydick 2008; Aligica and Boettke 2009). I will say more about this body of work in Chapter 5. Arguably, it is now the most important and dynamic room in the entire disciplinary suite. The Nobel Prize Committee has repeatedly recently agreed with this, emphasizing my point that this so-called "new" institutional economics can hardly be regarded as counter-establishment or 'heterodox.'

In light of all this, my advice to a reader who wants to avoid confusing herself and others is to drop all references to 'neoclassical' and 'heterodox' economics unless she is referring to work done between 1947 and 1980. We are all just economists now (Coyle 2007).

Let us then turn away from exercises in normative semantics and get back to matters of substance – specifically, the modeling of the informational asymmetries that characterize almost all actual markets. The major theoretical innovators in this area, duly rewarded by the Nobel Committee, are George Akerlof (1940–), Michael Spence (1943–) and Joseph Stiglitz (1943–). The most famous dramatization of the impact of an informational asymmetry in a simple market is Akerlof's (1970) analysis of a stylized used-car market. In Akerlof's model, sellers of used cars have private information about the tendencies of their vehicles to break down. The fact that owners of faulty cars ("lemons") are more likely to want to sell them than are owners of non-lemons means that the appearance of a used car on the market carries the information that it has a higher-than-average probability of being a lemon. Hopeful marketers of non-lemons will proclaim the quality of their offerings, but because promoters of lemons are incentivized to proclaim the same thing, no one's quality advertisements are believed by canny buyers. Therefore all used cars must be marketed at prices adjusted down to reflect the higher-than-average probability that a car on that market is a lemon. Now suppose that most non-lemons are worth more to their owners than that adjusted price. In that case, there will be almost no non-lemons offered for sale and the price of used cars will fall further, reflecting the fact that any used car for sale is almost certain to be a lemon. This creates the inefficiency of a 'missing market': there are pairs of buyers and sellers who could carry out mutually profitable transactions, but do not do so because the sellers of non-lemons cannot successfully *signal* their private information over the noise created by agents with incentives to disguise lemons as non-lemons, and the potential buyers cannot *screen* honest from dishonest signals.

Akerlof's model is a nice example of the way in which the construction of a model of a non-actual market illuminates the workings of actual markets (Sugden 2000a). In most real-world jurisdictions there is in fact a brisk trade in used cars. It is facilitated by a variety of institutions, mainly companies that serve as intermediaries for buying and re-selling both lemons and non-lemons. Because these companies market many cars over extended periods of time, they have incentives to establish reputations with end-use buyers for setting appropriate lemon and non-lemon prices. This requires them to carefully inspect cars offered for sale to them and to study and verify repair histories, thereby screening the hidden private information of lemon-floggers. But of course both sellers and end-use buyers must contribute to the intermediaries' profits; the principal service sold by used car dealerships is covering enough of the cost of screening to bring the otherwise missing market to life. Information that makes markets work is itself a commodity that is traded and valued on the market. (In addition, used car dealerships add the value common to all retailers of providing buyers and sellers with convenient places and times for finding one another. This reminds us that in all actual markets, unlike fictional perfectly competitive ones, there are transaction costs that market facilitators get paid to reduce. *That is why all non-ephemeral real markets are themselves institutions.*)

The two most important kinds of markets to which the economics of asymmetric information was first applied were labor markets (Spence 1973, 1974) and credit and insurance markets (Rothschild and Stiglitz 1976; Dixit and Stiglitz 1977; Stiglitz and Weiss 1981). The basic strategic interaction between a job candidate and her prospective employer is that the former either wants to signal to the latter that she is talented and conscientious, or else prevent the employer from screening her false assurances on these points. That is, she has private information about herself that she wants to signal if it increases her market value and hide if it lowers her market value. The employer, knowing that proclaiming herself to be brilliant, loyal and tireless is a dominant strategy for the candidate, disregards her self-advertisement. This creates market space for intermediaries such as universities, which sell accreditations that job seekers can only earn by meeting thresholds for intelligence and persistence. As for people seeking credit or insurance, they have incentives to present themselves to providers as being at low risk for insolvency, carelessness, death or illness regardless of the facts about which they have private information, so banks and insurers will discount these presentations and be stingier than they should be with those who are actually good prospects. Market-making intermediaries in this instance include rating agencies that keep track of people's records of debt repayment and ratios of expenditure to income.

It may not be obvious why GT is necessary to model the economics of information asymmetries. I will therefore modify an example from Dixit and Skeath (2004, pp. 280–292). This example is typical of models from industrial organization economics, which as previously noted was the first branch of microeconomics taken over by applications of GT. Imagine a start-up firm A moving into a market dominated by a single incumbent D. D might have sufficient cash and access to capital to try to resist A's entry by locking in suppliers or starting a price war, but this is private information of D's. Suppose that D's probability of being able to raise enough capital to protect its monopoly is .25. If A enters and D resists the result is a mutually destructive price war that earns the payoffs (–10, –10) against the two firms' respective ordinal utility scales. If A enters and D doesn't resist, let the outcome be (5, –5). But of course D is best off if A doesn't enter. The key question is whether D can send a signal that A will believe. If D signals when it can resist but A judges that D is likely to be bluffing, the destructive price war will result. This risk is made serious by the fact that a weak firm has stronger incentive to signal intention to resist entry, hoping it can save itself by successfully bluffing, than a strong firm does. A signal that is free to send cannot possibly carry any conviction in this set of circumstances. D's signal, to constitute a strategic move, must involve some real costs for it. A full set of outcomes corresponding to the constraints just stated is shown as Figure 3.16.

D's financiers, who determine that D has a .25 probability of being able to fight, make decisions relevant to the game conditions but do not otherwise effect its outcome. Their strategies, based on their risk preferences and market and performance forecasts, are already factored into the lending rates that give rise to the probabilities attached to the branches from node 1. They are therefore associated with a parametric conditioning move by 'Nature' at node 1. Nature is game theorists' standard terminology for an exogenous mover in a game. In specification of outcomes we don't include payoffs to Nature.

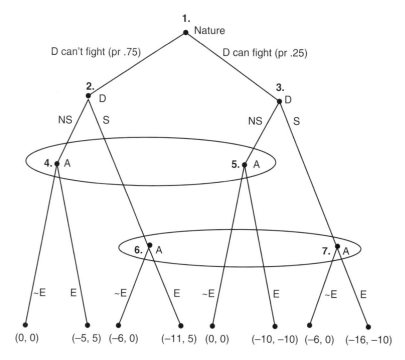

Figure 3.16 An entrant-incumbent game with separating equilibrium

At nodes 2 and 3 D chooses between taking an action that would signal its intention to resist entry. A observes this signal but doesn't know whether D is actually capable of fighting. Therefore, A chooses between entering and not entering from two information sets: one around nodes 4 and 5 when A observes no signal from D, and one around nodes 6 and 7 when D signals.

Let us conjecture that D signals if it is able to resist and does not signal if it is unable to resist; and that A enters if D doesn't signal but stays out of the market if D signals. Is this pair of conjectures an equilibrium in beliefs?

If A finds itself at nodes 6 or 7 it infers from its conjecture about D's strategy that it is at node 7. In that case not entering is its best reply. If A finds itself at nodes 4 or 5, it infers from its conjecture that it is at node 4. In that case entering is its best reply. Now suppose that D has a .75 probability of being able to resist. If it signals, then A will infer that it is at node 7 and will not enter. D prefers this to entry from node 7. If D doesn't signal, A will infer that it's at node 4 when it's really at node 5. This will induce it to enter, giving D a worse payoff than D gets from signaling. Thus if D is able to resist it will signal. Now suppose instead that D is unable to resist. If it signals then A will infer from its conjecture that it's at node 6 when it's actually at node 7. A will therefore enter, giving D a payoff of –10. If D does not signal, A will infer correctly that it's at node 4 and will enter, giving D a payoff of –5. This is better than the payoff D gets when it tries to bluff. Thus the conjecture is a *separating equilibrium*: the incumbent will signal only if it isn't bluffing and the prospective entrant should believe a signal if it observes one. We would not predict a wasteful price or other capital-destroying war in this case.

Dixit and Skeath then change the imagined payoffs, in a way still consistent with the strategic constraints as previously stated, as shown in Figure 3.17.

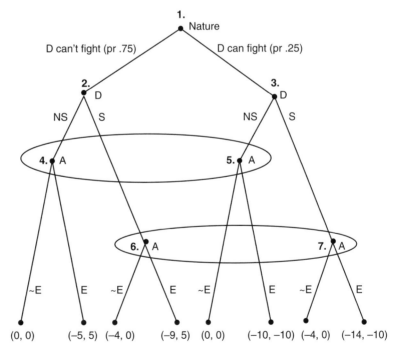

Figure 3.17   An entrant-incumbent game with pooling equilibrium

Suppose A plays as before. Now if D is unable to fight, it gets a payoff of −5 if it doesn't signal and A therefore enters. But if D signals from node 2 then A infers wrongly that it's at node 7. A therefore stays out and gives D a payoff of −4. Thus D has an incentive to bluff and A should ignore any signal it observes. Thus we have a *pooling equilibrium* in which both well-resourced and poorly resourced incumbents signal resistance, and capital will be wastefully thrown into fires by investors (to the short-run benefit of consumers). We can also construct a pooling equilibrium in which D never signals, even when it can fight. If A conjectures that D never signals, then A maintains a standing hypothesis of a .75 probability that D can't fight. Then when A chooses entry it earns an expected payoff of $(-10 \times .25) + (5 \times .75) = 1.25$. When A chooses to stay out its expected payoff is 0. Therefore unless A is (sufficiently) risk averse it will always enter. In response to an entrant that always plays enter, not signaling is a dominant strategy for D: well-resourced D gets −14 from signaling and −10 from not signaling, while poorly resourced D gets −9 from signaling and −5 from not signaling. Once again we will get a mutually destructive war whenever D is strong enough to fight.

In general equilibrium models the pooling equilibria couldn't arise, because capital markets would anticipate them and adjust financing rates to eliminate them. But general equilibrium presupposes that all private information has been screened. In actual financial markets, as Stiglitz and others have demonstrated in numerous studies, private information abounds. Use of some forms of private information in such markets is generally legally proscribed – the government here aiming to reduce transaction costs as a public service – but as sanctions must be general and each investor is particular, the design and implementation of a perfectly efficient and effective regulatory regime is generally impossible. In real credit markets there are normally multiple short-run partial equlibria, of which few may be stable in the long-run and none may be resistant to exogenous shocks of kinds that are highly probable in medium or long-runs.

The reader should now have at least a conceptual grasp of why GT is essential to the analysis of actual microeconomic markets, and of why institutional dynamics that mainly determine the flow and distribution of less-than-fully-public information can seldom be left out of models that are intended to guide policy decisions by agents.

3.10 Institutions and coordination

In the previous section we saw how some institutions arise as intermediaries between agents who have some interests in common – specifically, interests in having a market in which to transact – but whose objectives are otherwise in conflict. But we also saw that this is not quite the whole story about the economic rationales of institutions; consider again the used-car dealership that sells screening services, but also gets some of its value by letting it be known that a selection of screened used cars can be found at Honest Dan's during normal business hours. This second aspect of the institutional function is referred to by economists as *coordination.*

A *pure coordination game* occurs whenever the utility of two or more players is maximized by their doing the same thing, and where such correspondence is more important to them than *what*, in particular, they both do. A standard example arises with rules of the road: 'All drive on the left' and 'All drive on the right' are both NE, since no one benefits by unilaterally adopting a minority strategy in this simple game. But neither NE is more efficient than the other. In such games there is no temptation to use refinements of NE, for example equilibrium in beliefs, as solution criteria. If players make conjectures they test against Bayes's rule, any strategy that is a best reply to any vector of mixed strategies available in NE is said to be *rationalizable.* That is, a player can find a set of systems of beliefs for the other players such that any history of the game along an equilibrium path is consistent with that set of systems. Pure coordination games are characterized by non-unique vectors of rationalizable strategies. In such situations, players may try to predict equilibria by searching for *focal points*, that is, features of some strategies that they expect will be salient to other players, and that they expect other players will expect to be salient to them. In the most famous example due to Nobel laureate Thomas Schelling (1921–) (1960), if two people want to meet on a given day in a big city but can't contact each other to arrange a specific time and place, both might improve their chances of success by going to the city's most prominent downtown plaza or architectural landmark at noon. Factors that select focal points depend on agents' psychological, cultural, legal or even philosophical histories.[25]

---

[25] For a recent survey of the history and current state of thought about focal point dynamics, see Cronk and Leech (2012).

Solving coordination problems is crucial to almost all aspects of social life, so the applications of GT to this class of phenomena extends outside of economics and across all of the social sciences as well as the behavioral disciplines within biology, that is, ecology and ethology. Fashion, political ideology, organized religion, ethnic and national identification, and other devices for collective mobilization are all fundamentally coordination mechanisms. In Chapter 5, I will argue that the distinctive individual selves that almost all modern humans cultivate and defend are devices for pre-empting ranges of (impure) coordination problems, and that this insight is crucial, but historically often overlooked, in the philosophy of economics.

In the realm of typical market interactions, pure coordination games are relatively rare, but games that involve a coordinative *aspect* are ubiquitous. In a mutually beneficial trade, the parties prefer different prices (the buyer preferring low and the seller preferring high), but both can realize their benefits only if they coordinate on *some* price.

Of particular interest in this connection are large financial asset markets. These can be conceptualized as large-n (i.e., many party) coordination games in which traders try to avoid coordinating their valuations with other current participants but to coordinate them as closely as possible with *future* participants. That is, each trader wants to buy assets that others don't yet know they will value more highly later, and to sell assets that others don't yet know they will value less highly later. In consequence, such markets are the most economically important instances in which informational dynamics dominate valuation associated directly with consumption. In addition, in modern economies these markets are the ultimate Hayekian institutions: the information about relative values that they transmit through prices coordinates whole societies in their allocation of productive resources. Whenever a number of traders large enough to be visible at the scale of aggregate market valuations buy (sell) an asset, they thereby signal to other traders that they have private information indicating that the asset is worth more (less) than previously public information had suggested. Put another way, market trading makes private information public. But, as almost everyone in the world has been vividly reminded since 2007, these informational dynamics lead naturally to instability. If agents have more confidence in others' private information than they have in their own – which is usually wise, given the weight of numbers (Chamley 2004) – then they will tend to abandon their own strategies and copy strategies they observe to be widespread. But agents who do this withhold from revelation whatever aspects of their private information are in fact sound, thus giving rise to informational inefficiency. Accumulation of such inefficiencies consistently leads to over-valuation of some assets, and under some circumstances generates over-valuation of whole asset classes (e.g., US equities before 1929, residential property in most OECD countries before 2006). This contributes to the familiar phenomenon of bubbles that spectacularly crash and impoverish people through the resulting sudden contractions in the supply of capital. (See Kindleberger 1978 for the classic history of bubbles.)

The application of GT to the theory of coordination in large asset markets is still in the early stages of development. Cooper (1999) elegantly synthesizes what has been well established so far. The extension of GT that constructs the equilibrium dynamics of bubbles and crashes, and other macro-scale phenomena generated by micro-scale coordination games, is known as *global game theory* (Carlsson and van Damme 1993; Morris and Shin 2003). In a global game, players receive slightly noisy, non-public, signals about uncertain states of the economy. If players have correct beliefs about the sources of noise, when each one observes her own signal she can estimate the distributions of signal values received by other players. Not knowing their background beliefs, she assumes that these are randomly distributed about the unit interval, because in her ignorance this is the least arbitrary prior. On this basis the player estimates the probable distribution of actions by others, and chooses her best reply. Following Morris and Shin's (2003, p. 86) exposition, suppose we have the game shown as Figure 3.18. Each player $i, j, \ldots, n$ observes a signal $x_i = \theta + \sigma \varepsilon_i$, where the ε_i are eight-dimensional noise terms. σ parameterizes an incomplete information game. If the payoff vector $\theta \in \Re^8$ is drawn according to a strictly positive, continuously differentiable, bounded density on $\Re^8$, and the noise terms for each player are drawn according to a continuous density with bounded support, independently of θ, then as $\sigma \to 0$ any sequence of strategy profiles that survives iterated elimination of strictly dominated strategies converges to a unique limit, independent of the noise distribution, which includes the unique NE of the underlying complete information game if it exists, and the risk-dominant NE if there is more than one strict NE.

	1	0
1	θ_1, θ_2	θ_3, θ_4
0	θ_5, θ_6	θ_7, θ_8

Figure 3.18   Incomplete information game with payoff vector $\theta \in \mathfrak{R}^8$

Morris and Shin (1998) develop a global game in which a bank run – all depositors wanting to withdraw their funds at the same time – becomes a unique equilibrium if a parameter driving the expected rate of return for longer-term depositors falls below a specifiable threshold. Such modeling is potentially valuable to market regulators, since it offers the promise of indicating when exogenous intervention might be justified to avoid a value-destroying crash.

This point provides another basis for emphasizing the importance of institutions in economics. Abetting coordination by providing publicly visible signals is among the basic functions of the *majority* of human institutions, both formal and informal. As an example of the former, a currency supported by laws mandating its acceptance by registered businesses allows agents to store their wealth in a liquid and generally fungible medium. What it means for something to be money is that users are coordinated in their expectations that others will accept it as payment. An example of an enormously influential informal institution is the socially accepted weekly calendar, which allows people to efficiently organize their availability for business transactions at the same time as one another, and also coordinate their leisure hours. Thus entertainment services can be efficiently marketed, while business time wasted searching for suppliers who have gone fishing is minimized. The market itself is often conceived in a way that abstracts from specific institutions, as meaning simply all the information about valuations encoded in histories of exchanges. But when we talk about 'actual markets' in an applied context, we are invariably referring to structures that are stabilized and identified by mixtures of formal and informal institutions, for example firms, named products, posted prices, and legal specifications of responsibilities and rights recognized as belonging to occupants of commercial roles. Laws and regulations governing who gets to do what with resources – that is, the network of property control in a society – is the most fundamental institutional understructure of its economy.

An economy with an under-developed infrastructure of institutions for assigning ownership rights, structuring market participants' expectations and sanctioning breaches of contracts and other promises is typically inefficient to the point of trapping most of its participants in poverty. Acemoglu and Robinson (2012) synthesize decades of scholarship by development specialists to make a persuasive case that missing or ineffective governance institutions are the overwhelmingly most important factor in explaining why national income averages around the world are not smoothly distributed, but instead form clusters around three widely separated points. Affluence of the kind found in OECD countries such as Canada, Sweden and South Korea, with per capita income in the neighborhood of $40,000 per annum, is one equilibrium in a society-wide coordination game. Widespread poverty of the sort that blights Haiti, Sierra Leone and Cambodia, where per capita income is less than $1,000 per annum, is another such equilibrium. A third equilibrium state with per capita income in the area of $10,000 per annum and high levels of income and wealth inequality, is shared by middle-income countries such as Mexico, Russia and South Africa. This third cluster seems to arise because educational, medical, and financial institutions accessible only to limited numbers of wealthy households turn out to be easier to stabilize than more widespread public goods, of the kind that allow most people to build marketable specialized knowledge or skills. These loosely defined outcomes are said to be equilibria not because countries never move between them, but because such transitions are much less frequent than any model that does not recognize a central role for institutional coordination would predict.

The logic of coordination is also relevant to macroeconomic policy in the narrow sense of Section 2.9. Outside of general equilibrium models – so, in real economies – there are multiple equilibria with respect to levels and allocations of investment and profit-taking by shareholders. Keynes was the first to argue that inefficiencies characteristic of depressions arise when agents adjust their expectations of one another's propensity to invest around lower levels. Such cascades of mutual readjustment lead to equilibria referred to as liquidity traps. Monetarists subsequently promoted the view, which has been adopted by most central banks, that a positive rate of inflation is useful for discouraging households and firms from holding too much cash. The operative mechanism here is *expectations* about inflation rather than inflation per se. But any given historical rate of inflation is consistent with multiple sets of expectations depending on agents' implicit models of the economy. Central banks therefore indicate, as clearly and consistently as possible, target bands within which they will aim to keep inflation. This is supposed to coordinate households' and firms' expectations so that they can agree on predicted rates of return on investments when they negotiate contracts and joint ventures.[26]

3.11   Institutions and commitment

In general equilibrium no agent can be made worse off by an expansion in her range of options for choice. If a new option is dominated in her preference ordering by existing options she can simply decline to exercise the added opportunity. If, on the other hand, the new option dominates her existing alternatives as represented by her utility function, then we would predict that she would maximize her welfare by choosing the novelty.

This logical principle collapses when agents confront non-parametric choice problems as represented by games. In a wide range of extensive-form games, players can improve their outcomes by taking actions that make it impossible for them to subsequently take what would be their best actions in the corresponding strategic-move games. (Since the difference between an extensive-form game and its corresponding strategic-form game resides in the former's informational structure, this indicates that we are as usual dealing in the general domain of informational phenomena.) This possibility arises because, unlike the case in general equilibrium or perfect competition, there is no restriction on how reductions in an agent i's option set might influence the expectations, and hence the actions, of agents $j, ..., n$ who are strategically

---

[26]   Critics of such *inflation targeting* have argued that, since the onset of the 2008–09 financial crises, central banks have been aiming at inflation rates that are too low to make adequate inroads against unemployment. This criticism is compatible with the idea that central banks should coordinate expectations on higher rates of inflation. Most libertarians, on the other hand, object to inflation targeting in principle, since it doesn't leave the cost of capital to be determined entirely by market forces.

entangled with *i*. Such self-pre-empting actions by agents in their own interests are referred to as *commitments*.

Consider the following hypothetical example. Suppose agent *i* owns a piece of land adjacent to agent *j*'s property, and *i* wants to expand his lot by buying *j*'s. Unfortunately for *i*, *j* refuses to sell at the price *i* is willing to pay. If *i* and *j* decide simultaneously – *j* posts a selling price and *i* independently gives his agent an asking price – there will be no sale. This might lead *i* to try to change *j*'s incentives by playing an opening move in which *i* announces that he'll build a putrid-smelling sewage disposal plant on his land beside *j*'s unless *j* sells. This threat if taken seriously should make *j*'s property less valuable to her, thereby lowering the price she demands. Since it is crucial to the point of *i*'s action that *j* know he has taken it when she chooses her strategy, the threat relies on the informational dynamics of the interaction as represented in the extensive form of the game. But as described thus far the threat can have no effect compatible with the rules of non-cooperative GT. If *j* still refuses to sell, it is not then in *i*'s interest to carry out his threat, because in damaging *j*, *i* also damages himself. Since *j* knows this, *j* should regard *i*'s threat as incredible and ignore it.

However, *i* could *make* the threat credible if there is some way in which he could *commit* himself to carrying it out in the event that *j* is recalcitrant. Suppose, for example, that *i* signed a legally binding contract with some farmers promising to supply them with treated sewage (fertilizer) from his plant, but including an escape clause in the contract releasing him from his obligation if and only if he can double his lot size and so put it to some other use before a specified date. Now his threat to *j* is credible: if she doesn't sell, *i* is committed to building the sewage plant. Since *j* knows this, *j* might now have an incentive to sell her land at a price acceptable to *i*.

Commitment is often secured through the value to a player of her own *reputation*. Indeed, this is by far the most important mechanism for commitment in most markets. For example, a used car dealer tempted to pass a lemon off on a guileless buyer for the price of a good car may refrain from doing so because, if the subsequently disappointed buyer reports the behavior publicly, the dealer's ability to gain future profits from the role of intermediary in the market may collapse. This, then, is commitment that relies directly on the value of information.

The most important institutions for facilitating commitment in markets are structures that make games transparent to observers, so that reputation effects can accrue. For example, in developed countries businesses often contribute resources to establish 'better business' bureaus to which unhappy customers can report inadequately serviced sales contracts. That businesses thus underwrite their own watchdogs may appear at first glance to be noble public-mindedness. Although many business owners may be genuinely public-minded, this attitude cannot simply be inferred from their contributions. The commitment device represented by the existence of the bureau protects the long-run profitability of all the contributing businesses from the temptations they encounter to save expenses through under-performance. (The businesses avoid a PD, in which each tries to free ride on the contributions of others, because failure to contribute also sends a reputation damaging signal to potential customers.) On the other side of the ledger where public welfare is concerned, companies trying to maintain price-fixing cartels in public procurement markets must punish any of their members that gain contracts by pricing below the cartel's agreed level. They are hampered in this, however, by the absence of legal institutions for carrying out such punishments. In consequence, most industrial cartels tend to be unstable unless they can co-opt politicians, and even those that do enjoy help from corrupt public officials are unstable if they have more than five members. As Selten (1973) showed, the cost of punishing that is necessary to deter defection from a cartel is systematically related to the number of firms among which the surplus from price-fixing must be divided. In consequence, punishment is not supportable as an NE strategy once cartel profits must be divided among six or more members. Competition authorities therefore should not worry about investigating for collusion in industries with that level of concentration or lower.

As another example of the importance of institutions in preventing commitment that threatens public welfare, consider again the example of the game in which one agent i tries to secure the property of another agent j by threatening to otherwise act to reduce its value. This is made possible by i's ability to commit to imposing a *negative externality* on agent j – that is, a harm to j that is unilaterally imposed on her through an arrangement between other parties (that is, i and the farmers who want fertilizer). In the imaginary environment of perfect competition all such externalities are ruled out by definitional fiat: all values affected by all exchanges are assumed to be incorporated in the exchanges in question. In actual markets, externalities cannot be defined out of existence, and their influence can produce ubiquitous inefficiencies. The majority of commercial regulations are designed to force agents to pay, in the form of risk of punishment, for negative externalities they do or could inflict. In our imaginary example, i might be restrained by laws requiring him to pay for pollution that affects property other than his own. In most cities zoning regulations discourage agents from manipulating prices in real estate markets in the way we imagine agent i doing.

3.12 Experimentation

GT is only one of three major new technologies that have transformed economics over the past three decades. The second is the widespread adoption of experimental methods. That this occurred at the same time as the rise of GT is not an accident. GT allows for rigorous modeling of a wide range of small-scale markets, of the kind that can be built in a lab or isolated for manipulation in the field.

I will not review the history of experimental economics here. The interested reader can consult Kagel and Roth (1995) for a comprehensive review of work up to its year of publication. Guala (2005) provides a coarser-grained review, on a topic-by-topic basis, embedded in the normative context of philosophy of science. In the present section, I will confine attention to a few philosophical and methodological themes that are relevant to the general argument of this book.

Experimental economics is a mansion of many rooms, some of which have attracted excited attention in popular media and are therefore sometimes mistaken for the whole structure. A frequently encountered narrative, promoted in sources such as Thaler (1992) and Ariely (2008), goes roughly as follows. (The reader, or anyone extracting quotations without context, is cautioned that I do not endorse the narrative.) For most of its history economists held back the road to enlightenment in their own discipline by clinging to a Cartesian methodology in which results were formally deduced from allegedly obvious premises. These were derived initially from introspection and 'common sense,' and then later from the implausible hypothesis that individual people are selfish maximizers of personal utility functions that emphasize material wealth, who make use of all available information in their environments and always model it correctly without introducing any errors or idiosyncratic distortions of objective statistics and probabilities. Recently, however, methodological liberation has dawned and more and more economists – open-minded younger ones, especially – have entered the ranks of genuine empirical scientists by designing and running experiments. This has led them to discover that the previously received wisdom was an old bag of mythology. Experiments reveal most people to be altruistic to a greater or lesser degree. They typically ignore at least some available information, especially information that conflicts with flattering self-delusions they nurse. They are shockingly bad statistical reasoners, at least when they aren't pressured by benign bureaucrats into slowing down and thinking carefully, and their representations of distributions and frequencies are fun-house mirror distortions of the objective ones described by statistical theory. In consequence of this replacement of mythical economic agents by models of actual people, traditional 'neoclassical' economic theories have been swept away in a 'paradigm shift' that represents economic behavior as it really is, 'warts and all.' But all things considered, the trade-off in self-imagery the narrative invites us to enjoy is flattering. It asks us to recognize that we aren't very good at statistics and that we are easily fooled, especially by ourselves. On the other hand, we are reassured that we are not the greedy, miserly robots constantly seeking opportunities to put one over on one another that economists formerly imagined us to be. Instead we are warm-hearted bumblers who want to have lots of friends and to be well regarded by them.

Most of Chapter 4 will be directly or indirectly devoted to consideration of this Pinocchio story in which the wooden puppet heart-warmingly becomes a real boy. For the moment I am concerned only with its relationship to the new methods and tools that have come into use in economics since 1980. To the extent that someone believes the Pinocchio story, they must necessarily suppose that the explosion of experimental activity is the revolutionary engine that has transformed economics. Readers with this view might indeed be wondering impatiently why I have spent many pages discussing obsolete topics like utility maximization and revealed preference. Why did I not simply start clean with the real science, the experimental evidence?

For reasons I will explore in Chapter 4, I do not see that any fundamental revisions in general, foundational economic theory have resulted directly from experimental evidence. Experimentation has indeed transformed the character of the discipline – not by refuting former received wisdom, but by allowing it to be applied to policy problems, and related to the wider scientific worldview, built on the technical foundations provided by the past masters such as Samuelson, Savage, Frisch, Haavelmo and Tinbergen.

The reason that few economists performed experiments before 1980 was not that they hadn't noticed that experimentation is generally crucial to scientific achievement. It was that they were too far short of yet having detailed theories of isolated small markets. But the decades of theory development had, by the 1970s, at last produced a range of questions about the abstract subject of market behavior that were clear enough to be worth empirically testing through painstaking experimental designs. The first two such questions I consider most important were:

(1) What factors facilitate (and why), and what factors impede (and why), the discovery and stability of competitive equilibrium in markets where institutional rules are relatively simple and prices are relatively transparent?

(2) Where informational structure is less institutionally constrained and transparent, how do people's subjective representations of risk and probability interact with the relative value assignments summarized by utility functions?

Question (1), and the family of sub-questions it quickly begot, were gradually rendered sharp enough for the eventual design of experimental investigation by the tradition of theory development running from Pareto through Samuelson and the first generation of post-war mathematical economists, especially Arrow. This was the question taken up by the leading pioneer of economic experimentation, Vernon Smith.[27] As Smith (2008) emphasizes, an essential inspiration for his framing of the question in terms of informational dynamics and institutional constraints[28] and supports was Hayek. Meanwhile theorists,

---

[27] Smith inherited the challenge from his teacher Edward Chamberlain (1899–1967).

[28] This framing, by Smith's own account, sharpened over the course of his experimental work; it did not precede his career fully formed.

including an economist as strongly associated with hyper-rationalistic theory as Gary Becker, from early on contributed crucial translations of the mathematics of consistent incentives into techniques for controlling incentives in the laboratory (Becker, DeGroot and Marschak 1964[29]).

Question (2) is the fundamental problem bequeathed to economists by Savage. Like the experimental market research program launched by Smith, laboratory and field investigations of choice under uncertainty, in both parametric and nonparametric conditions, thrives. (For a frontier tour of recent insights and new theoretical controversies they open, see Cox and Harrison 2008.) Vital to progress in this area is steadily increasing sophistication in econometric technologies that facilitate joint estimation of risk preferences, time preferences and subjective probability judgments (Andersen et al. 2008; Harrison et al. 2012). Some of these results will be discussed in Chapter 4. Especially important there will be work aimed at empirical estimation of heterogeneous distributions of choice functions at the pooled population level.

As I have noted at several previous points, economics has from its inception been motivated at least as much by policy concerns as by disinterested curiosity. A flourishing area that combines applied GT with experimental investigations is known as *mechanism design* (Hurwicz and Reiter 2006). Mechanism designers aim to identify micro-scale institutional rules that induce agents to waste less utility – that is, to be more efficient – in their interactions within specified contexts such as firms or bureaucracies. The best known examples of designed economic mechanisms to date have been auctions for privatizing publicly controlled assets – for example, mobile communications spectrum licenses – in ways intended to realize predetermined goals such as maximization of government revenue, competition within industries, service quality, or propensity of firms to invest in technological innovation (Klemperer 2004; Milgrom 2004; for critical philosophical discussion, Alexandrova and Northcott 2009). The philosopher of economics Julian Reiss (2007, pp. 96–105) has criticized economists working in auction design for

---

[29] The 'BDM' technique for controlling incentives developed in the cited paper is often still proclaimed to be the best way of aligning laboratory subjects' incentives with experimenters' questions. Due to questions that have arisen since 1964 about the relationship between utility and subjective representations of risk and probability, this is not correct. However, BDM is the ancestor of a range of subsequent, experimentally honed, refinements that continue to be improved upon as active targets of empirical *and* theoretical research.

sometimes substituting their own ideas of what constitutes sound goals for those intended by the public authorities. One might also legitimately worry about the welfare consequences of inducing competing interest groups to extract further resources in order to fund arms races between their competing game theorist consultants. But these are both concerns arising from the *success* of economic theory and experimentation in modeling behavior in institutions. Scientific and engineering achievements in all fields typically confront political and legal processes with new challenges resulting from unanticipated consequences. If we did *not* encounter such challenges arising from the work of economists, this would in itself give us reason to doubt that it was delivering the practical outputs touted by its creators.

Economic experimentation not only takes place in laboratories. Recent years have seen a rapid rise to prominence of experiments being taken into the field. For a typology of field experiments, including hybrid types that mix elements of field and lab methodologies, see Harrison and List (2004). The choice between lab and field basically involves trading off *external validity* – the extent to which an experiment reproduces the causal and other structural relations of the target system being modeled – against the experimenter's ability to *control* and observe subject behavior. As Harrison and List argue, since field and lab experimentation are seldom mutually exclusive alternatives, the natural way to manage the trade-off is to combine them.

Currently the most active area of such work is development economics (DE). This arose as a specialized branch of economics only during the period of decolonization in Africa and Asia, when for a mix of humanitarian and strategic geopolitical reasons leaders of wealthy countries conceived the hope of accelerating the industrial growth and prosperity of poorer countries. DE is in one sense as old as modern economics; the basic concern of Smith and Ricardo, after all, had been the enhancement of national wealth through more efficient international trade policies. However, post-war DE theorists argued that poor countries could sharply accelerate their rate of 'convergence' to 'first world' status by incentivizing or forcing concentrations of investment capital by means of barriers to financial transfers and trade. This approach, grounded more in hope than in economic science,[30] had demonstrably failed,

---

[30] The idea that industrialization can be accelerated through autarchy and forced capital accumulation originated with the economists of the early Soviet Union, then was ironically borrowed by

indeed generally backfired and pushed intended beneficiaries deeper into poverty, by the mid-1970s. A subsequent emphasis on liberalizing trade and deregulating domestic markets has frequently also led to disappointments. In the case of both policy frameworks, problems were less narrowly economic than institutional. Protection of 'infant industries' and maintenance of strong currencies encouraged corruption and bloated state bureaucracies. The later emphasis on liberal trade policies and privatizations produced destabilizing political resentment when rapid change created losers who lacked the safety nets to be able to patiently wait for freer markets to work promised magic.

In some instances – Chile, Uruguay, Indonesia and Turkey being some recent cases in point – the establishment of stronger private market institutions supported by more robust rule of law does appear to be having the desired effect. Arguably, development through liberalization of the trade and domestic business environment *is* generally effective *when* it is politically possible to actually effect it – but the rub is that these political conditions are unusual. A number of other poor countries, primarily in Asia, successfully accelerated development by combining an emphasis on international trade promotion through profit-driven companies with state-led capital concentration (Lin 2012). In general, DE remains the branch of applied economics in which there is the least consensus on general propositions. In my opinion, the deepest cause of this is the fact that wherever DE policy has been mainly conceived by external benefactors it has been overwhelmed by lack of political legitimacy. The record of homemade economic reform, usually along lines anticipated by Adam Smith, has been much more frequently successful (Rodrik 2007).[31]

Western development engineers as an intended tool of competition against the USSR in the Cold War. The Soviet experience suggests that the strategy can indeed succeed if accompanied by a general militarization of all social institutions, particularly the labour market. Under Stalin's dictatorship this included the extensive use of slave labour. The economic case for humane and democratic development through state mobilization of capital was championed by the Argentinean applied economist and agency chief Raul Prebisch. See Dosman (2008).

[31] In referring to Smith, I do *not* allude to a policy of handing over national economic strategy to private shareholders and their boards and managers. Successful economic development indeed requires resort to private exchange and production markets as the primary means of allocating capital and setting prices. Best policy also emphasizes strengthening civic organization and social capital, as Smith knew. Bringing this up to date means promoting state investment in infrastructure, education, health care, research and innovation, empowerment of women, and fostering of institutions to help young people enter the labour market as soon as possible after they leave full-time schooling. Cultivation of a professional ethos in the civil service also appears to be a *sine qua non* (Acemoglu and Robinson 2012).

The rise of experimental DE must be understood against this backdrop of perceived failure of large-scale policy themes. By the beginning of the twenty-first century, a rough consensus had emerged among DE specialists that institutional engineering at the scale of whole countries was in principle a path to frustration (Easterly 2001). The focus has instead shifted to incentive-changing interventions at the scale of villages or specific groups within communities (e.g., farmers, teachers, parents of young children). This locally focused work can in turn be divided into two broad sets. One set, for which Eleanor Ostrom received a Nobel Prize in 2011, concentrates on testing the consequences of policies in applied GT models (Ostrom 1990; Wydick 2008; Aligica and Boettke 2009); essentially it is social (as opposed to commercial) mechanism design. The other set involves administering *randomized controlled trials* (RCTs), in which people in the intended class of policy beneficiaries are randomly sorted into experimental and control groups (Banerjee and Duflo 2011). The experimental group enjoys, or as the case may be, suffers from, the intervention (borrowing from the language of RCTs in medical research, 'is treated') while the latter is left alone. Experimental and control subjects are then visited and surveyed at pre-determined intervals and compared, often using a panel (longitudinal) structure for the data.

The relationship between economic theory and social mechanism design is relatively uncontroversial: this is standard microeconomic GT. Ideally it should be accompanied by experimental elicitation of risk and time preferences (Andersen et al. 2008), since these are almost always relevant to modeling equilibrium responses to policy incentives. The relationship between RCTs and economic theory is more strained, and contested. A leading attraction claimed for RCTs is that they allow for direct testing of causal relationships between treatment variables and outcome variables. In consequence, it is alleged, their design and estimation need not be conditional on structural economic theories and data are allowed to "speak for themselves" (Angrist and Pischke 2009). Critics (Deaton 2010; Harrison 2011b) question these claims. Estimation of linear models using ordinary least squares regressions – the standard form of analysis when structural modeling and econometrics are eschewed – tests only average effects in populations, and is sensitive to strong assumptions about the absence of background common causes, unobserved complementary causal influences, and feedback relationships between treatments and effects. The rhetoric with which RCT methods in DE are promoted often appeals to suspicion of economic theory for incorporating "too many assumptions." Such populism does not reflect well on the scientific value system of those who exploit the rhetoric. Among its side effects is that it has so far generally discouraged implementers of RCTs from combining them with theoretically informed efforts to estimate population-scale distributions of risk and time preferences, or subjective beliefs about probability à la Savage. Policy engineers lacking these data, now that methods for obtaining them are readily available in economics departments around the world, put themselves in the position of unnecessarily flying blind. To be clear, the value of RCT methodology to many development policy questions is not in doubt; the point is that economists should not become so enthusiastic about this tool that they discard their other ones. This recommendation might sound trite and sanctimonious. However, structural modeling and estimation are much more difficult and time consuming than linear modeling and estimation; in consequence their use constitutes a 'hard straight road' from which researchers under pressure of policy contexts are tempted to take shortcuts.

RCT-based experimentation is analytically related to, though less methodologically controversial than, atheoretic reliance on pseudo-experimental randomization, in which the theorist searches for so-called instrumental variables that are correlated with an hypothesized causal variable in a linear model but uncorrelated with the error term in the model (Angrist and Pischke 2009). This approach, which has been massively popularized under the embarrassing label of "Freakonomics" by the celebrity economist Steven Levitt (Levitt and Dubner 2006), represents a radical flight from the use of economic theory to undergird empirical study. I join critics such as Leamer (2010), Keane (2010) and Rust (2010) in regarding it with disquiet.[32] Validly instrumental variables for linear models should surely be exploited where they happen to turn

---

[32] Where Levitt's specific influence is concerned, "disquiet" is an understatement. Some highly tendentious and important claims paraded before millions of readers by Levitt and Dubner – such as the suggestion that liberal abortion law in the US has reduced crime by removing potential criminals from the population – have been shown to rely on demonstrably incorrect econometrics (Foote and Goetz 2008). For the record, I favor liberal abortion policy; but announcing morally startling results based on sloppy science is a truly terrible way to advocate it. See McCrary (2002) for another remarkable technical mistake by Levitt.

up, but they are far too rare to be relied upon as a general replacement for structural modeling. Yet many young economists are not learning the difficult techniques required for such modeling. This puts economic theory at risk just as the technology for fully realizing its scientific promise comes into our collective possession. I will return to this issue briefly in the next section.

I summarize this section as follows. The rise of experimentation in economics has complemented GT as one of its major sources of enrichment over the past two decades. Experimentation allows questions (1) and (2), inherited from the best economic theory of the past, to be subjected to much more direct empirical investigation than was formerly possible. These empirical questions in turn jointly bear on what I identified in Chapter 2 as the currently most important question for the *philosophy* of economics, viz

> Are the principles of normative decision theory, or at least those principles most relevant to identification of relative opportunity costs and oppor- tunity values, more closely approximated by individual people making choices in relative isolation, or by groups of people making choices in certain sorts of institutional contexts?

However, progress on all of these questions will not be forthcoming if the focus on experiments is allowed to *displace* theory rather than apply and inform it. In their excellent critical guidebook to experimental economics, Bardsley et al. (2010) celebrate the fact that experimen- tation in economics is increasingly being used to inductively *discover* new economic phenomena for further investigation, as opposed to merely being used to *test* the predictions of already developed theories. I endorse this perspective; good science is opportunistic by nature, and relies on both top-down (theory driven) and bottom-up (data driven) investigations. But a science that *abandons* its theory invites degen- eration and loss of generality and epistemic power. Philosophers of science can helpfully involve themselves in this current high-stakes controversy among economists.

3.13   A note on econometrics and computational tools

The reader will have clearly gathered by now that in my opinion the widespread image of economics as overly dependent on a priori theory and insufficiently sensitive to data is severely out of date. But even readers who already recognized, with Solow (1997, p. 37), that economists have always been "obsessed with data," might be very surprised at the suggestion that theory might be at risk of neglect by economists, as suggested above. It has become part of the stereotype of economists that they pay more attention to worlds deduced from abstract assumptions than to models of the actual world built up inductively from observations. In the best-known joke about an economist, he advises fellow castaways on a desert island who have retrieved a can of vegetables that floated onto the beach to "assume a can-opener."

The objective basis of this image is historically thin. No historical economist of any note has defended a Platonic or Cartesian methodology according to which propositions about the objective empirical world are to be derived from a priori truths about pure mathematical abstractions. The Austrian methodologists who might seem to come closest to this, including Lionel Robbins (1935), were not Cartesians but Kantians. In keeping with that philosophy, they thought of the fundamental structural relationships of economics, expressed in formal axioms, as conceptual filters that make the meaningful organization of observations possible. But even for them the ultimate point of the exercise was to test policies against data.

The strongest basis in institutional reality for the "assume a can-opener" stereotype is that there was indeed a moment, between the mid-1950s and the mid-1970s, when the highest possible prestige in the discipline was attached to proving the formal existence of properties of general equilibrium models. The previous chapter furnished part of the story of how such activity came to be regarded as the purest kind of economics, even though it has little to do with economic behavior. After decades of establishing distance from psychology, the trajectory of disciplinary development overshot and briefly risked floating away from science as a whole.[33] But for at least the past thirty years, the overwhelming majority of papers published in economics journals have been analyzes of empirical data.

Most stereotypes are exaggerations of rough truths. However, the stereotype of the economist is no longer an exaggeration but a *reversal* of reality; no other social science privileges empiricist methodology to

---

[33] I should add that in my opinion this pathology never became as malignant in economics as it now is in analytic metaphysics.

the extent that economics does. The confused popular image of economists stems from a circumstance that was mentioned in both the present chapter and the preceding one. During the crisis of the 1930s and the heady days of optimism about technocratic social management after 1945, economists became publicly visible in debates over sweeping questions about governance and general welfare. But in the days before game theory, as we have seen, they had little practical advice to offer to capitalists or managers. The challenges faced by such strategists stem mainly from the *heterogeneity* of people, motivations and circumstances. Such heterogeneity is in turn the precondition for the asymmetries in information that most actual economic activity is about exploiting, reducing, amplifying or managing. Economists were forced to confine their attention to highly abstract levels of generalization until the development of GT provided them with the mathematics for modeling the interactions of heterogeneous agents.

These mathematics, however, were not sufficient in themselves for the transformations in economics described in this chapter. Another necessary condition was the explosion in computational power and speed that became available to researchers through the invention and commercialization of microprocessing technology. In 1980 almost no economists had digital computers or large databases of statistics available to them in their offices. By 1990 almost all did. This radically altered their capacity set. Part of the basis for change has resided in the greater *quantities* of empirical information that can be usefully integrated. But the more profoundly influential transformation has been in the range and complexity of operations that can be performed upon data to reveal statistical patterns that in previous generations would have remained irretrievably hidden in it.[34]

Deterministic causal relationships can often be modeled by hand, using mathematics one can write out on a blackboard or piece of paper. These models typically require the idealization that every specific patient of the relationship – every instance of the dependent variable – responds identically to any given magnitude of application of the causal agent. Thus such models often discourage attention to effects of variation within classes of explananda. In classical mechanics,

---

[34] Morgan (1990, pp. 138–139) quotes Bean (1929) as recommending that an economist budget eight hours to calculate a four-variable multiple regression.

the original exemplar of a deterministic theory, all bodies are inter-changeable except with respect to the variables of the model, mass, velocity, and acceleration. But where we have reason to expect our explananda to respond heterogeneously to changes in independent variables, taken one at a time, then deterministic relationships typically give way to stochastic ones.

Historically, models that incorporated stochastic causal relationships were regarded as essentially incomplete. Until the twentieth century, philosophers generally supposed that deterministic causation governs reality at all scales, but that as analysts refine causal vectors into finer partitions of variables, underlying deterministic structures eventually become too difficult for beings with limited representational and computational power to calculate. According to this classical scientific metaphysic, the social and other domains of 'higher-order' complexity merely appear to us to be irreducibly statistical. In the days when it was plausible to think that classical mechanics might be a reducing platform for all causation, as Kant for example supposed, this was probably the best scientifically grounded hypothesis. But modern quantum physics has suggested an alternative possibility: that the metaphysical structure of the world is stochastic 'all the way down' (Ladyman and Ross 2013).[35] The open question today is not whether quantum fluctuations themselves are irreducibly statistical; that has been settled for decades now. The question, rather, is whether deterministic models at higher scales are ever more than approximate descriptions that involve ignoring heterogeneous response at the scales on which the variables in the models are distinguished.[36] Literal determinism having turned out to be false in fundamental physics, it clearly cannot be regarded as a principle of reason to be imposed as a regulative expectation elsewhere in science. The question becomes an empirical one about the form that refinements of modeling will take as science progresses. Humphreys (2004) identifies a range of indicators that future science might mainly consist of the development of statistical models that can only be operated on by large electronic computers, and which *displace*

---

[35] Remarkably, this hypothesis was formulated and defended decades *before* quantum mechanics, on the basis of taking evolutionary dynamics as more fundamental than static laws of classical physics, by the philosopher C.S. Peirce (1839–1914). See Hacking (1990, Chapter 23.)

[36] Philosophers often like to say that quantum stochasticity doesn't 'percolate up' to macro scales. This is a glib formulation of a lazy idea. See Ladyman and Ross (2007, Chapter 3).

closed-form mathematical models of the kind that conscious biological processes can handle.

In the late nineteenth and early twentieth centuries, economists took the possibility of an irreducibly stochastic world no more seriously than most scientists. (Among those who actively resisted the possibility was, famously, Einstein.) As Morgan (1990) documents, this had a significant impact on the history of the relationship between economic theory and probability theory. Economists analyzing demand data from the perspective of standard theory were aware of a persistent gap between theoretical predictions and observations. In general, three kinds of hypotheses can be offered to account for this gap. The first two presuppose that there is a deterministic 'true model' (in standard parlance following Frisch and Waugh 1933), but that either (1) measurements of variables typically involve errors, or (2) structural models are incomplete in the sense of missing some relevant independent variables. The third possible hypothesis is that the relationships among the variables are in fact irreducibly probabilistic; the true model includes stochastic effects, and the gap can, in an ideal case, be merely an artifact of the finitude of any real data set (Morgan 1990, p. 193). It is important to note that hypothesis (3) could not be operationalized – so in terms of Chapter 1 amounted to idle philosophical speculation – until Frisch (1933) showed how to manipulate *dynamical* microeconomic relationships. Prior to that, empirical evaluation of models could only be conducted through the method now used to train undergraduates, comparative statics (comparing rest positions of variables at different measurement time points). Samuelson (1947, p. 284) referred to Frisch's achievement as "a revolution of thought."

Hypotheses (1)–(3) are not mutually exclusive at the level of application. Obviously, stochastic models can contain errors in variables or errors in equations. And economists do not express implicit philosophical preferences when they decide which hypothesis to focus their attention on. But economists' collective practice reflects the general eclipse of pre-quantum prejudices throughout science. Few economists today are methodologically uncomfortable, as their predecessors were, with stochastic models.

This change in the zeitgeist, which has been incremental and almost entirely unreflective (as is normal with changes in the philosophical backdrop to science), has allowed the emergence of a sensibility among many economists that would have shocked Pareto. In this louche sensibility, statistics supplants mathematics as being all the foundations the economist needs. In a few quarters, statistics even supplants economic theory (Keane 2010). The majority of research activity carried out today by academic economists is a mix of applied statistics and applied theory. In the applications of non-academic economists (i.e., those who advise banks and investment houses), theory typically plays a role comparable to that of the vermouth in James Bond's martinis. In this methodological respect, economics resembles the contemporary physics/applied physics/engineering nexus quite closely.

For the more self-reflective economist, there is an available philosophical conception, offered by a great laureate, to go with what Pareto would have regarded as the louche attitude. Morgan (1990, p. 251) credits Haavelmo (1944) with first expressing the fully modern attitude to the minimalist view of the role of theory in economics. Theory, Haavelmo maintains, serves the function of guiding the economist on how she should expect to find observations distributed in truly representative samples.

It is no coincidence in this connection that Haavelmo's 1944 paper, along with Frisch and Waugh (1933), is widely taken (including by Morgan 1990, p. 150) to have been one of the two key founding texts of modern econometrics, the hybrid discipline that aims to fuse economic and statistical theory. In early days the fusion was more often an ideal than an actuality. This partly stemmed from details of Frisch and Waugh's methodology, which emphasized the distinction between *identifying* an economic model (economics), on the one hand, and, on the other, *estimating* its fit to data (econometrics). Economists continue to draw this obviously useful distinction. But since the Nobel-winning achievements of Daniel McFadden (1937–), James Heckman (1944–), Robert Engle (1942–) and Clive Granger (1934–2009), the ideal has increasingly corresponded to reality: in the best contemporary econometrics, identification and estimation are carried out jointly. This is the difficult art, essential for rigorously testing structural models against data, that some younger economists increasingly eschew learning, particularly if they are beguiled by the methods of quasi-experimentation.

There is some irony in the background to this concern. Before 1980, the growth of econometric theory was limited by a constraint on the demand side: there was little point in pursuing the hypothetical basis for new techniques that economists would be unable to use because of practical limits on computation. According to Morgan (1990, p. 251), the hugely influential post-war Cowles Commission researchers explicitly saw themselves as implementing Haavelmo's conception of economic method, but struggled to produce convincing examples of success due to computational restrictions. Once microprocessors removed the demand constraint, and at the same time provided a vastly more efficient way of packaging the supply, the explosion of new econometric ideas pioneered by McFadden and the others quickly followed. These ideas are built into technology such as STATA™, an ever-expanding software package for data representation and analysis that is now as essential to most economists as matrix theory. This is the source of the irony to which I alluded above. STATA hides much of the rich integration of economic and statistical theory on which it based beneath the explicit view of the user. But this doesn't free the young economist to spend more time reading the classics: becoming a STATA expert is a time-consuming – but highly rewarding – investment, and a major upgrade emerges every couple of years. Thus young economists are under significant pressure to master STATA but, except in the top American graduate programs, are often given correspondingly little incentive to absorb subtle nuances of theory. In this regard the theoretical richness of modern econometrics that makes STATA and related technologies possible undermines appreciation and knowledge of its details.

It is tempting in these circumstances to view economic theory as a ladder that the well-practiced economist can kick away. Suppose that the domain of social causation is in fact a relatively unsystematically structured but complex network of stochastic waves of influence and feedback. It might then be tempting to think that the best methodology for social science is to simply estimate specific, narrow causal channels using the quasi-experimentalist methods – drop efforts to construct and apply general models, and content oneself with a salad bowl of small-scope estimated relationships. The problem here is that in the absence of strongly convincing evidence for this minimalist social metaphysic, we would simply be abandoning ambitions for what has traditionally been the primary aim of scientific inquiry: maximally general, powerful theories that *explain* observations by unifying them under a concise set of principles governing the channels by which incentives influence choices in markets.

Moreover, to argue against the value of economic theory and structural modeling by appeal to the power of instrumental variables to help us estimate narrow causal relationships is not as metaphysically modest as it might seem at first glance. To see why, let us consider the quasi-experimentalist approach in a bit more detail than we did in Section 3.7.

Suppose we want to estimate the influence of a variable x_t on an outcome variable y_t. Suppose furthermore that x_t is expected to be correlated with confounding variables W_t: $w_{t1}, \ldots, w_{tk}$ that also influence y_t. So we have an endogeneity problem unless we have a model that structurally represents the parametric relationships among y_t, x_t and w_t – or unless we can find an instrumental variable (IV) v_t that is measurably correlated with x_t but not with W_t and that exerts its influence on y_t strictly through x_t. For example, suppose we allocated a group of addicts to treatment on the basis of their surnames and then ran out of funding for new clinic spaces after the M's had been placed. Then surname could be an IV for the influence of clinic placement on, say, earnings at $t2$.[37] We would estimate

$$y_t = \alpha + \beta_0 + \beta_1' v_t + \theta' w_t + \varepsilon_t$$

where ε is the usual error term we hope is a randomly distributed bundle of variables uncorrelated with anything else in the equation.

If there is any heterogeneity in the response in y_t, to v_t, as there is likely to be in our example, then an estimation based on ordinary least squares regression will be biased. The quasi-experimental methodology here advises us to use the Wald estimator (see Angrist and Pischke 2009, pp. 127–138), since our IV is bivariate and both y_t and v_t are subject to measurement error. If these errors are serially uncorrelated, not correlated with each other, homoskedastic and have finite variance, then the Wald estimator allows us to estimate the average effect of treatment on the addicts.

Economists who have criticized quasi-experimental methodology have pointed out a number of practical difficulties that must be overcome

---

[37] Note that this won't work if our sample is from South Africa, where most Black people's surnames start with M. The ubiquity of worries like this reminds us of the importance of situational knowledge in assessing a proposed IV.

in this sort of case. The conditions on consistency of the Wald estimator are demanding (Wald 1940, Harrison 2011b). Errors must be serially uncorrelated, not correlated with each other, homoskedastic and have finite variance. Wald himself advised against using his estimator for prediction. There will typically be new confounding variables dragged in with an IV, adding to the potential 'sprawl' of causal relationships and non-relationships we need to know something about. But let us set these issues to one side in pursuit of the philosophical point we are after.

Ladyman and Ross (2007) invoke metaphysically minimalist rhetoric similar to that of quasi-experimental methodologists when they say that causation is just influence that changes measurement values (and predicts such changes out of sample). But to think that quasi-experimental method allows one to accurately model the world without resort to structural restrictions incorporates a quite *bold* metaphysical hypothesis to the effect that all causes operating on a given outcome variable are elements of a single vector that is amenable to simultaneous linear estimation. Ladyman and Ross refer to a world that fits that general restriction as 'causally flat.' We then argue (2007, chapter 5) that the world is *not* generally causally flat, and that that is why inter-domain reductions both within and across sciences go through only occasionally. This is indeed approximately equivalent to what we mean when we claim that ontology is scale-relative. Scale-relativity is impossible to represent in a set of linear equations.

As we saw in Section 3.7, if the economist avails herself of economic theory then she doesn't need to resort to Wald estimation with IVs to handle heterogeneity in response variables. She can use mixture modeling instead. Recall that mixture model estimation finds the distribution of weights across the structural theories in a mixture that maximizes the likelihood of observing the data. But of course the economist must decide which models to include in her mixture, and she can never be *sure* that there isn't a better mixture, perhaps including models that no one has yet thought of, which would bring her closer to the true model of the data-generating process she is studying.

With this we bring our philosophical survey of economics up to date. The general conclusions are as follows. Economics has been significantly transformed over the past three decades. The primary contributors to this transformation have been game theory, the emergence of economic experimentation as a mainstream pursuit, and the explosion of computational power that has triggered advances in econometrics. All of these developments, taken together, have allowed economists to build and test more complex models that can incorporate heterogeneity in agents' responses to changes in incentives, to an extent unavailable to previous generations of researchers. Heterogeneity is of crucial importance to markets, because it is the basis for the information asymmetries that make markets dynamic, innovative and creative – and that also creates scope for regulation that improves, as opposed to only stifling, efficiency.

Contrary to widespread talk of paradigm shifts and revolution, these new developments have been built on the theoretical platform inherited from Hicks, Samuelson, von Neumann, Savage, Frisch, Tinbergen and Haavelmo. The core ideas of the most important speculative economists of the previous century, Hayek, Keynes and Schumpeter, have been sharpened into rigorous modeling instruments and vindicated in the most important way an idea can be: by being turned into empirical research programs.

So far, however, we have considered economics largely as if it were a self-contained domain of inquiry. Of course, we should expect the network of conceptual and evidential relationships to be more densely connected within the network than at and across its borders; that is what being a distinguishable discipline consists in. But recall from Chapter 1 that the point of philosophy of science is to unify the naturalistic worldview by identifying ways in which the whole of scientific knowledge goes beyond the sum of knowledge delivered by its disciplines in isolation. From the perspective on economics developed over the past two chapters, let us now examine relations with the neighbors.

4 How Economics and Psychology Differ

4.1 Back to Jevons?

In Chapter 2 we saw that some early marginalists, particularly Jevons and Edgeworth, expected economics to be crucially informed by the anticipated development of a rigorous, axiomatically structured psychophysics. We then followed the progression by which economic theory separated itself from psychological foundations, culminating in RPT and its exclusive focus on observed behavior as the basis for modeling responses to shifts in incentives. But now, we are repeatedly told by excited popular science publications,[1] we live at the dawn of the transformation of our entire collective view of our own thought and behavior by cognitive science, increasingly grounded in neuroscience. A working prototype of the technology of which Edgeworth dreamed, in the form of neuroimaging machines, is finally upon us. Now, it is said, when people make incentivized choices and compare relative valuations of alternatives, we can watch their neurons carry out these operations, and thereby understand them.

In this context it has become fashionable among some scholars, and in the part of the general public that has opinions on economic methodology, to regard the separation of economic theory from psychology as a mistake to be put right (Camerer, Loewenstein and Prelec 2005). Jevons's expectation concerning the most appropriate trajectory of economic theory and method is often taken to be simply *obvious*. As the

---

[1] Examples pulled from a large pool are Thaler (1992) and Ariely (2008). In their wake travels a flotilla of books by financial journalists (e.g., Zweig 2007) explaining why economics that is allegedly better grounded in psychology and neuroscience would help people follow wiser investment strategies than most do.

neuroeconomist Paul Zak (2008, p. 301) puts it, 'Economic decisions are made in the brain, not the toe or the elbow.'

We can extract a generic high-level argument sketch shared by those authors who urge us to take up pitchforks against the long tyranny of Pareto, Hicks, Samuelson and Savage. It goes as follows:

(1) Economists have historically modeled an individual person's choice between competing alternatives as if it were normally consistent, far-sighted, uninfluenced by shifting moods and emotions, and mainly guided by sound estimation of the relative extent to which each alternative would improve or reduce the chooser's lifetime material wealth.

(2) New psychological and neuroscientific evidence shows that most people's choices between competing alternatives are regularly inconsistent, often short-sighted, constantly influenced by shifting moods and emotions, reflect factually inaccurate, statistically unsound and unstable estimations of relative valuations, and furthermore veer unsteadily between prioritizing the chooser's own well-being and emphasizing the implications of the choices for other people, particularly other people with whom choosers are personally related.

(3) Therefore, most conventional economic wisdom is profoundly mistaken, and it is no wonder that economists make false predictions, fail to anticipate collective disasters such as market crashes, and seldom give advice that reliably helps people to become and remain happy or wealthy. If its usefulness and scientific accuracy are to be improved, economic theory must be re-written from the ground up so that its starting assumptions match the actual psychology of real people as reflected in their choices.

A reader of Chapters 2 and 3 of this book should see that premise (1) is a deeply misleading statement about the actual history of mainstream economic thought since Pareto's time. In this chapter we will take up issues relevant to evaluating premise (2) and the conclusion of the argument sketch, (3). But the primary business of the chapter will consist in explaining how the argument depends upon taking for granted a particular set of assumptions concerning what economics *should be* about and *should be* useful for. It incorporates, that is to say, a certain philosophy of economics, in the sense of philosophy defended in Chapter 1: it amounts to a view about how economics should be related to one of its neighboring disciplines, namely psychology.

4.2 The rise of cognitive science and the eclipse of behaviorism

During the first half of the twentieth century, the most influential school of thought in academic psychology, particularly in America, was behaviorism. Behaviorism is not a single, unified doctrine, and the views of leading behaviorists have evolved as their research program has advanced. Some behaviorists have emphasized practical considerations, stressing the need to ground psychological theory in controllable observation and then arguing that hypothesized latent processes generally fail to meet this standard. There has also been a strong strand of conceptually motivated behaviorism, which we can divide into two sub-strands. *Eliminative* behaviorists (e.g., Skinner 1971) argue that the ontology of inner mental processes that contribute to the causation of behavior is a fundamentally confused folk construct and should be replaced by a new scientifically derived ontology based on various kinds of environmental conditioning. *Ecological* behaviorists (e.g., Gibson 1979) argue instead that objects of apparent interior reflection and control are all elaborations on perceptual tracking of information extracted from ecological constraints.

It has been common for accounts of economic theory written from outside mainstream economics to interpret RPT as an application of behaviorism. As discussed in Chapter 2, Samuelson's favored semantic policy was to eliminate the preference construct from economics altogether. This practice would of course match the recommendations of an eliminative behaviorist (Ross 2005). However, as discussed in Chapter 2, although Samuelson interacted with behaviorist psychologists and philosophers, he did not regard them as motivating influences on his development of RPT. The logical order of Samuelson's thought did not begin with psychology and proceed to economics; it started and ended with economics. 'Choice,' for methodologically self-aware revealed preference theorists, has a crucial second property in addition to being relatively directly observable: it involves allocation of scarce resources and so is part of market dynamics. This is directly related to the axiomatic construction of revealed preferences as expressing necessarily *consistent* valuation: only choices at least stochastically respecting this constraint can straightforwardly provide the basis for the coordination of market expectations that emerge as prices and as shared estimations of opportunity costs. By contrast, psychologists never imagined that choices as they understood them must express consistent valuations. According to Skinner, the very idea of choice is an illusion.

In light of this, the most accurate generalization about the relationship between economics and psychology as of the mid-1950s is that their conceptual structures were separate but broadly compatible. Economists modeled incentivized choices, usually at aggregate scales. They defined the concepts of consumer theory using axioms that describe an idealized individual decision-maker, but did not look for or expect to find empirical instances of processes corresponding to such decisions (as reflected in Friedman's methodological doctrine emphasizing 'as if' economic agency). Psychologists, on the other hand, cast their theories in terms of conditioning rather than in terms of deliberation and choice. The mainstreams of both disciplines shared an aversion to theories that postulated latent processes as causes of behavior.

But beginning in the 1960s, and with overwhelming force by the late 1970s, psychology underwent a profound change, typically characterized as 'the cognitive revolution.' Led in the first place from linguistics, but thereafter fuelled mainly by computational models of information processing and later by functional neuroscience, mainstream psychology turned into one of the primary mansions of the interdisciplinary complex known as cognitive science. (For a philosophical history, see, Flanagan 1991.) The ambition of cognitive science is to identify the computational architecture of the mind and to explain behavior as causally produced by that architecture, given informational inputs transformed by the brain into representations formatted for processing by the architecture in question. In this context it became increasingly difficult for economists to go on casually regarding the foundations of economics and psychology as distinct but mutually consistent. New questions began to be asked. Should economists start introducing variables for latent states and processes into their models of the effects of incentive changes on choices? Or should they emphasize reasons for treating cognitive models as black boxes whose contents don't matter when agents are under competitive pressure to conform their behavior to axioms of rationality?

In Chapter 3 we traced the profound impact on economics, from the 1970s onward, of models of asymmetric information, and we saw how this attention to information emerged mainly from intellectual dynamics internal to economics. As we also observed, more and more economists became persuaded of the importance of empirical experimentation. In light of these developments, it is hardly surprising that there has been a steady trend toward acceptance of economic models that incorporate latent processes. However, the blind dynamic of semantic selection in academia operated as if guided by a trickster with a malicious wit. The growing subset of economists who saw themselves as abandoning *behaviorism* in economics became universally labeled as *behavioral* economists!

This forces us, if we are to avoid intractable referential confusion, to engage in some linguistic legislative innovation. Henceforth, I will use 'behaviorism' in the usual way, to refer to theorists, whether economists, psychologists or philosophers, who seek to minimize reliance on hypothesized latent processes. I will refer to economists who *reject* RPT in favor of modeling preference as a latent construct, and therefore as distinct from choice observations, as *behavioralists* or *behavioral economists*. Many economists who conduct behavioral experiments – notably, with respect to economists whose names have appeared in this book, Vernon Smith, Charlie Plott, Ken Binmore and Glenn Harrison – are *not* behavioralists, because they continue to understand preference according to RPT. This does not imply that they reject all recourse to latent processes; none of those just named do so, with Harrison in particular seeing it as one of the key objectives of experimental research to identify such processes.[2] Thus the general class of *experimental economists* denotes a philosophically heterogeneous group that includes both behavioralists and anti-behavioralists. Recently, two well-known economists who model phenomena of interest to experimentalists (e.g., addiction), Faruk Gul and Wolfgang Pesendorfer (2008) have

---

[2] Harrison (private correspondence) stresses here his emphasis on 'weak' (roughly: fit for empirical progress) as opposed to 'strong' (roughly: sufficient to decisively reject a class of powerful model restrictions) identification. See Manski (1995).

vigorously defended behaviorism. This effectively forces them (see, Ross 2011 and Hands 2013) to reiterate Friedman's methodological doctrine according to which the relationship between the restrictions on model domains and empirical reality is irrelevant to the value of a model, and predictive success (in some underspecified sense) is all that matters. For reasons I will diagnose later in this chapter, many economists find this position attractive, even though it can't possibly adequately characterize most actual work going on in economists' laboratories (Harrison and Ross 2010). Thus we have behavioralists (e.g., Camerer, Loewenstein and Prelec), anti-behavioralist behaviorists (Gul and Pesendorfer) and anti-behavioralist anti-behaviorists (Smith etc.). I will promote the perspective of the third group. But discussion will acquire a Monty Pythonesque flavor if I go on labeling their view using the double negation. I will therefore refer to them using a label which I hope will gain the approval of my colleagues in this camp: *neo-- Samuelsonians*. To reiterate the view positively: neo-Samuelsonians agree that latent cognitive processes play roles in generating economic data. But they affirm RPT and interpret preferences as summaries of, rather than causes of, economic choices.

One much publicized behavioralist theme on which I will not spend much time is experimental 'refutation' of the alleged egoism of standard economic theory. The agents of that theory maximize 'their own' utility functions. On one interpretation this statement is tauto- logical: an economic agent is individuated in the first place by a utility function, so there is no logical room for a utility function to 'belong' to any entity but the agent defined by reference to it. However, behav- ioralists often interpret the statement as involving commitment to the empirical proposition that economic agents care only about their own welfare. On that understanding, if utility is in addition interpreted as a psychological magnitude then one can object that people often seem motivated to increase the utility of others, either in addition to or instead of their private gains. This is widely taken to be demonstrated by obser- vations in various experimental games, particularly 'ultimatum,' 'trust' and 'dictator' games in which subjects are tasked with offering money to other subjects under varying conditions.

In the standard ultimatum game setting, Player I is endowed with a pot of money by the experimenter and allowed to choose a proportion to offer to Player II. Player II then chooses between accepting and rejecting the offer. If Player II accepts, then the pot is divided as per the terms of Player I's proposed division. If Player II rejects, the pot is withdrawn and neither player gets anything. Behavioralists typically allege that 'game theory' predicts that Player I should offer only the smallest practical increment – perhaps 1 cent – to Player II, on grounds that 'rationality' obliges Player II to prefer this tiny positive sum to nothing, so Player II will accept and Player I will maximize her reward. Then it is triumphantly reported that in actual experiments with this game, most subjects in the Player I role offer between 20 percent and 50 percent of the pot, offers below 50 percent are sometimes refused by subjects in the Player II role, and offers below 40 percent are usually refused.

Of course, as we saw in Chapter 3, game theory makes no empirical predictions independent of the specification of players' utility functions. The prediction attributed above to 'game theory' is the SPE of a one-shot game in which both players care about money, neither player cares about the other player's welfare or feelings, and Player II attaches no value to demonstrating that he is a proud agent. Ultimatum game experiments show, as if any such demonstration were needed, that this does not describe utility functions operated by most people. There is no axiom in the formal theory of the economic agent, or in any standard formalization of game theory, that stipulates that agents are narrowly selfish in their concerns, let alone an axiom according to which people treat maximization of utility as equivalent to maximization of monetary gains. Some individual economists have perhaps imagined that people are narrowly selfish on the basis of idiosyncratic philosophical theses about human nature; but no such economist could ever have correctly claimed to have derived such a philosophy from economic theory or from evidence analyzed using that theory. According to standard economic theory, any agent i can reveal preferences favoring – or disfavoring – the well-being of another agent j to any extent whatsoever.

Suggestions by populist behavioral economists that they have 'discovered' that people are not narrowly selfish are therefore of no significance. However, some behavioral economists go further and claim to have furnished experimental evidence for widespread *specific* preferences, with specific parametric structure, for social norms of fairness, altruism, and dispositions to defend such norms by bearing costs to punish violators (Fehr and Schmidt 1999; Fehr and Gächter 2000, 2002; Fehr and Gintis 2007; Gintis 2009). Evidence that such utility functions, as observed in specific experiments, generalize to new cases is extremely weak at best (Binmore and Shaked 2010). Indeed, it may be regarded as empirically *refuted* by experiments that some of these very behavioralist authors conducted in small relatively closed cultures around the world. These experimenters found that norms of fairness and altruism – 'social preferences' as they are commonly called – are highly variable and strongly influenced by the forms of production and distribution dominant in the cultures in question (Henrich et al. 2004). Binmore (2010) argues that this finding suggests that in one-shot ultimatum game experiments with less exotic subjects in laboratories, people simply apply the norms they have learned in pot-dividing situations they have encountered outside the lab. This leads them to play a one-shot ultimatum game as if it is a stage of a repeated ultimatum game. SPE is then no longer the relevant solution assumption; and *any* division of the pot that sums to 100 percent is an NE. Binmore et al. (2007) provide rigorous experimental evidence for this conjecture. They introduce a stochastic element to the game, so that players receive their rewards with less than certainty. This furnishes the experimenters with a control lever they can use to vary the feasibility and efficiency of the NE. They then find that they can condition subjects to learn any NE, and that once subjects have been conditioned away from the application of norms they bring into the lab, subjects find efficient NE slowly but relentlessly.

We will revisit this issue in Chapter 5, because it fits more properly into consideration of the nexus between economics and sociology than into a chapter on the boundary between economics and psychology. I have reviewed it here simply because 'the discovery of social preferences' is among the main accomplishments typically attributed to behavioral economics; and so it is important to point out that there is no such accomplishment to credit.

The core psychological thesis from which behavioralists begin is *bounded rationality*. This concept, brainchild of the late Nobel laureate Herbert Simon (1916–2001) (1957), has its direct intellectual origins in the early foundations of cognitive science. No real computational process is instantaneous and effortless, like the idealized computation of prices in Walras's model of market equilibration. Actual computation involves processing stages and consumes scarce resources of time and energy. A rational agent will therefore limit the amount of information processing in which she engages, in consequence of which her choices will typically be based on less than all the relevant information available by ideal inference from the data she could access. Recognition of this fact *inspires* behavioralism but does not *imply* it, since neo-Samuelsonians accept it also.[3]

The next behavioralist step is to follow Jevons and Edgeworth in modeling individuals as optimizers of subjective value under scarcity, but with one or another modification that blocks the road taken by Pareto. Behavioralists modify *either* the standard theory of subjective value itself *or* add a distinctive theory of the optimizing process, *or* both. This leads to a tripartite classification of behavioralism, following Davis (2010). I will consider the three branches in turn, devoting most attention to the first branch because it has been the most influential and also, in my opinion, the one that has generated the most confusion about the boundary between economics and psychology.

4.3 Biases, frames and prospects

The most important behavioralist sub-tradition was pioneered by Daniel Kahneman (1934–), Amos Tversky (1937–1996) and their collaborators (Kahneman et al. 1982; Kahneman 2011). This approach begins by emphasizing that choice problems are processed in finite real time relative to the perceptual *frames* in which they are considered. Frames are dimensional and parameter restrictions on choice problem spaces imposed psychologically by choosers. For example, someone might frame her choice between pizza for lunch and salad for lunch as constrained by the principle 'compare meals that pass acceptability thresholds on taste and price only with respect to their comparative calorie loads.' The 'editing' of the problem so as to restrict the subsequent choice problem to a single dimension of comparison simplifies cognitive load, or at least so behavioralists allege.

Kahneman and his co-authors distinguish between two broad types of response to choice problems. Under emotionally relaxed conditions with low time pressure most people can analyze the comparative consequence of using different available decision frames. Kahneman (2011)

---

[3] For that matter, so do behaviorist economists. But they consider it irrelevant to economics.

refers to this as 'slow thinking.' As the urgency – temporal or emotional or both – of a problem rises, people tend to revert to 'fast thinking.' In this decision-making style, people automatically deploy established frames. These frames may have been entrenched phylogenetically, co-adapted with brain structures by natural selection because of their past frequency of keeping disaster at bay across a wide range of fitness-relevant challenges faced by our ancestors.[4] Or they may have been established by habitual use, having once been chosen by slow thinking in application to similar but non-identical problems. Behavioralists generally associate slow thinking with deliberate decision and fast thinking with automatic pattern matching and pattern completion by the neural networks of the brain.

We may consider an example buttressed by both applied neuroscience research and computational learning theory. Neurons in the mammalian ventral striatal area of the brain can be trained to predict stochastic reward deliverances using a form of conditioned learning known as temporal difference learning, generalized as 'Q-learning' (Sutton and Bartow 1998; Schultz et al. 1997). This allows identified neurons in monkeys, for example, to track changing Nash equilibria (NE) in games with no NE in pure strategies (Dorris and Glimcher 2004). However, this mechanism can serve agents' welfare poorly when the stochastic processes generating rewards are truly random. Ross et al. (2008) argue that the human striatal mechanism cannot learn that there is nothing to learn from playing slot machines. This puts people at risk of gambling addiction, which most people see they should avoid by recourse to slow thinking involving mathematics. Such analysis reveals that the expected value of playing a slot machine is negative. But such thinking is, for many people who enjoy the suspense involved in gambling, and for whom the expected *utility* of a round of slot machine play might therefore be positive, only a necessary rather than a sufficient condition for keeping addiction at bay. Ainslie (1975, 1992, 2001) argues that *framing* choices involving potentially addictive substances as implicating future series of similar choices is also crucial. In a frame where

---

[4] For example, if you detect a long tubular coiled object on the ground in your peripheral visual field, behave as if you believe it's a dangerous snake. By reference to objective frequencies, it probably isn't a snake at all, and if it is it probably isn't dangerous. But the consequences of the false positive error are usually minimal and the consequences of the false negative error might be fatal.

someone is choosing only between presently gambling and presently not gambling, the former might be preferred. However, if the choice is instead framed as between being a gambler *in general* and not being a gambler *in general* the latter might be recognized as having higher utility, and as being incompatible with gambling at any *particular* time, including now. Ainslie's work furnishes the most psychologically and philosophically insightful treatment of the devices by which people manage and regulate the framing of their choices.

Savage's expected utility theory (EUT), as discussed in Chapter 3, assumes frame-independence. Binmore (2009) argues that actual people typically choose according to patterns that stochastically approximate EUT in decision contexts in which expected frequencies of all relevant variables can be estimated with known error, and in which learning has been sufficient to allow intuitive identification of the roughly true EUT model. EUT identification and estimation by individual choosers can be bypassed in problem contexts for which institutions have inscribed cues for cumulative learning by many people. For example, millions of small investors buy sensible stock portfolios, despite doing no research on individual public companies, because they can decode reputational signals and hire investment services that offer sound funds at reasonable transaction fees. However, psychologists typically place experimental subjects in carefully contrived predicaments where they have no solution technologies available to them except their raw brains. Since psychologists are usually interested in the computational capacities of all or part of the brain, this *in vitro* methodology makes sense. In such circumstances it cannot be assumed that most people will choose as if they consistently follow Savage's manual. One alternative possibility is that people in such choice settings simply make what are, from the economist's perspective, random errors. Another general possibility is that they exhibit patterns that can be characterized as systematic bias with respect to accurate statistical representation and preference structures conforming to WARP. The aim of the Kahneman-Tversky research program has been to discover and model such biases.

The most famous of the biases modeled by Kahneman and Tversky are consolidated in *prospect theory*, a model of individual choice that behavioralists typically claim to be more empirically adequate than EUT. The original version of prospect theory, proposed in Kahneman and Tversky (1979), emphasized the distinction between editing and evaluation, as in the example above. Here I will restrict attention to the subsequent form of the theory, cumulative prospect theory (CPT), as offered in Tversky and Kahneman (1992). Because this is an extensional theory rather than a processing theory – that is to say, dropping reliance on stages in a hypothetical computation – it admits much more easily of direct comparison with mainstream economists' models. (Original prospect theory is incompatible with general utility maximization because it allows for violations of the dominance axiom given three or more possible choice outcomes.) For a technical history of prospect theory set within the general context of models of utility functions, see Wakker (2010).

In models of people's choices from sets of alternative lotteries (see Chapter 3), if we impose the assumption that people choose in accordance with the Savage axioms, then we obtain as a robust result that most people are moderately risk averse. This is consistent with a much-discussed fact about financial asset markets, that over timescales of ten years or more equities deliver higher returns than the main alternative, less risky, asset classes: bonds, real estate and cash. In the EUT framework, risk aversion can be decomposed into three components that vary partly independently: aversion to variability in the distribution of returns (*classic risk aversion*), aversion to skewness in such distributions (*prudence*), and aversion to kurtosis in distributions (*temperance*). A superior fit with the rich load of experimental and market data is achieved by adjusting EUT to add *rank dependence* (Quiggin 1982; Yaari 1987), allowing that some choosers, in some situations, choose as if they become more pessimistic about probabilities as the outcomes associated with the probabilities ascend in their preference orderings. Characterized differently, people who choose lotteries in accordance with rank-dependent expected utility theory (RDEU) behave as if they rank order outcomes with respect to whether they do or do not deliver utility or expected utility (respectively) at levels greater than various cumulative thresholds.

One might motivate supplementing EUT with RDEU by reference not only to empirical adequacy but to psychology. It is plausible to think that most people care more about not dropping into utility levels they regard as relatively catastrophic than they care about achieving symmetrically higher utility within various 'comfort zones.' The fact that most economists do not regard introduction of RDEU into choice modeling as a radical methodological departure thus suggests that economists are not entirely insensitive to the importance of achieving a unified view of behavior. However, moving from RDEU to CPT *does* carry us across a methodological fault-line into behavioralism. Why?

Preference structures as modeled by EUT and RDEU are insensitive to the point on the wealth gradient from which other points are evaluated. By contrast, what CPT adds to EUT is RDEU plus *loss aversion*, in utilities or probabilities or both. CPT incorporates the hypothesis that people are more averse to losses than they are attracted to gains that are equal in monetary terms, which in turn implies that they will take greater risks when they frame at least one potential outcome of a choice as a loss than when they frame all potential outcomes as gains. One immediate consequence of this is that a person's utility function is held to be relative to a baseline, or status quo, endowment. Recall from Chapter 3 how the justification of von Neumann-Morgenstern cardinality was constructed without involving reference to absolute magnitudes of utility, by identifying highest-ranked and lowest-ranked outcomes from a set and then calibrating all outcomes in between by reference to these endpoints. CPT ensures consistency of the utility function – that is, avoids dominance violations – by combining two rank-dependent functions, one in the gain frame and one in the loss frame, and then assuming semi-differentiability around zero and comparing the right derivative at zero to the left derivative at zero. One then constructs the CPT utility function by cumulatively iterating RDEU from the top down in the gain frame and from the bottom up in the loss frame (hence the 'cumulative' in CPT). This entails that the overall utility function is extremely sensitive to the location of the point where the two cumulative functions meet, i.e., the reference point denoted by zero. As Wakker (2010, p. 247) notes, 'the global measures of utility loss aversion depend on extremely local properties of utility functionals.'

One can in fact model loss aversion in two different ways, as utility loss aversion above or as *probabilistic* loss aversion. In utility loss aversion we might have

$$U(x) = u(x) \quad \text{if } x \geq \$0$$
$$U(x) = -\lambda u(-x) \quad \text{if } x < \$0$$
$$\lambda > 1$$

where \$0 is the reference point. Alternatively, we could represent differential attitudes to gains and losses if we allow an agent to assign different probability weightings to them, i.e., $\omega(p) = p^{\gamma+}$ for gains and $\omega(p) = p^{\gamma-}$ for losses. But whenever differential probability weighting is *not* allowed for, i.e., when $\gamma^{+} = \gamma^{-}$, then all differences in risk preferences as between gains and losses must be represented by λ.

What, in economic terms, is a reference or status quo point? In some financial market application it might be imagined to be the point at which an actual agent has zero wealth in the world, such that all points below it involve bankruptcy. This can be referred to as the *real loss domain*. But economists are not allowed to run experiments that drive some subjects into bankruptcy. And in any event, CPT is typically appealed to, as we have seen, as a foundation stone for behavioralist interpretations of utility that are frame-relative. Thus in experiments that aim to test CPT against alternative utility models, one must postulate $-\lambda$ or $\omega(p) = p^{\gamma-}$ in a loss *frame*, that is, in a real gain domain that one believes subjects represent as losses within the context of the experiment. Typically, subjects in such experiments are given endowments – often as rewards for some expenditure of aversive effort or some minor intellectual achievement, so that they might hopefully represent the endowments as earned – which might then be partially or wholly given back by the experimenter as outcomes of lottery choices. Then an outcome in which the subject walks away with exactly the endowment is modeled as the reference point.

This kind of procedure seems to depend on heroic assumptions about the extent to which the experimenter can control latent representations of subjects. Might not some subjects, if they are in fact averse to losses, represent their pre-endowment wealth level as the reference point? Might others, perhaps made sophisticated by experience with large investments in volatile asset markets, not identify the loss frame with the real loss domain? Confidence that all subjects' reference points are fixed at the endowment level by the experimental procedure is required by the sensitivity, noted above, of the utility measure to the behavior of the function around zero. Few if any behavioralist experimenters go to any trouble to substantiate the requisite confidence.

It is common in behavioralist pot-boilers for loss aversion to be claimed as an established empirical fact (see, e.g., Zweig 2007, pp. 194–196). However, as Harrison and Swarthout (2013) show, no published empirical study to date has in fact tested CPT against alternative utility models using the conditions that would be required to show that loss aversion is a typical property of human preferences over risky options. That is, no experiment has offered subjects real, salient incentives over both gain and loss frames, and left it empirically open as to whether apparently loss averse responses might stem from utility loss aversion or probability loss aversion. Thus studies that *claim* to have demonstrated the superiority of CPT over EUT have at best shown that revealed human preference over risky alternatives is often better characterized by RDEU; and RDEU does not in itself lead us toward behavioralism.

Policy critics who are convinced that prospect theory provides an empirically correct description of most or all human decision-making do not deny that in competitive markets agents who follow EUT instead will be more likely to end up with more wealth. Many behavioralists advocate 'nudge paternalism' (Camerer et al. 2003; Sunstein and Thaler 2003a, 2003b), according to which policy-makers should aim to create incentives that induce boundedly rational agents to more closely approximate the behavior of unboundedly rational agents where doing so would be 'best for them.' The book by Zweig (2007), deriving advice for investors from behavioral economics and neuroeconomics, is explicitly constructed so as to yield tips for avoiding what is taken to come naturally, but which will result in poor investment decisions, viz., fast thinking.

This illustrates a peculiarity of CPT as (in part) a theory of the utility function. When a person's behavior is characterized in terms of EUT or RDEU, there is no evident basis for saying that the revealed preferences are in any sense wrong *as* generalizations of the person's subjective sense of what is best for her. Of course, these preferences might reflect false beliefs about facts or probabilities. But no one has ever denied that education is, up to a point at least, good for people. Where CPT is concerned, the relativity of preferences to a reference point allows for a different order of correction: the third-party analyst can pronounce on what the person would do if alternatives were evaluated from a different reference point. This makes obvious practical sense given that people's reference points obviously *do* move around with changes of circumstance. You are now young, and decide what your rate of savings should be from that perspective. Reducing your immediate liquidity feels like a loss, so according to the prospect theorist you are more reluctant to part with it than you would be if you followed the advice of Savage. But I, the analyst with an urge to help you, know that when you retire, and review your current options from that future reference point, the consumption to which you by then will have become accustomed will feature in your loss frame, and you will regret that you formerly counted it in the gain frame. Thus I might suppose I can legitimately nudge, or perhaps even force, you to buy some long bonds or an annuity. As far as your present agency is concerned, I thereby side with an ideally maximizing model of you against the model of you that, according to the behavioralist, actually describes you.

Nudge paternalism is controversial even among economists who are convinced that CPT is the most empirically adequate account of most human preference. In Chapter 5, I will indicate my normative reasons for rejecting nudge paternalism, which are independent of the evidence claimed by behavioralists. For the moment, let us note the case of an economist, Gilles Saint Paul (2011), whose normative stance against paternalism combines with empirical endorsement of behavioralism to lead him to reject the soundness of basing personal policy advice on utility analysis. This reminds us that the value of all the uses to which economics can be put is potentially at stake when we assess the claims of behavioralists.

4.4   Frugal heuristics

The school of researchers led by Gerd Gigerenzer (see, Gigerenzer et al. 1999) apply bounded rationality with a still *more* strongly revisionist attitude toward its normative aspect. Their research aims at identifying ranges of problems in which the use of simple heuristic rules outperforms statistical analyzes across relatively subtle variations in the paramaterizations of problems. Statistical models may often over-specify decision problems relative to classes of logical near-relatives. This raises two problems for the practical decision-maker. First, time constraints often make it rationally sub-optimal (perhaps severely so) for the individual to develop a new analysis tailored to the exact parameters of each specific problem. Second, even if time and cognitive resource capacity allowed for this more expensive procedure, ampliative learning and generalization, of the kind embodied in wider-ranging simple rules, would tend to be neglected. Gigerenzer and his co-authors concentrate on common heuristics that, they try to demonstrate, have recurrent applications in wide problem classes. But the most convincing uses of heuristic reasoning are based on idiosyncratic learning and representations.

For example, suppose I'm wondering whether I should buy resource stocks during a period of depressed commodity prices. Someone might try to convince me that my decision should optimally be based on building a detailed valuation model of each stock I could buy. But I doubt that that is true. Even if I were putting enough money at stake to justify the prodigious commitment of time involved in all this research and analysis, I would expect my models to be too sensitive to specific parameterizations in which I'd have low confidence. In fact I do sometimes buy resource stocks, and I do so in hopes of increasing my family's wealth. I use a two-step approach. In step one, deciding whether to buy *any* resource stocks now, I rely, as for all financial asset transaction decisions, on a very general model of market dynamics that I regard as the one best supported by evidence, based on Frydman and Goldberg (2007). If the conclusion of this step is that resource stocks as a class are expected to be profitable within my investment time frame, then step two does not involve considering every available resource stock. I consider only the tiny subset of resource companies with managements I know something about, and which have seemed in the recent past to display the approximate blend of risk awareness and aggressiveness in adapting to market change that I have learned to favor. This two-step process is far from purely qualitative; I need to check various impressions I have against numbers and mini-models of pieces of the general problem. And my heuristic is certainly informed by economic theory.

Behavioralists often strike an attitude toward normative economic rationality that has been spread through scientific and semi-popular culture by evolutionary psychologists. On this view, we can understand the evolutionary pressures that stabilized actual, boundedly rational, behavior in the same way that we understand people's dispositions to eat more fat and sugar than is good for them, or to take extravagant youthful risks while being watched by peers. That is, dispositions that were fitness-promoting in types of situations that were important to the biological fitness of our hunter-gatherer ancestors have stabilized into habits of thought – perhaps supported by evolved features of neural architecture – that are in turn reflected in common heuristics for decisions. These inherited representational structures, it is argued, direct people away from rational optimization in contexts, such as financial asset markets and food courts, in which the special constraints of the ancestral problem setting have been lifted. This attitude comports naturally with nudge paternalism, leading behavioralists to try to identify policies that counteract the residual habits of fast thinking that have become outdated.

The frugal heuristics school, however, distinguishes itself among behavioralists by rejecting this view. Gigerenzer and his group instead emphasize the normative rationality of using heuristics, instead of statistical models constructed with a stress on exact fidelity to objective problem structures. Thus the frugal heuristics criticism of EUT-based or RDEU-based decision theories, to the extent that it is valid, applies with enhanced force against CPT. We noted in the previous section that CPT adds two or three complications to EUT: rank-dependence plus either or both of two forms of loss aversion. In consequence CPT tends to outperform EUT in fitting within-sample choice data because its extra parameters provide more degrees of freedom. (As we saw, though, this advantage evaporates against RDEU.) Critics from the frugal heuristics school emphasize, along with other critics, that the extra flexibility becomes a disadvantage where out-of-sample prediction is concerned (Camerer 1995). In addition, the simpler functional form of EUT is more robust against estimation errors (Hey and Orme 1994). Simple heuristics avoid this criticism by something like stipulation; they are identified on the basis of out-performing (both descriptively and normatively) model-based alternatives within the task domains over which they have been learned.

This points us to the way in which the foundations of the frugal heuristics approach lie in psychology rather than economics. Generalization of the approach depends upon construction of a principled ontology of problem domains, a task which falls to cognitive science. This challenge surfaced in artificial intelligence (AI) over three decades ago as the *frame problem* (Pylyshyn 1987, 1996). Efforts to build general-purpose intelligence into computers kept resulting in designs that either made stereotypically program-bound errors (e.g., the robot's instructions told it that it couldn't walk on water, but not that it couldn't *run* on water) or searched indefinitely large possibility spaces before acting (e.g., verify that your color is irrelevant to how you get across water, verify that the language you speak is irrelevant, verify that the current temperature in Bolivia is irrelevant unless you're in Bolivia, verify that you're not in Bolivia, etc.). AI designers appealed precisely to Simon's reflections on bounded rationality to try to engineer around this dilemma by structuring knowledge into frames. The idea is that when an AI system encounters a problem, it first locates the problem in a frame, which restricts the range of relevant background conditions it must examine in generating and testing a solution. For example: if I must cross deep water using my own body, activate a pre-loaded **swimming** frame. These efforts quickly led to a regress: the frame problem re-emerges one level higher up. If the system's frames are too general they don't help much, and if they're too specific the system needs a great many of them and faces the problem of searching through the big set to determine which one applies to a given new problem.

The frame problem almost certainly has no *general* solution. Every mind that has ever functioned successfully in a dynamic environment is one special solution to the frame problem, customized to that environment. By 'environment' we mean the set of long-standing problem-spaces with which the system has co-evolved. There is no evident reason to deny that there might be unboundedly many such possible solutions, especially as solution-environment matices become complex and incorporate self-amplifying processes.

Insofar as they must rely only on the resources of their own brains, people surely are boundedly rational. And there are strong reasons to believe that in consequence a typical person often solves novel problems by resort to heuristics that represent her current, specific, embodied solution to the frame problem. (As she learns, she will come to embody new solutions.) But if we conceptualize economics as the enterprise of seeking general knowledge about markets, then it is difficult to see how we might be led to more powerful economics by basing it on a research track within cognitive science that explores a problem which likely lacks even a relatively general solution, either theoretical or instantiated. This point might be taken as support for an intuition that economic processes and structures are too irreducibly complex to generally model. It isn't possible to produce a convincing a priori argument against that intuition. (As pointed out in Chapter 1, it isn't possible to produce a convincing a priori argument against *any* intuition about empirical reality.) With respect to any scientific enterprise, the intuition is simply defeatism.

4.5 Preference construction

Behavioralists who apply prospect theory or frugal heuristics accounts presuppose that preferences precede choices. Often they maintain that preferences *cause* choices. In this they reject the neo-Samuelsonian understanding of preferences as generalizations of mutually consistent sets of choices. The standard versions of behavioralist and neo-Samuelsonian modeling approaches treat preference sets as static.

Davis (2010) distinguishes a third behavioralist tradition that is characterized by treating preferences as intrinsically dynamic. Such *constructed preference* models, developed by Lichtenstein and Slovic (2006) and their followers, represent preferences as evolving, path-dependent responses to interactions between frames and the consequences of choices made within them. For example, I enter into the market for a new car thinking that I prefer Jaguars to all other brands. I then learn that, relative to my ex ante expectations, Lotuses are attractively priced. There is no conflict with standard preference theory if I buy a Lotus because it turns out to cost less than a Jaguar. Nor, slightly more subtly, is there any need for revision if the Lotus costs more than the Jaguar, but the discovery about the price leads me to widen the dimensions of the choice set to consider features I hadn't thought would be relevant, such as ease of parking on crowded streets or the comparative quality of the audio systems. But constructed preference theorists ask us to consider more nuanced relationships between representations of choices and preferences. Perhaps I had, ex ante, grouped types of cars into equivalence classes for purposes of comparison. My preference for Jaguars was in fact based on comparing them only with other types I'd considered actually buying. When I discover that the more expensive Lotus is not *so* much more expensive as to be beyond what I regard as a rationalizable quantum of opportunity cost for a car, I compare Jaguars and Lotuses for the first time; and then perhaps I discover, by observing my own choice, that I prefer Lotuses. Most readers will probably not find this description of an imagined psychological process implausible, at least as a folk story. It might be a good account for even a hard-nosed economist to trot out when she comes home unexpectedly with a Lotus and a larger charge on the household credit card than she and her partner had discussed.

Preference construction clearly involves commitment to behavioralism if it is thought, as it sometimes is, to undermine the significance of utility function maximization as a basis for modeling choice. But let us try to hold our hats on our heads in this rather light wind. The modeling value of utility function maximization depends on the *extent* to which preferences are thought to be dynamically unstable. Let us first consider one limiting case: no choice a person makes provides any basis for predicting any other choice they will make. In that case, echoing the point on which I quoted Coleman in Chapter 2, there would be no empirical basis for applying the concepts of preference or choice at all. So now consider the other limiting case: the entire history of a person's choices across her lifetime, from infancy through decrepitude, maximizes one utility function according to SARP (see Chapter 2). No economist, or indeed sane person, would imagine that this could apply to any normal human biography. Evidently, therefore, every possibly useful application of GARP to an individual person's choices is to some restricted temporal window on those choices. Constructed preference theorists can be understood in this context as researchers who compare choices of one and the same biological person *across* boundaries between these windows. (My preferred way of talking about this is in terms of transitions in economic agency within a person; see, Ross 2005.) There is no general reason why this cannot be done using elements of standard, non-behavioralist economic theory, specifically RPT, game theory, and overlapping generations modeling (Ross 2012c). (We need overlapping generations because earlier temporal agents that a person instantiates typically care about the specific welfare of later temporal agents she expects to instantiate, and because later selves inherit the resource stock and interpersonal contractual obligations, debts and credits of earlier selves. We need game theory because the sub-agents a person instantiates interact strategically [Strotz 1956; Ainslie 1992; Ross 2005; Bénabou and Tirole 2004; Fudenberg and Levine 2006].)

This response to the motivation for preference construction is not entirely adequate in itself. With respect to the homely example about car preferences, if I must be modeled as a new agent after I discover such features of myself as liking Lotuses more than I'd previously noticed, then suspicion arises that neo-Samuelsonian method will require modeling me as undergoing at least one shift in agent identity per month, if not more often. That consequence, generalized, seems highly theoretically inconvenient.

This objection points to a broader point, which will merit further philosophical discussion later in this chapter. If an analyst in fact sets out to model the economic agency transitions of a single specific individual, they will generally arrive at more accurate and relevant predictions, and produce more enlightened explanations, from the vantage point of psychology. Carefully designed and tested behavioralist models in the constructed preference literature are examples of this – and they go on being examples of it even if their authors mislabel them as 'economics.' However, when an analyst includes intrapersonal economic agency transitions in her model of a strategically interacting *group* of people, she should avoid idiosyncratic agent construction and should use the tools of neo-Samuelsonian economics. In such contexts it is not only *enough* to assume but scientifically *better* to assume simply that if Lotuses come to cost less relative to the other cars among which market research reveals that consumers generally group them, then there will be higher market demand for Lotuses. I therefore deny that recognition of dynamic preferences necessarily involves one in behavioralism.

That said, Ross (2005) argues that intrapersonal economic agency change, which should be modeled as such, is routinely motivated by forces operating from outside the individual. This will be the subject of Section 4.7. Ainslie (1992, 2001) can be read as offering insightful generalizations about the subjective psychological consequences of such pressures. This relationship illustrates unification – with the economist identifying a phenomenon from one scale of analysis that the psychologist then models at the appropriate *different* scale – without cross-disciplinary reduction. If you want to know whether market dynamics will make it more likely that I, as a statistically identified member of some reference population, will switch from buying Jaguars to buying Lotuses, you should engage in economics. If my spouse is trying to guess whether there might be Lotuses in our household's future, she would be better advised to reflect on the possibility using her knowledge as an expert on my psychology.

4.6 Architectures and mechanisms for bounded rationality: neuroeconomics

The intellectual origins of bounded rationality models unquestionably lie in cognitive science, specifically through the thought and inspiration of Simon and of the psychologist Ward Edwards (1928–2005). Interpretations of the processing or architectural basis of the models have, perhaps in consequence, co-varied with the general evolution of preferred frameworks in cognitive science generally. (That is to say, evolution of the models has been much more heavily influenced by wider trends in cognitive science than by discoveries in experimental economics.) In the 1970s and early 1980s it was common to understand frames and heuristics as arising from the widely proclaimed functional modularity of cognition. Modules, according to the influential account of Fodor (1983), enable fast, automatic thinking, while 'central systems' can in principle optimize – but more slowly – because they have access to all information available through perception and inference. Under the influence of parallel distributed processing ('connectionist') models of cognitive architecture (Rummelhart and McClelland 1986; Clark 1989) that became popular beginning in the late 1980s, these processing associations have tended to be reversed. Now it is common in cognitive science for fast thinking to be attributed to the distributed subconscious completion of patterns from cues by spreading activation in neural networks, while slow thinking is associated with symbolic, serial processing, often supposed to be localized in frontal brain areas.[5] The extent to which mental processing is functionally modularized is a crucial one for models of bounded rationality, since this would provide a possible independent empirical constraint on the identification of boundaries between frames. But we find the opposite of consensus on this question among cognitive scientists, with every logically possible view having at least some distinguished defenders.

More recently, increasing numbers of behavioral economists have embraced the accelerating takeover of cognitive science by cognitive

---

[5] This characterization of a reversal in associations is intended as a highly abstract profile at the 'zeitgeist' level, not as an account of rigorous hypothesis revision by cognitive scientists. Many connectionists have argued that anatomically homogeneous neural networks can support functionally articulated and stratified modules; so there is no inherent tension in hypothesizing that fast thinking is based *simultaneously* on distributed network activation and modularity.

neuroscience. This dominance has come about for three reasons, which vary in soundness. The first, and strongest, basis is several decades of advances in modeling the computation of information performed by single neurons and by connected groups of neurons. The primary empirical ground for this work is direct probing of neurocellular activity in awake non-human animals. This method of data gathering cannot be applied to humans, other than those who remain conscious during brain surgery. However, there are excellent reasons to believe that the general principles of interneuronal communication are the same in all mammals. The second source of the new dominance of cognitive science by neuroscience is the invention of techniques for non-invasive *indirect* observation of neural activity in real time while human experimental subjects perform directed tasks. The most important of these *neuroimaging* technologies is functional magnetic resonance imaging (fMRI), which relies on inferences about neurocellular informational processing in subjects whose heads are placed in strong magnetic fields. Observable changes in the resonance[6] of such fields are correlated with shifts in relative volumes of oxygeneated intracranial blood flow in the subjects. These shifts are in turn related to *some* extent to variations in functional cognitive activity. However, as noted above, different theories of mental architecture make strongly divergent conjectures about the depth and power of this relationship. The third source of neuroscience's status as the queen of the cognitive sciences is the one for which we should have the least respect. The enduring Western metaphysic favors reductionistic, inside-to-outside, causal models over models that involve multidirectional influence propagation across multiple scales of mutually constraining processes. Neuroscience dominates cognitive science for the same philosophical reason that molecular genetics dominates biology (Mitchell 2003), which also contributes to some economists' faith that macroeconomics must have microfoundations. But philosophical habits do not constitute scientific evidence *in any respect*. Metaphysical reductionism is a cultural prejudice, not a general fact.

In and at the boundary between economics and psychology, the expectation of neuroscientific foundations has inspired investment in

---

[6] This refers to the extent to which oscillations in a magnetic field match the spin frequency of the atomic nucleus. The degree of such synchronization determines the absorption of energy by the nucleus from the field.

a group of related – sometimes only loosely related – research programs that are institutionally allied under the banner of *neuroeconomics*. The most convenient tour of this cluster of research programs is provided by Glimcher et al. (2009). Ross (2012d) offers a critical methodological survey. An influential early call for grounding a strongly revisionist, aggressively anti-Samuelsonian behavioralism in neuroeconomics was published by Camerer, Loewenstein and Prelec in 2005. These authors identify mental functions directly with classes of neural computations that are suggested to be localizable in specific brain regions. The neural computations in question are then hypothesized to be the basic causes of patterns of economic choice. This chapter thus stands as among the most frank and unqualified proposals for bolting economics to psychological, and then ultimately to neurological, foundations in the non-populist literature. The extent to which Camerer and his colleagues pre-judge difficult and still open empirical questions about neural architecture is nothing short of breathtaking. Readers familiar with debates in naturalistic philosophy of mind will be equally struck by the brazen confidence of the authors' reductionism. The speculations of this manifesto have nevertheless been frequently reported, especially in popular and cross-disciplinary literature, as if they were well-confirmed facts.

We will take up the relevant philosophical issues in Section 4.8. But first I will summarize what can be said, at a very general level, about the current state of relevant scientific knowledge if one prefers not to let speculation slip free of the constraints of careful observation and rigorous analysis.

Ross (2008b, 2012d) distinguishes two primary sub-programs within neuroeconomics, which can and should be assessed independently of one another.

One program, *neurocellular economics*, grows out of applied computational learning theory. Such theorists recognized in the 1990s that a relatively encapsulated information circuit in the mammalian midbrain, which evolved long before hominids, implements the integration of conditioned learning across sensory modalities. Through reverse engineering from behavioral capacities, scientists inferred that although single-modality conditioning of specialized neurons can be the basis for such processes as perceptual learning in the visual system, a mobile animal that seeks out its own resources must be able to compare the opportunity costs of alternative contingencies that can only be compared along abstract dimensions. For example, food seeking and predator avoidance are typically in tension with one another, and both compete for an animal's attention with cues for mating opportunities. But these contingencies are likely to be tracked by processors of information from different sense organs in different circumstances. The relevance of the conceptual vocabulary of economics to this general design problem is straightforward. When theorists discovered in the 1990s that the neurotransmitter *dopamine* encodes relative abstract reward value by changes in its tonic level and phasic uptake rate in striatal and orbitofrontal areas of the brain (Schultz et al. 1997), they soon began to refer to this chemical as the brain's 'common reward currency' (Montague and Berns 2002). This goes beyond mere analogy mongering if it fruitfully guides formal modeling. The application of the core economic concept of opportunity cost is literal; and since the dopamine reward circuit engages in risky trial-and-error learning, models of capital accumulation also apply. By recording neural firing patterns across striatal dopamine synapses while rats and monkeys performed voluntary choice tasks under controlled reward contingencies, scientists were able to construct a general value function that both describes the conditioning, and identifies it with its neurochemical implementation (ibid; Montague et al. 2006). The neuroscientist Paul Glimcher (2003, 2011) then argued that since standard Samuelsonian economics is the elegant axiomatization of relative valuation response to changing prices, and a natural reward return on voluntary action is therefore a kind of non-monetary price signal, economic theory was the most powerful mathematical framework for generalizing the model of the dopamine circuit.

Glimcher (2011) defines a new modeling target he calls *subjective value* (SV). SVs are real number magnitudes $0 \leq SV \leq 1000$ that scale action potentials per second. In order to make them measurable by fMRI, which can resolve distinctions only between large groups of neurons called *voxels*, SVs are defined as the mean firing rates of voxels. This means that they are linearly proportional to the blood-oxygen-level dependence (BOLD) signals that fMRI aims (successfully or not, as the case may be) to identify. SVs, with finite range ≥ 0 and finite but typically large variance, are encoded cardinally in firing rates relative to a baseline. Glimcher's ambitious empirical hypothesis is that SVs are always stochastically consistent with choice, even when expected utilities are not. The axioms of the theory of SV specify its relationship to GARP. The most important difference is that Glimcher drops the independence axiom of GARP, rendering the theory of SV unsuitable as a basis for aggregate welfare modeling.

Glimcher's hypothesis is the first relatively rigorous formulation of a Jevonsian reduction of economics to psychophysics. It models a quantity, SV, which cannot be identified with neo-Samuelsonian utility but is isomorphic to it in specifiable respects. (It is itself a pending project, waiting for mathematical economists working away from the laboratory, to explore the details of this relationship. For a start see, Caplin and Dean 2009.) Thus the use to which economic theory is put is not merely suggestive and analogical, but substantive. As with the ordinalist utility of the second generation of marginalists (see Chapter 2), it cannot subserve interpersonal welfare comparison, emphasizing the way in which it naturally anchors its value measure in properties of individual agents rather than couplings of individuals and their social environments. It produces a formal cousin-concept to utility that could in principle, and is claimed by Glimcher to in fact be, a *cause* of choice rather than a representation of choice as in RPT.

An important aspect of the neuroeconomic concept of reward is that it is distinguished from hedonic pleasure. This is based not on conceptual analysis but on evidence that reward and pleasure responses are processed in different brain areas (Berridge and Robinson 1998; Berns et al. 2001). The reward system responds positively to some stimuli, such as hot peppers and the taste of alcohol, that are associated with aversion responses in circuits associated with feelings of warmth, sweetness and tactile delight. In general, where reward and pleasure responses conflict, reward is the dominant influence on behavior. This seems to rest on the fact that most people can ignore pleasant distractions if they have incentive to do so, whereas rewarding distractions are highly compelling of attention. For example, many nicotine addicts eventually find the experience of consuming cigarettes unpleasant, but suffer from uncomfortable visceral cravings if they abstain. In light of this, when we say that Glimcher's empirical hypothesis that SV stochastically determines human choice revives Jevons's and Edgeworth's psychophysical understanding of utility, this should be qualified by noting that the Benthamite association of utility with hedonic pleasure is dropped. In consequence, many of the anti-utilitarian polemics by 1930s economists that fed the development of RPT fall beside the point of current debates.

Ross (2012d) indicates other, distinctively contemporary, reasons for skepticism about Glimcher's empirical hypothesis. The most important of these reasons are simply applications of the *general* basis, to be discussed later in the current chapter, for resisting any Jevonsian reduction of economics to psychology or functional neuroscience. Indeed, Glimcher's hypothesis is the most robust target for that general argument. This reflects the fact that Glimcher has, for the first time in the history of economics, produced a version of the Jevonsian program with clear empirical content, so critique need not engage only with shadows.

A major limitation in Glimcher's hypothesis, which he acknowledges (Glimcher 2011, pp. 381–388), is that it seems only applicable to choices that are computed and exercise their behavioral effects through sub-conscious processes operating on short time scales that are not mediated by the agent's use of public symbol-systems for framing and integration of the choice problem. We will further reflect on the implications of this in Section 4.8. In consequence, either Glimcher's hypothesis applies only to one part of the input vector leading to standard economic choices, or he is advancing the radical claim that public symbolic mediation is merely a kind of disturbance field around the core, fundamental engine of choice determination. His rhetoric strongly suggests the second interpretation.

A less damaging, and much less far-reaching criticism of Glimcher's version of neuroeconomics takes aim at its reliance on fMRI. I say that this is less damaging because little of the spirit, or the formal substance, of Glimcher's hypothesis would necessarily have to be surrendered if the populations of neurons with respect to which SVs were measured came to be identified with something other than fMRI voxels, and if neuronal firing rates were measured without intermediation through BOLD signals. Clearly, Glimcher's hypothesis about human choice could not be tested in the absence of *some* means of non-invasively recording human neural activity that allows identification of relationships between specific neurotransmitters and behavioral functions.

But neurotransmitters have a variety of distinguishing properties besides their specific concentration variations in different brain areas, on which identification by fMRI depends. Most obviously, they have different molecular structures. Thus one would have to be implausibly pessimistic about future technological developments to doubt that Glimcher's hypothesis will be able to be re-framed, at some point, with respect to a more robust data-gathering method than fMRI.

A similar defense cannot be offered of the other main strand of neuroeconomics, which Ross (2008b) labels 'Behavioral Economics in the Scanner' (BES). This is the style of neuroeconomics that has captured popular attention and is the main motivation for excited pronouncements on a new basis for financial guidance such as Zweig (2007). BES has spawned a naïve pseudoscience of 'neuromarketing' that purports to be able to 'look into' people's brains and discover the concealed springs of their commercial preferences. Lindstrom (2008) is a popular manifestation, and Zurowicki (2010) an academic one, of exuberant conjecture fueled by frothy combinations of sophomoric philosophy of mind and careless statistical analysis. This populist muck rides atop a wave of dubious articles in the most prestigious of scientific journals, particularly *Nature*, *Science* and *Neuron*. They remind us that the institutions of academic review are imperfect guardians of rigor, especially when interdisciplinarity leaves it unclear as to exactly which methodological constraints authors should be required to respect.

This dubious, largely atheoretical literature is almost entirely based on reports of correlations between, on the one hand, performance by experimental subjects on tasks that try to isolate aspects of comparative reward and/or action valuation and, on the other hand, evidence of differential activity levels in specific brain areas. As a basis for inference, this resembles an alien scientist reporting that, on Earth, low-rise buildings with unusual concentrations of large oval tables and ceiling-mounted PowerPoint projectors are the causes of new policy proposals.

Interpretation of fMRI data involves complex chains of inference: from observed changes in magnetic fields to hypotheses about intracranial blood flow to hypotheses about changes in firing rates in large groups of neurons, all conditioned on background models of relationships between cognitive architecture and processing dynamics.

The relevant inferences are seldom constrained by rigorous econometric principles. In particular, outputs of earlier stages of analysis are frequently treated as if they were data, with standard errors from the earlier stages allowed to drop out of calculations (Harrison 2008). Furthermore, it is universally recognized that the background models of informational dynamics in the brain are at best incomplete. Due to the high cost of scanner time, subject pools are typically tiny by the standards of the best experimental economics, and statistical power is achieved by taking many 'observations' of each brain. This practice amplifies the potential effects of inter-subject heterogeneity with respect to functional neural organization, which appears to be heavily shaped by idiosyncratic learning histories. It is vanishingly rare in this literature for experimental design to be driven by structural models; most of it instead simply consists of enumerating discovered correlations and hypothesizing feigned quasi-causal stories about them using vague relationships such as 'linked to' or 'implicated in.' (See, Ross 2012d pp. 66–69 for an example drawn from BES-style study of the influence of emotions on economic choices.)

These fuzzy hypotheses are frequently arrived at through reasoning that self-critical neuroeconomists (Poldrack 2006; Phelps 2009) have identified as involving a 'fallacy of reverse inference.' This fallacy arises when a neuroeconomist first infers that a particular brain area A was more active than its baseline rate during a subject's execution of a task of type b, then appeals to earlier results showing A to be correlated with some functional process type c (e.g., 'emotional registration' or 'loss magnitude estimation'), and on the basis of all this concludes that the execution of b involves c. This is at least the *kind* of conclusion that might interest an economist, since it potentially informs construction of a structural model of a response function. But it is clearly invalid unless there is independent evidence that A is uniquely selected to support function c. Such evidence exists for some specialized aspects of early-stage perceptual processing and midbrain reward value computation. Such evidence generally does *not* exist for integrative cognitive functions and frontal-cortical brain areas. The distinctively human parts of the brain seem, in general, not to work that way; multiple brain areas are 'implicated' in most tasks, and most brain areas are 'implicated' in multiple functions (Uttal 2003).

Ross (2013c) summarizes what, in my opinion, we can currently regard as empirically well-motivated hypotheses about economic value computation in the brain[7]:

(1) Comparison of the value of alternative short-term, highly stimulus-bound, prospective rewards involves, as a necessary condition, activity in the ventral striatum.

(2) Value computation in the midbrain more generally is closely integrated with comparison of the values of alternative immediate actions, and under some circumstances these computations prime motor responses without close (or perhaps any) governance by frontal areas or areas that are implicated in symbolic or otherwise reflective reporting by subjects.

(3) Midbrain value computation is stochastic rather than deterministic. This in principle eliminates what would otherwise be mysteries about the learning of updated valuations in light of new experience, about the typically graduated nature of such learning (as contrasted with sudden gestalt-type transitions), and about the ability of people and other animals (certainly other mammals) to stay close to optimal response patterns in strategic interactions that require use of mixes of strategies. Existing mathematical and statistical models of this learning usefully answer a number of 'how possibly?' questions but cannot yet be regarded as empirically confirmed general theories. (See, Lee and Wang 2009, and Ross 2012d for some technical details.)

(4) The principal neurotransmitter that implements these mainly striatal computations is dopamine.

(5) Other neurotransmitter activity in orbitofrontal and other more recently evolved areas often inhibits or suppresses dopaminergic control of whole-organism behavioral response. Serotonin and GABA are among these neurotransmitters.

These provisional claims to knowledge have been achieved by the work of the neurocellular economists, Glimcher, Schultz, Montague, Dayan

---

[7] The version of the summary produced here involves some editing and streamlining of the original statement to fit the context of this book. A reader who wishes to closely criticize the summary should consult the uncondensed version.

and others. They are contrasted with a summary of main limitations in understanding of the neuroscience of choice, limitations that almost entirely vitiate the BES research program:

(i) Almost nothing is currently known about the neural processing aspects of computation of comparative values of alternative rewards or actions that depend on symbolic representation of choice problems – for example, choice between financial assets.

(ii) Almost nothing is currently known about the neural basis for computation of comparative values of alternative rewards or actions that are not tightly stimulus-bound or are evaluated over lengthy time scales (i.e., scales of 3 minutes or more, rather than seconds) – for example, choice between brands of automobiles, vacations, academic majors or spouses.

(iii) The roles of various brain regions that appear to interact systematically with the striatal-orbitofrontal reward valuation circuit[8] have not yet been closely modeled, and advances in our understanding of them likely await invention of a more refined non-invasive observation technology than fMRI.

(iv) There is no consensual model of cognitive architecture for reward or action value processing beyond the striatum; and even models of the functional architecture within striatum (e.g, of processing relationships between ventral and dorsal striatum) remain speculative.

It should clearly not be controversial that economic choice by humans requires them to use their brains, and that unified understanding of choice will need to address mutual constraints that economic and neural information-processing dynamics impose on one another. At the present time only the modest precursors to that understanding are in place.

In summary, as of this writing we find a body of neuroeconomics in the BES vein that is not likely to be accepted in the longer-run as based on good science. Neurocellular economics, on the other hand, has allowed for specification of a testable version of Jevons's conjecture.

---

[8] The extent of aptness of the 'circuit' metaphor for value processing pathways is itself open to interrogation.

The version has not yet been tested against a range of human choices. I would be surprised if it passes most such tests when they are eventually performed. Were it to do so, the neo-Samuelsonian philosophy of economics would necessarily give way to a variety of behavioralism.

4.7 Intertemporal preference stability

It is widely believed among behavioralists and their audiences that people in general discount future value *hyperbolically* rather than *exponentially*. If people are assumed to have additively separable intertemporal utility functions, then this predicts that people will either tend to reverse preferences as points of reward consumption become closer in time, or will have to exercise strategic self-control to preserve consistency if this is something they value (perhaps because they are in an environment where competing agents will try to take advantage of their inconsistency to cause them losses). The most important theorist of hyperbolic discounting, George Ainslie (2012), thinks that it is of limited importance to economics because people usually do exercise strategic self-control in market contexts, especially markets in which values are captured by monetary prices. However, it is much more common for behavioralists to claim that most or many actual human choice patterns, both inside and outside market contexts, are non-exponential and under suitable framing manipulations will reveal temporally inconsistent preferences.

Samuelson (1937) originated the linear intertemporal discount function that has been standard in economics ever since. This is given by:

$$v_i = A_i e^{-kD_i} \tag{1}$$

where v_i, A_i, and D_i represent, respectively, the present value of a delayed reward, the amount of a delayed reward, and the delay of the reward; e is the base of the natural logarithms; and the parameter $0 > k > 1$ is a constant that represents the agent's idiosyncratic attitude to the effect of time on the reward's value. A higher value of k implies steeper discounting, that is, a greater negative effect of time on value. Samuelson did not claim that this function was based on empirical evidence, or even that it is a plausible empirical generalization about people. Instead, he took it to be of interest because it lends itself to soluble representation of policy alternatives. No matter how strongly present-focused an agent might be, choice-behavior in accordance with (1) is intertemporally consistent: whatever preferences she has at the time of choice will remain her preferences at a later time of consumption.

Against this benchmark we can raise questions about how best to model a variety of common behaviors in which preferences seem to reverse merely because the time of consumption moves closer to the present. Many people prefer at time t_1 that at future times $t_2, ..., t_n$ they will not drink alcohol to excess, make reckless impulse purchases, underinvest in their pensions, or procrastinate. Then, when temptations of these kinds arrive, they choose in ways that seem to conflict with these earlier preferences. Of course, an economist interpreting preference according to RPT will want to see more by way of evidence for reversal than the agent's mere verbal forecast at t_1 of her later preferences. But addicts, for example, often do spend resources to make later addictive consumption less likely, then undo this attempted commitment when the crunch comes. It is not open to serious doubt that most people wrestle, at least from time to time, with some self-management problems of this kind.

The history of debates about intertemporal preference consistency has involved both economists and psychologists for over half a century, and provides fertile ground for exploring the complexities of the interdisciplinary relationship – the proper role, as I have stressed, for the philosopher of economics. It was an economist, Robert Strotz (1956), who drew attention to a fact, long recognized by novelists, that people cultivate strategies for managing their own predictable changes of preference. The main point of Strotz's analysis was that intertemporal preference consistency is only assured by an exponential discount function. Another economist, Nobel laureate Thomas Schelling (1978, 1980, 1984) described the subtle self-management of motivations and opportunities in the implementation of such personal policies as initiating and maintaining abstinence from smoking. For example, a smoker might promise to pay fines levied by his friends and family if they caught him smoking. Were people generally accurately modeled as intertemporally unified economic agents who discount exponentially, such self-manipulation would make no sense. The terms of

Schelling's discussions are similar to those of the experimental psychiatrist George Ainslie (1975, 1992, 2001). Ainslie has placed greatest stress on the importance of achieving self-control through a variety of framing he refers to as *reward bundling*. For example, if an agent faces a choice between going jogging in the wind and rain today or staying inside with a cup of cocoa, the latter alternative might appear clearly utility maximizing. But this choice might be taken by the person as predicting that she will never jog in bad weather, which would appreciably impair her preferred fitness regimen. If she therefore frames today's choice as being over the alternatives 'be the sort of person who jogs every day come what may' and 'be the sort of person who jogs only when it's nice out,' she may choose to brave the elements. Ainslie (1992) coined the term *picoeconomics* to refer to the study of these framing dynamics, which he joins Schelling in modeling as bargaining games among 'interests' that compete for control of a whole person's behavior.

Ainslie accounts for preference ambivalence on the basis of a drastically modified representation of the personal discount function. Based on experimental work with pigeons, Ainslie (1992) argued that the default intertemporal discount function for animals, including people, is given not by the exponential function (1) but by a hyperbolic function as described by (among other variants found in the literature) Mazur's (1987) formula (2):

$$v_i = \frac{A_i}{1 + kD_i} \tag{2}$$

This function is referred to as 'hyperbolic' because it is steeper close to the point of choice and flattens with respect to points further out into the future, with its change of slope describing a hyperbola. Hyperbolic intertemporal discounting is compatible with intertemporal preference reversals when agents choose between smaller, sooner rewards (SSRs) and larger, later ones (LLRs). A pair of temporally spaced rewards a $[t_1]$, b $[t_2]$ for which the person's ordinal ranking is $b > a$ at a point t_2 in the future, relative to the current choice point t_1, where the slope of the discount function is relatively gentle, may swivel into the relation $a > b$ as t_1 moves into the past and the temporally approaching t_2 slides up onto the more immediate part of the curve where discounting is steeper.

Here b is an LLR – say, reviewing one's investment portfolio – and a is an SSR – for example, watching a movie.

Ainslie refers to the equilibria people sometimes achieve through bundling, which allow them to choose as if they were exponential discounters, as *personal rules.* A demanding such personal rule would be a ban on all unproductive entertainment when any LLRs are in competition with this kind of SSR. However, Ainslie argues that this is unlikely to be an equilibrium policy because it will tend to make enjoyment of entertainment impossible always, which will cause the person's interest in relaxing to 'rebel' and overthrow the rule. A more stable alternative rule might allow entertainment only after 9 pm each evening. Even this rule might fail to be enforceable if it does not allow for loopholes, e.g., attractive invitations by friends or romantic partners to events beginning at 7 pm. But this in turn creates a higher-order picoeconomic problem, rationalization of loophole widening – for example, actively sending hints that an invitation would be welcome. According to Ainslie, there is no permanent, general solution to the problem of operating personal rules; there are merely varying degrees of stability in practice.

Most commentators on Ainslie's work (e.g., those represented in Ainslie 2005) find this third-person phenomenology to be consistent with everyday experience. One can nevertheless ask whether a coherent modeling approach results from borrowing tools from economics to represent it.

At some qualitative level the prospects for interdisciplinary conceptual and modeling unification offered by picoeconomics seem promising. The state of a person who governs her choices using a stable personal rule that causes her little anxiety and needs minimal effort to maintain has illuminating elements in common with a well-adapted regulatory framework that coordinates agents in games and allows them to get on smoothly with joint projects. If a person believes that 'her brain' discounts hyperbolically, then she might also believe that maintenance of her personal rule guards her against choices that would undermine her long-range well-being. In this case her confidence in her personal rule has the characteristics of a valuable capital investment. If the rule is broken in the immediate instance, then this asset is damaged or destroyed in the present, where the picoeconomist models discounting as steep, and so the value of keeping the rule intact might dominate the value of the competing SSR.

The economist will struggle, however, to take Ainslie's economic metaphors literally, in the sense of incorporating them into formal theories for use in specifying tests to identify relationships among experimentally controllable variables. A first problem is that the value functions implied by hyperbolic discounting do not necessarily converge as new behavioral data are observed. In such cases a model cannot be used to restrict econometric estimation. Second, according to Ainslie, hyperbolic discounting is a latent process, since he claims that it characterizes a person's underlying dynamics of valuation even when she governs her behavior by reference to a personal rule that makes her actual choices consistent with exponential discounting. RPT is not compatible with this kind of separation between interior and observed preference.

Behavioralists who have no allegiance to RPT are of course not troubled by this concern. Indeed this is among the most important sites of difference between the behavioralist and the neo-Samuelsonian. However, as economists, behavioralists *are* motivated to address the first problem with picoeconomics, intractability to asymptotic estimation, identified above. Models due to O'Donoghue and Rabin (1999, 2001), Bénabou and Tirole (2004) and Fudenberg and Levine (2006) follow Ainslie in modeling varieties of intertemporal preference ambivalence by analyzing people into complex communities of sub-personal economic agents. These models facilitate asymptotic estimation by resort to an alternative form of discount function called 'quasi-hyperbolic' or 'β – δ,' which was borrowed from Phelps and Pollack (1968) and applied to individual agent modeling by Laibson (1997). This class of functions is expressed by

$$v_i = A_i \beta \delta^D \tag{3}$$

where v_i, A_i and D retain the interpretations as from (1) above, β is a constant discount factor for all delayed rewards, and δ is a per-period exponential discount factor. Where β = 1 the equation reduces to standard exponential discounting. Where β < 1 discounting is initially steeper up to some inflection point, then flattens. β – δ discounting predicts that value drops precipitously from no delay to a one-period delay, but then declines more gradually (and exponentially) over all periods thereafter.

A widely publicized recent claim, often reported as a fact in populist behavioralist accounts, is that β and δ discounting is implemented in distinct groups of neurons in the human brain. The evidence cited for this is a 2004 fMRI study by McClure et al. However, Glimcher et al. (2007) designed an extension of the study that the authors argue to be more consistent with Ainslie's view that neurons in general implement hyperbolic discounting. For reasons I will review in Section 4.8, I think that this interpretation of the data needs important qualification. But even if we set neuroeconomics to one side here, we can still ask whether β – δ discounting is a useful approximation of the hyperbolic discounting model that gets around the asymptotic convergence problem through a technical patch.

In experimentally comparing alternative discounting models, recognition of the likelihood of heterogeneity of utility functions in empirical choice samples should caution us against running 'horse races' that are designed to declare one model the winner and another the loser with respect to performance in estimating a data set. This point was noted earlier with respect to experimental estimation of risk preferences, and it applies even more clearly in the case of discounting functions. Hyperbolic and quasi-hyperbolic models typically have more degrees of freedom than exponential functions, in which cases horse race designs will be biased against the latter. As with the risk preference work discussed in Section 3.7 above, we should instead favor use of mixture models or other methods that allow identification of different coexisting forms of discounting in choice data sets. Sopher and Sheth (2006) and Andersen et al. (2011) have performed SSR/LLR choice experiments on groups of subjects and then analyzed the data using such techniques. The heterogeneity these studies detect allows for two interpretations. Perhaps, on the one hand, there are different types of subjects, where each type always discounts according to one of functions (1), (2), or (3) above respectively. On the other hand, perhaps most or many subjects each discount in accordance with different functions under different circumstances.

Sopher and Sheth, comparing only exponential and hyperbolic discounting in their data, find little support for hyperbolic discounting. They do, however, report a substantial proportion of variance they attribute to 'error.' Andersen et al. (2011), in a sample of 413 Danish adults choosing between cash lotteries, estimate a mixture model that finds the maximally likely proportions of exponential, $\beta - \delta$ and smooth[9] hyperbolic discounting. They find that by far the largest share of the choices are best modeled as exponentially discounted, while a small subsample is best modeled by the hyperbolic function and no subsample is best modeled by the $\beta - \delta$ function. Such hyperbolic discounting as Andersen et al. do pick up is not significantly steeper than the median rates among the exponentially discounted choices. Andersen et al. also re-analyze data from previous studies that reported hyperbolic discounting. This reveals that support for hyperbolic models is confined to studies that used university students as subjects. This might lead one to speculate that students impose a distinctive framing on SSR/LLR choices because of the ecologically unusual differences between their expected present and future wealth levels. Another possible (not mutually exclusive) hypothesis would advert to unusual integration of experimental income with background wealth among students because their reserves are supported up to security thresholds by family resources or student loans that do not straightforwardly trade off against other earnings.

These results arise in the context of an earlier insight and empirical demonstration by the same group of researchers. For any functional form used to model intertemporal discounting, pooled rates across samples will appear to be vastly steeper than they really are if allowance is not made in estimation for the fact that most people are risk averse. Andersen et al. (2008) introduce and demonstrate, in the context of a real experiment, a technique for jointly estimating subjects' intertemporal discounting rates and the curvature of their utility functions over uncertain monetary outcomes. Consequences in terms of magnitudes are dramatic: average discounting rate estimates fall from 25.2 percent per annum without controlling for utility curvature to 10.1 percent with utility curvature jointly estimated. Subsequent measurements by the same authors in other samples (e.g., Andersen et al. 2011) have yielded even stronger contrasts. This dissolves what Ainslie (1992) had long identified as a puzzle for hyperbolic discounting models. Despite the drumbeat of reports by behavioralists that their experimental subjects manifest extreme preferences for present over future consumption,

---

[9] They use a specification due to Read (2001) and descended from Mazur (1987).

monetary interest rates in most countries remain in the moderate range of 1 percent to 10 percent per annum most of the time.

Thus I cannot agree with most behavioralists that the stylized fact that people discount future rewards hyperbolically, or even steeply, is supported by the most careful economic experiments. It must be noted that this does not necessarily embarrass Ainslie, who has avoided associating his theory with behavioralist dogma. If, as Ainslie proposes, most people have developed effective personal rules, then they should be expected to intertemporally bundle SSRs and LLRs and therefore to choose as if they were exponential discounters. Ainslie's thesis is in fact that hyperbolic discounting is latent but infrequently expressed in choices involving significant stakes, except in pathological cases such as addicts choosing between immediate rewards to which they are addicted and later rewards to which they are not.

On its face, Ainslie's hypothesis looks to be incompatible with RPT. Insofar as an individual utility function is derived from choices over monetary rewards, one such function differs from another mainly with respect to risk preference and time preference structure. In that case, by RPT, if a set of choices is best modeled by a function that incorporates exponential time discounting then we have no basis for positing latent hyperbolic discounting. I said in Section 4.2, however, that neo-Samuelsonians are not behaviorists, and do not deny that data-generating processes they model involve latent cognitive operations. The difference between the behavioralist and the neo-Samuelsonian here is that the latter will not build non-exponential discounting into a utility function unless this is manifest in choice. The observed evidence for latent hyperbolic discounting to which Ainslie appeals is self-commitment behavior and other actions apparently designed to establish and maintain personal rules. In my opinion it adds nothing to the rigor of picoeconomics, and invites methodological confusion, to label a latent tendency to frame choices myopically as a kind of 'discounting'. After all, the well-developed formal model of discounting fits it awkwardly at best. Is there any reason to believe that there is any such phenomenon as 'discounting' that is independent of modeling construction? Some behavioral patterns, manifest in choice, are usefully generalized by discounting models. Why insist on roping in other behavioral patterns that seem better generalized by different – psychological rather than economic – models?

One answer to this question is given by Glimcher et al. (2007) when they claim to have found evidence of groups of neurons that compute hyperbolic discounting functions. Note that this attribution, running as it necessarily does beyond relatively theory-neutral observation, is rendered into a serious methodological proposal by the *combination* of the empirical data (if we put aside doubts about the reliability of functional inferences from BOLD signals) and the theory of SV that Glimcher (2011) uses to embed the data. Recall that Glimcher's empirical hypothesis that choice is determined by neural processes that compare SVs provides a testable and non-metaphorical basis for a Jevonsian unification of microeconomics and psychology that would reduce the former to the latter. As with all such reductions in science, Glimcher's requires conceptual revision of elements in the model being reduced. In theories incorporating RPT, utility cannot be a *cause* of choice, since a utility function merely generalizes properties of a set of choices (Binmore 2009). SV, the construct to which Glimcher proposes to reduce utility (minus, as we saw, its independence property), is explicitly claimed to be the core causal factor for choice.

The above dialectic offers Glimcher's robust causal preference theory as a basis for defending Ainslie's use of an economic concept, discounting, to model a family of latent psychological phenomena. Interestingly, Ainslie himself (2013), resists this way of 'rescuing' his semantic preference for 'discounting.' The divergent sub-personal interests that give rise to picoeconomic dynamics are, according to him, *virtual*, and should not be identified with specific neural assemblages. I agree with him about this. Furthermore, I think that the general philosophy of mind reflected in Ainslie's resistence to neuroeconomic reduction of picoeconomics is crucial to articulating a general view of the relationship between economics and psychology that, in turn, justifies neo-Samuelsonian rejection of behavioralism. I turn now, and for the remainder of the chapter, to these overtly philosophical issues.

4.8 Ecological rationality, externalism and the intentional stance

In Section 4.6 we noted that, as recognized by Glimcher (2011), comparisons of the values of symbolically represented, relatively abstract rewards delivered over complex time schedules seem to require a more complex model of cognitive processing than comparisons of relatively tightly stimulus-bound rewards. Given a choice between chocolate and vanilla ice cream I usually take vanilla, and always do so if there's a sauce to pour on it. It is plausible that this computation can be managed largely or entirely by a midbrain reward valuation circuit that my brain shares with brains of animals that don't traffic in symbolic representation. The suggestion seems much less plausible when the choice under consideration is between whether to accept one job offer or another, whether to tell a student that her thesis is ready for submission or that she should run a few more robustness tests, or whether to authorize removal of life support for an unconscious terminally ill parent or engage in low-probability search for interventions that might offer a bit more decent-quality life. These three decisions are all ones that I wouldn't try to make without quite a lot of explicit *talking*, both with other people and to myself. The most important aspects are relatively abstract. It is doubtful that I could represent them at all, let alone set out to comparatively value them, if my cultural environment didn't provide a stable semantic field for referentially identifying and re-identifying them. In this respect the decisions are embedded in basic social institutions. (They are also embedded in secondary, specific, social relationships: I'll discuss choice 1 with my wife and friends, choice 2 with other members of the student's supervisory committee, and choice 3 with relatives and doctors. But this level is in principle dispensable. The basic level is not.)

Models in psychology and functional neuroscience – henceforth, for brevity, 'cognitive science' – tend to begin with information processing at the level of individuals, implicitly treating outputs of such processing as potential inputs to social interactions. (Of course, all cognitive scientists recognize that social interactions feed back into individual thought.) Economists marinated in the rhetoric of methodological individualism, when asked to describe their methods in philosophical terms, typically say that they take the same approach. But I think that this answer is based on a lazy tendency to not reflect carefully on what they, as economists, actually do. (The typical answer sometimes also reflects allegiance to ideology. But ideological reasoning is just a special kind of cognitive laziness.)

Most data that economists gather, analyze and model are aggregate data: market prices and volumes, or changes in rates or in rates of change of new hirings or asset purchases or patent applications or college loans or manufactured exports, etc. As my examples indicate, this is true in microeconomics as well as in macroeconomics, where it is obvious. Economists regard these representations as appropriate dependent variables for *their* attention, rather than for the attention of other kinds of scientists, because and strictly to the extent that the representations are regarded as subject to choice. What this means in practice is that economists take the variables to be sensitive to changes in relevant incentives – typically shifts in opportunity costs at the market or population level. It very seldom means – again, *in practice* – explicitly represented and individually computed triumph of one alternative over others. By contrast this typically *is* what choice means, in practice, in cognitive science – and, crucially to a main issue of the present chapter, in behavioral economics.

This point is profoundly obscured by the fact that, under the vital influence of Savage (see Chapter 3), economists are trained experts in idealized models of rational decision that are rhetorically, but casually rather than formally, associated with stylized individual people. The words 'casually' and 'stylized' refer to the fact that most economists aren't, and don't want to be, philosophers, even in the limited sense of philosophy I have defended. (That is, they don't worry very much about the relationship of economics to other disciplines.) If pressed to explain the 'deep' causal basis of choice at the level of markets or populations, they are likely to appeal to models of individual decision-making. This can lead easily to a very portentous assumption that *stability* and *informational efficiency* of population-level choices in markets arises from the *rationality* of individual decisions. To economists with these intellectual habits, reports by cognitive scientists that individual people's decisions are heavily influenced by idiosyncratic and 'irrational' framing effects will seem to be obviously on topic, and, if true, to portend a paradigm shift away from commitment to 'rationality.'

This leads directly to the sort of tension we encountered in Section 4.7. If most people frame their individual choices in a way that leads to hyperbolic discounting, why aren't most interest rates in the neighborhood of 1,000 percent or more? These are the sorts of rates implied by the discounting experiments typically emphasized by behavioralists.

Neo-Samuelsonian philosophy of economics blocks the above slide into behavioralism by avoiding the lazy assumption that market efficiencies are typically or necessarily products of individual rationality. Binmore (2009) reminds us of Savage's insistence that his decision theory cannot be used to successfully track the consequences of incentive changes in what he calls 'large worlds' – that is, environments dominated by uncertainty about probabilities and probability structures. The kinds of markets in which Savage decision theory gains straightforward purchase are 'small worlds,' in which institutionalized constraints tightly limit agents' goals and narrow the domains of the beliefs and conjectures that matter to their actions. The leading example of a small world for the applied economist is a market with a small number of participants known to all, mechanisms for clearly transmitting price information on the basis of offers and sales, and rules that incentivize participants to reveal private information. The modern theoretical tools for modeling and studying such markets were reviewed in Chapter 3.

As was also discussed in that chapter, since the expansion of their toolkit provided by game theory, modern information processing capacity and richer econometrics, economists have become increasingly interested in worlds that are not small in Binmore's sense. Macroscale labor markets, coalition-formation markets driven by politics and regulation (the main source of determinants for international trade), markets for innovation and entrepreneurship, financial markets, insurance and risk management markets – all of these abound with uncertainty. Savage decision theory is vital to modeling them because it provides the bedrock we must modify as we introduce factors that represent responses to the uncertainty. Binmore's point, however, is that in such markets we are likely to go badly wrong if we expect outcomes that are Nash equilibria of games among individual Savage decision-makers each successfully comparing their expected utilities under every possible strategy vector. Nevertheless, complex large-world markets *do* present sufficient stability and regularity to provide traction for informative economic analysis. What explains this, if modeling each participant as a Savage decision-maker does not?

The answer given by the neo-Samuelsonian Nobel laureate Vernon Smith (2008) appeals to 'ecological rationality.' Smith attributes this idea, with justice, to Hayek. But it has best been articulated by an anthropologist, Edwin Hutchins (1995), and a philosopher, Andy Clark (1997). Clark's account is particularly relevant in the present context, because it rests on deeper themes in the relationship between psychology and attributions of rationality that are essential to a fully adequate philosophy of economics. The themes in question were first explored in detail by philosophers Daniel Dennett (1969, 1978, 1987) and Tyler Burge (1986), and have since become the mainstream view in the philosophy of mind and cognitive science (Ross 1997, 2013b). I refer here to a doctrine about the meaning of the semantics of thought known as *externalism*. These two philosophical theses, ecological rationality and externalism about the mind, can be synthesized to construct an understanding of economic agency as an *interface pattern*, following terminology introduced in Chapter 2. Specifically, such agency is the pattern that arises when individual human minds are embedded in market structures.

I will begin with ecological rationality. As Hayek articulated most clearly and forcefully, a human society is a massive distributed information processor. Its evolutionary dynamics continuously produce structures that help individual people, households and small associations to coordinate their behavior, and the structures in question are reproduced and maintained *because* they do that. Consider, for example, the care that is paid to maintaining stable, shared names for bits of functional geography such as streets, towns and lakes. Much more subtly, every participant in a modern market society is continuously told how to shop by the rigorously controlled infrastructure of the retail environment, which encodes a multitude of behavioral expectations. Rationality of consumers' behavior is largely maintained by the simple punishment signal of social disapproval of behavior that others can't quickly recognize as within the bounds of expectation. Scarcity, competition and the need to coordinate then generate institutions that tether these bounds of expectation to relative efficiency.

Consider an example that is of fundamental economic importance. In modern asset markets, most small individual investors maintain reasonably well-diversified portfolios – some safe stocks, some riskier stocks, some bonds, some cash and some real estate – despite doing little or no research on factors underlying asset values, and being incapable of performing the relevant calculations if they did do such research. Instead they take crude advice from asset managers. These people are themselves functionaries, not creative modelers, but they have relatively refined institutional scaffolding (e.g., Bloombergs, recommendations emerging from analysts' meetings etc.) to which they have first-order access relative to their clients. If the system were strongly hierarchical, with a single master source of unmediated information that institutionalizes expectations by passing commands and data down a linear chain, it would not be so theoretically interesting; individual rational optimization would simply be traced back to the wizard at the origin point. Hedge funds to some extent really do work this way; but they are atypical. In most market-management institutions knowledge and expertise are diffuse and the primary response channel is simply copying of observed choices, with some experimental variation that is driven by the goal of increasing wealth. That slender tether is sufficient to maintain widespread basic economic rationality as long as the institutional constraints don't disintegrate.

Of course, that economic institutions keep chaos at bay does not imply that they converge to efficiency frontiers. In late 2008 the world was reminded of the distributed nature of ecological rationality in asset markets when CEOs of major financial institutions generally turned out not to understand the investment strategies of which they had been the legally responsible administrators. Large groups of people coordinated by institutional scaffolding do not produce global dynamic rationality in the sense of becoming optimally insured against systemic risks. At any given time some piece of scaffolding that, in retrospect, might have transmitted information about a threatening system failure might have failed to evolve. Distributed choice structures thus do not achieve the miracle of generally *solving* the computationally intractable problem of large worlds that formal rational decision theory cannot; but they enormously loosen the constraints of bounded rationality through massive redundancy of information storage and experimentation.

We will return to the large-scale social dynamics of markets in Chapter 5. For the moment, our focus is on the scale of individual behavior where economics meets psychology. Many economists who have not reflected on the philosophy of psychology will be inclined to say at this point that market institutions, by entrenching individual people in networks of mutual expectations and inducing them to reveal private information, cause people to respond to changes in incentives *as if* they had broadly consistent and complete preferences and beliefs. In fact, this common philosophizing typically continues, their actual preferences and beliefs are a jumble of confusion and contradiction. At this point the economist can move in one of two directions methodologically. On the one hand she might claim that the latent confusions and contradictions will tend to statistically cancel out, allowing her to abstract away from them and ignore psychology. This economist will proceed operationally as if eliminative behaviorism prevailed, that is, as if 'real' preferences and beliefs simply don't matter to economics. This is the methodology of Gul and Pesendorfer (2008). Another economist might alternatively think that she should refine her models by endogenizing *systematic* aspects of latent preference inconsistency and missing or false beliefs, so that she can ground her accounts of phenomena at the market/social scale in generalizations about individual people. This is of course the philosophical path that leads to behavioralist methodology.

I think that this methodological fork represents a false dichotomy. It rests on an assumption that preferences and beliefs are *internal* states of people that have existence and meaning independent of social and institutional context and which should be studied in the way that psychologists and neuroscientists generally do, by isolating people in labs and 'looking inside.' But the most common perspective in the philosophy of mind, externalism, denies this assumption. Just as economic agency denotes an interface pattern between minds and markets, so the mind itself, as understood by externalists, is an interface pattern that describes systematic relationships between brains and socially related people.

During the first few years in which researchers first started referring to themselves as cognitive scientists – roughly from the mid-1970s to the end of the 1980s – it was common to model the human mind by very close analogy to first-generation computer architectures. That is, it was often supposed that mental operations were rule-based computations over objects individuated by a syntactically structured neural code, often referred to as 'the language of thought' (Fodor 1975). Philosophers and artificial intelligence researchers engaged in heated, largely a priori, debates over how this syntax supported a semantics – i.e., how it was meaningfully related to objects external to the thinker and to actions (see, Pinker and Mehler 1988). Most proposed solutions to this problem assumed that the mental program operates on *propositions* – representations of states of affairs that could be true or false, such as 'Muskrats are large water-dwelling voles' or 'Economic methodologists are extravagantly paid' – by making them the objects of *mental attitudes* such as beliefs and desires. Thus my attitude to the phylogeny of muskrats consists in bringing the first proposition within the scope of a belief operator, while the second proposition might fall within the scope of a desire operator in my mental ecology and its denial within the scope of a belief operator (alas).

It is important to note that most advocates of this computer model of mind were not reductionists. Specifically, they typically argued that various neural states could implement any given propositional attitude under different – but regulated – circumstances. Thus the mind was regarded as software that runs on the hardware of the brain. This furnished philosophers with a satisfying story about the *ontology* of the mental, according to which minds are not identical to brains but are virtual objects implemented in brains. The principle that different pieces of neural hardware could support the same or similar mental software allowed philosophers to understand how two agents with different brains could be said to share the same belief: each applies their syntactically distinct belief operator to a respective class of neural events, in each respective brain, that have common semantics because they play similar computational roles in the overall mental programs of the two thinkers.

This *internalist functionalist* philosophy of mind is not sufficiently precise in its empirical claims to be subject to scientific confirmation or refutation. For many philosophical purposes it remains a serviceable metaphor. But taken very literally it has a consequence that could be empirically investigated by cognitive scientists, namely, that beliefs and desires expressed using natural languages should have discrete, identifiable analogs in brains that neuroscience could identify. Suppose in this philosophical context that one thinks of preferences as propositional attitudes. Then one arrives at the view of the psychology of preference that Jevons vaguely assumed and that Glimcher has now made relatively precise. A person i has a preference $P(x): x = r > s$, where x ranges over states of affairs individuated by sentences in natural language, at time t, if and only if there is an identifiable neural state or event in i's brain at t that is the translation into the language of thought – that is, a neural theory of preference implementation – of a natural language sentence that states the proposition that i prefers r to s.

Daniel Dennett rejected this literal neurocomputational form of functionalism about the mental from the moment it started to emerge in the literature. (See, Dennett 1969.) There is not space here to survey his wide-ranging suite of philosophical counter-arguments; an interested reader can consult Zawidzki (2007). In advance of technological developments in AI that came along in the 1980s, these arguments persuaded only a minority of philosophers. What was more important was that Dennett provided an alternative way of understanding the ontology of the mind and of propositional attitudes, to which theorists – particularly scientists – could turn when they doubt, as most now do, that there are internal states of brains that systematically co-vary with propositional meaning in such a way as to support the hypothesis of a language of thought.

Certainly brains process information, and in that sense are computers. But the distinction between operators and passive data structures, crucial to the enterprise of early AI, does not appear to apply to them. Brains are dynamic neuroelectrical and chemical systems embedded in wider environmental dynamics (Port and van Gelder 1995; Eliasmith and Anderson 2002). They are poorly modeled by schemas that attempt to draw clear distinctions between perceptual inputs and active outputs (Friston and Kiebel 2009; Friston et al. 2011). Most importantly, states of brains are not *symbols* in any sense that interestingly resembles words or icons (Keijzer 2001). No state in my brain *means* 'muskrat' or 'economic methodologist.' My brain has learned to *recognize* muskrats, in that events in it cause me to behave in certain predictable ways when my environment draws my attention to muskrat-related patterns (e.g., I see a muskrat or someone says they're wearing a muskrat coat, or I read the word 'muskrat').

The statements above might at first glance seem naturally congenial to eliminative behaviorists who hold that mind and propositional attitudes are merely artifacts of folk psychology with no scientific standing. This is how the philosopher Alex Rosenberg (1992), in a classic criticism of economic methodology, interprets the situation. Rosenberg argues that economists are committed to modeling behavior as conditioned by rational adjustments of preferences and beliefs to changes in incentive structures and information. He does not imagine that economists are necessarily committed to methodological individualism, or to extremely demanding rationality criteria such as the REH (see Chapter 3). However, he argues that a truly scientific psychology, especially one based firmly in advancing neuroscience, has no place for folk concepts such as rationality and propositional attitudes. Thus, he concludes, the entire edifice of economics rests on an obsolete, pre-scientific ontology.

This criticism, if valid, would undermine behavioralism as thoroughly as it would the neo-Samuelsonian approach defended in this book.

In direct response to Rosenberg, I argue in Ross (1994) that Dennett's understanding of the ontology of propositional attitudes offers the way out of this cul-de-sac. Propositional attitudes, according to Dennett (1991a), are *real patterns* at the scale of *social* organization, as opposed to approximate descriptions of states or events at the scale of individual psychology. This proposal will strike most people, including most economists, as radical and counter-intuitive. However, it is surely no *more* surprising than the eliminativist behaviorist's suggestion, which has been part of the intellectual landscape since the 1940s, and which is often taken to have been Samuelson's view, that rationality and propositional attitudes are simply *myths*. By contrast, Dennett argues that they are real but importantly different from most people's naïve view of them. As noted above, Dennett's alternative has gradually become the dominant opinion in the philosophy of mind. (An up-to-date and very thorough development of the position can be found in a series of books by Radu Bogdan [1997, 2000, 2009, 2010, 2013].)

The view unfortunately lacks a standard label. I will here follow my own precedent (Ross 2005) and refer to it as *intentional-stance functionalism*. It begins from a hypothesis about the function of mental concepts that caused them to evolve as a part of every normal person's behavioral repertoire. In order to coordinate their expectations, people must model one another as goal-directed systems. Furthermore, they must do so by reference to goals and means of achieving goals that they can share. This implies that each individual projects their conception of the world as a domain for *normative* action – a domain of *goals*, goal-derived *problems* and *sensible solutions* to those problems – onto other people and then explains and predicts their actions and statements by reference to this framework. But individuals don't do this independently of one another. Since the very point of it is to enable coordination, each person must try to broadly match her normative projections to those of others. The process is thus an equilibrating one that could in principle be modeled as a conditional game. Nor do any individuals ever play this game from ground zero. Children join games that are already in dynamic equilibrium among adults, and then learn the boundaries on interpretive practices that are culturally allowed – in that other people don't dismiss them and their authors as crazy – from their parents.

Expressing this in Dennett's language, people learn to adopt *the intentional stance* toward one another. That is, they learn to model one another's behavior using everyday canons of rationality. I see my neighbor, who I know is not an actor, leave his house and get into his car dressed as a pirate. I infer that he probably believes he's been invited to a costume party, desires to attend that party, and believes he can successfully get there in his car. On this basis I might generate all sorts of further expectations. If I know that he is very conscientious, I might conclude from his taking his car that he won't be doing much drinking at the party. Let us zoom in more closely on this last inference. I am *not* necessarily inferring that my neighbor has experienced an internal psychological state with a content (in 'the language of thought') that would best be translated into English as 'I will not drink much tonight' or 'I should not drink much tonight.' Perhaps conscientiousness is a long-standing disposition of my neighbor, and he never actively thinks about drinking at all when he has his car out. Nevertheless, it seems that statements I could make (if I had some reason to) including 'My neighbor desires not to drink much tonight' and 'My neighbor believes he won't drink much tonight,' are true. What *makes* them true are not discrete states of my neighbor's brain but general patterns in his behavior with respect to certain socially salient sets of alternatives. The same point holds for all of the intentional-state ascriptions I make to rationalize my neighbor's behavior in the hypothesized case. Has he ever framed to himself the belief 'I can successfully get to the party in my car'? This is possible, but it would hardly be typical, so is certainly not what I assume about him. But does he have that belief? His behavior makes it evident that he does.

The considerations above so far tell only against the hypothesis that the contents of internal states typically derive from conscious self-repre-sentations of those contents. The story would be compatible with a less extravagant form of internalist functionalism if we supposed that when people take the intentional stance toward one another, they are reasoning by analogy from their first-person observations of their own minds as causal engines of their behavior. In the hypothetical story above, the internalist would hypothesize that I entertain an implicit premise to the effect that 'My neighbor is experiencing the same or very similar internal psychological states as I would if I were conscientious and driving to a party'; and then some story is told about how I am directly acquainted with the relevant states in myself.[10] The core thesis of intentional-stance functionalism is that this has the relationship between ascriptions of mental content to others and expressions of one's own mental content backwards. People do not first observe themselves 'from the inside' and then project what they find there onto others. Rather, people observe how others behave, are under normative pressure to model their own behavior in terms that will make sense to others given those patterns, and so they take the intentional stance toward their own nervous systems and try to regulate them accordingly. Since a non-infant person observes far more of her own behavior than she observes anyone else's, and observes more of her own behavior than anyone else does, her biography of herself from the intentional stance is uniquely rich and detailed. It is, indeed, a more detailed network of expectations and remembered stories than even the most skillful novelist can construct around a character. In continuously taking the intentional stance toward herself, a person *creates* a self that is rational in the psychological sense, that is, does things that the person herself expects that others will be able to make sense of by reference to generally comprehended norms. (Experience will teach her that in many circumstances, especially novel ones, this might require a lot of explanation and might not succeed. What matters is that she tries. A person who ceases trying to appear rational, in socially structured terms, to *herself* is a person whose self-stability is disintegrating.)

This loosely rational agent that the person works at being is not a *fiction* that 'hides' the 'real' bundle of rational neural activity occurring within. Self-construction and self-maintenance are embedded in behavior. The person will typically actually *do* what she can rationalize and avoid doing what she can't rationalize. Others will often successfully discourage her from repeating behavior she can't persuasively rationalize to others. My neighbor's belief that conscientiousness is obligatory and incompatible with drinking and driving is a pattern in his behavior that an observer must identify if they want to successfully predict his responses when

---

[10] Philosophers struggle mightily to flesh out analyzes of this kind of acquaintance in ways that can withstand conceptual criticism. I don't think that they succeed. We can also note that this view of the relationship between intentional descriptions and behavior is explicitly offered by Lionel Robbins (1935) as part of his account of our knowledge of economic rationality. It is a peculiar aspect of Robbins's philosophy of economics that he denies that projection of intentionality from self-awareness can support inferences about relative preference intensities. In consequence he joins behaviorists in denying that interpersonal comparisons of utility are possible, while rejecting behaviorism itself.

people at the party offer him drinks. But by hypothesis this belief is not an occurrent state in his brain. It is a *relationship* between him and a social environment structured by norms and mutual expectations. Thus the belief is a kind of *virtual* state. Being virtual is not a way of being fictitious; it is a way of being real. If one needs to track a pattern in order to explain and predict actual events, that pattern is real.[11]

Contentful mental states as understood by intentional-stance functionalist are not *episodic* causes of behavior. When I act on the basis of a belief I do not first call up or create an occurrence in my brain that is a representation of that belief in the 'language of thought.' Mental states are, at that scale of analysis, after-the-fact rationalizations of behavior. But this does not entail that mental states are causally inert (*epiphenomena*, as philosophers say) on the road to action. Their causal effect arises on a longer scale. The need for a person to conform future actions to the rationalized patterns of her past actions constrains the set of actions that survive sub-cognitive processing of episodic choice sets. Because multiple possible actions at the episodic scale are typically rationalizable, the agent's self-narrative seldom *determines* action at that scale; but in restricting action, narratives figure in the *explanation* of action *patterns*. This is why it is perfectly coherent to talk of an agent surprising herself, along with her strategic interactants, in a game with mixed-strategy NE or a range of QRE: the specific action was not predicted by a prior rationalization, though the utility function that selects the operative mixed strategy NE or QRE strategy set is so predicted, and derivable from careful observations of a relevant range of the agent's behavior.

The key message of intentional-stance functionalism in the context of this book is that beliefs and desires – and psychological preferences – should not be expected to reduce to states or events that can be characterized only in terms of properties internal to individuals or their brains. This is the main reason why I do not expect Glimcher's hypothesis, that SV as he defines it determines choice behavior, to be borne out. And that in turn is my main reason for denying that economists would well serve the advancement of their discipline by turning and retreating back up the path of theoretical development that lead away from Jevons and toward Samuelson.

---

[11] Ladyman and Ross (2007, Chapter 5) argue that that is all that 'being real' amounts to for *anything*, including material objects.

As recently argued in detail by Lagueux (2010), the everyday psychological rationality that structures the framework of beliefs, desires and other mental states – that is, the concept of mind in general – is *not* equivalent to rationality in the technical sense of GARP. Almost no one demands that they or others organize all of their behavior in such a way as to facilitate modeling it as constrained maximization of a single utility function. Everyday rationality is not only insufficient for economic rationality, it isn't even necessary for it. As I argue at length in Ross (2005), very simple nervous systems such as those of insects conform more closely to GARP than whole human beings do, and yet insects are not rational in the psychological sense because they do not take the intentional stance toward anything. 'Economic rationality' in the sense of GARP is *not* a refinement of, or 'improvement' on, psychological rationality. It is something different altogether. For this reason I think that economists and their critics would be able to keep a clearer grip on methodological and philosophical issues that matter to their practice if they dropped the use of the word 'rationality' when they are referring to utility maximization. A dogged reader who cares to check will see that I surveyed current practice in economics in Chapter 3 without having to use the concept of rationality in any first-order sense (that is, except in characterizing some methodological opinions of others with whom I disagree).

Both psychologists and economists study choice behavior, that is, behavior that is goal-regulated and responsive to changes in incentives. But they study it at fundamentally different scales.[12] Psychologists who study individual behavior, and of course neuroscientists, are often interested in how human and other animal brains respond when placed in socially unstructured circumstances and forced to 'fend for themselves.' This is part of the explanation – the deepest part – of why disciplinary norms in psychology allow experimental subjects to be deceived, while economics journal editors and Ph.D. supervisors do not. If one wants to learn about human behavioral variation at the scale of individual idiosyncrasy, psychology is the discipline to consult. If one wants to learn about the structures of markets under different conditions, one should turn to economics.

---

[12] Psychologists study many phenomena that are *not* choice phenomena. Economists study *only* choice phenomena.

On this view of the difference between the disciplines, behavioral economists are scientists who study comparative valuation, like economists do, but have decided to take up psychology *rather than* economics. (Of course, I don't deny that one and the same scientist could sometimes do economics and sometimes do psychology.[13]) But I think that it would be a positive development for methodological clarity if the label 'behavioral economics' semantically evolved into the label 'psychology of reward valuation.' Of course neo-Samuelsonian economists, taking heterogeneity of utility functions seriously as a key property of data-generating processes at market scales, will continue to perform experiments using individual human (and non-human animal) subjects. But their methods differ in telltale ways from those typical of behavioral economists. Neo-Samuelsonians typically require larger subject pools because their aim is to use econometric estimation to reveal the structure of heterogeneity *with respect to maximization of expected utility* within populations. We can contrast this with the objective of most work in 'behavioral economics' to explain central tendencies in a population by reference to cognitive dispositions or biases common to individual members of the population. This reflects different policy motivations. The neo-Samuelsonian experimental economist aims to predict the consequences of heterogeneity for policies or interventions at the population scale; the behavioralist is typically more interested in prospects for useful advice that might be given to individuals.

Experimental economists often pool their data elicited from individuals and estimate distributions of responses that are silent on the question of whether observed heterogeneity is based on different *types* of people or on divergent tendencies *within* individuals to manifest varying ranges of response as independent variables or parameters in a model change. Consider the use of mixture models for maximum likelihood estimation, as reviewed in Chapter 3. Economists who take up these tools signify recognition of the significance to economics of psychological variation, without this leading them to abandon their distinctive disciplinary concerns to start studying the psychological *sources* of the variation.

Economists and psychologists study different aspects of the same world, and there is substantial scope for mutual exchange of information.

---

[13] For example, I am a co-author on Kincaid et al. (2013), which is unabashedly psychology.

Economic incentives must be established and stabilized by institutions, and institutions in turn make demands on cognitive structures and capacities of participants that may be more or less reasonable and sustainable. To take an extreme example, Stalin's regime in the Soviet Union extracted high aggregate productivity from a large population by institutionalizing one core incentive, namely fear of being enslaved in the Gulag or shot. There is no principle of economics accordingly to which this might not have worked indefinitely; but the evidence is that it was too psychologically stressful and exhausting to continue supporting output growth for long. Stalin's successors almost certainly prolonged the life of their system for decades by switching to a normal mix of sticks and carrots. A twenty-first-century example might turn out to arise from the widening inequality that is accompanying the current rapid displacement of middling human skills by pattern-recognition software and industrial robots (Brynjolfsson and McAfee 2012). It violates no generalization of economics to hypothesize that a small minority of rich people could indefinitely enjoy high profits from selling services to one another while welfare of the majority stagnates or slides backwards. This is important knowledge to be derived from economic modeling, because it warns us not to imagine that market dynamics will naturally correct the trend to rising inequality by themselves. But if psychologists suggest that human psychological responses to status erosion and injustice will undermine any such equilibrium, policy-makers and investors should also pay attention to them.

4.9   Neo-Samuelsonian economics summarized

Neo-Samuelsonians take the need for experimentation in economics seriously because they recognize that economic choices are produced by heterogeneous data-generating processes. However, unlike behavioralists they continue to understand preferences as summaries of choices, as axiomatized by GARP. This implies that they do not identify choice with causal processes in brains that include neural implementations of discrete beliefs and desires – or preferences – as elements of the causal basis. Choice behavior, for a neo-Samuelsonian, is simply any behavior that is systematically (but typically stochastically) related to changes in incentives. The causal basis of choice behavior, at the individual scale but also at the aggregate scales that economists mainly study, includes channeling structures in the social and institutional environment that are often not explicitly represented in choosers' nervous systems, let alone in conscious awareness.

Leading neo-Samuelsonians such as Vernon Smith have emphasized the ecological dimension of economic rationality. GARP might not usefully characterize much interesting behavior emitted by an individual human brain in isolation, yet support out-of-sample predictions, generalizations and explanations when people interact within market structures that are institutionalized and generate information that 'raw brains' cannot. However, I suggest that the neo-Samuelsonian attitude, though clearly articulated by economists such as Binmore, has fared relatively badly in rhetorical competition with behavioralism because most of its promoters have failed to attend to the need to support their view on the basis of a reasonable philosophy of mind. Resisting identification of choice processes with purported neural implementations of folk psychological concepts of rational deliberation, neo-Samuelsonians have tended to fall back on eliminative behaviorism as if there were no other available option. Binmore (1994, p. 183 n. 5), for example, says 'I think it unlikely that Adam Smith's moral sentiments ... all have genuine physiological referents. Under certain circumstances our bodies pump chemicals into our bloodstream. We then invent myths in seeking to explain to ourselves what we are experiencing.' But this readily leads to refusal to pay attention to psychologists, as exemplified by Gul and Pesendorfer's (2008) revival of Friedman's inadequate methodology. This methodology is not merely *philosophically* inadequate. As Harrison (2008) explains, it leads economists to restrict attention to closed-form models that are useless for identifying patterns of importance in real empirical choice data generated by experiments. Heterogeneity calls for structural modeling, and heterogeneity is both empirically incontrovertible and important.

Fortunately there is an alternative to neural reductionism of folk psychology, on the one hand, and eliminative behaviorism, on the other hand. The alternative in question is not esoteric or shallowly developed: it is the view of the ontology of mind that has become dominant among philosophers of psychology. According to this view, intentional-stance functionalism, minds and their elements – including beliefs and preferences – are virtual objects constructed collectively by people who must coordinate their expectations in the face of massive informational complexity. People learn to be rational in the psychological sense, relaying on institutionalized social ecology. 'Belief' and 'preference' describe patterns in socially regulated behavior, not internal representations. 'Preference,' specifically, describes patterns in choice behavior.

However, choice patterns conforming to GARP are not 'ideal' refinements of psychological rationality. Psychological rationality prevails in all social interactions involving normal people; but GARP becomes a useful modeling framework only when behavior is conditioned by market institutions. This leads us to consider a second main dimension of the place of economics in the unified scientific worldview: its relationship to sociology. To that we turn in the next, and final, chapter.

5 Economics as a Social Science

5.1 The metaphysics of economic aggregation

I have argued in the preceding chapters that although the normative theory of rational individual decision-making is a crucial conceptual and formal tool for economists, economics is not best viewed as an extension of that theory. I have furthermore aimed to set economics firmly apart from psychology by emphasizing that whereas psychologists are fundamentally concerned with the idiosyncratic information processing dynamics of individuals, typically abstracted from their social environments, economists explore what happens when people and other goal-directed agents faced with scarcity of resources are coordinated by social and institutional structures to focus on prospects for specialization, exchange and competition. Summarizing, I have argued that, despite important connections, psychology is not in its core a social science, whereas economics is.

As I have acknowledged, the majority of contemporary economists at least pay lip-service to methodological individualism (MI), and teach economics to undergraduates as if it is built on individual decision theory. I have argued, however, that the increasing diversity of social research programs in economics is not consistent with taking this casual psychologistic individualism too seriously as a working philosophy of economics. This opinion of mine is far from an unprecedented heresy; a number of past masters have shared it.

In Chapter 2, I quoted Samuelson denying that the formal foundations of RPT are in turn the foundations of economics, even though the axioms of RPT are used to structure the economic concept of choice. Hildenbrand (1994), who shares my interest in detaching economics from alleged foundations in assumptions about individual behavior, finds repeated rhetorical inspiration in Samuelson's most immediate theoretical precursor, J.R. Hicks. From Hicks's most important treatise, *Value and Capital* (1939b) comes this:

> [E]conomics is not, in the end, much interested in the behaviour of single individuals. Its concern is with the behaviour of groups. A study of individual demand is only a means to the study of market demand. (Hicks 1939b, p. 34)

A second Hicks remark on this theme cited by Hildenbrand is:

> [T]he preference hypothesis only acquires a *prima facie* plausibility when it is applied to a statistical average ... [T]o assume that an actual person, the Mr. Brown or Mr. Jones who lives round the corner, does in fact act in such a way does not deserve a moment's consideration. (Hicks 1956, p. 55)

This remark synopsizes a fundamental methodological view of the earliest macroeconomists. Haavelmo (1944) argued that the aim of an economic theory is to accurately predict how observations should be distributed in true samples; theory should not be expected to add value to sets of choice responses too small or narrowly drawn to exhibit central tendencies. We noted earlier that self-conscious macroeconomics, that is, the explicit idea that the economics of the aggregate scale might be based on distinctive conceptual principles, arose in the general theoretical ferment of the 1930s. Methodological individualists often bypass views such as Hicks's and Haavelmo's, perhaps on grounds that no philosophical point can be established simply from the fact that a special group of economists decided, for practical reasons, to ignore the ontological foundations attended to by their colleagues. Against this it must be emphasized that the goal of the first macroeconomists was to synthesize microeconomics and macroeconomics as complementary aspects of *one* science – precisely what Samuelson thought he had achieved.

The word 'macroeconomics' was coined by Ragnar Frisch – who also gave us 'econometrics' – in 1933. His conception, which was established as a dominant activity of policy-oriented economists by Tinbergen, grew out of a tradition of work in economics that has not previously been mentioned in this book: the modeling of temporal fluctuations in aggregate indicators of economic activity such as rates of investment, employment of labor and manufacturing capacity, and household savings and consumption expenditure. As Mary Morgan (1990) emphasizes, such *business cycle* research serves as an ideal foil to the tradition of demand modeling that receives the lion's share of attention from philosophers of economics, and that has also been extensively discussed in this book. On Morgan's persuasive telling, the roots of econometrics – the most important methodological channel connecting economic theory with empirical data – lies in the intermingling of technical challenges from these two sub-fields, business cycle and demand modeling, which from the perspective of philosophical epistemology could hardly be less similar to one another.

I will turn to the fascinations of business cycle research in Section 5.2. Delving into it immediately would distract from the current topic of aggregation, because in one straightforward sense the macroeconomic tradition of Frisch, Tinbergen and Haavelmo sidesteps the issue by focusing in the first place on concepts that have no reference at the scale of an individual agent.[1] It begs the question as to whether macroeconomics needs microfoundations to *assume* that macroeconomists at least ultimately owe an account of aggregation. By contrast, as we saw in Chapter 2, since Jevons's time demand modeling has typically begun with the stylized individual agent. However, as I have been arguing throughout the book, the main motivating target of the enterprise is understanding, prediction and explanation of the demand side of markets. Thus demand theorists have from the outset confronted the problem of how to aggregate demand functions, which has in turn been understood as the basic step in aggregating agents into economies.

The overwhelming majority of philosophers who have commented on demand aggregation have focused exclusively on paths from individual demand functions of the form[2]

$$f^i(p,x) \in \mathbb{R}^l_+ \, (commodity \; space) \qquad (1)$$

---

[1] This is in contrast to the macroeconomics stemming from Keynes. The basic elements of Keynes's theory, such as the preference for liquidity, *can* be regarded as properties of individual agents. This is precisely what made Keynesian economics vulnerable to the later rational expectations critique.

[2] My formulation follows Hildenbrand (2008), except that Hildenbrand assumes aggregation over households, the normal atoms of actual applied microeconomics, whereas in the current context where metaphysics are at issue I assume aggregation over individual agents.

where p is a price vector and x^i is i's income (assumed to be equivalent to i's total expenditure), to mean demand across a population I:

$$\frac{1}{|i|}\sum i \in I^{f^i(p,x^i)} \tag{2}$$

In treatments emphasizing foundations, f^i is derived from a specification of a revealed preference function. This approach features in the standard existence proof of general equilibrium (GE). Thus for philosophers who follow Hausman (1992) in viewing economics as an extension of individual preference theory and who depict GE as the theoretical crown jewel of the discipline, the above statement of aggregation is canonical.

However, as Hildenbrand (2008) observes, "[I]n macroeconomics or in applied demand analysis the notion of aggregate demand is quite different." Along with a price vector, variables include non-aggregated statistics such as income distributions and measures of income inequality; there are no individual-specific (or household-specific) variables. The point of *practical* aggregation theory is then to relate models of prices and statistical variables to models constructed according to the template in (2) above. Given within-population heterogeneity, there is no general solution to this problem, but only specific functions relating microeconomic demand characteristics of parts of the population to the population-scale statistics. In such exercises it is *not* standardly imposed as a condition that demand functions be derivable from constrained utility maximization.

The individualistic approach in aggregation theory is classically exemplified by Gorman (1953). He investigates the formal conditions under which economic rationality of individual consumers is preserved under aggregation, so that the consumption side of a whole economy could be modeled as a representative agent. The conditions in question are found to be extremely stringent and empirically implausible. The opposite logic is explored, in quite different ways, by Becker (1962), Gode and Sunder (1993) and Hildenbrand (1994). Becker (1962) showed that a fundamental property of the standard model of the market – the 'law of demand,' according to which downward sloping demand for any good given constant real income – depends on no claim about the procedural or computational rationality of the consumers in the market; it can be established instead from the assumption that households with smaller budgets, and therefore smaller opportunity sets, consume less. In a similar vein, Gode and Sunder (1993) simulate 'zero intelligence' agents that participate in a double auction experiment subject to budget constraints and are constrained to mindlessly obey two very simple rules. These are that sellers do not charge more than their marginal cost, and buyers do not make negative offers or offers above a fixed ceiling. Otherwise the agents bid randomly. The efficiency of these simulated markets matches that achieved by human subjects. This is widely taken as suggestive of the idea that efficiency of outcomes in such markets may result from the ecological rationality of the institutional rules, rather than sophisticated 'inboard' computations.[3]

Hildenbrand (1994) is particularly illuminating in this area. His aim is to identify conditions under which the law of demand can be inferred without recourse to any behavioral assumptions at all, or even to structural modeling of consumers. The law of demand is not plausible as an empirical claim about all individual consumers with respect to all goods. Goods purchased for the sake of conspicuous consumption, for example, are so-called Giffin goods in at least part of their possible price range for some consumers: people aiming to signal their wealth by carrying handbags known to be expensive would demand fewer of them if their price declined, at least below some threshold. This might even hold – though genuine empirical examples are elusive (Deaton and Muellbauer 1980) – if we properly model demand by reference to utility instead of money. Plausibly, part of the satisfaction of owning an original work of art is that it is very expensive, independent of an investment value it is taken to have based on expected price appreciation. But the law of demand is intended to apply to markets, not to individual consumers: it claims that no good is Giffin in the aggregate.

Hildenbrand derives the law of demand roughly as follows. (I say 'roughly' because Hildenbrand's constructions are mathematical, and natural language cannot be used to exactly represent the contents of mathematical statements except in very simple cases.) Consider first the abstract idea of *compensated* demand, which economists use to distinguish two standard effects of price changes. Imagine that when the price of a good that an agent consumes increases, the agent's

---

[3] Sunder (2003) discusses generalizations of this result, and further economic applications.

income is augmented by an amount corresponding to the increase. This abstraction allows us to disentangle substitution effects of price changes from income effects; in the case of real, uncompensated demand there is both a change in relative prices of goods *and* a change in the agent's budget constraint. Now apply the idea of compensated demand at the aggregate level. For example, imagine that the price of bread rises by $1, and each household with an interest in bread gets $1 added to their income. We use this hypothetical construction to characterize the property of *metonymy*: when households that formerly had incomes of $1 have their incomes increased to $1 + ε, suppose that the *distribution* of their consumption resembles the distribution of consumption of the households that already earned $1 + ε. Hildenbrand shows that if the heterogeneity of households' consumption patterns increases with their incomes, then given metonymy in compensated demand the law of demand holds for *uncompensated* demand. Lewbel (1994, p. 1833) states the intuition as "some goods may be Giffen goods for some people, but there are no Giffen goods in the aggregate if people's tastes are sufficiently varied such that no one good is Giffen for too many consumers." But as always we should be careful about intuitive formulations of technical results. As Lewbel points out, his gloss refers to the tastes of people and so is behavioral in spirit, whereas the whole point of Hildenbrand's argument is to restrict attention to properties of markets.

Hildenbrand then shows that the relationship he models between incomes and dispersion of consumption patterns fits times series of British and French household consumption data over several decades, thus explaining the conformity of these everyday large markets to the law of demand.

Before drawing philosophical morals from Hildenbrand's exercise, let me quote his own methodological remarks about it:

> Traditional aggregation theory analyzes the problem of whether the implications of rational individual behavior are preserved – or to what extent they are preserved – if one goes from an individual household to a large population. Thus the key questions are: What is preserved? What is inherited? The accepted view in the literature is that, in general, one loses structure by aggregation. Only with restrictive additional assumptions on the distribution of household characteristics can this loss of structure be avoided.

Following Hicks, I now would like to take the opposite view in claiming that Wald's axiom [about monotonicity of demand functions] is better justified for aggregate behavior, that is to say, for mean demand, than for individual behavior. In claiming this, I base my arguments essentially on the hypothesis of increasing dispersion (Hildenbrand 1994, p. 119).

...

Let me emphasize that the hypothesis of increasing spread of household demand does not imply a specific restriction on the behavior of any particular individual household. The hypothesis refers to the whole population of households, which is thought of as being large. (Ibid., p. 128)

Note, then, that Hildenbrand's result is not simply a special application of a general claim that in large populations idiosyncratic departures from economic rationality are 'washed out' by the law of large numbers. Rather, a specific kind of heterogeneity is responsible for the population-level regularity. The law of demand as Hildenbrand constructs it is not a property of households (or, obviously, of individuals) *at all*; it is a property of markets.

From the fact that the law of demand might hold independently of behavioral dispositions of individuals, it obviously cannot be concluded that the same point applies to all market regularities of interest to economists. As Lewbel (1994, p. 1836) observes, "regularities or structure *both* in the behaviour of individuals and in the distributions of individuals contribute to the regularities found in aggregate data, and both Gorman's and Hildenbrand's approaches are unnecessarily restrictive." Recall from Chapter 4 what distinguishes the neo-Samuelsonian economic methodology from that of the eliminative behaviorist. The former is open-minded about which conditioning variables, parameterized and otherwise, may appear on the right-hand side of an economic model. An economic model specifies a data-generating process, and some aspects of such processes may be latent and unobservable. So the neo-Samuelsonian is willing to include not only behavioral elements in models, but also cognitive and even neural elements if these improve reach and power. What distinguishes her from the behavioralist is that she defines choices – the left-hand variables in her models – not in terms of deliberative or sub-cognitive computational processes, but as changes in allocations of resources (including time) in response to changes in incentives. The economists I cited in Chapter 4 as exemplifying the neo-Samuelsonian attitude – Vernon Smith, Binmore, Harrison etc. – also assume that economic models will typically feature irreducibly aggregate-scale elements on their right-hand sides. Indeed, I think we can go a step further: *no* adequate model of an empirical economic phenomenon is devoid of such elements. And here is an asymmetry. Hildenbrand's theory of market demand gives us an example of an empirically successful economic model that is devoid of individual-scale elements. Thus no economic model is simply equivalent to a psychological model; some economic models incorporate hypotheses derived from psychology; and some economic models are entirely innocent of psychological ideas.

In consequence of this asymmetry, we should expect the relationship of economics to other aggregate-scale social sciences, such as sociology, to differ in principle from the relationship between economics and psychology.

5.2 Business cycles

I return now to elaboration on Morgan's (1990) important point about the two tributaries that fed the modern river of econometrics, with over-emphasis on one stream having produced a distorted picture of economics among philosophers. Demand modeling, as we saw in Chapter 2, has historically been characterized by relatively settled theory driven mainly by a priori reasoning. This has been possible because there has been general agreement on what demand *is*: the structuring of agents' goals in response to resource constraints. Then the theoretical problem has been taken to consist in specifying this concept with sufficient rigor for model identification. Demand theory thus often resembles analytic philosophy, which may have encouraged philosophers' tendency to treat it as the methodological core of economics.

By contrast, it has always been an open question what business cycles might be, or even whether they should be regarded as genuine parts of the furniture of the world. That aggregate economic indicators fluctuate is doubted by no one; the issue is which of the following philosophical perspectives one should best adopt with respect to these fluctuations:

(1) Local trends notwithstanding, indicators fluctuate randomly and independently of one another in the limit. More specifically, there is no moving set of measurement variables such that if one finds that the cluster of values has one set of coefficients, one thereby gains information to the effect that another set of coefficients is further away in time than any other.

(2) Some indicators cyclically co-vary statistically while others oppose one another in changes of direction and magnitude; but these patterns emerge from interactions among an open set of underlying factors, including anything from psychological dynamics to weather changes, that are respectively tracked by disparate sciences and cannot be shoehorned into any stable set of generalizations.

(3) Recurrently important patterns in changes of indicator values result directly from regularities studied by some groups of scientists other than macroeconomists – perhaps microeconomists, perhaps psychologists, perhaps political analysts. Apparent macroeconomic patterns that do not have this characteristic are illusions.

(4) Macroeconomic patterns resemble those studied by physicists who work at the scale of classical objects. More specifically, indicator fluctuations have recurrent wavelike dynamics. These patterns can only be conceived beyond a certain scale of aggregation, but are governed by discoverable endogenous regularities.

To someone who endorses (1) macroeconomics is as misconceived and pointless as astrology. Unsurprisingly, this view has never had much presence in economics. It flies in the face of practical experience from a wide range of times and places – e.g., of economy-wide unemployment almost always rising relatively soon after durable goods inventories begin climbing, or of residential property prices stagnating relatively soon after bond market yield curves invert. (2), on the other hand, has many adherents, especially skeptics from outside of the economics profession. It is also not unknown for views like (2) to be propounded by ungenerous microeconomists in off-the-record conversations among themselves. (3) is the view of those who think that sound macroeconomics requires microfoundations. This includes both mainstream economists who seek the foundations in standard microeconomics, and behavioralists who look to psychology for foundations. According to those who find (4) most plausible, business cycles are real patterns, and as such are worthy objects of scientific study in their own right.

This is an issue that philosophers should find fascinating for reasons of their own, and which should motivate them to transcend the obsession with decision theoretic foundations in the philosophy of economics literature. Business cycles are epistemologically intriguing conjectured objects. If they can be observed, this can only be by means of statistical analysis. It is likewise only statistical analysis that could demonstrate them to be illusory or reducible to micro-scale regularities. In typical discussions in general epistemology of science, it is standard practice to presuppose *some* form of evidence – sometimes 'direct' perception, sometimes well-established deterministic laws – that is at least partly independent of statistical modeling. But where business cycle research is concerned there is no such foothold to be had.

Different philosophical temperaments react to this situation in different ways. A philosopher who thinks that a sound science must be characterizable in terms of one or another of the standard epistemological frameworks is apt to be suspicious of the very idea that there could be a science of macroeconomics. On the other extreme, Ladyman and Ross (2012) argue that the epistemological situation of macroeconomics exemplifies that of most sciences – and particularly quantum physics – now that possession of modern computational power invites us to discard the fiction that important sectors of reality are accurately described by non-stochastic generalizations stated in closed-form mathematical theories. Borrowing a rhetorical trope from Wittgenstein, Ladyman and Ross argue that the world in general resembles the domain of macroeconomics in being "the totality of non-redundant statistics."

In keeping with the philosophy of science sketched in Chapter 1, I do not think that the question of whether business cycles are real patterns can be solved from the philosopher's – or, for that matter, the pure economic theorist's – armchair. To someone who defends the pursuit of microfoundations on the basis of general reductionist principles, a philosopher of science can offer a similarly general rebuttal, along the lines of Batterman (2002) and Ladyman and Ross (2007): even macro-scale physical objects do not decompose into micro-scale physical objects, so the suggestion that such decomposition is a general goal of science is untenable. However, the important arguments for and against explaining fluctuations by reference to processes less abstract than business cycles are economic, not metaphysical. Taking the question fully seriously requires immersing oneself in macroeconomic modeling and assessing the extent to which practice forces commitment to irreducible regularities in relationships among aggregate variables. Necessarily, this involves one in the domain of policy. Debates about business cycles are not practically avoidable, and so cannot be regarded as mere intellectual exercises. For example, few people beyond radical free marketeers would regard it as prudent to abolish central banks. But if we think it is advisable to have central banks then presumably we also think that central bankers should have well-motivated general opinions about which data they should pay attention to in choosing monetary policies, and about which relationships in their data they should treat as reliable targets of manipulation.

Akerlof and Shiller (2009) present the behavioralist view on this question: central bankers, according to them, should monitor contagious social emotions because business cycles arise as a result of recurrent dynamics in social psychology.[4] According to this account, pervasively optimistic and pessimistic attitudes spread and wane in populations like viruses. When most people expect most other people to be optimistic, they anticipate high aggregate rates of investment relative to saving. As such widespread anticipation predicts an asset boom, it encourages more optimism, which in turn motivates more investment. Market indicators characteristic of booms – rising average prices, average wages, government revenues, corporate profits, and values of equities – are all lifted on this wave of coordinated happy expectations. But at some point those who are fearful of being caught out by market correction begin spreading fear and pessimism to others. Eventually a self-amplifying vicious circle replaces the formerly self-amplifying virtuous one, and the population converges, with accelerating speed as contagion spreads, on gloomy expectations. Prices and wages consequently stop rising, product inventories start backlogging, investment rates decline, unemployment rises and asset markets

---

[4] The discussion of Akerlof and Shiller's account here drastically compresses a fuller critical treatment provided in Ross (2010).

become bearish. Misappropriating a phrase that Keynes used to mean something different, Akerlof and Shiller explain business cycles as arising in this way from changes in aggregate "animal spirits." If they are right, then it seems that central bankers should conduct monetary policy by consulting social psychologists. Of course, the social psychologists would only be able to furnish useful advice if they had a general theory that allowed them to predict the timing of public mood swings.

Social psychologists in fact have no theory of this kind. From a practical point of view, it thus seems that the animal spirits theory of business cycles has little to recommend it. Of course, this does not in itself show that business cycles are not expressions of, and thus caused by, cycles in aggregate psychological mood. However, I am aware of absolutely no statistical evidence for such a causal hypothesis. Leamer (2009) points out that immediately after September 11, 2001, one of the few occasions when an exogenous event demonstrably coordinated the US population on pessimistic expectations about the future, including expectations about health and stability of market values, all other standard indicators continued to signal the strong recovery from the dot-com recession that we now know was indeed underway.

If the behavioralist account of business cycles is *not* intended as a causal hypothesis, then on a general interpretation it is a mere redescription. Of course most people do have confident expectations during booms and pessimistic expectations during recessions; but this is precisely what we want business cycle theory to *explain* in the first place. A more charitable way of interpreting Akerlof and Shiller's conception of a swing to pessimism is as a specific, in principle measurable, relaxation of the rational expectations hypothesis to reflect effects of self-fulfilling beliefs (i.e., "I've become anxious; so others who know everything I do should also be anxious or be about to become anxious; so we should all expect one another to sell assets; so I should sell my assets"). Models of such effects, which can be quantitatively compared against data with models based on the real business cycle framework (Kydland and Prescott 1982; Long and Plosser 1983), have been familiar since Farmer and Guo (1994). Far from implying methodological revolution, developing and testing such hypotheses is firmly in the heartland of establishment macroeconomics. But this work is not aimed at explaining the causes or structure of business cycles. It is, rather, part of a literature investigating the question of which business cycle models are and aren't compatible with different versions of the REH.

Notwithstanding Akerlof and Shiller's embarrassingly extravagant rhetoric on behalf of their psychological account of business cycles,[5] I thus do not think that behavioralism will displace the primary methodological contest in business cycle modeling, which is between microfoundations advocates, on the one hand, and believers in irreducible aggregate-scale patterns and structures, on the other hand.

As stressed before, this debate is not one that we can expect to resolve through mere theoretical reflection. I will nevertheless state the approach I currently regard as most promising, that of Roman Frydman and Michael Goldberg (2007, 2011), as an illustration of a specific ontological attitude consistent with perspective (4) above. This opinion of mine is not based on methodological or philosophical first principles; rather, it represents my holistic judgment about which of a range of available economists' models makes best sense of the most data from the history of markets. Space precludes review of many insights derived from other models, for example that of Phelps (1994) on multiple structural equilibria in labor markets, that provide complementary enrichment of understanding.

Frydman and Goldberg begin from the premise that Knight's and Keynes's distinction between *risk* and *uncertainty*[6] is crucial to an adequate macroeconomics. Where market participants have enough information to be able to quantitatively estimate the risk of buying or selling an asset, we should expect that asset's price to reflect the distribution of risk preferences in the heterogeneous population of investors.

---

[5] "In telling how the economy really works," they proclaim, "we accomplish what existing economic theory has not. We provide a theory that explains fully and naturally how the U.S. economy, and indeed the world economy, has fallen into the current crisis. And – of perhaps even greater interest – such a theory then allows us to understand what needs to be done to extricate ourselves from the crisis" (Akerlof and Shiller 2009, pp. 6–7). What we need to do is cheer one another up.

[6] See Chapter 2. This distinction can be further refined. Glenn Harrison (personal communication) offers the following tripartite categorization. "If an individual has some belief distribution over an outcome and reduces it to the average probability, then we say that the individual faces *subjective risk*. However, if the shape of the distribution, apart from the mean, matters for the decisions made, then we say that the individual is also reacting to *uncertainty*. Finally, if the individual does not have enough information to form a subjective belief distribution, then we say that the individual is also reacting to *ambiguity*." For context see Harrison (2011a). What Knight and Keynes meant by 'uncertainty' is closest to what Harrison means by 'ambiguity'. That they made a cruder partition of the conceptual space here stems from the fact that they wrote before Savage came along.

Of course this distribution cannot be known a priori and its empirical estimation is challenging; but as we saw in Chapter 3, methods for dealing with such challenges are currently the site of fertile development in both economic and econometric theory. But with respect to long investment horizons, much information that everyone knows will be important to asset values is simply unavailable. In the terminology of Savage, as revived by Binmore (2009) and discussed in Chapter 4, we enter 'large worlds' in which Bayesian probability estimation lacks sufficient empirical oxygen to be applied. Investors in such settings tend, stochastically, to follow the advice of David Hume and act as if the future will resemble the past with respect to the least volatile domain of relevant information that they have: the relative fundamental value of companies, based on the quality of management and productive technologies. This predominance of *value investors* explains why large asset markets are relatively stable *most* of the time. (It should be emphasized that such stability presupposes the background stability of legal, administrative and information-disseminating institutions.)

This form of Humean conservatism in beliefs tends to lead value investors to adopt similar strategies to one another.[7] But this implies some inefficiency: when a value investor wants to sell because the time has come to consume her gains – for example, when she needs to liquidate some holdings to spend on her retirement – she would find her expected profit hard to realize if everyone else in the market attached the same value to her portfolio in every period as she does. Fortunately markets also feature short-run speculative traders who are *not* focused on fundamentals. Such traders keep markets active, and thereby make them (usually) ready sources of capital for the real economy. However, this helpful availability of gamblers generates a prevailing asymmetry of coordination between risk-averse and more risk-tolerant investors. Because the bulk of capital is held by conservative value investors, movements above historical benchmarks tend to reach their peaks by way of long, gradual climbs. Traders focused on fundamentals become anxious to sell when asset values appear not to be justified by underlying earnings; and since there are more of them, and their beliefs are coordinated, downward corrections are typically

---

[7] Thus, if it were the whole story then we would expect that macroeconomic models featuring a single representative agent would be recommended for analysis.

faster and sharper than the upward drifts that give rise to them. Here gamblers don't help; on average, only half of the speculative traders will hold long positions in the assets the value investors want to sell. (Of course, the gamblers who took early short positions in these assets will have helped *themselves*, perhaps spectacularly if the market correction is very fast and drastic, as in 2008.) Thus *realistically* – as opposed to ideally – efficient markets tend from time to time to painfully crash. Periodic financial crises, on this account, are not a sign of some 'irrationality' somewhere in markets; they are instead a price we all pay for enjoying the benefits of having broad, deep, highly integrated markets that allocate risk highly efficiently but also, as a downside, tend to coordinate risk-averse investors more than they coordinate risk-neutral or risk-loving ones.

Frydman and Goldberg refer to their general account as "Imperfect Knowledge Economics" (IKE), and to the asset valuation model that is its main working part as "endogenous prospect theory." In the model, value investors are loss averse but adjust their *level* of loss aversion in light of their experience with specific ratios of the asymmetry between long upswings and faster downward corrections. Since this is based on benchmarks as (evolving) reference points, rather than on calculation of lifetime net wealth differentials, it really is about loss *framing* rather than actual losses. Thus Frydman and Goldberg are correct to identify their model as, in this respect, an extension of (cumulative) prospect theory. In Chapter 4, I explained that in lottery choice experiments rank dependent utility seems to be able to account for the behavioral data that prospect theorists have used to motivate the hypothesis of loss aversion. It is an open possibility, as far as I can see, that the same point may apply to IKE. If this is the case, then the door remains open to an entirely non-behavioralist account of the phenomenon, which Keynes made central to practical macroeconomics, of *liquidity preference* – the premium investors pay to keep options open, but which under some circumstances can trap economies in equilibria with low rates of both investment and consumption, as in the 1930s. It would be ill-advised methodology to try to investigate this by studying the psychologies of individual investors. What is called for instead is estimating mixture models of heterogeneous investors, some of whom have rank-dependent utility functions, against large volumes of historical asset market data. That is, even if we set out to investigate Frydman and

Goldberg's theory using laboratory experiments with investors as one of our core methods, the hypothesis should be framed and tested at the aggregate, not the individual, scale.

To explain why, in general, asset markets periodically crash is *not* a basis for explaining why a *given* market crash occurred *when* it did. Nor is it to explain which classes of agents suffered the greatest losses in a specific crash, and which agents escaped unscathed or even grew their wealth. Economics is far from unusual among sciences in this respect. Contrary to Karl Popper's (1959, 1963) conviction that science is driven forward by bold predictions that are falsifiable by events, most sciences do much better at explaining regularities and identifying co-trending sets of variables than at clearly predicting singular events. For example, Darwinian selection theory is a mighty engine for explaining recurrent patterns in the history of the distribution of organism characteristics, but it is not a reliable generator of predictions of the emergence of specific new species. Any given such speciation event is a low-probability occurrence even conditional on the *true* theory that actually explains it. (Of course it will typically have even lower probability conditional on any alternative false theory.) This insight from the philosophy of science might have given pause to the many commentators, including some distinguished economists (e.g., Krugman 2009), who claimed that the 2008–2009 financial crisis refuted core aspects of mainstream business cycle theory because most economists allegedly did not foresee the event.

More specifically, Krugman and other critics assert that the financial crisis refutes macroeconomic theories that incorporate the rational expectations hypothesis (REH). For reasons explained in earlier chapters, the phrase 'rational expectations' is not the label one would choose if the aim were to maximize semantic transparency. Clearly, some or other specification of expectations must be central to any economic model. Economic agency just *is* the gathering and processing of information for the sake of refining expectations in hopes of improving expected payoffs from choices of resource allocations. And economic inter-action – market behavior – just *is* the strategic coordination of reciprocal expectations among economic agents, a perspective that game theory makes beautifully salient. As for 'rationality,' expectations are perfectly idle if the objectives against which they're framed are not *approximately* consistent over time frames scaled to the implementation horizons of normal human projects. But 'rational' in 'rational expectations' refers to the relative *accuracy* of agents' information, not to choice consistency.

Clearly most people do not spend whatever resources they would have to in order to operate with the most accurate information they possibly could bring to bear in all circumstances; and no version of the REH taken seriously by economists says that they do. The REH is, rather, a restriction on the extent to which the economist should allow that some agents – particularly policy-makers and would-be arbitragers in markets – can manipulate other agents' ignorance when those very manipulations incentivize the manipulated to become better informed. This restriction is consistent with many specific models of expectations. As one would therefore expect, both the theoretical and empirical literatures in economics are replete with such models; and different models perform better in different empirical applications, because actual people have well-stocked toolkits of expectations-refining tricks, habits and heuristics that are influenced by their varying cultures, institutions and incentives.

It is no doubt true that some economists have, at least rhetorically, treated the principle that no individual can systematically outperform a large financial market's asset price forecasts (that is, the Efficient Markets Hypothesis) as if it implied the patently false claim that market prices must always imply *correct* estimates of value (where 'correct' refers to comparison of forecasts with actual future states). *That* confusion was indeed 'refuted' by the 2008–09 crisis – as if anyone needed so dramatic a refuter when every recession, however mild, has already contributed plenty of counter-evidence. But as for *reasonable* expectations models embedded in macroeconomic theories, some were cast into doubt by the painful recent experiences and some were not. Analogously, some currently well-regarded models of adaptation in population ecology are going to be winnowed out when climate change presents scientists with hitherto unavailable observations; other models will survive this confrontation with new facts. That sort of *gentle* Popperian process – falsificationism without bold conjectures or dramatic moments of refutation – *is* how science normally makes progress.

However, when critics heaped scorn on the macroeconomics establishment over the occurrence of the financial crisis, their intended focus was usually less on specific models than on a more diffuse culture of overconfidence they discerned among economists. Had the crisis indeed struck most economists as an utter bolt from the blue this debunking attitude would have been justified. But few economists I know were either amazed or even particularly surprised by what happened in late 2008 and thereafter. Richard Posner (2009, pp. 77–78) points out that the most influential sources of sophisticated economic journalism, the sources actually read by almost all finance executives, clearly recognized well before 2008 that residential real estate in the US was over-valued and that correction of this potentially involved magnitudes big enough to trigger a major financial crisis. Posner particularly cites *The Economist* as having been "obsessed" with the housing bubble and with its threat to the real global economy, from as far back as 2003. The main (anonymous) sources of predictions retailed by the journalists at *The Economist* are, as one might think, economists. Furthermore, the mechanisms of crisis transmission *The Economist* identified were exactly those that were in fact tripped during 2007–2008: the spread of mortgage-backed securities through the asset books of global financial institutions, the increasing correlation of risk caused by the manufacture of opaque derivatives based on these securities, and the amplification of this risk by credit default swaps. The problem is that anyone who acted on this prediction in 2003 would have lost money because the bubble still had three more years of growth in front of it. The moment when, in my experience, most economists began to expect the real estate market correction to be violent instead of gentle *and* to produce a general crisis in capital availability across the economy was when a major French bank went under in August 2007 and reported that it could not determine the proportion of loans on its book that were linked to non-performing mortgages. It still surprises me that 13 more months elapsed before the bankruptcy of Lehmann Brothers caused inter-bank lending to freeze and brought on the Great Recession.

A reader who wants to see how systematic study of structural relationships among macroeconomic variables can yield *understanding* of events such as recessions, even in the absence of any deterministic theory that would allow their timing to be predicted, should consult Leamer (2009). Through dogged attention to patterns in the timing of changes in various aggregate indicators, Leamer musters a persuasive argument for the conclusion that of the ten major episodes of negative growth in the US since World War II, eight were associated with interest rates being set too low for too long and triggering over-coordination by consumers on purchases of homes and durable goods (e.g., cars). If this is the *normal* pattern associated with recessions, then we know something about the danger signals to watch for when trying to forecast new ones. But Leamer's analysis also suggests that this generalization, however illuminating, has exceptions. The 1953 recession, he argues, had a different basis, namely a sudden contraction in defense spending following the relatively sudden and unexpected end of the Korean War (which was itself brought about by the sudden and unexpected event of the death of the Soviet dictator Stalin). The 2001 recession had yet another *sui generis* origin, the race for supply-side positions in the new internet services market, which generated a level of aggregate investment that could not be supported by fast enough aggregate revenues.

Note that work of this relatively atheoretical kind is not in tension with a general structural perspective such as that offered by Frydman and Goldberg. Leamer does not address the question of which general models of expectations are and aren't compatible with his empirical analyzes. But that is a natural thing to wonder about. If the US Federal Reserve has recurrently let bubbles inflate through overly loose monetary policy, why does it not learn from experience? Why do consumers not notice that when house prices start rising faster than rental prices and incomes, they should postpone buying?

Xavier Ragot (2012) suggests one of the many available sensible weakenings of the REH. Instead of urging that no agent in a model should be allowed to be unappraised of anything known to the economist who builds the model, Ragot recommends that "if the economist builds a theory or model in which the agents fail to do something that it is in their interests to do, then the economist must justify why they did not do it" (pp. 187–188). This reflects Simon's famous point that since gathering and processing information are costly activities, agents need adequate incentives to engage in them; but institutional settings may often fail to furnish the requisite incentives. In the case of the run-up to the financial crisis, one can safely surmise that most senior bankers at least read *The Economist*. However, after the crisis set in, when banks were forced to distinguish non-performing from performing and potentially recoverable loans on their books, the opaque structures of many of the securities they held turned out to make that information recovery extremely difficult and time-consuming. And even then they would not have subjected themselves to gruelling 'stress testing' exercises[8] had governments not forced them to do so. To have engaged in this work before the crash, when shareholders would have punished any financial institution that stopped delivering the heady value appreciation prevailing in the industry, would have required a strongly motivating fear of insolvency leading to bankruptcy. However, subsequent events also showed that with the exception of the politically unlucky Lehmann Brothers and the genuinely deranged banks of Iceland, such fear would have been misplaced. For the majority of institutions, effective insolvency did *not* lead to bankruptcy, thanks to bailouts from government that most economists and financial managers had anticipated.[9] One might think – I do think – that the leadership of the largest financial institutions showed an alarming lack of professional concern for their client relationships before, and for that matter since, 2008. But I do *not* think a convincing case can be made that they were 'irrational' in some fundamental sense that henceforth must be reflected in a revamped economic modeling methodology. As for the Federal Reserve and the mass of consumers, I think it is clear that they lacked an accurate model of the incentives influencing the banks, and consequently did not recognize that interest rates were much too low.

This is not to say that the dramatic economic events that continue to roil the world as I write in 2013 offer no basis for fertile methodological reflection. The crisis, I have argued, did not show that there is anything profoundly wrong with economics as a science. However, a reasonably thorough understanding of the causes and dynamics of the crisis cannot be provided merely by best-practice economic modeling of business cycles (whatever best practice is thought to be). Some factors that have been cited as important causal factors for the crisis, such as global imbalances in savings rates between Western and Eastern economies combined with increasing global correlation of risks (Pettis 2013), are best captured in economic models. But other causal factors that may be equally important, including capture of asset ratings agencies by financial institutions and the rising income

---

[8] This refers to simulations in which sets of assets are studied to determine what would happen to their values under various hypothetical exogenous shocks, such as sudden increases in interest rates or violent exchange rate movements.

[9] The majority of economists were surprised when the US government did *not* rescue Lehman Brothers. If the Bush administration could have had that moment of decision back with the advantage of hindsight, they almost certainly would have acted differently.

inequalities that have eroded middle class household savings in wealthy countries (Rajan 2010), require the attention of political scientists and sociologists. Lurking among the fundamental conditioning influences on all business cycle modeling at all times are the forces of demographics. A major source of the collapse of household savings in wealthy countries is the ageing of their populations – as people retire they need to spend what they have saved. And it is difficult to imagine how most European countries or Japan can possibly restore their pre-crisis wealth while their labor productivity declines for the most elementary and inexorable of reasons. Finally, the deeply alarming worldwide phenomenon of increasing youth unemployment almost certainly has its most important (though not only) causal root in massive structural adjustments on both the demand and supply sides of labor markets driven by the commercialization of artificial intelligence and robotics (Brynjolfsson and McAfee 2012).

It is understandable that in the immediate wake of a considerable economic disaster business cycle research is preoccupied with the particular characteristics of crises that choke off credit markets (see Reinhart and Rogoff 2009). But if we step back from this preoccupation, we find that the history of business cycle theory delivers a payoff that is of deeper significance to our philosophical project of wondering how economics fits into the wider project of the social and behavioral sciences.

5.3   The two driving forces of economic dynamics

There is a contingent, empirical reason why it is possible for economists to discover highly general structural truths about the dynamics of markets. That is, there is a reason why economics is more than a mere summary of historical episodes. The reason in question is based on a contingent fact about the social world. This is that two exogenous forces are, at least throughout the period since the beginning of industrialization, overwhelmingly dominant drivers of economic change and primary determinants of available sets of local equilibria. The existence of just *two* such forces explains why large-scale economies are not so complex and nonreproducible in their dynamics as to confound efforts at formulating any general theory. The specific nature of these two forces is also important to the argument for understanding economics as a social science rather than as an extension of the theory of individual decision-making.

The two forces in question are demographic and technological change.

I will consider technology first. As Schumpeter (1911/1982) first articulated comprehensively,[10] if market institutions exist to allocate capital to competing firms on the basis of their comparative productivity, then firms can reliably be expected to invest in invention and commercialization of new methods of production, and in new devices for generating utility, that will continuously disrupt existing relationships between supply and demand. The institutional prerequisite is crucial, and must include institutions for preventing oligopolies from locking out new competitors through fostering market suppressing regulation (Acemoglu and Robinson 2012). This prerequisite is frequently unfulfilled at local scales; national and municipal governments are typically captured to some extent by cartels of producers. However, globalization – by which I refer to the tendency of markets in separate jurisdictions to fuse through cross-border exchanges, which has been occurring since the beginning of industrial capitalism in north-western Europe – ensures that the quiet lives of oligopolies protected by politicians tend to be brief. So technological change forces economic change sufficiently reliably to rise above the noisy flux of other causal forces as a primary generator of real economic patterns.

There is an air of paradox in saying that the source of continuous *disruption* of business equilibria is a primary basis for the *regularities* that provide traction for relatively general economic theory. It was Schumpeter's genius to see through this apparent paradox. Economies that are driven on macro scales by a large and fluctuating range of micro-scale influences will, from the modeler's point of view, drift aimlessly within wide but shallow basins of equilibria. This situation arguably describes pre-industrial economies (except on very long timescales), and makes it unsurprising that scientific economics emerged only with the rise of capitalism and industrialization. But once technological innovation is harnessed to a continuous collective

---

[10] Schumpeter had an idiosyncratic and highly implausible econophysical theory of business cycles. Fortunately, the insight for which he is most famous does not depend on it.

search for productivity improvements, economic change begins to approximate a deterministic system – albeit a highly stochastic one,[11] with vanishing predictability as scales of analysis shrink. The key to the (stochastic) determinism of the Schumpeterian economic process is that technological knowledge once achieved is rarely forgotten, so contingent barriers to productivity growth are always temporary. The process of economic development therefore does not simply drift: markets become machines that search possibility spaces for productivity improvements. Capitalist competition is a ratchet that turns in one direction, and thereby invites statistical modeling and generalization.

This story is important to explaining why economics is a *social* science and why methodological individualism is profoundly mistaken as a basis for its ontology. At the micro scale of, say, the competition between two neighboring pizzerias, theoretical economics should not be expected to be the best source of predictions or explanations. Facts about the psychological dispositions of the pizzeria owners, and their respective places in local ethnographic networks, are the appropriate foci of attention for predicting and explaining how they fare against one another. However, as scales increase, attention to the elements that feature in economic models generates steadily increasing epistemological yield. Long before we reach the scale of macroeconomics – for example, at the scale where we analyze the whole fast-food sector in a city – microeconomists working in industrial organization (IO) theory can bring game theory to bear to understand general relationships between industry structures, asymmetric strategic incentives between incumbent and entering firms, forms of access to finance, and the probabilities that firms will invest in and commercialize product and production system innovations. (Sutton [2001] is the most sophisticated and enlightening source of methodological reflection on this kind of work.) What makes this modeling possible, and gives it empirical purchase as a primary basis for policy decisions by competition authorities and designers of taxation schemes, is the maintained assumption throughout that productivity enhancement is the goal of technological

---

[11] As quantum theory in physics has made clear, a system can be stochastic in the sense that all equations describing it involve conditional probabilities other than zero or one, but also deterministic in the sense that the model does not leave out any influencing factors.

innovation, and that more productive technology will ultimately displace less productive technology.

The second dominant exogenous driver of economic dynamics, population demographics, likewise directs our attention to large-scale social modeling. Economic modeling would be very different from what it is if each generation of people reliably produced just enough offspring to replace itself, or to generate a modest and steady rate of growth that tracked rates of increase in wealth-building productivity. Again, in such a hypothetical world the basic causes of differences among market equilibria would – if we set technological progress aside – be a host of irregular historical contingencies related in highly complex and circumstance-dependent ways. But the actual world, at least since the industrial revolution, has been characterized by a succession of strong demographic responses to technological change, which then equally powerfully react back on the structures of production and distribution.

In the first stages of industrialization there was a steady increase in demand for concentrations of unskilled labor. Relatively disempowered women were induced by the institutional structures of patriarchy to rear this labor supply, and populations surged. But, predictably, the skill levels demanded by ever more sophisticated technology steadily rose. This had a number of profound consequences. Mass education was provided using state-collected funds so workers could read, write, count and be conditioned to let their lives be governed by clocks. This created a citizenry that was more effective in exercising political participation, which in turn induced elites who needed cooperative labor, and who were anxious to avoid forced experiments in industrial communism, to accede to the grand bargain represented by the modern welfare state. However, starting in the most advanced industrial countries after the 1970s, further technological change began shifting production back to less labor-intensive methods. This, in conjunction with the incorporation of women into formal labor market participation, which was also a consequence of mass education and improved social security, has led to declining mean family sizes. This decline now predicts falling per capita productivity as the population structure in almost all wealthy countries, along with China and Russia, tilts dramatically in favor of older people. In addition, it is not clear that anyone knows how to effectively adapt the existing institutions of mass publicly funded education systems to instill the higher skills levels demanded by the production side of the increasingly knowledge-intensive economy. In consequence we confront a spreading global phenomenon in which producers adopt more capital-intensive methods despite rising youth unemployment, because large proportions of the in-principle available labor supply lacks the skills or discipline needed to add economic value. This leads wealthy families to withdraw their support from public education while they carry the costs of educating their own offspring privately. The unsurprising result, at least in the short term, is rising inequality, declining population shares in middle classes, and erosion of the fiscal basis needed to maintain social insurance.[12]

Again, it is possible to develop general economic models of these phenomena because, at large enough scales of aggregation, the causal weight of effects of demographic change overwhelm the host of more complex micro-scale influences. And, again, the explanatory and predictive power of such modeling declines as scales of analysis get smaller. If my neighbor wants to understand why her son is continuously unable to impress potential employers in job interviews, she should focus primarily on his style of personal presentation and the extent to which he realistically perceives his capacities when he applies for positions. If she wants expert help with this problem, she should consult an employment counselor or psychologist, not an economist. But when the Minister of Industrial Development wonders why her schemes to encourage youth employment are proving even less effective than those of her predecessors, despite the fact that her government is allocating substantially more resources to them, it is precisely a carefully built set of economic models she should consult, not a panel of psychologists who could design mass workshops on interview preparation.

Many readers will object at this point that themes such as increasing alienation from labor market participation among poorly educated young people are at least as much sociological phenomena as economic ones. Less wealthy parents are unable to send their children to suffi-ciently effective schools in large part because they collectively lack the political power to force the tax increases that would be needed to pay for them. Long experience with such powerlessness perhaps gives rise

---

[12] Libertarians imagine that the optimal level of state-funded social insurance is zero. This is bad economics. People who face irrecoverable ruin at their first major illness or injury are much less likely to invest in their own human capital; and that is a serious source of inefficiency.

to cultural trends that emphasize alternative paths to social status, such as heroic substance abuse among young men or network strengthening through encouragement of ethnic polarization, which further undermine pro-educational values. Such aspects of social dynamics have been the focus of sociological study since the dawn of that discipline; and it is not difficult to make the case that they matter at least as much to understanding social reality as consideration of the effects of the latest sources of marginal productivity improvements on labor market structures.

A typical mainstream economist before the 1970s would have rejected this last claim. I conjecture that the main reason for this skeptical attitude to sociology was that economics as a discipline had then embraced mathematical analysis for a few decades while many – though certainly not all – sociologists continued to mainly produce narratives. The narratives in question were not biographical stories about individuals; no discipline has been more self-conscious than sociology about being a *social* science. But a common sociological method was based on identification with the empirically grounded, but also imaginatively constructed, subjectivity of various types of people that sociologists identified with *social roles*. 'Ideal types' of role players, to use the venerable terminology of the great early sociologist Max Weber (1864–1920), were essentially representative agents of sub-populations such as industrial workers or office clerks or young housewives. Because they were characterized much more thickly than economists' representative agents – who were merely walking ordinal utility functions with fixed productive capacities – their interactions were represented as being much more complex and difficult to capture in mathematical models.

We can look back on this period of methodological estrangement between economists and sociologists with equal sympathy for the prevailing attitudes of both sides. As explained in Chapter 2, economists working before the fusion of game theory with information theory, or the development of the capacity for estimating models of large statistical data sets, were largely restricted to comparing the overall welfare efficiency of different allocative regimes. This implied that they simply could not be in the business of thick social explanation. But it also implies that it would have been perverse for sociologists to have emulated economists' methods, as that would have simply amounted to giving up on the sociologist's ambitions. At the same time, the prosaic descriptive narratives that served as the exemplars of great sociology were not very effective methodological templates for lesser mortals than Weber, Durkheim or Goffman. Though I recognize that many will disagree with what I am about to say, and though space limitations deter me from embarking on the many pages of discussion that would be required to make it more than a tendentious assertion, I do not think that standard sociology before the 1970s succeeded in establishing anything that can literally be regarded as a scientific generalization. Most economists sensed this; and many were rude about it.

The situation just described is now as dead as dodo birds. On the one hand, contemporary sociology is mainly driven by statistical analysis of large empirical data sets. If someone wants to make a good career as a sociologist, they need to master the highly technical discipline of critical population survey design and implementation. On the other hand, a glance at any recent issue of the leading general economics journals – for example, the *American Economic Review* – will find that the majority of articles model sets of heterogeneous agents with rich demographic texture. An economist is as likely as a sociologist to want to know why some children drop out of high school while others sacrifice most of their play time to build CVs that might someday get them into MIT, or why young unemployed African-American men are more likely than their sisters to become too discouraged to continue searching for jobs. Sociologists generally do not refer to their toolbox of data analysis technologies as 'econometrics,' but differences in underlying foundations of these techniques are more semantic than substantive. My own university has a thriving institution called the Centre for Social Science Research in which economists and sociologists collaborate on empirical projects. When I go to their seminars I would battle to tell the one group apart from the other were it not for the uninteresting accident that I am the dean to the economists, who are in the business school, but not to the sociologists, who are in the humanities school.

The sociologist John Levi Martin (2009) makes the interesting point that sociologists have largely transitioned from representing structural relationships using graph theory to matrix notation, which has been the norm among economists for many decades. According to Martin, this has not been motivated by an implicit aim among sociologists to turn themselves into economists, but by a recognition that it allows for representation of absent influences instead of only actual positive or negative ones. That it also allows for representation of quantitatively measurable influences – where empirically appropriate – might have only begun as an unintended side benefit, but one that is now routinely exploited in sociological practice.

There is reason to believe, then, that economics and sociology are undergoing fusion, and that this is to be welcomed. However, merely noting that economists and sociologists are increasingly using similar tools to study similar – or the same – problems does not yet address philosophical issues around the structure of potential disciplinary unification. To this I now turn.

5.4   Unifying economics and sociology

Writers have disputed over the justification, nature and location of the boundary between economics and sociology since the institutional birth of the two disciplines in the late nineteenth century. Most of those who have favoured eradication of the boundary have supposed, sometimes explicitly, that this should happen through *conquest* from one side or the other. Fine and Milonakis (2009), in their excited jeremiad against imperialistic economists, find no shortage of fodder for their paranoia in thoughtless comments by economists over the decades to the effect that since any human motivation can be the argument of a utility function, all sociological propositions must either be imprecise nonsense or can be translated into economic models. I call such comments 'thoughtless' because they are circular: what makes a model *interestingly* 'economic' is not, in the first place, what formalism can be used to represent it. One could describe macro-scale physical objects using utility functions (e.g., such objects 'optimize' by following geodesic paths in spacetime), but one would not thereby turn relativistic physics into economics. Most casual economists' rhetoric about displacing sociology is merely an expression of tribalism within the institutional structure of academia. On the other side, one can find uncompromising critics of mainstream economics – for example Lawson (1997), and Addleson (1997) – who demand that economists abandon their focus on markets and equilibria and effectively turn themselves into sociologists as traditionally conceived.

This 'traditional conception' has its clearest and most influential roots in Max Weber's (1949) understanding of the differences between economics and sociology. According to Weber, economics begins with behavioral descriptions of isolated individuals and derives social relationships from them (Udehn 2001, pp. 100–101). Sociologists, by contrast, begin with the co-construction of the meaning and significance of actions and outcomes by diads or groups. As Udehn (ibid.) points out, this conception of the disciplinary boundary became unsustainable once microeconomics came to be dominated by game theory. Equilibrium solutions to games, as we saw in Chapter 3, are vectors of relationships among intentional programs of action, not aggregations of individual decisions. Following Harsanyi (1977) and Shubik (1982), we can say that a game is not specified unless one has identified its rules; and the 'rules of a game' are invariably idealizations of social institutions. Gintis (2009) takes a similar view, arguing that were sociologists to base their models on information-theoretically interpreted game theory, while economists generally recognized the gratuitousness and empirical inadequacy of models based strictly on narrowly selfish optimization, then all of the social sciences would be automatically unified.

I think it is true that if the social scientist's fundamental box of tools includes game theory *and* if strategies of game players are interpreted on the basis of an externalist philosophy of intentionality as described in Chapter 4, then in a highly abstract sense the social sciences are duly unified. But we cannot be content to stop with such elevated conceptual pronouncements. This is like announcing that all sciences are unified by the recognition that they all model real statistical patterns (Ladyman and Ross 2012). That is correct, but it is *mere* philosophy. Making the philosophical point scientifically relevant requires attention to methodological issues. Economics and psychology are unified at the purely philosophical level of analysis but remain separate disciplines because they are methodologically distinct and aim to explain different aspects of social reality. By contrast, economics and sociology study the same subject matter and their remaining methodological differences are *only* institutional.

The key methodological ambiguity that arises when sociological theorists debate their relationship to economics centers around the centrality of markets in economics. I have been insisting throughout this book that market structures and processes are the basic subject matter of economics. Thus sociologists such as Martin (2009) who consider it crucial that *their* subject matter transcends markets will be immediately skeptical concerning my claims about disciplinary unification.

A useful way of getting straight to the heart of this issue is to focus on conflicting interpretations of one of the great general methodological treatises in sociology, James Coleman's *Foundations of Social Theory* (1990). Coleman explicitly constructs sociology as the science of generalized *social exchange*. Martin vehemently rejects this construction. I will not aim here to fashion a reconciliation between Coleman and Martin on all points that divide them, which would require another book. However, I will aim to eliminate the gulf between them on a very general methodological level that is sufficient to establish my unification thesis, and in a way that does not force me to claim that Martin is wrong about the character of his discipline.

On Coleman's account, among the basic assets that are allocated in a social structure are *rights* to *control* actions of agents. 'Rights to control' refers to institutionalized norms of legitimation. Kidnappers control the actions of their victims, but not on the basis of any allocated rights. By contrast, a CEO controls (many) actions of the employees of the company she directs, and a wide range of institutional structures and forces supports her entitlement to this control. Legitimately controlling agents are often collective; (many of) the CEO's actions are controlled by no particular individual, but they are controlled by the joint agency of the Board of Directors, which exerts its agency according to constituting rules.

Sociology is often thought by skeptical economists to reach beyond suitably observable foundational elements because it treats *power* and *social roles* as basic constructs. Such economists would balk at Coleman's foundational treatment of rights to control. The CEO has socially legitimated power over her firm's employees and her Board has socially legitimated power over her. But her power attaches neither to her nor to her employees as *people*. She may not tell her employees how to raise their children or what films they can watch or what they can and can't eat for breakfast, except insofar as these choices interfere with their performance of their corporate responsibilities (i.e., she *can* instruct them not to have vodka for breakfast on workdays). When a person leaves the employment of the company, the CEO's power over him dissolves altogether. Thus the power asymmetry is associated with *roles* that the specific people occupy, rather than with the people *qua* people. The institutionalism that I defended in Chapter 3 is the basis of my response to the economist who thinks that power and social roles are mere verbal glosses on more fundamental behavioral elements (or, as a sociologist would be more likely to put it, *reifications*). Economic theory that is not built up analytically from foundations in individual decision theory – as I have spent most of this book arguing it should not be – doesn't get off the ground unless a legal framework establishing property rights is presupposed. The property rights that legitimate certain relationships between people in certain roles (shareholder, homeowner, etc.) and material or financial objects are foundationally on all fours with the control rights that legitimate certain relationships among social roles occupied by people. As for power, this has been treated as a primitive element in the economic theory of bargaining since Nash (1950b); see Binmore (1998, chapter 1; 2005, pp. 40–42, 179–183). Notwithstanding various rules different societies use for legitimizing transfers of power, power is always and everywhere fundamentally a function of the extent of an agent's control over others' actions and over property.

This foundational symmetry between property rights and rights to social control is the core basis for Coleman's unified model of social theory. These rights provide the basis for social *value*:

> The value of an event lies in the interests powerful actors have in the event ... The value of a resource differs from an interest that a given actor has in it, for the value is a property of the resource in the system as a whole ... The value of a resource lies in what an actor who controls it can gain from exchanging it. (Coleman 1990, p. 133)

Social interaction as Coleman models it then consists of cooperative exchanges in which agents exercise their rights for one another's advantage. Some of these exchanges occur in monetized markets: companies direct their employees to perform services for customers, lessors grant temporary use of property, agents exchange ownership of property for cash. Other exchanges involve non-monetized assets: property is bartered, circles of friends contribute their time, sweat and vehicles to help one another move, politicians and lobbyists exert their network influence on one another's behalf. And of course, to the extent that their interests are not aligned, agents use resources they control to compete with one another. Coleman's general model of social analysis is an equilibrium account:

> Control over goods and events, and the systemic functioning, is dependent on a balance of power among those who are interested in gaining control. That functioning consists of actors using resources under their control to gain control of other resources of greater interest to them, in competition with others also interested in gaining control of the same resources. The equilibrium that is achieved is one in which each actor's resources are pitted against, or balanced against, the resources of other actors in the system. (ibid., p. 899)

Coleman's picture has been criticized by some sociologists for allegedly incorporating methodological individualism (MI) (e.g., Fine and Milonakis 2009). On the other hand, Udehn (2001, p. 304) interprets his position as "structural-individualism," because the most powerful social actors according to Coleman are firms and bureaucracies; and such actors "have interests of their own, interests which are distinct from the interests of the natural persons, who occupy positions in the corporate actors. Thus 'corporate actors are, in their actions, motivated towards purposes of their own – very often purely growth – for which membership benefits are viewed merely as constraints' (Coleman, 1974: 29)" (Udehn 2001, p. 296).

I want to avoid bogging down here in debates that revolve mainly around subtle distinctions between different meanings attached in the meta-sociological literature to 'individualism' and 'structuralism.' Udehn views Coleman as a kind of individualist because Coleman so described himself; and the point of this self-labeling was to signal rejection of "holism" and "collectivism." Holists and collectivists are characterized as people who view social structure as orthogonal to *all* agency, as a different category of being altogether. One might be tempted to claim that positions of this kind couldn't possibly apply to any economists, as they require an esoteric metaphysics and a disinterest in the concept of choice; but I am not so sure. Perhaps Hildenbrand, with his rigorous avoidance of any behavioral elements in his analysis of market demand, is an instance of a holistic economist.

The reason I think we can bypass these issues is that the basis of the anti-individualism defended in this book is not a thesis about the general nature of social causation, as are each of the various doctrines distinguished by Udehn that feature in the standard debates over social ontology in the methodology of sociology literature. Rather, what I am rejecting when I attack individualistic explanation is the idea that people have intentional states, specifically preferences and beliefs, that remain assignable properties of them in isolation from the normative expectations of others with whom they interact. Individuals, I claim, are products of social structure, not components into which social structure can be analyzed. This simply removes from serious consideration the kind of individualism that has often been rhetorically associated with economics by libertarian ideologues, and which is incompatible with explanatory principles used across the social sciences. That clears the way for reconciliation of economics with sociology *regardless* of which subtle metaphysical spin one extracts from the classic debates. I am not convinced that these debates, like other exercises in analytic philosophy, have much bearing on how anyone actually goes about practicing empirical social science. They also appear orthogonal to what bothers Martin (2009) about Coleman, which is the latter's emphasis on *exchange* as fundamental.

Let me begin my discussion of Martin's book by saying that I am treating it here as the current state-of-the-art review of the foundations of sociology, and thus as a primary source for investigating what economists should learn from their sister discipline. I will turn to these learning points, however, only following some critical remarks about Martin's understanding of markets.

Martin is not a particularly polemical writer. However, one tendency in sociological method clearly sets his teeth on edge. I quote him at length:

> Our understanding of the structure of … dyadic exchange has been (somewhat ironically) seriously hampered by the obsessive interest with understanding social life in terms of exchange found in the social sciences. To make a long story short, there is something about capitalist society that leads many people to be easily convinced that exchange is the be-all and end-all of society. Consequently, there are recurrent waves of fanatical exchange theorizing, all foundering on the same ideological

shoal. This is the dogma that all exchanges must be equal. To be fair, there is some analytic reason to wish for such an axiom: if it is true, it can be used to identify utilities not obvious at the start – plus, we can hope to always be able to talk our poorer neighbours out of killing us. Further, when social structures exist to *make* this true, social interaction is dramatically changed. However, the conviction that it is *always* true is perhaps the single least intelligent thing that can be said about exchange.

The recurrent assumption that exchanges are always equal is particularly foolish since it does not even flow from the postulates of rational action (postulates that are indeed frequently useful, though the one thing we know about them is that they are not strictly true). These postulates do not even allow us to derive the often assumed conclusion … that for any freely made exchange, the costs cannot outweigh the benefits for either party. The costs of exchanges very frequently do outweigh the benefits to one party in a rational interaction; they simply are less than the costs entailed in *not* making an exchange. This is generally the case for exchanges between unequal parties in the absence of a true market, and we will see the importance of this in our analysis of patronage structures below.

(Martin 2009, pp. 77–78)

There is a lot to unpack here. Economists reading these passages are apt to see as most salient the familiar sociologist's emphasis on power differentials, and the accompanying suggestion that economists ignore these by assuming that every party to any market transaction is 'free' to simply walk away from it if it does not increase their utility.

Economists are of course aware that some transactions result from mafia-style 'offers you can't refuse.' It is indeed an over-worn half-joke in introductory economics to ask students to imagine a person held up by an armed mugger who presents him with the *choice* "Your money or your life?" I have emphasized the word 'choice' here because that is the very point of telling the story: we want the students to see that although the victim will likely have nothing to deliberate about, and indeed has no freedom in a non-technical sense, his handing over of his wallet *does* reveal that he prefers being alive and wallet-less to being dead. In the only sense of choice that matters in economics, namely that the behavior is sensitive to incentives, a choice it is. We can see this merely by imagining a likely course of events if the hypothetical victim were on his way to jump off the subway platform, and thinks that getting shot is a less awful form of demise.

Nothing in Coleman's exchange-based account of social structure implies that all participants, or most participants, or for that matter *any* participants, in exchanges of rights to control typically get the best outcome they possibly could. Experience with game theory, as any contemporary theorist of markets must have, shows immediately that many real-life situations modeled as Nash equilibria are miserable outcomes for some parties. Some such situations, for example long labor strikes that result from rational but poorly informed mutual conjectures about fallback positions, produce bad outcomes for both bargaining sides and no compensating upsides for anyone. Far from denying that such exchanges occur, economists who model labor disputes have taken recurring interest in them (Kennan and Wilson 1989).

We can obtain a more sophisticated sense of Martin's issue here by focusing on his reference to "hope" that we will "always be able to talk our poorer neighbours out of killing us." This has a direct referent (whether or not Martin intended it) in the game-theoretic political economy literature. Binmore (1998) uses Nash bargaining theory to show that in the absence of coalition formation, agents who bargain with each other from positions of unequal power will eventually converge on the solution that the political philosopher John Rawls (1971) recommended as being in accordance with the liberal conception of justice. Binmore's result indeed hinges on the proposition that there is some offer that can be made to the poor which they prefer to the outcome they obtain when they riot and burn down the society. Perhaps this presumes a heartier brace of enlightenment rationality than general facts warrant. However, it is important to point out that in Binmore's multi-stage (evolutionary) game the optimistic result is not mainly driven by enlightenment confidence. It is driven instead by the fact that the very poor require what is, to them, very substantial compensation for continuing to bargain from one round to the next in the earlier going. In consequence they get better off from round to round. Then the principal point of the model is to identify conditions under which the evolution of egalitarian norms as the poor get relatively richer prevents the initially rich from breaking off talks as soon as they're confident that the initially poor have acquired too much to lose to still have a credible threat to break off negotiations. What matters for present purposes is not whether Binmore's model does or does not shed light on real processes of normative adjustment. The point is rather that this exchange model, of precisely the kind that excites Martin's sarcasm, depends on the adjustment of norms for managing transactions in which inequality threatens stability. So here in the very heartland of mathematicized exchange-based models of social structure, Martin's critical presumption about the kind of theory he opposes is violated.

Martin in fact has a more specific motivation for being skeptical about exchange models. This is his conviction that among the primary drivers of the development of social structure are networks of what he calls 'patronage networks.' The idea here is that people with high social status are often required to give more to their political clients than they get back in return in order to maintain their status as patrons. Martin's main examples of this are drawn from pre-capitalist societies, which might encourage some economists to doubt their relevance. We can repair this deficit, however, by considering the fact that many relatively wealthy people in modern developed countries put in weekly work hours that are far above the mean. Economists tend to be drawn first to the hypothesis that this is because the opportunity cost of such leisure time as these people take is correspondingly far above the mean. But there is no shortage of very hard-working people whose main income arises from dividends or interest or rents and would thus continue to accrue if they did little or nothing. It intuitively *seems* that such people care more about patronizing their shareholders and employees than about their narrow self-interest. (Of course, as Schumpeter [1942] supposed, they might also gain personal utility from building business empires that is independent of monetary income or wealth.)

Martin's empirical hypothesis is reasonable, then. But it represents no challenge to standard economic modeling, which, as discussed in Chapter 2, allows that utility can derive from anything an agent values, including status or feelings of self-worth that derive from exercises of patronage (see Cox et al. 2008). There are various indications in Martin's text that when he refers to exchange, he presupposes a narrow conception of markets associated with perfect competition. For example, he argues that matching games, for example between potential employers and employees, or between potential spouses, do not involve exchanges and are not set in markets (Martin 2009, p. 71). In a footnote (49) he refers to "the frequent confusion of such pairing structures with a price-making market," and then says "But the restrictive conditions necessary for a pure market need not be invoked when we simply see interaction follow a spatial logic induced by a popularity tournament." These semantics, according to which whatever is not a *Walrasian* market is not a market at all, are sometimes deployed by economists, including non-dogmatic ones. For example, the methodologically open-minded, highly empirically focused Edward Leamer (2009, pp. 143–146) explains the fact that wages are sticky (i.e., tend not to fall during recessions) by saying that most employer-employee relationships in manufacturing (as contrasted with agriculture) are thick and personal, and so should not be modeled as "market" phenomena. Leamer, unlike Martin, is explicit that he confines 'markets' to Walrasian price-setting processes. But 'market' is never used this narrowly in the contemporary game-theoretic literature on 'labor markets' (Fields 2009). These economists generally account for the stickiness of 'labor markets' exactly as Leamer does. Martin would have to say that they are modeling a network of patronage relationships. Would he say they have thereby turned into sociologists?

This unsubtle semantic ambiguity is a nice expression of my main point in this section. The explanatory interests *and* the empirical research programs of economists and sociologists are becoming so indistinguishable that we cannot even predict a scholar's use of basic terminology from his or her institutional disciplinary affiliation. The residue of former genuine, non-semantic divergences persists in the merely semantic disagreement; but in our example we have 'market' being used in one sense (Walrasian only) by one economist and one sociologist (Leamer and Martin respectively) and also in the other sense (anything modeled with game theory) by one economist and one sociologist (Fields and Coleman respectively).

I am not claiming that nothing *at all* still distinguishes economists from sociologists. Young sociologists enjoy a richer menu of philosophical material in their graduate courses, which among other things inclines them to draw analytical conceptual distinctions that most economists ignore. One of Martin's central concerns is to develop a theory of structure as pre-institutional. The idea here is as follows. *Structure* arises when people become interchangeable within roles. The inventory auditor at a plant does what any inventory auditor is expected by others to do, not what Joseph E. Bloggs is expected to do by the experts on Bloggs, namely Bloggs's family and friends. Similarly, at the dawn of the division of labor according to Ofek (2001), a late *Homo erectus* fire-keeper did what any fire-keeper was expected to do. But, Martin argues, the modern Bloggs has room for cognitive maneuver that the individual Paleolithic fire-keeper – or the medieval apprentice – did not. Bloggs can dissociate himself from his structural role. For example, he can frame the idea that "I could go and be an auditor for a different company," or more radically, with a nod at Monty Python, "I could go and be a lion tamer." In Martin's conceptual scheme, this dissociation marks the coming of *institutional* structure (Martin 2009, p. 337).

Economists have not traditionally distinguished between structures and institutions in this way (or in any other way). The absence of this distinction in most economics, I contend, is responsible for the two main respects in which, to external critics, economists have seemed to be saddled with empirically impoverished models of agency. First, it has led them to ignore the importance of the fact that a person does not simply converge on one model of economic agency when pressures from market forces and institutions constrain her choices. The relationship between people and economic agents is more complex: a typical person transitions among different normatively governed agents, with different utility functions. (This is part of the reason why we do better empirical economics when, in modeling choice data at the population level, we avoid imposing the restriction that each experimental subject is identified with one utility function; see Chapters 3 and 4.) Second, failure to draw Martin's distinction has blocked most economists from seeing that the *normative* individualism they typically find compelling in policy contexts is best understood if it is *not* confused with an empirically false *descriptive* individualism that imagines that people might have economic preferences that are exogenous to social interaction.

But economists are beginning to transcend these limitations; and in doing so they are closing the last remaining open water between their discipline and sociology. I will close the book with these two developments, in turn.

5.5   Team reasoning and conditional games

An important class of games I mentioned in Chapter 3, but on which discussion was deferred until now, are games of *pure coordination*. These games are of particular interest to sociologists because, as first argued by the philosopher David Lewis (1969), they are ideal settings for displaying the logic of social conventions.[13] The classic example of a Pure Coordination game is that underlying driving conventions. Imagine people freely choosing whether to drive on the right-hand or the left-hand side of the road. To simplify – in a way which doesn't distort the logic at all – imagine that the society in question includes only two people. Then we could represent their game in strategic form as in Figure 5.1.

This game has two pure-strategy Nash Equilibria (NE): (L, L) and (R, R). It has a mixed-strategy NE in randomization by both drivers, but this will typically be unstable because it is Pareto-dominated by the two pure-strategy NE. (I say it is merely 'typically' unstable because I have driven in Cairo.) It should make no difference to the players which of the two conventions they adopt, one of which they will likely codify into law so that they establish who is at fault when overtaking on a single-lane road causes a head-on collision. (To imagine this, relax the 2-person society simplification for a moment; I am not asking you to contemplate the society's extinction.) This example is relatively trivial, but there are many more interesting social situations well-modeled by its logic. Why do so many people go downtown on Saturday night? Answer: Because so many others do. What makes one part of town count as 'downtown'? Answer: The fact that that is where people who want to enjoy doing a lot of matching (for shopping, partying, deal-making, bling display etc.) go.[14]

	II	
	L	R
L	1, 1	0, 0
R	0, 0	1, 1

Figure 5.1   A Pure Coordination game

---

[13] In fact, Lewis argued for the stronger thesis that all conventions are solutions to Pure Coordination games. I reject this thesis for reasons given in Ross (2008a).

[14] Recall from Section 5.4 that these are among the games that, on Martin's (2009) narrow use of the concept of a market, don't count as markets. This helps to show just *how* restricted Martin's concept is. According to it, downtown is not a market phenomenon.

The principles of GT say nothing about how players should select strategies so as to converge on one NE in a Pure Coordination game. Empirically, people and other animals find efficient outcomes in circumstances that appear to be best modeled as pure coordination games at far better than chance in all circumstances that have been studied. The Nobel laureate Thomas Schelling (1921–) (1960) argued that they do this by exploiting *focal points*. A focal point is simply some shared information players of a coordination game have about the relative salience of features of alternative equilibria to other players. For example, if you want to buy a make of car that will be easy to repair and trade in for a decent price because lots of other people are buying it, pay attention to comparative advertising frequencies. Most examples of focal point logic in the literature are cuter but less economically significant than this one. For example, suppose you lose track of your spouse, and your cellphone, while on vacation in Manhattan, before you've selected a hotel. How should you think about where to go in hopes of meeting her? This is a Pure Coordination game if it only matters that find one another *somewhere*, but don't care where exactly. You should solve this problem by asking yourself whether there's a particular place she'd expect you to think that she'd regard as salient for the two of you. Is there a spot in Manhattan one of you has recently described to the other as their favorite? Do you have a photo in your bedroom of the two of you posing in front of a New York landmark? If, as a couple, you have no history in Manhattan, perhaps you should go to the Empire State Building. (For nice experimental investigations, see Mehta et al. 1994.)

In this example you solve your Pure Coordination game through individual psychological modeling. In a Coordination game involving many people – say, we're going to protest *en masse* against the dictator, so all want to blend in together, so choose red clothes, or at least definitely *not* yellow clothes or green clothes – people seek solutions by generalizing what they know about typical individual psychological models. You will not find any useful axioms in formal game theory or microeconomics or Savage decision theory. This has led philosophers to construct a silly literature wondering whether 'rationality' has any role to play in the solutions to Pure Coordination games (for reviews and criticism, see Bickhard 2008 and Ross 2008a). Such literature has had a useful consequence the philosophers did not intend, in work done by game theorists.

The philosopher Margaret Gilbert (1989), in the context of worrying pointlessly over whether the concept of 'convention' is best analyzed in terms of coordination, argues that 'game theory' is the wrong kind of tool for the job because, among other problems, it is 'individualistic'; whereas conventions are essentially social phenomena. This concern about allegedly individualistic foundations of GT has been echoed by economists Robert Sugden (1993, 2000b, 2003) and Michael Bacharach (2006). In particular it motivated Bacharach to propose a theory of *team reasoning*, which was completed by Sugden, along with Nathalie Gold, when Bacharach tragically died at the peak of his career. Team reasoning is an important idea with a wealth of empirical applications, notwithstanding the muddled philosophical context in which Bacharach and his executors present it.[15] Indeed, it is one of the two key foundation stones for completing the unification of economics and sociology.

Let us leave coordination games for a moment and consider the philosopher's favorite game, the one-shot Prisoner's Dilemma (PD) (from Section 3.6). For ease of reference, consider again the strategic form as in Figure 5.2.

As usual, C denotes the strategy of 'cooperating' and D denotes 'defecting.' Many people – not just philosophers – find it incredible when a game theorist tells them that 'rational' players must choose so as to yield the outcome (D, D). The explanation seems to require appeal to very strong forms of both descriptive and normative individualism. After all, if the players attached higher value to the social good than to their individual welfare, they could then do better individually too; game-theoretic 'rationality,' it is objected, yields behavior that is perverse even from the individually optimizing point of view. Sugden

	II	
	C	D
C	2, 2	0, 3
D	3, 0	1, 1

Figure 5.2 One-shot PD, strategic form

---

[15] I blame the muddle on philosophers, not on them.

(1993) seems to have been first to suggest that *truly* rational players here, including non-altruistic ones, would reason *as a team*, that is, would ask 'What is best for *us*?' instead of 'What is best for *me*?'

As Binmore (1994) strenuously argued – and as the general philosophical literature seems subsequently to have acknowledged – this line of criticism confused GT as mathematics with questions about which GT models are most typically applicable to people and their situations. If players value the welfare of the team over and above their 'individual' returns then these must be represented in their utility functions. In the game of Figure 5.2, if the players' concern for 'the team' were strong enough to induce a switch in strategies from D to C, then the payoffs in the (cardinally interpreted) upper left cell would have to be raised to at least 3. (*At* 3, players would be indifferent between cooperating and defecting.) The resulting game, shown in Figure 5.3, is no longer a PD; it is an Assurance game. The fact that there is now an NE where both players cooperate thus does not refute the *mathematical* fact that (D, D) is the unique NE in the one-shot PD.

Bacharach's executors (Sugden and Gold, in Bacharach 2006 pp. 171–173), unlike Hollis and Sugden (1993), get this right, agreeing that players can only cooperate in a one-shot PD if someone makes an error. But, Bacharach, Sugden and Gold argue, *human* game players will often or usually avoid framing situations in such a way that the game of Figure 5.2 is the right model of their circumstances. A situation that 'individualistic' agents would frame as the game of Figure 5.2 might be framed by 'team reasoning' agents as the game of Figure 5.3. We must acknowledge that the welfare of the team might make a difference to payoffs without making *enough* of a difference to trump the lure of unilateral defection – suppose it bumped them only to 2.5 for each player. Then the game would remain a PD. This point is important, since in

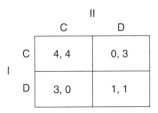

Figure 5.3   One-shot Assurance game, strategic form

experiments in which subjects play sequences of one-shot PDs[16] majorities of subjects begin by cooperating but learn to defect as the experiments progress.[17] On Bacharach's account of this phenomenon, these subjects initially frame the game as team reasoners. However, a minority of subjects frame it as individualistic reasoners and defect, taking free riders' profits. The team reasoners then re-frame the situation to defend themselves. This introduces a crucial aspect of Bacharach's account. Individualistic reasoners and team reasoners are not claimed to be different types of human game players. People, Bacharach maintains, flip back and forth between individualistic agency and participation in team agency.

Now let us return to coordination games. The game of Figure 5.1 actually represents a situation in which the players are either narrowly individualistic or haven't recognized that their team is better off if they jointly stabilize their strategies around one of the NE choices. Then, just as the PD is transformed into an Assurance game by team reasoning, so the Pure Coordination game of Figure 5.1 is transformed into the Hi-Lo game that we encountered back in Section 3.6, represented here as Figure 5.4.

Notice here that the transformation requires more than *mere* team reasoning. The players still need focal points to know which of the two Pure Coordination game equilibria offers the less risky prospect for social stabilization (Binmore 2008). In fact, Bacharach and his executors are interested in the relationship between Pure Coordination games and Hi-Lo games for a special reason. It does not seem to imply any criticism

		II	
		L	R
U		2, 2	0, 0
D		0, 0	1, 1

I (appears to the left of the U/D rows)

Figure 5.4 Hi-Lo game, strategic form

---

[16] *Not* repeated PDs, because opponents in the experiments change from round to round.

[17] Though see Friedman and Oprea (2012) for evidence that capacity to respond rapidly is a crucial neglected conditioning variable here.

of NE as a solution concept that it doesn't favor one strategy vector over another in a Pure Coordination game. However, NE *also* doesn't favor the choice of (U, L) over (D, R) in the Hi-Lo game of Figure 5.4, because (D, R) is also an NE. At this point Bacharach and friends adopt the philosophical reasoning of the refinement program. (See Section 3.6.) Surely, they complain, 'rationality' recommends (U, L). Therefore, axioms for team reasoning should be built into refined foundations of GT.

I am no more persuaded by this instance of refinement reasoning than by any other. It is not among the specifications on GT as a mathematical technology to capture an intuitive concept of 'rationality.' And we do not, in any event, need to add team reasoning axioms to GT in order to derive (U, L) as the solution to the Hi-Lo game of Figure 5.4. We need instead merely remind ourselves that the strategic form of a game provides relatively sparse information. We can represent the game of Figure 5.4 in extensive form using Figure 5.5.

The informational interpretation of GT is then all we need. If both players conjecture that the other reasons in accord with Bayesian logic, then the only consistent set of conjectures is that I will choose U and II will choose L.

If the urge to refine NE is not a compelling motivation for seeking a formal theory of team *reasoning*, there are nevertheless strong grounds for wanting a mathematical account of team-centered choice. *If* people's choices reveal preferences that are conditional on the welfare of groups with which they wholly or partly identify their agency, we want to be able to identify the implied utility functions in estimating models of behavior. We won't be able to do that if our theory is

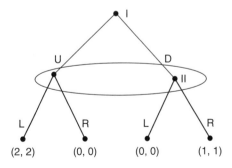

Figure 5.5 Hi-Lo game, extensive form, simultaneous moves

entirely psychological. (This point is consistent with thinking that the best *evidence* for the existence of team-centered choice is psychological, and with hypothesizing that some elements of the data-generating processes yielding team-centered choices are typically latent.)

Do people's choices reveal team-centered preferences? I think it is overwhelmingly empirically persuasive that people are often strongly motivated by consideration of the welfare of groups to which they belong. Sometimes this is very explicit. Members of sports teams are under considerable pressure to choose actions that maximize prospects for victory over actions that augment their personal statistics. Of course this can be represented as merely enlightened *self*-interest – fans boo players whom they detect playing selfishly, and players have strong incentives to avoid being disliked by fans. But a similar retrenchment maneuver is harder to push convincingly in the case of soldiers. Though trying to persuade soldiers to sacrifice their lives in the interests of their countries is not generally very effective, they can regularly be induced to storm into probable death out of solidarity with their buddies, or when enemies directly menace their home towns and families.

In any event, we must remind ourselves that economic theory *in no way* encourages us to try to reduce all motives to selfish ones. Nor is economic theory committed to any doctrine about the scale of agency. People are psychologically complex, and incorporate bundles of sub-personal interests that economists do not hesitate to model as agents (O'Donoghue and Rabin 2001; Prelec and Bodner 2003; Bénabou and Tirole 2004; Benhabib and Bisin 2004; Fudenberg and Levine 2006; Bernheim and Rangel 2008; see Ross 2005 for general methodological discussion). And the agents that figure most commonly in applied economic models are not individual people but firms and households. In international economics the agents are usually governments. Thus there is no consideration at all that should stand in our way of attempting to formally represent team-centered choice. Of course, we *do* urgently want any such theory to be technically integrated with RPT and GT. Thus it should not *directly* be a theory of team *reasoning*; it should be a theory of choice conditional on the existence of a team.

Theory satisfying these desiderata has recently been provided by Wynn Stirling (2012). Stirling aims to formalize, and to derive equilibrium conditions for, a notion of group preference that is not an aggregation of individual preferences.[18] Nor is the idea that of a transcendent 'group will' that is imposed as the basis for an outcome in light of normative considerations extrinsic to individual decisions. The intuitive target Stirling has in mind is instead that of processes by which people derive their *actual* preferences partly on the basis of the comparative consequences for group dynamics of different possible profiles of preferences they could each hypothetically reveal.

The intuitive idea is as follows. People may often – perhaps typically – defer full resolution of their preferences until they learn about the preferences of others. Examples can be relatively crude or more subtle. On the simpler end of the spectrum is Stirling's own first example, adapted from Keeney and Raiffa (1976), in which a farmer forms a clear preference among different climate conditions for a land purchase only after, and partly in light of, learning the preferences of his wife. This little thought experiment is plausible enough, but not entirely satisfactory because it is readily conflated with vague ideas we might have about *fusion* of agency in long and deep marriages. We can construct a better example. Imagine a company Chairwoman consulting her risk-averse Board about whether they should pursue a dangerous hostile takeover bid. Consider two possible procedures she might use: in process (i) she sends each member an individual email about the idea a week prior to the meeting; in process (ii) she springs it on them collectively *at* the meeting. It will surely be conceded that the two processes might yield different outcomes, and that one reason for this might be that on process (i), but not (ii), some members might entrench personal opinions they would not have time to settle into if they received information about one another's willingness to challenge the Chair in public at the same time as they heard the idea for the first time. In both imagined cases there are, at the moment of voting, sets of individual preferences. But it is more likely that some preferences in the second set were *conditional* on preferences of others. A conditional preference as Stirling defines it is a preference that is influenced by information about the preferences of (specified) others.

---

[18] Theories of aggregation of individual preferences are, in effect, theories of constitutions or decision procedures for groups, and are properly part of political economy. Arrow (1951) famously showed that no such aggregation procedure can be consistent unless it allows one member of the group to have dictatorial authority. For the classic study of preference aggregation in the wake of Arrow, see Sen (1971).

A second notion formalized in Stirling's theory is *concordance.* This refers to the extent of controversy or discord to which a set of preferences, including a set of conditional preferences, leads. Members or leaders of teams do not always want to maximize concordance by engineering all internal games as Assurance or Hi-Lo (though they will likely always want to eliminate PDs). For example, a manager might want to encourage a degree of competition among profit centers in a firm, while wanting the cost centers to identify completely with the team as a whole.

Stirling formally defines representation theorems for three kinds of ordered utility functions: conditional utility, concordant utility and conditional concordant utility. These may be applied to agents of any scale, so both to individuals and to teams. Then the core of the formal development is the theory that aggregates individuals' conditional concordant preferences to build a model of team choice that is not exogenously imposed on individual team members, but derives from their preferences. Stirling's aggregation procedure is subject to five constraints[19]:

(1) **Conditioning**: A team member's preference ordering may be influenced by the preferences of other team members, i.e., may be conditional. (Note that influence may be set to zero, in which case the conditional preference ordering collapses to the categorical preference ordering of classical GT.)

(2) **Endogeny**: A concordant ordering for a group must be determined by the social interactions of its sub-groups. This condition distinguishes conditional game theory from cooperative game theory; see Chapter 3. It also ensures that the theory is not 'holist' or 'collectivist' in its implications, in the senses disparaged by Coleman.

(3) **Acyclicity**: Social influence relationships are not reciprocal. This will initially strike readers as a strange condition; surely most

---

[19] In stating these constraints I paraphrase Stirling rather than quoting him verbatim. This is partly because Stirling refers to 'groups' where I refer to 'teams'. Stirling does not cite Bacharach (2006), so does not set his work within the team reasoning context. I have indicated my sympathy with one possible reason for avoiding such a context: what we should really want is a theory of individual choice in the context of teams, not a theory of team *reasoning*. But the concept of a team is more precise than the concept of a mere 'group'; and, as I have indicated, I think that many of the empirical considerations adduced by Bacharach and his executors provide excellent motivation for welcoming Stirling's technical achievement as providing a tool for social scientists.

social influence relationships among people *are* reciprocal. Here, however, we must remind ourselves of our freedom to choose ontologies when we apply formal models. A perfectly symmetrical reciprocal social influence relationship is simply a single fused agent. Furthermore, the acyclicity requirement is not as restrictive as it appears, because it only bars an agent j influenced by i from *directly* influencing i. j can influence k who can influence i. The point of the restriction is to allow for representation in directed graphs.

(4) **Exchangeability**: Concordant preference orderings are invariant under representational transformations that are equivalent with respect to information about conditional preferences.

(5) **Monotonicity**: If one sub-team prefers alternative A to B and all other sub-teams are indifferent between A and B, then the team must not prefer B to A.

The aggregation theorem that Stirling proves under these restrictions follows a general result for updating utility theory in light of new information that was developed by Abbas (2003).

Individual team members each calculate the team preference by aggregating conditional concordant preferences. Then the analyst applies *marginalization*. Let χ^n be a team. Let $\chi^m = \{X_{j_1}, \dots, X_{jm}\}$ and $X^k = \{X_{i_1}, \dots, X_{ik}\}$ be disjoint sub-teams of χ^n. Then the marginal concordant utility of χ^m with respect to the sub-team $\{\chi^m, \chi^k\}$ is obtained by summing over $\mathcal{A}^k$, yielding

$$U_{x_m}(\alpha_m) = \sum_{\alpha_k} Ux_m x_k(\alpha_m, \alpha_k)$$

and the marginal utility of the individual team-member X_i is given by

$$U_{x_i}(a_i) = \sum_{\sim a_i} U_{x_n}(a_1, \dots, a_n)$$

where the notation $\sum \sim a_i$ means that the sum is taken over all arguments except a_i (Stirling 2012, p. 62). This operation produces the *non-conditional* preferences of individual agent i, *ex post* – that is, updated in light of her conditional concordant preferences and the information on which they are conditioned, namely, the conditional concordant preferences of the team. Once all *ex post* preferences of agents have been calculated, the resulting games in which they are involved can be solved by standard analysis.

Stirling's construction is, as he says, a true generalization of standard utility theory so as to make non-conditioned ("categorical") utility a special case. It provides a basis for formalization of team utility, which can be compared with any of the following: the pre-conditioned categorical utility of an individual or sub-team; the conditional utility of an individual or sub-team; or the conditional concordant utility of an individual or sub-team. Once every individual's preferences in a team choice problem have been marginalized, NE or SPE analysis can be proposed as solutions to the problem given full information about social influences. Situations of incomplete information can be solved using Bayes-Nash or sequential equilibrium.

I suggest that Stirling's theory provides the formal basis for the unification of economics and sociology. This does not necessarily imply that the distinct methodological inheritances of the disciplines will or should be lost. The social influence relationships that are expressed in Stirling's formalization as conditional preferences will typically be based on evidence from thick narrative accounts of the kind with which sociologists are more comfortable than most economists. However, even in this area the disciplinary boundary is visibly eroding. Bates et al. (1998) have produced a methodological handbook, built around case studies, for what they call 'analytic narratives.' These are exercises that integrate thick description of specific episodes in the vast history of social dynamics with game-theoretic models that are intended to discipline the argumentative rigor of causal hypotheses based on inferences about agents' motives and about the information on which they relied in making choices. Reciprocally, the GT models and solutions are themselves testable against traditional historical evidence: proposed game equilibria should be expected to be instantiated as actual historical institutions, and where no plausible such expression is manifest in records, this casts doubt on the modeling. Avner Greif (2006) provides a fully extended and much-cited application of the approach to explain differences in the contributions of, and consequences for, different Mediterranean cities as seaborne trade networks expanded during the medieval period. The explanations provided by

Greif's account are cultural and institutional, and in that specific sense sociological; yet in being reciprocally supported by GT modeling they ensure that we are not asked to implicitly imagine that historical actors were fools who could not learn or seek and appreciate available information that was relevant to their interests. Greif's work has been treated by leading development economists as an important methodological contribution to their sub-discipline; see, for example, Acemoglu and Robinson (2012) on the persistence of poverty in contemporary least-developed countries.

It is pointless to ask whether analytic narratives are economics or sociology. I expect that many sociologists might be cautious or skeptical about treating accounts such as Greif's as exemplary, on grounds that using traditional GT as the core, test-bed technology reflects a residual commitment to individualism. But of course conditional GT was not yet available to Greif or his co-authors in Bates et al. (1998). The analytic narratives of the coming years can be enriched by Stirling's more accommodating mathematics. As such work rolls out, I see no reason why it should be approached any differently depending on whether a researcher was trained in an economics department or a sociology department. Nor do I see that the elders of either tribe will then have any basis for claiming to have methodologically colonized the other.

5.6 Descriptive anti-individualism and normative individualism

The majority of contemporary economists are liberals. I do not here mean 'liberal' in the peculiar sense of US politics, where the word refers to anyone who is neither a free market ideologue nor a defender of theocracy nor a national chauvinist. I mean rather that most economists prefer policies that best promote the efficient aggregate use of productive resources *because* they believe that, in general, such efficiency generally best serves the flourishing of individual people as those individuals themselves conceive their flourishing. Even economists who are sympathetic to 'nudge' paternalism (see Section 4.3) emphasize the 'nudge' aspect because they reject full-blown paternalism that overrides individuals' conceptions of their own well-being. As economics is fundamentally a policy-driven science, these political sympathies are deeply entrenched in the work of most economists, rather than being incidental to it. But clearly they do not *derive from* any theoretical axioms of economics, which are not normative and are not even specifically concerned with people. Liberalism is a political philosophy, independent of scientific economics, that the majority of economists endorse and that strongly influences the choices they make about which problems to investigate. It also explains why, when they engage in welfare analysis, they insist on treating subjective preferences as decisive.

Here at the end of the book, I will not maintain a pretense of oracular distance by merely talking loftily about the opinions of 'most economists.' Though I am not a libertarian – because I do not think that individual liberty, or anything else, should generally trump all other goods – I am sufficiently devoted to individual moral sovereignty and sufficiently unimpressed with the nature of life in bureaucratically over-governed structures, that even nudge paternalism is too much paternalism for my taste. (Here I endorse considerations explored by Sugden [2008] and Saint Paul [2011]. It is an important source of joy and dignity to be able to learn from consequences of one's own ignorance.)

So I am a strong normative individualist. Yet I have spent this book arguing that economics is distinct from psychology, but not ultimately distinct from sociology, because whereas psychology is basically about individual people economics is not. And my primary basis for this claim is a set of philosophical arguments to the effect that although there are of course individual human *organisms* and individual human *brains,* the idea of an individual human *person* is a myth; people, as entities with goals to which utility functions can be ascribed in economic models, are created by social processes. Thus I am a descriptive anti-individualist. Is there not considerable tension between these two views of mine? How can I attach high normative importance to something that I think doesn't literally exist?

The short answer to this question is that human individuality is, like any object of normative aspiration, a regulative ideal. Individuality is something people strive to approximate, and if they so strive must work to protect, precisely because it is *not* natural and tends to be eroded by entropic pressures. (Bureaucracies, Hobbesian mafia structures, and repressive dogmatisms about preferred lifestyles, each of which undermines individualism, all *do* grow naturally.) It is possible to flesh out this short answer a bit more rigorously, by appeal to themes that have been explored in the earlier sections of this book. That is what I will do in this closing section. (A substantially more rigorous discussion is given in Ross 2013a.)

A core concept in social psychology, but which is almost entirely absent from economics, is *socialization* – the designation for socially governed processes of *personal formation* from infancy through early adulthood. Part of the explanation as to why economists have not modeled such processes is that, as I have argued throughout this book, they are not mainly interested in dynamics by which individual people establish and maintain their idiosyncracies. But another important part of the reason, which applies equally to sociology, stems from the fact that, in the modeling framework of economics, socialization implies changes in a person's utility function. Coleman (1990) describes the resulting problem as follows:

> Since psychological theory is so forthcoming with theories of psychological change, it is necessary to ask why economics – the social science for which a theory of purposive action has been most central – has never developed or borrowed from psychology a theory of internal change of individuals... One reason... is the difficulty of introducing a theory that is compatible with the central principle of action, maximization of utility. If an actor's goals, or what goods and events he regards as satisfying him or as having high utility for him, cannot be specified, then there is no basis for maximization. The theory of rational action of purposive action [sic] is a theory of instrumental rationality *given* a set of goals or ends or utilities. If a theory of internal change of actors is to be... consistent with the basic principles of action, it must do what appears to be impossible: to account for *changes* in utilities (or goals) on the basis of the principle of *maximization* of utility. (Coleman 1990, p. 515)

A central theme of Ross (2005) is that there is only one solution to this problem. Since an economic agent is identified with a utility function, but people's preferences are dynamically sculpted by socialization processes, an economic model of any relatively long stretch of a person's biography must depict the person as a *succession* of economic agents. Furthermore, each new agent is a product of strategic interactions between the ancestor agent and other people. Therefore an economic model of socialization will be game-theoretic and the person's trajectory through economic agency will be idealized as a sequence of equilibria. Ross (2006) and (2007a) add further details to the original account.

An infant's utility function at first ranges over only a few basic goods and their absence: nourishment, warmth, hugs, and mother's proximity. As the child's cognitive capacities grow, and support learning, this range expands. In consequence her preferences change: whereas she begins by preferring pabulum to hot dogs, by the age of 4 this has reversed. Later, perhaps, she comes to prefer pizza to hot dogs. The simple changes in this example are not merely consequences of genetically programmed maturation of taste sensitivity to adapt to changes in nutritional needs (though of course that is an important aspect). They also involve socialization. In contemporary North America, young children are expected to enjoy hot dogs and older children are expected to prefer pizza; and people adapt their preferences to social expectations.

Parents set a rich running example of social participation, and reward their offspring with smiles and other reinforcing tokens of approval when they respond in ways the parents interpret as interaction that is sensitive to their favored norms. One illuminating way of putting this is: they treat the baby as though she were a *person*, a narrator of a socially comprehensible *biography*, before she really is one or has fully developed the neural capacity to become one (McGeer 2001). The conditioned expectation that the small child will *become* a person pulls the baby along that path; children in healthy nurturing families are rewarded with attention and approval when they begin to display consistent interests linked with 'signature' styles of attachment to particular activities and kinds of objects. A typical mother, for example, will be proud of the fact that her small son is fascinated by different kinds of birds and will encourage him to show off his budding ornithological knowledge to adult acquaintances. From foundations in Pavlovian responses that increasingly come under self-representational control, by inventing and then behaviorally cultivating a standing mix of culturally mandated and idiosyncratic preferences,[20] the infant indeed becomes a person.

The development psychologist Phillippe Rochat (2009) says that between the ages of 2 and 5 years normal human children develop into what he calls "Homo negotiatus": agents who engage in reciprocal

---

[20] Different cultures draw the line between the mandated and the free preferences of people in widely varying places; but all draw it.

exchanges with others for coordination on joint projects, protection from threats, and mutual recognition of worth and value. They don't do this, according to Rochat, for the sake of optimizing their claims to material property, though they begin claiming ownership of objects at about 21 months on average. The hierarchy of priorities is rather the other way around: children claim and exchange objects in order to get and hold the attention of others, and they exchange property to proxy more abstract exchange of recognition. The objects of such recognition are selves. So the development into 'H. negotiatus' is the sculpting of the self.

Public language is the crucial technology for this process. Indeed, personhood, conscious self-representation and language learning are profoundly entangled with one another (Bruner 1986; Dennett 1991b; Ross 2005, 2007b; Hutto 2008; Bogdan 2009, 2010; Zawidzki 2013). When we say that an infant believes that her mother is angry, we don't thereby commit ourselves to the view that the infant yet represents to herself, in some hypothesized neural encoding, the socially coordi-nated concepts of motherhood or anger. We are instead describing the infant's behavioral patterns *as if* she were already a person. It is essential that we do this, because it is a necessary part of providing the infant with a template for personhood to develop into. This would all be fruitless if the child for some reason could not learn public language. As the child does learn language, she becomes able to grasp stories to which she can adapt her behavior. A milestone in self-development arises when the infant begins originating such stories – including imaginary stories – and applying them to *herself*. We should avoid falling into an incoherent picture of a pre-existing but non-articulated self who is then inserted into narratives by the child. Rather, the child talks to herself and her brain processes the linguistic input in the same way it does linguistic input from another person (i.e., via auditory processing circuits) and thereby *creates* a representation of a self who plays a special role in regulating action and thought. So, to re-cap and summarize: (1) parents use language to provide a normative develop-mental target of socially coordinated personhood for the pre-socialized infant organism; (2) as the infant's behavior adapts to normative expectations she becomes a *socially governed* organism; (3) as the infant learns to represent her behavior, and her behavioral options, to herself using the categories of public language, she creates a self that can eventually play the leading role in governing her own nervous system on behalf of the social norms in which she participates.

Dennett (1991b) provides an ideal analogy for all of this. A child is the principal *author* of herself in the same sense that a writer of fiction creates characters. As with a character in a novel (setting aside certain post-modern novels that draw attention to the rule by artfully violating it) the self must be relatively consistent. (Consider the frustration involved in reading a bad novel in which characters suddenly do and say things the reader can't make sense of in light of what they have done and said before.) Indeed, relative consistency in the eyes of others is the very *point* of the self. A socially viable self must, as it were, approximate economic agency.

If the child is the *principal* author of herself, it is crucial that she have the help of co-authors. Initially these co-authors should be overwhelmingly sympathetic and supportive. Human parents, who start the process of socialization and personal development, are co-authors of this kind. But children transfer principal co-authorship rights to peers well before the onset of adolescence (Harris 2007). This makes good strategic sense. Parents are too unconditionally supportive of the child's self-construction project to provide reliable feedback on which sorts of preferences and forms of personal expression will interact with the child's genetic endowments in such a way as to allow her to optimize her status in the prevailing social environment. Furthermore, it is the peers that ultimately *constitute* that environment.

Thus, as a matter of genetically guided normal development, from middle childhood through adolescence children experiment with personal identities during interactions with sub-cohorts. If an economist or game theorist was motivated to try to keep track of an individual child's progress in terms of economic agency – which, as I have argued, economists are generally *not* – then this economist would be forced to repeatedly adjust the utility functions in his models. Eventually, after adolescence, the process of preference experimentation slows and preferences stabilize *because others expect them to and will inflict social punishment if they don't*. People who are still emphasizing experiments with fundamental preferences make poor co-investors in sustained joint projects such as marriages, work teams and businesses.

On the other hand, people do not expect one another to stop adjusting their selves altogether. The world, after all, is dynamic and calls for adaptation and revision in the face of change. In general, people allow one another to effect changes in *core* aspects of themselves only if they follow culturally recognized (and culture-specific) scripts that make drastic adjustments comprehensible and well-patterned for others. In contemporary Western culture such scripts exist for first marriage and first parenthood, recovery from addiction, being converted to a religion, experiencing war or surviving near-fatal illness, and a few others. But purely endogenous *profound* changes are discouraged, because they disturb the expectations on which location of strategic equilibria depend.

In pre-modern societies this is most of the story. Entrenched social conventions in such societies make self-maintenance relatively easy. This, I suggest, is why such societies generally do not normatively celebrate individualism. Many such societies, on the contrary, strictly police and discourage cultivation of individualism beyond what is directly conducive to efficient specialization of labor, especially with regard to child-rearing and food gathering.

Modernity – meaning, essentially, capitalism and the acceleration of social change that it unleashes – introduces a profound difference in these dynamics. Capitalist economies and social orders generate vastly more information than any person or small group of people can process. Differentiation of people in such societies must be subtle, multi-dimensional and adaptive to novelty and organizational re-alignments. This returns our attention to the cognitive economics of Martens (2004), building on Hayek and Schumpeter, as discussed at the beginning of Chapter 3. In such environments, the challenge of self-maintenance becomes highly complex. A typical participant in an advanced capitalist society maintains several distinct sub-selves: one for the office, another for the family, perhaps others for sports or hobby clubs. Increasing numbers of people also operate yet further selves on Internet sites, often with different names. In some instances aliases are used because the activities in which online selves indulge are confusingly or embarrassingly inconsistent with the selves of the office or the home. But the more general explanation of online aliasing, I conjecture, is simply that it makes cognitive book-keeping of multiple self-hood easier. Facebook, interestingly, bans aliasing. This, I suggest, reflects the fact that Facebook is precisely in the business of inducing people to reveal and unify their different selves so that suppliers of goods and services can construct them as single, consistent economic agents for purposes of targeting advertising. Markets are the primary source of pressure for closer approximation of psychological individuals to economic agency, a point emphasized by Ainslie (2001).

Maintenance of selfhood in contemporary market societies is thus much more challenging than in pre-modern or agrarian societies. On the one hand, the very point of maintaining my self is to provide others with sufficiently stable expectations that they will be able to equilibrate their strategies with me, and so will choose me as an exchange partner in joint projects and commercial transactions. On the other hand, if I am *too* unwilling to adjust my self as circumstances change, I will be regarded as annoyingly or even offensively rigid, dull and undeserving of attention. Contemporary self-maintenance is thus a fine balancing act, which a typical person must recalibrate every day. In consequence, the market duly provides us with a plethora of assistance services: counseling facilities, self-help manuals, office team-building exercises, and so forth. Much more usefully, there is the gigantic business of fictional entertainments that allow us to imaginatively explore rich alternative worlds full of novel self templates into which we can safely project ourselves to find out what they're like.

This is why normative individualism is the appropriate ethics for contemporary capitalist societies. For each of us, in such societies, maintaining a set of selves that is unified in a common core but not so inflexibly as to make us boring or bored, or incapable of grasping new opportunities for learning and producing, is the primary preoccupation. Thus most people have core self-identification anchors – basic political and ethical orientations, religious affiliations, celebrations of the personalities of their intimate partners – that they value at least as highly as their biological survival. (How many people prefer to die when the alternative is forsaking their commitment to the value of their country or their religion or their spouse? For most of us such choices fortunately remain hypothetical. Yet we all think about them.) And thus also we love to contemplate and cultivate and try to deepen what is distinctive and – as contemporary English-speakers revealingly say – 'personal' about ourselves and others. The famous dystopias of the twentieth century – Zamyatin's *We*, Orwell's *1984*, Huxley's *Brave New World* – are for most people ultimate imaginative horrors *because* they depict environments in which individuality is suppressed. We read about North Korea, or the history of Stalin's Soviet Union, and shiver in the knowledge that others have endured, and still endure, such awful blighting of the very point of human lives.

None of this would make clear sense if maintenance of distinctive self-hood came easily to people. Normative individualism is the dominant ethic of capitalism *not* because distinctive preference profiles characterize each of us prior to analysis of our social interactions, but for the *opposite* reason. As biological organisms we have a set of preferences, varying through restricted ranges of types, independently of our participation in societies and markets. This set is of limited economic interest, though study of it by psychologists and neuroscientists sheds great light on our evolutionary history and physical ecology. Our economically interesting preferences, however, are generated in and by the social and material marketplaces where we interact, and which we best learn about by gathering and critically analyzing population-scale statistics. Against these huge social forces that shape our minds we struggle to remain (partial) authors of ourselves, and our moral valorizations celebrate the successes and mourn the failures in these struggles. In summary: *normative* individualism is explained by the fact that *descriptive* individualism is false.

That is a core principle of the philosophy of economics that I have described in this book. Economics has been widely thought to be distinguished from sociology because the former is committed to methodological individualism while the latter is not. But economic theory enjoins no individualistic doctrine, methodological or otherwise. In fact, economics and sociology merely divided the labor of unified social science during a period in which technology did not yet exist for simultaneously incorporating both common and asymmetric information at large scales. Economists have mainly been liberal celebrants of the moral sovereignty of individuals. This is not part of their theory, but a contingent fact about the biography of their discipline. It is a vitally important fact in explaining why they have emphasized the topical themes that they have, but that does not imply that their body of theory is unscientific ideology. Economists' prevailing liberalism explains their widespread rhetorical commitment to methodological individualism, but that is ultimately philosophical confusion.

Psychology, on the other hand, *is* mainly preoccupied with the dynamics of behavior at the scale of individuals. These dynamics create numerous constraints on population-scale behavior that is *choice* behavior – *aggregate* choice behavior – because it responds to changes in incentives. Thus economists are well advised to learn some psychology and incorporate it, carefully and selectively, into their models when achievement of empirically best model estimation depends on it. But economics does not fuse with psychology as it fuses with sociology.

References

Abbas, A. (2003). The algebra of utility inference. Cornell University Library working paper. http://arxiv.org/abs/cs/0310044.

Acemoglu, D., & Robinson, J. (2012). *Why Nations Fail*. New York: Crown.

Addleson, M. (1997). *Equilibrium Versus Understanding*. London: Routledge.

Afriat, S. (1967). The construction of utility functions from expenditure data. *International Economic Review* 8: 67–77.

Ainslie, G. (1975). Specious reward: A behavioral theory of impulsiveness and impulse control. *Psychological Bulletin* 82: 463–496.

Ainslie, G. (1992). *Picoeconomics*. Cambridge: Cambridge University Press.

Ainslie, G. (2001). *Breakdown of Will*. Cambridge: Cambridge University Press.

Ainslie, G. (2005). Précis of *Breakdown of Will*. *Behavioral and Brain Sciences* 28: 635–673.

Ainslie, G. (2012). Pure hyperbolic discount curves predict 'eyes open' self-control. *Theory and Decision* 73: 3–34.

Ainslie, G. (2013). Money as MacGuffin: A factor in gambling and other process addictions. In N. Levy, (ed.) *Addiction and Self-Control: Perspectives from Philosophy, Psychology, and Neuroscience*. Oxford University Press.

Akerlof, G. (1970). The market for 'lemons': Quality uncertainty and the market mechanism. *Quarterly Journal of Economics* 84: 488–500.

Akerlof, G., & Shiller, R. (2009). *Animal Spirits*. Princeton: Princeton University Press.

Alexandrova, A., & Northcott, R. (2009). Progress in economics: Lessons from the spectrum auctions. In H. Kincaid & D. Ross, eds, *The Oxford Handbook of Philosophy of Economics*, pp. 306–336. Oxford: Oxford University Press.

Aligica, P., & Boettke, P. (2009). *Challenging Institutional Analysis and Development: The Bloomington School*. London: Routledge.

Andersen, S., Harrison, G., Lau, M., & Rutström, E. (2008). Eliciting risk and time preferences. *Econometrica* 76: 583–618.

Andersen, S., Harrison, G., Lau, M., & Rutström, E. (2010). Behavioural econometrics for psychologists. *Journal of Economic Psychology* 31: 553–576.

Andersen, S., Harrison, G., Lau, M., & Rutström, E. (2011). Discounting behavior: A reconsideration. *Working Paper 2011-03*, Center for the Economic Analysis of Risk, Robinson College of Business, Georgia State University. http://cear.gsu.edu/papers/index.html

Angrist, J., & Pischke, J.-S. (2009). *Mostly Harmless Econometrics*. Princeton: Princeton University Press.

Ariely, D. (2008). *Predictably Irrational*. New York: Harper Collins.

Arrow, K. (1951). *Social Choice and Individual Values*. New York: Wiley.

Arrow, K. (1994). Methodological individualism and social knowledge. *Papers and Proceedings of the One Hundred Sixth Annual Meeting of the American Economic Association* 84: 1–9.

Arrow, K., & Debreu, G. (1954). Existence of equilibrium for a competitive economy. *Econometrica* 22: 265–290.

Ayer, A.J. (1936). *Language, Truth and Logic*. London: Victor Gollancz.

Bacharach, M. (2006). *Beyond Individual Choice*. Princeton: Princeton University Press.

Backhouse, R. (2002). *The Ordinary Business of Life*. Princeton: Princeton University Press.

Backhouse, R. (2010). *The Puzzle of Modern Economics*. Cambridge: Cambridge University Press.

Banerjee, A., & Duflo, E. (2011). *Poor Economics*. New York: Public Affairs.

Bardsley, N., Cubitt, R., Loomes, G., Moffatt, P., Starmer, C., & Sugden, R. (2010). *Experimental Economics: Rethinking the Rules*. Princeton: Princeton University Press.

Bates, R. (2001). *Prosperity and Violence*. New York: Norton.

Bates, R., Greif, A., Levi, M., Rosenthal, J.-L., & Weingast, B. (1998). *Analytic Narratives*. Princeton: Princeton University Press.

Batterman, R. (2002). *The Devil in the Details*. Oxford: Oxford University Press.

Bean, L. (1929). A simplified method of graphic curvilinear correlation. *Journal of the American Statistical Association* 24: 386–397.

Becker, G. (1962). Irrational behavior and economic theory. *Journal of Political Economy* 70: 1–13.

Becker, G., DeGroot, M., & Marschak, J. (1964). Measuring utility by a single-response sequential method. *Behavioral Science* 9: 226–232.

Bénabou, R., & Tirole, J. (2004). Willpower and personal rules. *Journal of Political Economy* 112: 848–886.

Benhabib, J., & Bisin, A. (2004). Modeling internal commitment mechanisms and self-control: A neuroeconomics approach to consumption-saving decisions. *Games and Economic Behavior* 52: 460–492.

Bergson, A. (1938). A reformulation of certain aspects of welfare economics. *Quarterly Journal of Economics* 52: 310–334.

Bernheim, B.D., & Rangel, A. (2008). Choice-theoretic foundations for behavioral welfare economics. In A. Caplin and A. Schotter, eds, *The Foundations* of *Positive and Normative Economics: A Handbook*, pp. 155–192. Oxford: Oxford University Press.

Berns, G., McClure, S., Pagnoni, G., & Montague, P.R. (2001). Predictability modulates human brain response to reward. *Journal of Neuroscience* 21: 2793–2798.

Berridge, K., & Robinson, T. (1998). What is the role of dopamine in reward: Hedonic impact, reward learning, or incentive salience? *Brain Research Reviews* 28: 309–369.

Bicchieri, C. (1993). *Rationality and Coordination*. Cambridge: Cambridge University Press.

Bickhard, M. (2008). Social ontology as convention. *Topoi* 27: 139–149.

Binmore, K. (1987). Modeling rational players I. *Economics and Philosophy* 3: 179–214.

Binmore, K. (1994). *Game Theory and the Social Contract Volume 1: Playing Fair*. Cambridge, MA: MIT Press.

Binmore, K. (1998). *Game Theory and the Social Contract, Volume 2: Just Playing*. Cambridge, MA: MIT Press.

Binmore, K. (2005). *Natural Justice*. Oxford: Oxford University Press.

Binmore, K. (2007). *Playing for Real*. Oxford: Oxford University Press.

Binmore, K. (2008). Do conventions need to be common knowledge? *Topoi* 27: 17–27.

Binmore, K. (2009). *Rational Decisions*. Princeton: Princeton University Press.

Binmore, K. (2010). Social norms or social preferences? *Mind and Society* 9: 139–157.

Binmore, K., & Shaked, A. (2010). Experimental economics: Where next? *Journal of Economic Behavior and Organization* 73: 87–100.

Binmore, K., Swierzbinski, J., Hsu, S., & Proulx, C. (2007). Focal points and bargaining. In K. Binmore, *Does Game Theory Work? The Bargaining Challenge*, pp. 67–101. Cambridge, MA: MIT Press.

Bogdan, R. (1997). *Interpreting Minds*. Cambridge, MA: MIT Press.

Bogdan, R. (2000). *Minding Minds*. Cambridge, MA: MIT Press.

Bogdan, R. (2009). *Predicative Minds*. Cambridge, MA: MIT Press.

Bogdan, R. (2010). *Our Own Minds*. Cambridge, MA: MIT Press.

Bogdan, R. (2013). *Mindvaults*. Cambridge, MA: MIT Press.

Bruner, J. (1986). *Actual Minds, Possible Worlds*. Cambridge, MA: Harvard University Press.

Bruni, L., & Sugden, R. (2007). The road not taken: How psychology was removed from economics and how it might be brought back. *The Economic Journal* 117: 146–173.

Brynjolfsson, E., & McAfee, A. (2012). *Race Against the Machine*. Seattle: Digital Frontier Press.

Bshary, R., & Noë, R. (2003). Biological markets: The ubiquitous influence of partner choice on the dynamics of cleaner fish – client reef fish interactions. In P. Hammerstein, (ed.) *Genetic and Cultural Evolution of Cooperation*, pp. 167–184. Cambridge, MA: MIT Press.

Burge, T. (1986). Individualism and psychology. *Philosophical Review* 95: 3–45.

Camerer, C. (1995). Individual decision making. In J. Kagel & A. Roth, eds, *The Handbook of Experimental Economics*, pp. 587–703. Princeton: Princeton University Press.

Camerer, C. (2003). *Behavioral Game Theory: Experiments in Strategic Interaction*. Princeton: Princeton University Press.

Camerer, C., Issacaroff, S., Loewenstein, G., O'Donaghue, T., & Rabin, M. (2003). Regulation for conservatives: Behavioral economics and the case for asymmetric paternalism. *University of Pennsylvania Law Review* 151: 1211–1254.

Camerer, C., Loewenstein, G., & Prelec, D. (2005). Neuroeconomics: How neuroscience can inform economics. *Journal of Economic Literature* 43: 9–64.

Caplin, A., & Dean, A. (2009). Axiomatic neuroeconomics. In P. Glimcher, C. Camerer, E. Fehr & R. Poldrack, eds, *Neuroeconomics: Decision Making and the Brain*, pp. 21–31. London: Elsevier.

Cappelen, H. (2012). *Philosophy Without Intuitions*. Oxford: Oxford University Press.

Carlsson, H., & van Damme, E. (1993). Global games and equilibrium selection. *Econometrica* 61: 989–1018.

Cartwright, N. (1989). *Nature's Capacities and their Measurement*. Oxford: Oxford University Press.

Cartwright, N. (1999). *The Dappled World*. Oxford: Oxford University Press.

Chamley, C. (2004). *Rational Herds*. Cambridge: Cambridge University Press.

Clark, A. (1989). *Microcognition*. Cambridge, MA: MIT Press.

Clark, A. (1997). *Being There*. Cambridge, MA: MIT Press.

Colander, D. (1996). The macrofoundations of micro. In D. Colander, (ed.) *Beyond Microfoundations*, pp. 57–68. Cambridge: Cambridge University Press.

Coleman, J. (1974). *Power and Structure of Society*. New York: Norton.

Coleman, J. (1990). *Foundations of Social Theory*. Cambridge, MA: Harvard University Press.

Cooper, R. (1999). *Coordination Games*. Cambridge: Cambridge University Press.

Cox, J., & Harrison, G., eds. (2008). *Risk Aversion in Experiments*. Bingley: Emerald.

Cox, J., Friedman, D., & Sadiraj, V. (2008). Revealed altruism. *Econometrica* 76: 31–69.

Coyle, D. (2007). *The Soulful Science.* Princeton: Princeton University Press.

Cronk, L., & Leech, B. (2012). *Meeting at Grand Central: Understanding the Social and Evolutionary Roots of Cooperation.* Princeton: Princeton University Press.

Danielson, P., (ed.) (1998). *Modeling Rationality, Morality and Evolution.* Oxford: Oxford University Press.

Davis, J. (2010). *Individuals and Identity in Economics.* Cambridge: Cambridge University Press.

Deaton, A. (2010). Instruments, randomization and learning about development. *Journal of Economic Literature* 48: 424–455.

Deaton, A., & Muellbauer, J. (1980). *Economics and Consumer Behavior.* Cambridge: Cambridge University Press.

Dennett, D. (1969). *Content and Consciousness.* London: Routledge & Kegan Paul.

Dennett, D. (1978). *Brainstorms.* Montgomery, VT: Harvester.

Dennett, D. (1987). *The Intentional Stance.* Cambridge, MA: MIT Press.

Dennett, D. (1991a). Real patterns. *Journal of Philosophy* 88: 27–51.

Dennett, D. (1991b). *Consciousness Explained.* Boston: Little Brown.

Dixit, A., & Skeath, S. (2004). *Games of Strategy*, 2nd edition. New York: Norton.

Dixit, A., & Stiglitz, J. (1977). Monopolistic competition and optimum product diversity. *American Economic Review* 67: 297–308.

Dixit, A., Skeath, S., & Reiley, D. (2009). *Games of Strategy*, 3rd edition. New York: Norton.

Dorris, M., & Glimcher, P. (2004). Activity in posterior parietal cortex is correlated with the relative selective desirability of action. *Neuron* 44: 365–378.

Dosman, E. (2008). *The Life and Times of Raul Prebisch 1901–1986.* Kingston, ON: Queen's University Press.

Dupré, J. (1993). *The Disorder of Things.* Cambridge, MA: Harvard University Press.

Easterly, W. (2001). *The Elusive Quest for Growth.* Cambridge, MA: MIT Press.

Edgeworth, F. (1881/1932). *Mathematical Psychics.* London: London School of Economics.

Eliasmith, C., & Anderson, C. (2002). *Neural Engineering: Computation, Representation and Dynamics in Neurobiological Systems.* Cambridge, MA: MIT Press.

Elster, J. (1985). *Making Sense of Marx.* Cambridge: Cambridge University Press.

Farmer, R., and Guo, J.-T. (1994). Real business cycles and the animal spirits hypothesis. *Journal of Economic Theory* 63: 42–72.

Feenstra, R. (2003). *Advanced International Trade: Theory and Evidence.* Princeton: Princeton University Press.

Fehr, E., & Gächter, S. (2000). Cooperation and punishment in public goods experiments. *American Economic Review* 90: 980–994.

Fehr, E., & Gächter, S. (2002). Altruistic punishment in humans. *Nature* 415: 137–140.

Fehr, E., & Gintis, H. (2007). Human motivation and social cooperation: Experimental and analytic foundations. *American Review of Sociology* 33: 43–64.

Fehr, E., & Schmidt, K. (1999). A theory of fairness, competition and cooperation. *Quarterly Journal of Economics* 114: 817–868.

Fields, G. (2009). Segmented labour market models in developing countries. In H. Kincaid & D. Ross, eds, *The Oxford Handbook of Philosophy of Economics*, pp. 476–507. Oxford: Oxford University Press.

Fine, B., & Milonakis, D. (2009). *From Economics Imperialism to Freakonomics*. London: Routledge.

Fisher, I. (1892/1925). *Mathematical Investigations in the Theory of Value and Price*. New Haven: Yale University Press.

Flanagan, O. (1991). *The Science of the Mind*, 2nd edition. Cambridge, MA: MIT Press.

Fodor, J. (1975). *The Language of Thought*. Cambridge, MA: Harvard University Press.

Fodor, J. (1983). *The Modularity of Mind*. Cambridge, MA: MIT Press.

Foote, C., & Goetz, C. (2008). The impact of legalized abortion on crime. Comment. *Quarterly Journal of Economics* 123: 407–423.

Frank, R. (2009). *Microeconomics and Behavior*. 8th edition. New York: McGraw-Hill.

Friedman, D., & Oprea, R. (2012). A continuous dilemma. *American Economic Review* 102: 337–363.

Friedman, M. (1953). *Essays in Positive Economics*. Chicago: University of Chicago Press.

Friedman, M. (1968). The role of monetary policy. *American Economic Review* 68: 1–17.

Friedman, M. (2000). *A Parting of the Ways*. Chicago: Open Court.

Frisch, R. (1933). Propagation problems and impulse problems in dynamic economics. In *Economic Essays in Honour of Gustav Cassel*, pp. 171–205. London: Allen and Unwin.

Frisch, R., & Waugh, F. (1933). Partial time regressions as compared with individual trends. *Econometrica* 1: 387–401.

Friston, K. & Kiebel, S. (2009). Cortical circuits for perceptual inference. *Neural Networks* 22: 1093–104.

Friston, K., Mattout, J. & Kilner, J. (2011). Action understanding and active inference. *Biological Cybernetics* 104: 137–60.

Frydman, R., & Goldberg, M. (2007). *Imperfect Knowledge Economics: Exchange Rates and Risk.* Princeton: Princeton University Press.

Frydman, R., & Goldberg, M. (2011). *Beyond Mechanical Markets.* Princeton: Princeton University Press.

Fudenberg, D., & Levine, D. (1998). *The Theory of Learning in Games.* Cambridge, MA: MIT Press.

Fudenberg, D., & Levine, D. (2006). A dual-self model of impulse control. *American Economic Review* 96: 1449–1476.

Fudenberg, D., & Tirole, D. (1991). *Game Theory.* Cambridge, MA: MIT Press.

Gauthier, D. (1986). *Morals By Agreement.* Oxford: Oxford University Press.

Ghemawat, P. (1998). *Games Businesses Play.* Cambridge, MA: MIT Press.

Gibson, J. (1979). *The Ecological Approach to Visual Perception.* Boston: Houghton Mifflin.

Gigerenzer, G., Todd, P., & the ABC Research Group (1999). *Simple Heuristics that Make Us Smart.* Oxford: Oxford University Press.

Gilbert, M. (1989). *On Social Facts.* Princeton: Princeton University Press.

Gintis, H. (2009). *The Bounds of Reason.* Princeton: Princeton University Press.

Giocoli, N. (2003). *Modeling Rational Agents.* Cheltenham: Edward Elgar.

Glimcher, P. (2003). *Decisions, Uncertainty and the Brain.* Cambridge, MA: MIT Press.

Glimcher, P. (2011). *Foundations of Neuroeconomic Analysis.* Oxford: Oxford University Press.

Glimcher, P., Camerer, C., Fehr, E., & Poldrack, R., eds (2009). *Neuroeconomics: Decision Making and the Brain.* Amsterdam: Elsevier.

Glimcher, P., Kable, J., & Louie, K. (2007). Neuroeconomic studies of impulsivity: Now or just as soon as possible? *American Economic Review* 97: 142–147.

Gode, D., & Sunder, S. (1993). Allocative efficiency of markets with zero-intelligence traders: Market as a partial substitute for individual rationality. *Journal of Political Economy* 101: 119–137.

Gorman, W. (1953). Community preference fields. *Econometrica* 21: 63–80.

Greif, A. (2006). *Institutions and the Path to the Modern Economy: Lessons From Medieval Trade.* Cambridge: Cambridge University Press.

Grossman, S., & Stiglitz, J. (1980). On the impossibility of informationally efficient markets. *American Economic Review* 70: 393–408.

Guala, F. (2005). *The Methodology of Experimental Economics.* Cambridge: Cambridge University Press.

Gul, F., & Pesendorfer, W. (2008). The case for mindless economics. In A. Caplin & A. Schotter, eds, *The Foundations of Positive and Normative Economics: A Handbook.* Oxford: Oxford University Press.

Haavelmo, T. (1944). The probability approach in econometrics. *Econometrica* 12, supplement.

Hacking, I. (1983). *Representing and Intervening.* Cambridge: Cambridge University Press.

Hacking, I. (1990). *The Taming of Chance.* Cambridge: Cambridge University Press.

Hájek, A. (2008). Dutch book arguments. In P. Anand, P. Pattanaik & C. Puppe eds, *The Oxford Handbook of Rational and Social Choice*, pp. 173-195. Oxford: Oxford University Press.

Hands, W. (2013). Foundations of contemporary revealed preference theory. *Erkenntnis* 78: 1081-1108.

Hands, W. (forthcoming). GP08 is the new F53: Gul and Pesendorfer's methodological essay from the viewpoint of Blaug's Popperian methodology. In M. Boumans & M. Klaes, eds *Mark Blaug.* London: Edward Elgar.

Harris, J. (2007). *No Two Alike.* New York: Norton.

Harrison, G. (2008). Neuroeconomics: A critical reconsideration. *Economics and Philosophy* 24: 303-344.

Harrison, G. (2011a). Experimental methods and the welfare evaluation of policy lotteries. *European Review of Agricultural Economics* 38: 335-360.

Harrison, G. (2011b). Randomisation and its discontents. *Journal of African Economics* 20: 626-652.

Harrison, G., & List, J. (2004). Field experiments. *Journal of Economic Literature* 42: 1013-1059.

Harrison, G., & Ross, D. (2010). The methodologies of neuroeconomics. *Journal of Economic Methodology* 17: 185-196.

Harrison, G., & Swarthout, T. (2013). Loss frames in the laboratory. In preparation.

Harrison, G., Jensen, J., Lau, M., & Rutherford, T. (2002). Policy reform without tears. In A. Fossati & W. Weigard, eds, *Policy Evaluation With Computable General Equilibrium Models*, pp. 20-36. London: Routledge.

Harrison, G., Martínez-Correa, J., Swarthout, T., & Ulm, E. (2012). Scoring rules for subjective probability distributions. Working paper, Center for Economic Analysis of Risk, Georgia State University. http://cear.gsu.edu/papers/index.html

Harsanyi, J. (1967). Games with incomplete information played by 'Bayesian' players, Parts I-III. *Management Science* 14: 159-182.

Harsanyi, J. (1977). *Rational Behavior and Bargaining Equilibrium in Games and Social Situations.* Cambridge: Cambridge University Press.

Hartley, J. (1997). *The Representative Agent in Macroeconomics.* London: Routledge.

Hausman, D. (1992). *The Inexact and Separate Science of Economics.* Cambridge: Cambridge University Press.

Hausman, D. (2011). *Preference, Value, Choice and Welfare.* Cambridge: Cambridge University Press.

Hayek, F. (1944). *The Road to Serfdom*. Chicago: University of Chicago Press.

Hayek, F. (1945). The use of knowledge in society. *American Economic Review* 35: 519–530.

Hayek, F. (1960). *The Constitution of Liberty*. Chicago: University of Chicago Press.

Henrich, J., Boyd, R., Bowles, S., Camerer, C., Fehr, E., & Gintis, H., eds (2004). *Foundations of Human Sociality*. Oxford: Oxford University Press.

Hey, J., & Orme, C. (1994). Investigating generalizations of expected utility theory using experimental data. *Econometrica* 62: 1291–1326.

Heyman, G. (2009). *Addiction: A Disorder of Choice*. Cambridge, MA: Harvard University Press.

Hicks, J. (1937). Mr Keynes and the 'Classics'; A suggested interpretation. *Econometrica* 5: 147–159.

Hicks, J. (1939a). The foundations of welfare economics. *Economic Journal* 49: 696–712.

Hicks, J. (1939b). *Value and Capital*. Oxford: Oxford University Press.

Hicks, J. (1956). *A Revision of Demand Theory*. Oxford: Oxford University Press.

Hicks, J., & Allen, R. (1934). A reconsideration of the theory of value. *Economica* 1: 52–76, 196–219.

Hildenbrand, W. (1994). *Market Demand*. Princeton: Princeton University Press.

Hildenbrand, W. (2008). Aggregation theory. In S. Durlauf & L. Blume, eds, *The New Palgrave Dictionary of Economics*, 2nd edition. London: Palgrave Macmillan.

Hollis, M., & Sugden, R. (1993). Rationality in action. *Mind* 102: 1–35.

Hoover, K. (2012). Man and machine in macroeconomics. CHOPE Working Paper No. 2012–07. http://ssrn.com/abstract=2144351

Houthakker, H. (1950). Revealed preference and the utility function. *Economica* 17: 159–174.

Humphreys, P. (2004). *Extending Ourselves*. Oxford: Oxford University Press.

Hurwicz, L., & Reiter, S. (2006). *Designing Economic Mechanisms*. Cambridge: Cambridge University Press.

Hutchins, E. (1995). *Cognition in the Wild*. Cambridge, MA: MIT Press.

Hutto, D. (2008). *Folk Psychological Narratives*. Cambridge, MA: MIT Press.

Ingrao, B., & Israel, G. (1990). *The Invisible Hand*. Cambridge, MA: MIT Press.

Irwin, D. (1997). *Against the Tide*. Princeton: Princeton University Press.

Jevons, W.S. (1871). *The Theory of Political Economy*. London: Macmillan.

Kagel, J., & Roth, A., eds (1995). *The Handbook of Experimental Economics*. Princeton: Princeton University Press.

Kahneman, D. (2011). *Thinking Fast and Slow*. New York: Farrar, Straus and Giroux.

Kahneman, D., & Tversky, A. (1979). Prospect theory: An analysis of decision under risk. *Econometrica* 47: 263–292.

Kahneman, D., Slovic, P., & Tversky, A. (1982). *Judgment Under Uncertainty: Heursitics and Biases.* Cambridge: Cambridge University Press.

Kaldor, N. (1939). Welfare propositions in economics and interpersonal comparisons of utility. *Economic Journal* 49: 549–51.

Keane, M. (2010). Structural vs. atheoretic approaches to econometrics. *Journal of Econometrics* 156: 3–20.

Keen, S. (2002). *De-bunking Economics.* New York: Zed Books.

Keeney, R., & Raiffa, H. (1976). *Decisions With Multiple Objectives.* New York: Wiley.

Keijzer, F. (2001). *Representation and Behavior.* Cambridge, MA: MIT Press.

Kennan, J., & Wilson, R. (1989). Strategic bargaining models and the interpretation of strike data. *Journal of Applied Econometrics* 4 (supplement): S87 – S130.

Keynes, J.M. (1921). *A Treatise on Probability.* London: Macmillan.

Keynes, J.M. (1936). *The General Theory of Employment, Interest and Money.* London: Macmillan.

Kincaid, H. (1997). *Individualism and the Unity of Science.* Lanham, MD: Rowman & Littlefield.

Kincaid, H., Daniels, R., Dellis, A., Hofmeyr, A., Rousseau, J., Sharp, C., & Ross, D. (2013). A taxometric analysis of the performance of the Problem Gambling Severity Index in a South African national urban prevalence sample. *International Journal of Gambling Studies* 29: 377–392.

Kindleberger, C. (1978). *Manias, Panics and Crashes: A History of Financial Crises.* Houndmills Basingstoke: Palgrave Macmillan.

Kitcher, P. (1981). Explanatory unification. *Philosophy of Science* 48: 507–531.

Kitcher, P. (1984). 1953 and all that: A tale of two sciences. *Philosophical Review* 93: 335–373.

Kitcher, P. (1989). Explanatory unification and the causal structure of the world. In P. Kitcher & W. Salmon, eds, *Scientific Explanation*, pp. 410–505. Minneapolis: University of Minnesota Press.

Kitcher, P. (1993). *The Advancement of Science.* Oxford: Oxford University Press.

Klemperer, P. (2004). *Auctions: Theory and Practice.* Princeton: Princeton University Press.

Knight, F. (1921). *Risk, Uncertainty and Profit.* Boston: Houghton Mifflin.

Kreps, D. (1990a). *Game Theory and Economic Modeling.* Oxford: Oxford University Press.

Kreps, D. (1990b). *A Course in Microeconomic Theory.* Princeton: Princeton University Press.

Krugman, P. (2009). How did economists get it so wrong? *The New York Times Magazine*, 6 September 2009, begins p. 36.

Kuhn, T. (1962). *The Structure of Scientific Revolutions*. Chicago: Chicago University Press.

Kydland, F., & Prescott, E. (1982). Time to build and aggregate fluctuations. *Econometrica* 50: 1345–1370.

Ladyman, J., & Ross, D. (2007). *Every Thing Must Go*. Oxford: Oxford University Press.

Ladyman, J., & Ross, D. (2013). The world in the data. In D. Ross, J. Ladyman & H. Kincaid, eds, *Scientific Metaphysics*, pp. 108–150. Oxford: Oxford University Press.

Lagueux, M. (2010). *Rationality and Explanation in Economics*. Oxford: Routledge.

Laibson, D. (1997). Golden eggs and hyperbolic discounting. *Quarterly Journal of Economics* 112: 443–477.

Lawson, T. (1997). *Economics and Reality*. London: Routledge.

Lawson, T. (2009). The current economic crisis: Its nature and the course of academic economics. *Cambridge Journal of Economics* 33: 759–777.

Leamer, E. (2009). *Macroeconomic Patterns and Stories*. Berlin: Springer.

Leamer, E. (2010). Tantalus on the road to asymtopia. *Journal of Economic Perspectives* 24: 31–46.

Ledyard, J. (1995). Public goods: A survey of experimental research. In J. Kagel & A. Roth, eds, *Handbook of Experimental Economics*, pp. 111–194. Princeton: Princeton University Press.

Lee, D., & Wang, X.-J. (2009). Mechanisms for stochastic decision making in the primate frontal cortex: Single-neuron recording and circuit modeling. In P. Glimcher, C. Camerer, E. Fehr & R. Poldrack, eds, *Neuroeconomics: Decision Making and the Brain*, pp. 481–501. London: Elsevier.

Legrain, P. (2002). *Open World*. London: Abacus.

Levitt, S., & Dubner, S. (2006). *Freakonomics*. New York: Morrow.

Lewbel, A. (1994). An examination of Werner Hildenbrand's *Market Demand*. *Journal of Economic Literature* 32: 1832–1841.

Lewis, D. (1969). *Convention*. Cambridge, MA: Harvard University Press.

Lichtenstein, S., & Slovic, P., eds (2006). *The Construction of Preference*. Cambridge: Cambridge University Press.

Lin, J. (2012). *The Quest for Prosperity*. Princeton: Princeton University Press.

Lindstrom, M. (2008). *Buyology*. New York: Crown.

Lipsey, R., & Lancaster, K. (1956). The general theory of second best. *Review of Economic Studies* 24: 11–32.

Long, J., & Plosser, C. (1983). Real business cycles. *Journal of Political Economy* 91: 39–69.

Lucas, R. (1976). Econometric policy evaluation: A critique. In K. Brunner & A. Meltzer, eds, *The Phillips Curve and Labor Markets*, pp. 19–46. London: Elsevier.

Mäki, U. (1992). On the method of isolation in economics. In C. Dilworth, (ed.) *Idealization IV: Intelligibility in Science*. Special issue of *Poznan Studies in the Philosophy of the Sciences and the Humanities* 26: 319–354.

Mäki, U. (2009). Realistic realism about unrealistic models. In H. Kincaid & D. Ross, eds, *The Oxford Handbook of Philosophy of Economics*, pp. 68–98. Oxford: Oxford University Press.

Mandeville, B. (1723 and 1728 [1997]). *The Fable of the Bees*. E. Hundert, (ed.) Indianapolis: Hackett.

Mandler, M. (1999). *Dilemmas in Economic Theory*. Oxford: Oxford University Press.

Manski, C. (1995). *Identification Problems in the Social Sciences*. Cambridge, MA: Harvard University Press.

Marshall, A. (1890). *The Principles of Economics*. London: Macmillan.

Martens, B. (2004). *The Cognitive Mechanics of Economic Development and Institutional Change*. London: Routledge.

Martin, J. (2009). *Social Structures*. Princeton: Princeton University Press.

Mazur, J. (1987). An adjusting procedure for studying delayed reinforcement. In M. Commons, J. Mazur, J. Nevin, & H. Rachlin, eds, *Quantitative Analysis of Behavior Vol. 5: The Effect of Delay and of Intervening Events on Reinforcement Value*, pp. 55–73. Hillsdale, NJ: Lawrence Erlbaum Associates.

McClamrock, R. (1995). *Existential Cognition*. Chicago: University of Chicago Press.

McClennen, E. (1990). *Rationality and Dynamic Choice*. Cambridge: Cambridge University Press.

McClure, S., Laibson, D., Loewenstein, G., & Cohen, J. (2004). Separate neural systems value immediate and delayed monetary rewards. *Science* 306: 503–507.

McCrary, J. (2002). Using electoral cycles in police hiring to estimate the effect of policy on crime. Comment. *American Economic Review* 92: 1236–1243.

McGeer, V. (2001). Psycho-practice, psycho-theory and the contrastive case of autism. *Journal of Consciousness Studies* 8: 109–132.

McKelvey, R., & Palfrey, T. (1995). Quantal response equilibria for normal form games. *Games and Economic Behavior* 10: 6–38.

McKelvey, R., & Palfrey, T. (1998). Quantal response equilibria for extensive form games. *Experimental Economics* 1: 9–41.

Mehta, J., Starmer, C., & Sugden, R. (1994). The nature of salience: An experimental investigation of pure coordination games. *American Economic Review* 84: 658–673.

Mercuro, N., & Medema, S. (2006). *Economics and the Law*. 2nd edition. Princeton: Princeton University Press.

Milgrom, P. (2004). *Putting Auction Theory to Work*. Cambridge: Cambridge University Press.

Mirowski, P. (1989). *More Heat Than Light*. New York: Cambridge University Press.

Mitchell, S. (2003). *Biological Complexity and Integrative Pluralism*. Cambridge: Cambridge University Press.

Montague, P.R, & Berns, G. (2002). Neural economics and the biological substrates of valuation. *Neuron* 36: 265–284.

Montague, P.R., King-Cassis, B., & Cohen, J. (2006). Imaging valuation models in human choice. *Annual Review of Neuroscience* 29: 417–448.

Morgan, M. (1990). *The History of Econometric Ideas*. Cambridge: Cambridge University Press.

Morris, S., & Shin, H.-S. (1998). Unique equilibrium in a model of self-fulfilling currency attacks. *American Economic Review* 88: 587–597.

Morris, S., & Shin, H.-S. (2003). Global games: Theory and applications. In M. Dewatripont, L. Hansen & S. Turnovsky, eds, *Advances in Economics and Econometrics, Theory and Applications, Eighth World Congress, Volume 1*, pp. 56–114. Cambridge: Cambridge University Press.

Mueller, D., (ed.) (1996). *Perspectives on Public Choice: A Handbook*. Cambridge: Cambridge University Press.

Muth, J. (1961). Rational expectations and the theory of price movements. *Econometrica* 29: 315–335.

Nash, J. (1950a). Equilibrium points in *n*-person games. *Proceedings of the National Academy of Sciences* 36: 48–49.

Nash, J. (1950b). The bargaining problem. *Econometrica* 18: 155–162.

Nash, J. (1951). Non-cooperative games. *Annals of Mathematics Journal* 54: 286–295.

Noë, R., van Hoof, J., & Hammerstein, P., eds (2001). *Economics in Nature*. Cambridge: Cambridge University Press.

North, D. (1990). *Institutions, Institutional Change and Economic Performance*. Cambridge: Cambridge University Press.

North, D. (2005). *Understanding the Process of Economic Change*. Princeton: Princeton University Press.

O'Donoghue, T., & Rabin, M. (1999). Incentives for procrastinators. *Quarterly Journal of Economics* 114: 769–816.

O'Donoghue, T., & Rabin, M. (2001). Choice and procrastination. *Quarterly Journal of Economics* 116: 121–160.

Ofek, H. (2001). *Second Nature*. Cambridge: Cambridge University Press.

Oppenheim, P., & Putnam, H. (1958). Unity of science as a working hypothesis. In H. Feigl, M. Scriven & G. Maxwell, eds, *Minnesota Studies in the Philosophy of Science Volume 2*, pp. 3–36. Minneapolis: University of Minnesota Press.

Ormerod, P. (1994). *The Death of Economics*. New York: Wiley.

Ostrom, E. (1990). *Governing the Commons*. Cambridge: Cambridge University Press.

Pareto, V. (1909/1971). *Manual of Political Economy*. New York: Augustus Kelly.

Pettis, M. (2013). *The Great Rebalancing*. Princeton: Princeton University Press.

Pettit, P., & Sugden, R. (1989). The backward induction paradox. *Journal of Philosophy* 86: 169–182.

Phelps, Edmund (1994). *Structural Slumps*. Cambridge, MA: Harvard University Press.

Phelps, Edmund, & Pollack, R. (1968). On second-best national saving and game equilibrium growth. *Review of Economic Studies* 35: 201–208.

Phelps, Elizabeth (2009). The study of emotions in neuroeconomics. In P. Glimcher, C. Camerer, E. Fehr & R. Poldrack, eds, *Neuroeconomics: Decision Making and the Brain*, pp. 233–250. London: Elsevier.

Phillips, W. (1958). The relationship between unemployment and the rate of change of money wages in the United Kingdom 1861–1957. *Economica* 25: 283–299.

Pinker, S., & Mehler, J., eds (1988). *Connections and Symbols*. Cambridge, MA: MIT Press.

Poldrack, R. (2006). Can cognitive processes be inferred from neuroimaging data? *Trends in Cognitive Science* 10: 59–63.

Popper, K. (1959). *The Logic of Scientific Discovery*. London: Hutchinson.

Popper, K. (1963). *Conjectures and Refutations: The Growth of Scientific Knowledge*. London: Routledge.

Port, R., & van Gelder, T. (1995). *Mind as Motion: Explorations in the Dynamics of Cognition*. Cambridge, MA: MIT Press.

Posner, R. (2009). *A Failure of Capitalism*. Cambridge, MA: Harvard University Press.

Pothos, E., & Busemeyer, J. (2013). Can quantum probability provide a new direction for cognitive modeling? *Behavioral and Brain Sciences* 36: 255–327.

Poundstone, W. (1992). *Prisoner's Dilemma*. New York: Doubleday.

Prelec, D., & Bodner, R. (2003). Self-signaling and self-control. In G. Loewenstein, D. Read & R. Baumeister, eds, *Time and Decision*, pp. 277–298. New York: Russell Sage Foundation.

Price, H., (ed.) (2007). *Causation, Physics and the Constitution of Reality: Russell's Republic Revisited*. Oxford: Oxford University Press.

Prinz, W. (2012). *Open Minds*. Cambridge, MA: MIT Press.

Pylyshyn, Z, (ed.) (1987). *The Robot's Dilemma*. Norwood, NJ: Ablex.

Pylyshyn, Z., (ed.) (1996). *The Robot's Dilemma Revisited*. New York: Praeger.

Quiggin, J. (1982). A theory of anticipated utility. *Journal of Economic Behavior and Organization* 3: 323–343.

Quiggin, J. (1993). *Generalized Expected Utility Theory. The Rank-Dependent Model*. Boston: Kluwer.

Quine, W.V.O. (1985). *The Time of My Life*. Cambridge, MA: MIT Press.

Ragot, X. (2012). The economics of the laboratory mouse: Where do we go from here? In R. Solow & J.-P. Touffut, eds, *What's Right With Macroeconomics?*, pp. 181–194. Cheltenham: Edward Elgar.

Rajan, R. (2010). *Fault Lines*. Princeton: Princeton University Press.

Rawls, J. (1971). *A Theory of Justice*. Cambridge, MA: Harvard University Press.

Read, D. (2001). Is time-discounting hyperbolic or subadditive? *Journal of Risk and Uncertainty* 23: 5–32.

Reinhart, C., & Rogoff, K. (2009). *This Time It's Different: Eight Centuries of Financial Folly*. Princeton: Princeton University Press.

Reiss, J. (2007). *Error in Economics*. London: Routledge.

Robbins, L. (1935). *An Essay on the Nature and Significance of Economic Science*, 2nd edition. London: Macmillan.

Robbins, L. (1938). Interpersonal comparisons of utility: A comment. *Economic Journal* 43: 635–641.

Robertson, D. (1957). *Lectures on Economic Principles, Volume 1*. London: Staples.

Rochat, P. (2009). *Others in Mind*. Oxford: Oxford University Press.

Rodrik, D. (2007). *One Economics, Many Recipes*. Princeton: Princeton University Press.

Rosenberg, A. (1992). *Economics: Mathematical Politics or Science of Diminishing Returns?* Chicago: University of Chicago Press.

Rosenberg, A. (2011). *The Atheist's Guide to Reality*. New York: Norton.

Ross, D. (1994). Real patterns and the ontological foundations of microeconomics. *Economics and Philosophy* 11: 113–136.

Ross, D. (1997). Externalism for everybody. *Canadian Journal of Philosophy*, 27: 271–284.

Ross, D. (2005). *Economic Theory and Cognitive Science: Microexplanation*. Cambridge, MA: MIT Press.

Ross, D. (2006). The economics and evolution of selves. *Cognitive Systems Research* 7: 246–258.

Ross, D. (2007a). Economics, cognitive science and social cognition. *Cognitive Systems Research* 9: 125–135.

Ross, D. (2007b). *H. sapiens* as ecologically special: What does language contribute? *Language Sciences* 29: 710–731.

Ross, D. (2008a). Classical game theory, socialization and the rationalization of conventions. *Topoi*, 27: 57–72.

Ross, D. (2008b). Two styles of neuroeconomics. *Economics and Philosophy* 24: 473–483.

Ross, D. (2010). Should the financial crisis inspire normative revision? *Journal of Economic Methodology* 17: 399–418.

Ross, D. (2011). Estranged parents and a schizophrenic child: Choice in economics, psychology and neuroeconomics. *Journal of Economic Methodology* 18: 215–229.

Ross, D. (2012a). Economic theory, anti-economics and political ideology. In U. Mäki, (ed.) *Handbook of the Philosophy of Science, Volume 13: Economics*, pp. 241–285. London: Elsevier.

Ross, D. (2012b). The economic agent: Not human, but important. In U. Mäki, (ed.) *Handbook of the Philosophy of Science, Volume 13: Economics*, pp. 691–735. London: Elsevier.

Ross, D. (2012c). Notes on coordination, game theory, and the evolutionary basis of language. *Interaction Studies* 13: 50–65.

Ross, D. (2012d). Neuroeconomics and economic methodology. In J. Davis & W.D. Hands, eds. *The Elgar Companion to Recent Economic Methodology*, pp. 61–93. London: Edward Elgar.

Ross, D. (2013a). The evolution of individualistic norms. In K. Sterelny, R. Joyce, B. Calcott & B. Fraser, eds, *Cooperation and its Evolution*, pp. 17–43. Cambridge, MA: MIT Press.

Ross, D. (2013b). A most rare achievement: Dennett's scientific discovery in *Content and Consciousness*. In C. Munoz-Suarez & F. De Brigard, eds, *Content and Consciousness 2.0*. London: Elsevier.

Ross, D. (2013c). Economics, cognitive science and scales of reality. Forthcoming.

Ross, D., & LaCasse, C. (1995). Toward a new philosophy of positive economics. *Dialogue* 35: 1–27.

Ross, D., Sharp, C., Vuchinich, R., & Spurrett, D. (2008). *Midbrain Mutiny: The Picoeconomics and Neuroeconomics of Disordered Gambling*. Cambridge, MA: MIT Press.

Rothschild, M., & Stiglitz, J. (1976). Equilibrium in competitive insurance markets: An essay on the economics of imperfect information. *Quarterly Journal of Economics* 90: 629–650.

Rubinstein, A. (2006). *Lecture Notes in Microeconomic Theory: The Economic Agent*. Princeton: Princeton University Press.

Rummelhart, D., & McClelland, J., eds. (1986). *Parallel Distributed Processing, Volume 1*. Cambridge, MA: MIT Press.

Russell, B. (1912). *The Problems of Philosophy*. London: Home University Library.

Rust, J. (2010). Comments on "Structural vs. atheoretic approaches to econometrics" by Michael Keane. *Journal of Econometrics* 156: 21–24,

Saint Paul, G. (2011). *The Tyranny of Utility*. Princeton: Princeton University Press.

Sally, D. (1995). Conversation and cooperation in social dilemmas: A meta-analysis of experiments from 1958 to 1992. *Rationality and Society* 7: 58–92.

Samuelson, P. (1937). A note on measurement of utility. *Review of Economic Studies* 4: 154–161.

Samuelson, P. (1938). A note on the pure theory of consumer's behaviour. *Economica* 5: 61–72.

Samuelson, P. (1947). *Foundations of Economic Analysis*. Enlarged edition (1983). Cambridge, MA: Harvard University Press.

Samuelson, P. (1948). Consumption theory in terms of revealed preference. *Economica* 15: 243–253.

Samuelson, P. (1958). An exact consumption-loan model of interest with or without the social contrivance of money. *Journal of Political Economy* 66: 467–82.

Samuelson, P., & Solow, R. (1960). Analytical aspects of anti-inflation policy. *American Economic Review* 50: 177–194.

Savage, L. (1954). *The Foundations of Statistics*. New York: Wiley.

Schelling, T. (1960). *The Strategy of Conflict*. Cambridge, MA: Harvard University Press.

Schelling, T. (1978). Economics, or the art of self-management. *American Economic Review* 68: 290–294.

Schelling, T. (1980). The intimate contest for self-command. *Public Interest* 60: 94–118.

Schelling, T. (1984). Self-command in practice, in policy, and in a theory of rational choice. *American Economic Review* 74: 1–11.

Schultz, W., Dayan, P., & Montague, P.R. (1997). A neural substrate of prediction and reward. *Science* 275: 1593–1599.

Schumpeter, J. (1911/1982). *The Theory of Economic Development*. Piscataway NJ: Transaction.

Schumpeter, J. (1942). *Capitalism, Socialism and Democracy*. New York: Harper and Row.

Selten, R. (1973). A simple model of imperfect competition where 4 are few and 6 are many. *International Journal of Game Theory* 2: 141–201.

Selten, R. (1975). Re-examination of the perfectness concept for equilibrium points in extensive games. *International Journal of Game Theory* 4: 22–55.

Sen, A. (1971). *Collective Choice and Social Welfare*. Amsterdam: North-Holland.

Shubik, M. (1982). *Game Theory in the Social Sciences: Concepts and Solutions*. Cambridge: Cambridge University Press.

Shy, O. (1995). *Industrial Organization: Theory and Applications*. Cambridge, MA: MIT Press.

Sidgwick, H. (1885). *The Scope and Method of Economic Science*. London: Macmillan.

Simon, H. (1957). *Models of Man: Social and Rational*. New York: Wiley.

Skidelsky, R. (2010). *Keynes: The Return of the Master*. New York: Public Affairs.

Skinner, B. (1971). *Beyond Freedom and Dignity*. New York: Alfred A. Knopf.

Skyrms, B. (1996). *Evolution of the Social Contract*. Cambridge: Cambridge University Press.

Skyrms, B. (2004). *The Stag Hunt and the Evolution of Social Structure*. Cambridge: Cambridge University Press.

Skyrms, B. (2010). *Signals*. Oxford: Oxford University Press.

Smith, A. (1759/1976). *Theory of Moral Sentiments*. Oxford: Oxford University Press.

Smith, A. (1776 / 1986). *The Wealth of Nations*. Harmondsworth: Penguin.

Smith, V. (2008). *Rationality in Economics*. Cambridge: Cambridge University Press.

Solow, R. (1997). How did economics get that way and what way did it get? *Daedalus* 126: 39–59.

Sopher, B., & Sheth, A. (2006). A deeper look at hyperbolic discounting. *Theory and Decision* 60: 219–255.

Spence, A.M. (1973). Job market signaling. *Quarterly Journal of Economics* 87: 355–374.

Spence, A.M. (1974). *Market Signaling: Informational Transfer in Hiring and Related Screening Processes*. Cambridge, MA: Harvard University Press.

Stiglitz, J., & Weiss, A. (1981). Credit rationing in markets with imperfect information. *American Economic Review* 71: 393–410.

Stirling, W. (2012). *Theory of Conditional Games*. Cambridge: Cambridge University Press.

Strotz, R. (1956). Myopia and inconsistency in dynamic utility maximization. *Review of Economic Studies* 23: 165–180.

Sugden, R. (1993). Thinking as a team: towards an explanation of nonselfish behavior. *Social Philosophy and Policy* 10: 69–89.

Sugden, R. (2000a). Credible worlds: The status of theoretical models in economics. *Journal of Economic Methodology* 7: 1–31.

Sugden, R. (2000b). Team preferences. *Economics and Philosophy* 16: 175–204.

Sugden, R. (2003). The logic of team reasoning. *Philosophical Explorations* 6: 165–181.

Sugden, R. (2008). Why incoherent preferences do not justify paternalism. *Constitutional Political Economy* 19: 226–248.

Sunder, S. (2003). Market as artifact: Aggregate efficiency from zero intelligence traders. In M. Augier & J. March, eds, *Models of a Man: Essays in Memory of Herbert A. Simon*, pp. 501–519. Cambridge, MA: MIT Press.

Sunstein, C., & Thaler, R. (2003a). Libertarian paternalism. *American Economic Review, Papers and Proceedings* 93: 175–179.

Sunstein, C., & Thaler, R. (2003b). Libertarian paternalism is not an oxymoron. *University of Chicago Law Review* 70: 1159–1202.

Sutton, J. (1991). *Sunk Costs and Market Structure*. Cambridge, MA: MIT Press.

Sutton, J. (2000). *Marshall's Tendencies*. Cambridge, MA: MIT Press.

Sutton, J. (2001). *Technology and Market Structure*. 2nd edition. Cambridge, MA: MIT Press.

Sutton, R., & Bartow, A. (1998). *Reinforcement Learning: An Introduction.* Cambridge, MA: MIT Press.

Taylor, L., & Black, S. (1974). Practical general equilibrium estimation of resources pulls under trade liberalization. *Journal of International Economics* 4: 37–58.

Thaler, R. (1992). *The Winner's Curse*. New York: Free Press.

Tversky, A., & Kahneman, D. (1992). Advances in prospect theory: Cumulative representation of uncertainty. *Journal of Risk and Uncertainty* 5: 297–323.

Udehn, L. (2001). *Methodological Individualism*. London: Routledge.

Uttal, W. (2003). *The New Phrenology: The Limits of Localizing Cognitive Processes in the Brain*. Cambridge, MA: MIT Press.

Von Neumann, J., & Morgenstern, O. (1944). *Theory of Games and Economic Behavior.* Princeton: Princeton University Press.

Wakker, P. (2010). *Prospect Theory for Risk and Uncertainty*. Cambridge: Cambridge University Press.

Wald, A. (1940). The fitting of straight lines if both variables are subject to error. *Annals of Mathematical Statistics* 11: 284–300.

Weber, M. (1949). *The Methodology of the Social Sciences*. New York: Free Press.

Weirich, P. (1998). *Equilibrium and Rationality*. Cambridge: Cambridge University Press.

Wilcox, N. (2008). Stochastic models for binary discrete choice under risk: A critical primer and econometric comparison. In J. Cox & G. Harrison, eds, *Risk Aversion in Experiments*, pp. 197–292. Bingley: Emerald.

Wilson, M. (2006). *Wandering Significance*. Oxford: Oxford University Press.

Wittgenstein, L. (1953). *Philosophical Investigations*. Oxford: Blackwell.

Wydick, B. (2008). *Games in Economic Development*. Cambridge: Cambridge University Press.

Yaari, M. (1987). The dual theory of choice under risk. *Econometrica* 55: 95–115.

Zak, P. (2008). The brains behind economics. *Journal of Economic Methodology* 15: 301–302.

Zawidzki, T. (2007). *Dennett*. Oxford: Oneworld.

Zawidzki, T. (2013). *Mindshaping*. Cambridge, MA: MIT Press.

Zurowicki, L. (2010). *Neuromarketing*. Heidelberg: Springer.

Zweig, J. (2007). *Your Money and Your Brain*. New York: Simon and Schuster.

Index

Printed and bound in the United States of America